Gold EXPERIENCE

B1

Preliminary for Schools

CB080295

Students' Book

Carolyn Barraclough
Suzanne Gaynor

Contents

	Listening	Speaking	Writing	Video
	Making plans *True/False*	**Talking about preferences** Making suggestions	**Write about a past activity**	
	Where you live *True/False*	**Giving personal information** Talking about where you live and what you like to do	**A personal profile**	**Welcome to our town**
	Learning a new skill Completing notes	**Phone trouble** Maintaining a phone conversation	**A funny story**	**A special talent**
	Gadgets Picture multiple choice	**Future technology and robots** Agreeing and disagreeing	**An email**	**The future is here!**
	Activities before school Three-option multiple choice	**Improving concentration** Explaining preferences and giving reasons	**A card**	**Pupil power!**
	Freerunning *True/False*	**Watching sport** Describing a photo	**An article**	**Just try it!**
	A good friend Three-option multiple choice	**Saying sorry** Apologising and responding	**An email (to apologise)**	**Horse whisperers**

Contents

	Listening	Speaking	Writing	Video
	Music Picture multiple choice	**Going to a performance** Making and responding to suggestions	**A review**	**We love classical music**
	An announcement Completing notes	**Travel stories** Telling stories and showing interest	**A blog entry (about something that happened on holiday)**	**Holiday survival tips**
	Strange but true facts Picture multiple choice	**Talking about strange facts** Asking for and expressing an opinion	**An article (about an exciting or interesting hobby)**	**Supernova, superstar**
	Interview with a make-up artist Three-option multiple choice	**Being a volunteer** Describing a photo and dealing with unknown words	**An application letter (for a volunteer job)**	**Be your own boss!**
	Green plans *True/False*	**Talking about plans to be greener** Taking turns	**A description of a place**	**Another world**
	Learning new skills Completing notes	**Talking about yourself** Talking about experiences, situations now and future plans	**A story**	**Challenge Toby!**

Starter

Buzz on the online noticeboard

Home | Discussions | Photos | Blogs | Messages | Questions

Orange and spiky! What do you think?
Rory, 15 minutes ago 🙂

It's brilliant. How did you do it? Dan

Amazing! Did you do it? Hannah

Thanks, Hannah. No, I didn't. My mate did it. He's a hairdresser. Rory

I prefer you with black hair 🙁 Liam

Laura, 55 minutes ago

He's lovely. Sam

Last week we lost him for two days in the garden. He was very hungry when we found him. Laura

That carrot's very big for him. Ben

My hamster hates carrots. Emma

Guess where I am?
Gemma, 2 hours ago

You look really sad. Get better soon! Molly

Oh no! Are you at the hospital now? Charlie

Yes, we got here two hours ago. We're waiting to see another doctor. Gemma

Ouch! Are you OK? Dan

I'm not sure. I fell at football practice last night. My leg hurts A LOT! 🙁 🙁 Gemma

No more football for you! Can I come round tonight? Dan

STARTER

Reading

1 Read the online noticeboard. How many posts …

1 include a photo?
2 have more than three replies?
3 want advice?
4 appeared in the last hour?

2 Find somebody who …

1 can't go on a picnic at the weekend.
2 doesn't like the colour of Rory's hair.
3 is doing something exciting tonight.
4 wants advice from friends.
5 has a pet that doesn't eat vegetables.
6 thinks music can help you to relax.
7 wants to go to a friend's house tonight.
8 had an accident last night.
9 isn't going to be at the picnic on Saturday.
10 didn't like what the family pet did with its food.

3 Without looking back at the posts, can you remember the following?

1 two animals
2 two jobs
3 two places
4 three sports
5 two types of food or drink
6 two words for feelings
7 two adjectives
8 two electronic gadgets

Search

Help! I can't sleep. What's wrong with me?

Emma, 2 days ago

You have to relax. Why don't you listen to music? Hannah

Are you worried about something? You should talk to your mum or your teacher. Molly

I always turn off my phone and computer before bed and watch something on TV. Then I'm relaxed. Sam

Don't forget! Picnic in the park for school Volleyball Club this Saturday. Dan

Good idea. I'll bring some popcorn and some juice. Melissa

Sorry guys. I'm playing basketball on Saturday. Nathan

Tonight we're sleeping with sharks! Best school trip ever at the Georgia Aquarium! Did you know, sharks are usually awake, even at night? I love sharks, but I won't get much sleep. ☹ Luke, 37 minutes ago

It's going to be amazing. Don't forget your camera. Jack

Listening

4 S.1 **Listen to a Skype conversation between friends. What is the main thing they talk about?**

future plans   general opinions   past events

5 S.2 **Listen to the rest of the conversation. Are the sentences (1–6) true (T) or false (F)?**

1 Two people are going to go to the beach
2 They are going to meet in the cinema.
3 The bus leaves at 1.45.
4 The girl is going to take some lemonade.
5 They are going to eat at the beach.
6 The girl will phone him before they meet.

Speaking

6 Work with a partner. Make a list of your favourite and least favourite weekend activities.

Favourite activities/Least favourite activities

7 Choose and plan a weekend activity together. Agree a place, a day and a time to meet.

Let's … What about … ? What time … ? Where … ?

Writing

8 Write a post about an activity you did last weekend. Use the first sentence and write 3–4 more sentences. Think about the following.

activities   food and drink   good or bad
when   where   who

I had a great time last weekend …

01 24/7 teens

READING

Power up

1 Think of two things you can say about the place where you live.

2 Ask and answer with a partner. What is life like for teenagers in these places? Is it similar to where you live? Why/Why not? Use these words and phrases.

boring cold DANGEROUS interesting in a small town in the city near the sea safe sunny

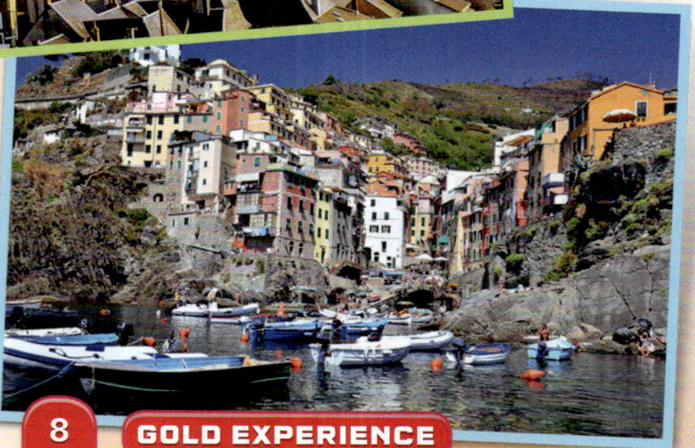

Read on

3 Read the first paragraph of an interview with Elena Martinez. Are the sentences (1–2) true (T) or false (F)?

1 Elena's family is Brazilian.
2 Elena lives in Brazil.

Welcome to my World

Thanks to satellite TV, web cams and social networking sites, you don't have to go 1) __________ far to meet teenagers from around the world. You can learn about, their school, their hobbies, their favourite food ... and much more. Elena Martinez is living in Rio de Janeiro for a year, but she speaks to her friends back home every day. We're talking to her on a video call now, and I want to find out more about Elena. What's she like? What's she interested in?

MW: Can you tell us about your family and where you live, Elena?
Elena: My dad's Argentinian and my mum comes from Wales. I've got an older sister, Rose, and a cat called Tigger. (He isn't very friendly!) We're living in Rio because my parents are working here at the moment. It's a busy city, but there are lots of parks, too. We live in a modern flat 2) __________ the beach, so I often go there with my friends. Brazil is always sunny, so being outdoors is a big 3) __________ of life here. Copacabana is my favourite beach – I love it! It's beautiful, the waves are huge and it's really popular with tourists. There are more than a million visitors here every year, and there are usually lots of them on the beach!

MW: What's your school like?
Elena: It's a long way from our flat, so I have to catch the bus at 6.30 a.m. We have lessons 4) __________ 7.45 a.m. to 3.30 p.m. and once a week I do art after school. I speak English and Spanish at home, and I'm learning Portuguese at school. The best thing about my school is where it is. It's 5) __________ by forest, and monkeys often run past the classrooms! There are also lots of blue butterflies – they're beautiful.
MW: How would you describe your Brazilian friends?
Elena: They love having fun, and they aren't shy at all. Most of them are really confident and they're all mad about football! When there's a football 6) __________ on TV, everything stops.
MW: What music are you and your friends listening to at the moment?
Elena: Lots of my friends are 7) __________ rap, but I don't like it much. I love guitar music, and at the moment I'm listening to a lot of songs by two Mexican guitarists, called Rodrigo y Gabriela.
MW: What's your favourite celebration in Brazil?
Elena: That's hard because there are lots of festivals in Rio! The Junina festival is fun because we dress up as girls from the country and wear straw hats. Musicians play country music and we dance all night. There's a lot of nice food 8) __________ my favourite brigadeiros – small chocolate sweets.
MW: Wow, Rio sounds amazing, Elena – you are lucky!
Elena: I know, sometimes I miss my friends in Wales, but I love it here!

4 **Read the interview. Choose the correct answer, A, B, C or D.**

	A	B	C	D
1	A even	B too	C such	D much
2	A near	B close	C next	D in front
3	A part	B piece	C slice	D bit
4	A around	B from	C before	D between
5	A located	B surrounded	C placed	D limited
6	A match	B contest	C race	D competition
7	A for	B in	C into	D about
8	A consisting	B containing	C involving	D including

5 **Find words that mean:**

1 very good or impressive *awesome*
2 very big
3 insects with big colourful wings
4 keen on
5 difficult
6 dried grass

Skill

Read the whole text quickly before you answer any questions.

Sum up

6 **What do you remember about Elena's life in Brazil?**

festivals hobbies home music school

She lives in a modern flat.
She loves brigadeiros. They're small chocolate sweets.

Speak up

7 **Is your life similar or different to Elena's? How?**

I like the beach.
I've got a sister.

SWITCH ON Welcome to our town page 15

VOCABULARY
Personal information

1 Match the words with the sentences.

calm serious shy

bossy lazy noisy rude

clever confident funny ~~lively~~ sporty

Someone who …

1 is happy and active is *lively*.
2 speaks or behaves in a way that isn't polite is …
3 makes people laugh is …
4 always tells other people what to do is …
5 doesn't like working is …
6 is intelligent is …
7 makes loud sounds in an annoying way is …
8 thinks about things a lot and doesn't laugh much is …
9 is often nervous with people they don't know is …
10 is relaxed and not angry is …
11 believes they can do things well is …
12 likes activities such as ball games or team games is …

2 Look at the words in Exercise 1 again. Answer the questions.

1 Why do you think they are in different groups?
2 Which words do you think are positive? Which are negative?

3 Choose the correct words to complete the conversation.

Nathan: Hi Alice. What are you doing?
Alice: Nothing. I'm staying at home today.
Nathan: You're so 1) *bossy/lazy*. Come on. There's a volleyball game at the park.
Alice: You know I'm not very 2) *rude/sporty*, Nathan. I'm staying here.
Nathan: Alice, you should go out. It's bad to stay inside all day.
Alice: Stop being so 3) *bossy/clever*. I need to relax and be 4) *calm/shy* for my exams next week.
Nathan: All right. Are you feeling 5) *confident/serious* about the exam?
Alice: Yes I am, but I need to revise. Now go to the park and leave me alone.
Nathan: OK, but don't be 6) *clever/rude!*
Alice: Please, leave me in peace, Nathan!

4 1.1 Listen and check your answers.

5 Match the sentence halves.

1 Tyler's very funny *d*
2 I'm excited about my party
3 Let's watch something else
4 Anna's frightened of the dark
5 The girls are interested in art,

a so the light is always on in her room.
b because I'm bored with this film.
c but they never paint at home.
d and he's brilliant at making jokes.
e because lots of people are coming.

Word XP

Are you talking about yourself or another person?
*good/brilliant **at** … bored **with**/fed up **with** … excited **about** … bad/terrible **at** … interested **in** … frightened **of** …*
Use an adjective + preposition + noun
*She's also interested **in** languages and dancing.*
*I'm fed up **with** this song.*
Or you can use an adjective + preposition + *-ing*.
*Jake's brilliant **at** cooking.*
*I'm excited **about** learning Spanish.*

6 Complete the second sentence so it has the same meaning as the first.

1 My cousin wants to know more about Chinese food.
My cousin is *interested in* Chinese food.
2 Jack's a really bad football player.
Jack's ____________ football.
3 My friends are looking forward to their holiday.
My friends are ____________ their holiday.
4 My little brother doesn't want to hear that story again.
My little brother is ____________ that story.
5 Max thinks big dogs are scary.
Max is ____________ big dogs.
6 Andrea can play chess very well.
Andrea's ____________ chess.

Game on

Work with a partner. Close your books. Write a list of all the words you remember from the page. Compare your list with your partner. You get one point for each correct word.

GRAMMAR

Grammar XP

p. 123

Talking about the present

Present simple

Use present simple for permanent states

*We **live** in a modern flat.*

for habits and repeated actions

*Once a week, I **do** art after school.*

Present continuous

Use present continuous for actions that are happening now

*We're **talking** to her on a video call now.*

for actions happening around now

*At the moment **I'm listening** to a lot of songs by two Mexican guitarists.*

Present simple and present continuous

You can contrast regular or permanent activities with activities happening now, today or around this time.

*Elena **is living** in Rio de Janeiro for a year, but she **speaks** to her friends back home every day.*

State verbs

Some verbs don't often use the continuous form: *feel, hate, hear, know, like, love, see, think, understand, want.*

*I **want** to find out more about Elena.*

*I **love** it!*

1 Choose the correct forms to complete the email.

About me!

Subject: About me!

Hi Harry,

Thanks for your email. Now I can tell you about myself.

At the moment I 1) *sit/'m sitting* in my bedroom in my grandparents' flat. I 2) *live/'m living* here with my mum and dad. I've got lots of friends, they 3) *aren't coming/don't come* to the flat. We 4) *'re meeting/meet* at the sports centre or in town. Today it 5) *snows/'s snowing* outside so I *stay/'m staying* at home. My friends and I 6) *are loving/love* winter because we 7) *go/'re going* skating. What about you?

8) *Does it snow/Is it snowing* in New York at the moment, too? 9) *What do you do/What are you doing* when it snows?

Speak soon,

Andy

2 Complete the sentences with the correct form of the verbs in brackets.

1. Amelia __wants__ to travel to South America this summer. (want)
2. Max and Will ________ their friends every day after school. (not see)
3. ________ you ________ the exercise? (understand)
4. I ________ for my camera, but I can't find it anywhere. (look)
5. We ________ going to the beach when there are lots of people. (not enjoy)
6. Oh no! It ________ and I haven't got my coat. (rain)

3 Complete the conversation with the correct form of the verbs in brackets.

video call | Call phone

Juliana, Argentina, 5 p.m.

Sophie, France, 10 p.m.

Juliana: How Sophie, how are you?

Sophie: I'm fine. What 1) __are__ you __doing__ (do) at the moment?

Juliana: Well, it's five o'clock in the afternoon in Argentina. I 2) ________ (sit) outside.

Sophie: Lucky you! It's ten o'clock at night here What time 3) ________ your classes ________ (finish)?

Juliana: School 4)________ (end) at two o'clock. That's why I 5) ________ (relax) now!

Sophie: My school day 6) ________ (start) at nine o'clock and 7) ________ (not finish) until five o'clock 🙂

Juliana: 8) ________ you ________ (study) now?

Sophie: Yes, I am. I 9) ________ (do) my English homework, but I'm fed up with it.

Juliana: Never mind. At least you 10) ________ (practise) your English now!

Write on

4 Write sentences about these topics.

1. where you live
2. what you do after school
3. what languages you speak
4. what you're doing now

I chat to my friends after school.
I'm doing my English homework.

LISTENING

Power up

1 **Match the words/phrases with the sentences. Use the picture to help you.**

latitude longitude the equator

QUICK QUIZ

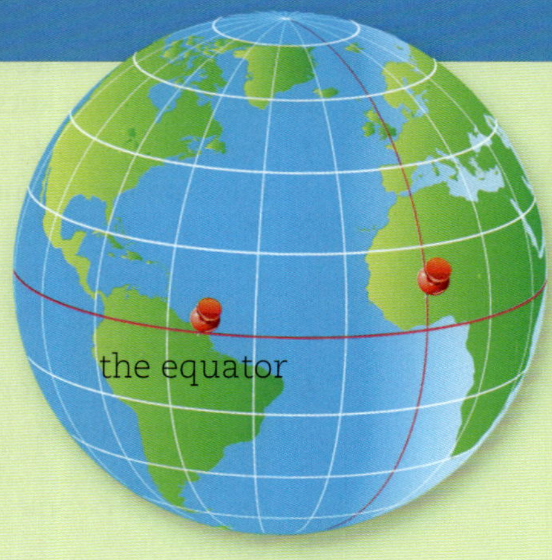

1. We use this to measure how far north or south a place is.
2. We use this to measure how far east or west a place is, and also to work out the time at that place.
3. This line around the earth is not north or south; it's at 0 degrees.

2 **Which of these two places is on the equator? Do you live north or south of these places?**

St Petersburg = 59.56 degrees north
Macapá = 0 degrees latitude

Listen up

3 1.2 **Listen and match each speaker to a city in Exercise 2.**

Alyona

Victor

4 1.3 **Listen again and check your answers.**

Exam

Are you listening for an attitude or opinion? Listen for attitude phrases, e.g. *I love/enjoy* or opinion words, e.g. *nice, interesting*.

5 1.4 **Listen again. Are the sentences (1–6) true (T) or false (F)?**

1 Victor likes Alyona's name.
2 Victor is interested in life in other countries.
3 Alyona dislikes summer nights because she can't sleep.
4 Victor prefers rainy weather.
5 Alyona doesn't mind the different seasons in Russia.
6 In Alyona's opinion, winter is boring.

Grammar XP

p. 123

Time expressions

Adverbs of frequency go after the verb *be*.

*The days and nights are **always** the same.*

Adverbs of frequency go before the present simple verb.

*I **usually** stay up late.*

Other time expressions usually go at the end of a sentence.

*It rains **most days**.*

6 **Put the words in the correct order to make sentences.**

1 It isn't / in June. / usually / dark
It isn't usually dark in June.
2 We enjoy / once a year. / 'white nights'
3 often / It / rains / in the middle of the day.
4 in the river / I like swimming / now and then.
5 My friends and I / once a week. / go surfing

7 **Write sentences about yourself. Use an adverb of frequency or these phrases.**

every week/weekend most days now and then once/twice/three times a year/week

1 see my friends
2 go on holiday
3 play a sport
4 go to the cinema

SPEAKING

Power up

1 What answers would you give to these questions?

What's your …

name?/family name?/
full name?/surname?

first name?/second name?/
middle name?/nickname?

How do you spell that?

Speak up

2 Work with a partner. Take it in turns to ask for and give the information to complete the table. Spell any difficult words. Check that the information is correct.

PERSONAL INFORMATION	
Name:	
Address:	
Town:	
Postcode:	
Email:	

What's your address?

How do you spell the street name?

C-u-m-h-u-r-i-y-e-t

Language XP

Giving reasons and examples

so one reason is (that) because for example

3 1.5 Listen to the first part of an interview. Who gives the best answer to the interviewer's question?

Where do you come from?

Where do you live?

Adrianna (Ada) Kaminski

Aydin Keran Sevim

4 Work with a partner. How can the other speaker in Exercise 3 improve? Think of examples, opinions and reasons the speaker can add to their answer.

5 1.6 Listen to the second part of an interview. Who gives the best answer to the interviewer's question?

What do you enjoy doing in your free time?

6 Work with a partner. How can the other speaker in Exercise 5 improve? Think of examples, opinions and reasons the speaker can add.

Exam

Are you talking about your interests and personal information? Be ready to give examples and reasons.

7 Work with a partner. Take it in turns to practise your own answers for the questions in Exercises 3 and 5.

8 Work with a partner. Student A, look at page 130. Student B, look at page 142. Follow the instructions.

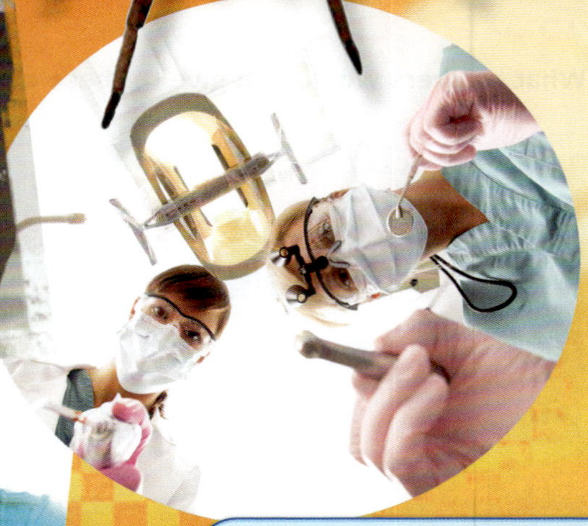

WRITING

Power up

1 **Work with a partner. Quickly say three adjectives that describe you.**

2 **Work with a partner. Take it in turns to talk about these phrases.**

- one thing you hate
- one thing you're fed up with
- one thing you're frightened of
- one thing you're keen on

I'm frightened of the dark.

3 **Read the advert and Camila's plan. Find the phrases in the plan which give the information the advert asks for in bold.**

Channel One is coming to film in your country.

We want to know more about YOU and **the place you live.**
For this programme, you can be **13–17**,
so lots of teenagers can take part!
We're looking for young people from many different countries.
Why should we choose you?
Send us your profile and plans for a short film about you!

A **A shot of me: I'm talking to the camera.**
Hi, I'm Camila Solanet. I'm fifteen and I come from the north of Argentina.
Some people think I'm quite shy, but in fact I'm a confident person. For example, I'm good at making friends.

B **A shot of my family: we're talking and laughing at a barbecue.**
My life is unusual because we live on quite a big ranch. We're not near a town, so my family is very important to me. We love having barbecues and telling stories on summer evenings!

C **A shot of our ranch and me: I'm riding a horse.**
We have a lot of horses, so I'm keen on horse-riding. I usually ride every morning. My country is big and beautiful and I love exploring it on horseback.

D **Another shot of me: I'm talking to the camera.**
Choose me because I'm a typical teenager, but I live in a very different place. Not many people have this lifestyle these days.

4 **Find four phrases with *quite* and *very* in Camila's plan.**

Language XP

We can use *quite* and *very* before adjectives. Use *very* to make an adjective stronger and *quite* to make an adjective less strong. If there is an article (*a/an*) before the adjective, then *quite* goes before the article.

Plan on

5 **Read Adam's profile notes. Complete the notes with these phrases.**

a very funny   a very old   ~~quite an exciting~~
quite interested   very keen on

1 I'm from Warsaw in Poland. It's quite an exciting city. There are a lot of things to do here.
2 My grandparents live in ________ part of the city. I know a lot of Warsaw's history.
3 I'm not ________ maths. I'm not very keen on science.
4 I'm ________ in acting. I like singing. I don't enjoy dancing.
5 Choose me. I'm ________ person. I can make you laugh.

6 **Join the sentences (1–5) in Exercise 5 with *and*, *but*, *or*, *because* or *so*.**

Write on

7 **Write a personal profile for a TV programme.**

Skill

Give plenty of information in each sentence. Join two short sentences with *and, but, or*, because or *so* to make one longer sentence.

Switch on

WELCOME TO OUR TOWN

1 **Guess the answer. Then watch and check.**

Rebecca, Emma and Toby are talking about where they live. Which four things will they mention?

A the park
B the shopping centre
C sports clubs
D dance clubs for young people
E public transport

2 **Are the sentences (1–6) true (T) or false (F)?**

1 Emma comes from a city.
2 Rebecca doesn't like shopping.
3 Toby's school doesn't have a girls' football team.
4 In Manchester you don't have to wait long for a bus or train.
5 There are lots of things to do in the evening where Rebecca and Toby live.
6 Rebecca doesn't think that her town needs a disco for under-18s.

3 **What is there to do in the evening where you live? Would you like to have more things to do? Why/Why not?**

Project

4 **Write your own video script for a short two-minute film about your town or village.**

1 Decide on these things
- What is there to do and see in your area?
- What is there for young people?
- What do you like about it?
- What would you like to improve?

2 Write your script.
3 Act it out.

Our town is surrounded by mountains, and lots of people go walking.
There aren't many shops, but there's a good sports centre. It's quiet at night. The town needs a cinema or a theatre.

02 Hello? Hello?

READING

Power up

1 Match these words for *Good morning*, to the correct language (1–7). How many do you know?

A bom dia
D 早安
E dzień dobry
B Καλημέρα
F صباح الخير
C доброе утро
G Buenos días

1 Arabic
2 Chinese
3 Greek
4 Polish
5 Portuguese
6 Spanish
7 Russian

2 Which languages have a different alphabet from English/from your language?

Read on

3 Read the text on page 17 quickly. Which countries and languages does it mention?

4 Read the text again. Are the sentences (1–10) true (T) or false (F)?

1 James didn't have a job when he left school. T
2 On the talent day people did a number of different tests.
3 The testers wanted to find people who were good at music.
4 James cooked food in a Turkish restaurant.
5 The winner of the prize was James.
6 Part of the prize was a trip abroad.
7 Arabic is not an easy language for most people.
8 James didn't learn many new words.
9 James' family were with him in Jordan.
10 James' TV interview was not very good.

Exam

Look for words and phrases in the text that have a similar or an opposite meaning from those in the question.

5 Find words in the text that mean the following.

1 not happy because you are thinking about a problem: w*orried*
2 sure that you can do something well: c __________
3 having a lot of rules: s __________
4 angry: c __________
5 a bit frightened; not calm: n __________
6 pleased with someone's success: p __________

Sum up

6 Work with a partner. Talk about …

1 the tests that James did on the talent day.
2 a thing that James did in the Turkish restaurant.
3 some things that were difficult about learning Arabic.
3 a thing that James did in Jordan.
4 the difference in James' life at the beginning and end of his story.

On the talent day, James did various tests. For example, …

Speak up

7 In your opinion, is James' talent a good one? What hidden talent would you like?

In my opinion, James' talent is …
I'd like to be able to …

Finding *your* talent!

Do you have a secret talent? Some people find their talent at school. Other people have a hidden talent which they discover later – often by accident!

When James Whinnery left school, he didn't know what to do, and his family were worried about his future. He wanted a job, but then he saw an advert for some talent tests. James believed he didn't have any talents, but he wanted to find out.

Nine hundred people went to the test centre and took part in various talent tests, such as opera singing, diving and remembering faces. Was James good at anything? A small group of people, including James, did well in the language test. James was surprised because he didn't study any languages at school. The testers wanted people with a good ear for sounds. 'Languages are like music,' explained one tester.

Next, James and his new friends learnt some Turkish. What can you learn in one day? First, they said greetings:, 'Merhaba' and 'Hosh geldiniz'. Then, they repeated lists of food words because their next challenge was to work in a Turkish restaurant! The language learners greeted customers and took food orders in Turkish. It was difficult to remember all the new words, but James was confident.

'Languages are like music'

In fact, James was the best Turkish speaker in the group. So, did he win a prize? Yes, he won an Arabic course and a five-week trip to Jordan. James didn't believe it! 'You never can tell,' he said. It was a fantastic chance to change his life. James moved to London to study Arabic – a very difficult language for most learners. The teachers were helpful, but strict. The alphabet and pronunciation weren't easy to understand, but James learned one hundred new words each day!

Life away from home was also strange, and James found it hard to study. When he had an interview on an Arabic radio station in London, he couldn't answer the interviewer's questions. James was cross with himself, but he carried on with his studies and travelled to Jordan.

James lived with a family in Jordan, so he spoke the language every day. On his last day, James was on TV for a twenty-minute interview in Arabic! At first, he was nervous because he remembered his terrible radio interview. The interviewer asked James lots of questions, and soon he was confident again. The interview was a success! 'If I can do that, I can do anything!' laughed James.

Back at home, James' family were all proud of him, and his life started to change. He is now studying to be an English teacher, and he wants to work in Japan so he can learn another difficult language!

SWITCH ON A special talent page 23

VOCABULARY
Language and communication

1 Complete the conversations (1–7) with these verbs. Use the meanings to help you.

mean = to have a meaning, definition or explanation
pronounce = to say a word with the correct sounds
repeat = to say or do something again
say = to speak words (to give information or opinions)
speak = to talk to people; to say and understand words of a language
translate = to change words from one language into another language
understand = to know what something means
explain = to tell someone about something so they can understand

1 **A:** Now, listen and ___repeat___ after me. 'Success'.
B: Success.
2 **A:** How do you ____________ 'difícil' in English?
B: Hard or difficult.
3 **A:** What does 'challenge' ____________ ?
B: Something new, exciting or difficult.
4 **A:** Can anyone ____________ Italian?
B: Yes, I can.
5 **A:** How do you ____________ 'competition'?
B: Com-pe-ti-tion. Repeat after me. Competition.
6 **A:** Can you ____________ 'worried'?
B: Yes, that's 'preocupado'.
7 **A:** I'm sorry, I don't ____________ this grammar.
B: Don't worry, I can ____________ it again.

2 2.1 **Listen and check your answers.**

3 Choose one verb to complete each pair of sentences.

1 talk/tell
1) ____________ us a story.
She didn't 2) ____________ me the answer.
My grandparents often 3) ____________about the old days.
If I have a problem, I 4) ____________ to my friends.
2 speak/say
We 5) ____________ two languages at home.
My sisters 6) ____________ in very quiet voices.
7) ____________ the alphabet in English.
Sorry, what did you 8) ____________ ?
3 hear/listen
Please 9) ____________ to your teacher.
10) ____________ ! This song is amazing.
Can you 11) ____________ me now?
Everyone is talking so I can't 12) ____________ the answer.

Word XP

Some verbs and prepositions go together.
listen to, talk to, speak to, explain (something) to + someone
*Who were you **talking to**?*
talk about, speak about + something
*What were you **talking about**?*

4 Choose the correct answer, A, B or C.

1 Our teacher sometimes ____________ us stories about her life in the UK.
A speaks **B** says **(C)** tells
2 It's difficult to ____________ that phrase because I don't know the meaning.
A talk **B** translate **C** listen
3 Can you ____________ the answer to us, please?
A explain **B** speak **C** understand
4 Nadia can ____________ Russian and English.
A tell **B** say **C** speak
5 Do you ____________ to your mum when you have a problem?
A say **B** talk **C** hear
6 A foreign language is useful if you want to ____________ to people from other countries.
A speak **B** pronounce **C** translate

Game on

Work with a partner. Take it in turns to say a word from the page. Your partner makes a sentence with the word in it.
A: *Listen.* **B:** *You never listen to me.*

GRAMMAR

Grammar XP

p. 135

Past simple

Use the past simple of the verb *be* for situations that finished in the past.

*James **was** on TV.*

*The alphabet and the pronunciation **weren't** easy.*

Use the past simple of regular and irregular verbs for:

a completed past action.

*Testers **discovered** that James **had** a real talent.*

*So, **did** he **win** a prize?*

one completed past action after another.

*They **greeted** customers and **took** food orders.*

a past habit or regular past event.

*James **learnt** one hundred new words each day!*

1 **Look again at the text on page 17. Make a list of regular and irregular past tense verbs in the text.**

2 **Make questions about James.**

1 have a job / James / before the programme / ?
Did James have a job before the programme?
2 James / in the first test / do well / ?
3 learn / what / language / for the restaurant / James / ?
4 James / what prize / win / ?
5 which / country / go to / he / ?
6 stay / he / with a family / ?

3 **Write answers to the questions in Exercise 2.**

4 **Look at the table. Make six sentences in the past about you.**

I My friend My teacher My friends	spoke (to) didn't speak (to) wrote didn't write phoned didn't phone talked to didn't talk to listened to didn't listen to understood didn't understand	(who?)	yesterday. last week. last month. two days ago. six weeks ago.

My friend phoned me last week.
I didn't understand my science lesson yesterday.

5 **Read Marisol's report. Complete the report with the correct form of the verbs in brackets.**

Home | stuff | About me | links | GO

Status | Photo | Check In

Classroom in the kitchen

Where did you go and why?

My grandparents are Mexican, but before this summer, I didn't 1) ___________ (speak) much Spanish. My brother and I 2) ___________ (go) to my grandparents' house in Mexico to change that.

How did you learn?

We 3) ___________ (live) in Merida for one month. We didn't use any books, but we didn't need them. My grandmother 4) ___________ (teach) us to cook in Spanish. We 5) ___________ (buy) food in the local shops, and we 6) ___________ (make) dinner together every day. We 7) ___________ (listen) to Mexican songs on the radio in the kitchen, too.

What did your grandfather teach you?

Some days, my grandfather 8) ___________ (take) us to interesting places. We 9) ___________ (talk) about the places in Spanish, and read tourist guides. One day, Granddad shut the car door on his finger. I 10) ___________ (hear) him say a new word. 'What does that mean, Granddad?' I asked. 'You don't need to know that word,' he told me! I'm not bilingual yet, but I'm good at communicating in Spanish.

Unlike · Comment 25 11

Write on

6 **Write one true sentence and one false sentence about last week. Swap with a partner and guess which sentence is true.**

LISTENING

Power up

1 **What's a good way to learn something new? Use these ideas.**

do a course
GET AN APP
look online
read books
talk to other people
watch someone else

2 **What's the best way for you to learn: a new dance, a computer game, English?**

Listen up

3 **2.2 Listen to the first part of a radio interview with Daniel. What summer camp did he go to?**

4 **2.3 Listen to the second part of the interview and complete the notes.**

Length of each course 1) *a week* Number of students at the camp: 2) ______
Ages of students: 3) ______
Daniel met students from 4) ______ and ______
On the first day, Daniel learned how to 5) ______ .
The competition prize was 6) ______ . Daniel's app helps people to 7) ______ . Daniel's favourite group in his app is 8) ______ .

Exam

Are you listening for information to complete your notes? For each question, write only the missing words or numbers that you hear. Don't try to use other words.

Grammar XP

p. 135

Past simple and past continuous

We use the past continuous to describe an action in progress in the past.

*Twelve students **were doing** the course.*
*How many students **were doing** course?*

We use the past simple when it interrupts an action in progress (past continuous) in the past.

*I was organising a basketball competition when **I had** an idea.*

We can use *while* instead of *when*, but only before the past continuous.

***While** I was organising a basketball competition, I had an idea.*

5 **Complete the message with the correct form of the verbs in brackets.**

I'm staying with a great family. This morning I had my first English class. I 1) *was waiting* (wait) outside the classroom when a girl 2) ______ (start) talking to me. Guess what? She was on the same plane as me yesterday! She 3) ______ (see) me at the airport while I 4) ______ (stand) at the bus stop. She had no idea I was coming to the same school. This morning we had a test. While I 5) ______ (do) it my phone 6) ______ (ring). Everybody looked at me!
More soon …

Like · Comment 5 1

6 **Work with a partner and discuss. What are your favourite apps? When do you use them?**

SPEAKING

Power up

1 **How do you and your friends usually arrange to do things?**

by email
by text
by phone
on a social networking site
other

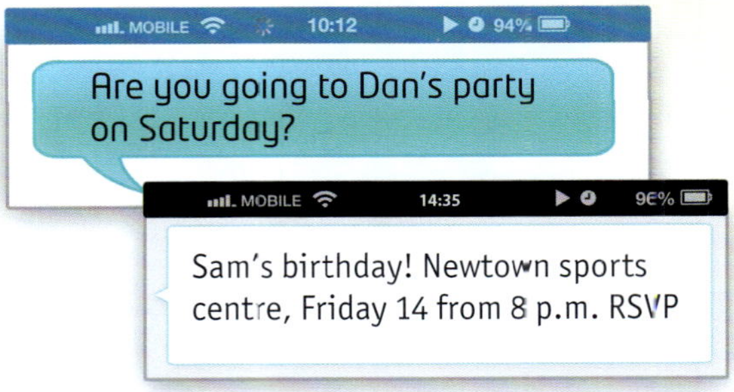

2 **What problems do you sometimes have when you try to arrange things?**

Speak up

3 **2.4 Listen to three short conversations. What is the problem in each conversation?**

4 **2.5 Listen again. Put the expressions in the order you hear them.**

Sorry. I couldn't hear you.
Thanks for calling.
Just a second. 1
We were cut off.
Hang on.
I haven't got a signal.

5 **Work with a partner. Look at the information on the role cards and practise the conversation. Use the Language XP box to help you.**

Student A
You're at a music festival. You decide to call a friend to arrange to meet them at eight o'clock, but there's a problem and you have to end the call.

Student B
Your friend calls from a music festival, but you can't hear them. You think there probably isn't a very good signal at the festival. When your friend calls you back, you still can't hear very well.

Student A
Say hello and say who you are. Tell your partner where you are and tell them what time to come.

Student B
Apologise and say you can't hear them well. Explain why.

Tell your partner to wait because you are going to move to a different place. Then call again.

Tell your partner it's better and you can hear them but ask them to speak louder.

Skill

You can't always hear or understand what people are saying. It's fine to ask people to speak louder or repeat things.

Language XP

Asking who's calling
Is that …?

Saying who's calling
It's …

Asking someone to wait
Just a second./Just a minute./Hang on.

Saying when there's a problem
Sorry, I can't hear you.
We were cut off.
I haven't got a signal.

Asking someone to talk louder or repeat
Can you speak/talk louder please?
What did you say?

6 **Work with a partner. Close your books and practise the conversation again.**

7 **Tell the rest of the class what happened when you had your conversation. Who called who and what was the problem?**

WRITING
Power up

1 **Why do these things sometimes happen when you are learning a language?**

you forget a word
you go red
you panic and say nothing
you say the wrong word

2 **Which English words do you find difficult to spell or pronounce?**

3 **Read the story. Find ten adjectives and two adverbs.**

About studentspot GO

My Student Life

Star Letter

A funny thing happened to me!

Last year, I was staying with a wonderful family in Scotland. The mum was very kind and cooked brilliant food. One day, we were eating a traditional Sunday lunch of roast chicken with potatoes and vegetables, and a brown sauce called gravy. It was delicious. While we were eating, I tried to make conversation and said, 'This kitchen is really good'. Everyone looked surprised. 'It's old now,' said the mum. 'My husband did it a few years ago.' Then I realised the word I wanted to say was 'chicken'. I always get kitchen and chicken confused because they sound the same. In the end, we all laughed.

4 **Rewrite the sentences (1–5) with these words.**

disgusting fantastic ~~furious~~ hilarious huge

1 The teacher was very angry.
The teacher was furious.
2 The pizza was very bad.
3 They lived in a really big house.
4 The film was very good.
5 John's joke was really funny.

Language XP

Use strong adjectives to make your writing more interesting.

awful *brilliant* *delicious (food)*
disgusting *fantastic* *furious* *hilarious*
huge *terrible* *wonderful*

You can also use an adverb to make an adjective stronger.

***really** kind* ***very** big* ***extremely** dangerous*

Don't use *very* or *extremely* with strong adjectives.

~~very~~ fantastic *~~extremely~~ brilliant*

5 **Which adjectives can you use with *very, really* or *extremely*?**

1 The history exam was difficult.
The history exam was very difficult.
2 Olivia is brilliant at languages.
3 Luke told us some funny jokes.
4 Guy and Anna made a delicious dinner.
5 The DVD was boring.
6 Emma wrote a fantastic story.

Plan on

6 Read the advert and answer the questions.

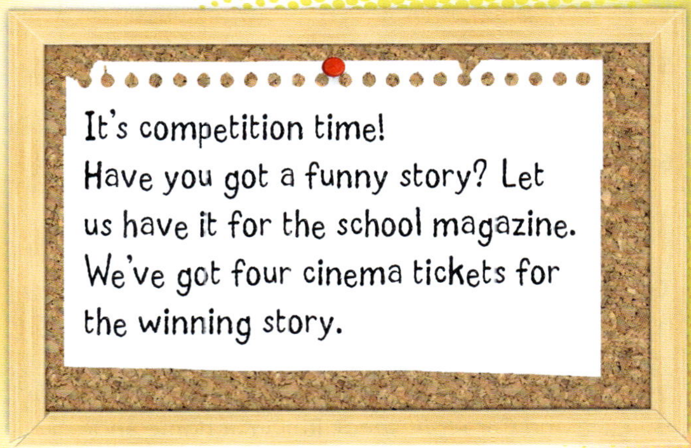

1 What kind of story does the competition want?
2 Who's going to read the story?
3 Where's the story going to appear?

7 Read the ideas for funny stories and add three more ideas.

I was talking to my friend when I fell off the chair.

I was singing in a school concert when I forgot the words.

It was the day of our school trip, but I got up late.

8 Choose an idea for a funny story in Exercise 7. Answer the questions.

1 When did it happen?
2 Where did it happen?
3 Who was there?
4 What was the main action?
5 What happened in the end?

Write on

9 Write a funny story for the school magazine. Write about 100 words. Begin like this.

A funny thing happened to me ...

Skill

Are you writing a story? First, think of an idea. Then, plan it, e.g. When? Where? Who? What happened in the end?

Switch on

A SPECIAL TALENT

1 Guess the answers. Then watch and check.

You're going to watch Tim speak some of the languages he knows.

1 How old is Tim in the video?
A 16 **B** 20
2 Will Tim speak your language?
A yes **B** no

2 Choose the correct answer, A, B or C.

1 Tim is a polyglot – he can speak many languages. How many does he know?
A 8 **B** nearly 20 **C** more than 20
2 Tim lives in a big city with people from many countries. Which city?
A Rio de Janeiro **B** New York **C** Sydney
3 According to the sub-titles, which language does Tim think has difficult pronunciation and grammar?
A Russian **B** Arabic **C** Turkish
4 Tim speaks the foreign languages in the order he learned them. Put these languages in the correct order, 1–3.
A Arabic **B** Russian **C** Turkish

3 Which of Tim's languages would you like to learn? Why?

Project

4 Write your own video script for a short two-minute film about learning a language.

1 Decide on these things:
- What language is your film about? (a language you know or you want to learn? sign language?)
- What problems will you talk about?
- What advice will you give on how to study this language?
- What 'props' will you need? (a board? a laptop? books? other people?)

2 Write your script.
3 Act it out.

Why don't you learn ...?
You should ... / You could ...

VOCABULARY

1 Match the sentence halves.

1 Mark is afraid *E*
2 They're fed up
3 Carla is brilliant
4 I'm interested
5 Jack is excited
6 My dad's terrible

A at dancing. She dances with the National Ballet.
B in languages. I'd like to learn Chinese.
C with the weather here. It rains all the time.
D at cooking. He always burns the food!
E of dogs. He doesn't like to be near them.
F about his holiday to Mexico. He loves travelling.

2 Complete the conversations with the correct word.

explain ~~mean~~ pronounce repeat translate understand

1 **A:** What does 'furious' __*mean*__ ?
B: Very angry.
2 **A:** Can you ________ your question please?
B: Yes, of course. What is the capital city of Brazil?
3 **A:** I don't ________ what Akiko's saying. What language is she speaking?
B: Japanese. She's from Tokyo.
4 **A:** Can you ________ this sentence from German to Polish?
B: No, I can't, I don't know Polish.
5 **A:** How do you ________ the name of this town?
B: Worcester? It's easy, Wors – ter.
6 **A:** Can you ________ how this app works, please?
B: Yes, let me show you.

3 Choose the correct answer, A, B, C or D.

1 My brother's very ________ . He always gets good marks in his school exams.
A shy (**B**) clever **C** sporty **D** bossy
2 You're so ________ ! Stop telling me what to do.
A serious **B** clever **C** bossy **D** lively
3 Rosie doesn't speak to many people at parties. She's not very ________ .
A confident **B** funny **C** rude **D** quiet
4 My cousins are very ________ . They never help my aunty do jobs in the house.
A noisy **B** calm **C** lazy **D** sporty
5 Can you be ________ , please? The baby's asleep.
A quiet **B** lively **C** noisy **D** bossy
6 Harriet never says 'please' and 'thank you'. She's very ________ .
A lively **B** rude **C** confident **D** shy

4 Choose the correct answer.

1 Rachel *said/told* that she was interested in learning Spanish.
2 Did you *listen/hear* the news about Mark?
3 Luca and Cara *talk/speak* Italian at home and English at school.
4 What did you *say/speak*? I can't hear you very well.
5 I was *hearing/listening* to the teacher, but I didn't understand what she meant.
6 I *said/told* Francesca about the party, but she can't go.

5 Complete the blog with the correct words.

~~at~~ confident in lively of repeat shy understand

home about

Rachel's stuff

My first week in Spain

When I first arrived at my language school in Playa del Carmen, I was really bad 1) __*at*__ speaking Spanish. I was also very 2) ________ and didn't want to talk to anyone. Now, a week later, I'm a different person! My Spanish still isn't brilliant, but I am 3) ________ enough to practise speaking. I'm not frightened 4) ________ making mistakes when I speak Spanish because all the people are so friendly here. The teachers are always happy to 5) ________ things if you don't 6) ________ the first time. It's a really 7) ________ school with lots of fun activities and trips for students. I'm really interested 8) ________ water sports and you can do surfing and sailing here. It's an amazing place to learn Spanish!

GRAMMAR

6 Put the words in the correct order to make sentences.

1 get up early / I / at the weekend. / usually
I usually get up early at the weekend.
2 go / once a year. / on holiday / We
3 play / now and then. / Ben and Holly / volleyball
4 after school / play / three times a week. / I / sport
5 go / My friends and I / once a month. / to the cinema
6 goes / Alicia / most weekends. / shopping

7 Complete the sentences and questions with the present simple or present continuous form of the verbs in brackets.

1 Luke isn't at school today. He *isn't feeling* very well. (not feel)
2 I ___________ my bike every day. (not ride)
3 My brother ___________ blonde hair and blue eyes. (have)
4 That smells really nice! What ___________ you ___________ ? (cook)
5 Grace and Noah ___________ to go on holiday to France. (want)
6 Hector ___________ with his grandparents while his parents are decorating their house. (live)
7 I ___________ this maths problem. (not understand)
8 Tim and Simon ___________ to some music on the computer at the moment. (listen)

8 Complete the past simple questions with the correct form of the verbs.

be be ~~be~~ enjoy give learn ~~watch~~ wear

1 What film *did* you *watch* at the cinema last night?
2 Why ___________ Jacob and Tom late for football practice yesterday?
3 ___________ they ___________ their trip to Paris last month?
4 When ___________ your sister's birthday?
5 ___________ you excited about the news?
6 ___________ Rebecca ___________ her new dress to the party last Friday?
7 Where ___________ you ___________ how to dance?
8 What homework ___________ your teacher ___________ you yesterday?

9 Complete the sentences. Use the past simple or past continuous of the verbs in brackets.

1 Where *was* Stephen *going* when you *saw* him outside the library? (go, see)
2 I ___________ football with my friends when I ___________ my leg. (play, break)
3 Oliver ___________ breakfast when he ___________ the news on the radio. (have, hear)
4 What ___________ you ___________ when the fire ___________ ? (do, start)
5 Emilia ___________ French when she ___________ Alice. (study, meet)
6 William ___________ asleep while he ___________ a film. (fall, watch)

10 Complete the conversation with the correct answer, A, B or C.

Tom: When did you move from Turkey to the UK?
Aysun: In 2010. My dad 1) ___________ a job in London.
Tom: Did you 2) ___________ English before you came here?
Aysun: Yes. I was good at English at my school in Turkey, but when I arrived in London, I 3) ___________ understand what people 4) ___________ ! Everybody spoke so fast.
Tom: And do you enjoy living in the UK?
Aysun: Yes. I've got some really good friends here, and I 5) ___________ the music in this country.
Tom: Is there anything you don't like?
Aysun: Well, I get fed up with the weather! Sometimes when it 6) ___________ and cold in July, I think about the Turkish summers!
Tom: And what do you do in your free time?
Aysun: I 7) ___________ the guitar and sing. I'm in a band, and at the moment, we 8) ___________ for a concert in our local park.
Tom: That sounds great – good luck!

1	**A** get	**B** was getting	**C** got (circled)
2	**A** know	**B** knew	**C** were knowing
3	**A** didn't	**B** don't	**C** wasn't
4	**A** are saying	**B** say	**C** were saying
5	**A** like	**B** 'm liking	**C** liked
6	**A** was raining	**B** 's raining	**C** rained
7	**A** played	**B** play	**C** 'm playing
8	**A** 're practising	**B** practise	**C** practised

03 Sounds of the future

READING

Power up

1 **Look at the photos. Do we hear, taste or smell these things? Sometimes more than one answer is possible.**

2 **Think of two things you like the sound, taste and smell of.**

Read on

3 **Read the news report quickly. What food does it mention?**

Sounds good, tastes good?

What's the first thing that you notice when you walk into your favourite pizza restaurant? Is it the smell of fresh pizza, or the sight of your favourite desserts? Food that looks or smells good will probably taste good, but what about sound? Is that important, too?

Scientists now believe that the taste of food can change when your brain hears different sounds, but it has to be the right kind of sound. When you switch on a microwave with popcorn in it, it soon starts to pop. Do you think, 'That sounds tasty!'? Not really, you probably think it's nearly ready, but it's when you smell it that you go to get the salt or the butter. Hearing the popcorn makes you think about it, but smelling it reminds you that it tastes good. So, what are the sounds that change how things taste?

In a recent experiment in a fish restaurant, customers wore headphones. They listened to the sound of the seaside while they ate. Did it make a difference? Yes, it did. Listening to the sea seemed to improve the taste of the food. It was fresher and saltier. When the restaurant tried the same experiment with the sound of farm animals, there was no difference in taste. The results are going to be useful for companies that make food. Perhaps they'll try to reduce the amount of unhealthy things, like salt and sugar in food. With the right music or sounds, perhaps we won't taste the difference.

Food companies are also beginning to see a connection between food and the sound the packet makes. Pick up a bag of your favourite crisps. What does it sound like? One crisp company recently changed the material that they used to make their crisp packets because research shows that a packet which makes the right noise will make customers think the crisps are fresher. Another idea is that playlists will begin to appear on food packets, so if you aren't keen on your greens, the right background sounds could help you learn to love them!

Will sound change the taste of our food? Tell us what you think.
(3 comments)

We'll see. I don't like fish, but I love listening to the sea. I'm going to try listening to some music when I next eat it. Perhaps I'll like it.
Tom, 15

It depends on the music. What happens if the music's terrible? Will the food taste terrible?
🙁🙁 **Will, 16**

I'm sure it will. I think I'll try it! I also read that in the future, fridges will make different sounds, so that people will think the food is fresher. That's so cool.
Olivia, 17

4 Read the news report again. Choose the correct answer, A, B, C or D.

1 What is the online article trying to do?
A find out if people like pizza
B explain how sound can change the taste of food
C compare different tastes and smells of food
D make people eat more green vegetables

2 What do you do when popcorn in the microwave begins to make noise?
A You plan what you will put on it.
B You start to smell it.
C You take it out of the microwave.
D You begin to imagine the taste of it.

3 What was the result of the experiment in the restaurant?
A The sounds of the seaside made the food taste better.
B The customers didn't like the food.
C The headphones spoiled the taste of the food.
D The customers preferred the sounds of the farm animals.

4 Why is the material of the packet important?
A Customers want it to sound and look right.
B Customers enjoy looking at the different materials.
C Customers think the food is good if it makes the right sound.
D Customers don't like noisy packets.

5 What does Olivia think of the idea of fridges that make different sounds?
A She doesn't like the idea.
B She hates the idea.
C She thinks it's a good idea.
D She's not sure about the idea.

Exam

Are you answering questions about a text? First, find the key words in the questions. Then, look for the key words in the text.

5 Find words in the news report that mean the following.

1 sweet food that you eat after the main part of your meal
2 the sound that popcorn makes when it is cooked
3 large organisations that make or sell products
4 make the amount of size of something less than it was before
5 white or brown sweet food
6 a list of songs or music for you to listen to

Sum up

6 Work with a partner. Explain the following in your own words.

1 the connection between the smell and taste of food
2 how sound can change how food tastes
3 why the sound of a packet of food is important

Speak up

7 Work with a partner and discuss. Do you agree that the right sound can change the taste of food? Why/Why not? What food would you like to try this experiment with?

SWITCH ON The future is here! page 23

VOCABULARY

Technology around the home

1 **Match these words with the technology (A–F) we can control with a phone app.**

air conditioning dishwasher fridge
microwave washing machine

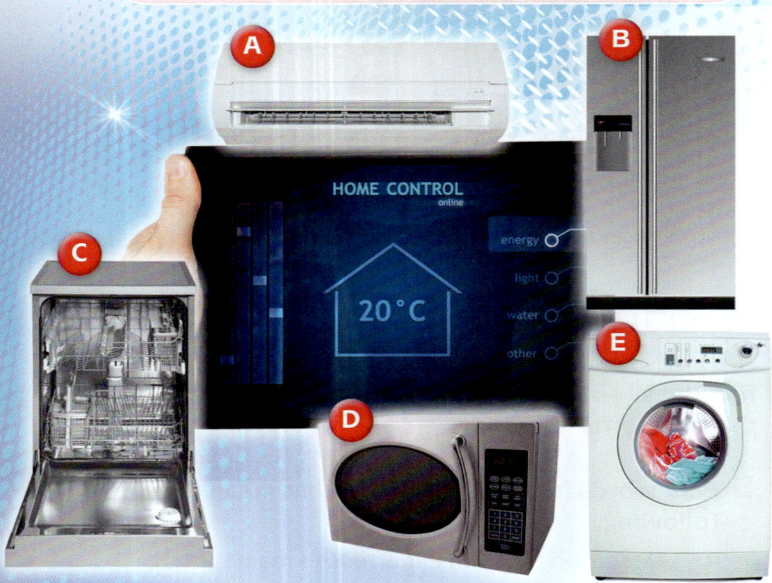

2 **Complete the sentences with these words/ phrases.**

3D TV hair straighteners hairdryer
headphones iron plug speakers

1 There was a problem with the _speakers_ at the party so they couldn't hear the music.
2 Ellie doesn't like her curly hair, so she uses her __________ on it every day.
3 I'm buying some new __________ because my old ones are too big for my ears.
4 Go and get the __________. It's cold, and you shouldn't go out with wet hair.
5 It's great watching action films on our new __________ because the picture is really good.
6 I don't know which __________ is for the computer. There are too many cables here.
7 Be careful when you use the __________ on those trousers. It's very hot.

3 3.1 **Listen to six sounds. What are they? Use some of the words in the boxes in Exercises 1 and 2.**

Word XP

Compound nouns

We can put two nouns together to make a compound noun. We usually do this in two ways, e.g. *washing machine* (two separate nouns), *hairdryer* (two nouns together).

4 **Make a list of the different compound nouns on the page.**

5 **Match these phrasal verbs with the correct meanings (1–6).**

pick up plug in switch off switch on
turn down turn up

1 connect a piece of equipment to the electricity supply: _plug in_
2 lift something or someone:
3 make the sound louder:
4 start the electricity supply to something:
5 make the sound quieter:
6 stop the electricity supply to something:

6 **Complete the second sentence with the phrasal verbs in Exercise 5.**

1 Don't leave your bedroom light on when you go out. _Switch off_ the light when you leave the room.
2 The music is too loud. Make it quieter, please. __________ the music, please. It's too loud.
3 They wanted to move the fridge, but it was heavy and they couldn't lift it.
They couldn't __________ the fridge because it was very heavy.
4 Can you start the dishwasher before you go out? Can you __________ the dishwasher before you go out?
5 Where can I connect my laptop to the electricity supply?
Where can I __________ my laptop?
6 The cake isn't cooking because the oven isn't hot enough.
The cake isn't cooking. Can you __________ the oven?

Game on

Work with a partner. On a piece of paper, take it in turns to draw a picture explaining one of the words or phrasal verbs from the page. Can your partner guess what the word or phrasal verb is?

GRAMMAR

Grammar XP

p. 136

Talking about the future

will

Use *will* for:

predictions.

*However, with the right music or sounds, perhaps we **won't taste** the difference.*

*Perhaps playlists **will begin to appear** on food packets.*

offers and immediate decisions.

***I'll get** the salt.*

*I think **I'll try** it.*

going to

Use *going to* for:

plans.

***I'm going to try** listening to some music when I next eat vegetables.*

things that we expect to happen because of something we know now

*The results **are going to be** useful for companies that make food.*

1 Choose the correct form to complete the conversations.

1 **A:** I can't find my hairdryer.
B: Oh sorry, it's in my bedroom. I*'m going to*/*'ll get* it for you.

2 **A:** Do you want to go out tonight?
B: No, thanks. I *'ll/'m going to* watch TV because my favourite programme is on.

3 **A:** The game is nearly over, and Nathan's won all the points.
B: Yes, he has. He *'ll/'s going to* win this match.

4 **A:** My speakers aren't working.
B: Just a minute. I *'ll/'m going to* have a look at them.

5 **A:** Are you OK?
B: Stop the car. I *'ll/'m going to* be sick!

6 **A:** Jake knows lots about computers.
B: Yes, he does. Perhaps he *'ll/'s going to* work with computers in the future.

2 Make sentences about you with *will* or *going to*.

1 Technology you will/won't have in your bedroom in the future.
I'll have a big 3-D TV.

2 The next thing you plan to buy with your money.

3 Plans you have for the weekend.

4 Something you are going to offer to do for your mum or dad tonight, to help them.

3 Read the email. Choose the correct word, A, B, C or D for each space.

Amazing screens

Hi Sam,

I had a great time at the weekend at the technology fair in London. I saw lots of things that 1) __________ have around the home in the future. There was an interactive 3-D TV, where monsters and scary things jump out of the screen! In the future, cinemas 2) __________ just have big screens – they'll have exciting interactive screens. Dad says 3) __________ going to happen for ages. 4) '__________ will be too expensive,' he says. 'People 5) __________ buy them,' but he's just too old. We also saw some fridges. They know when they are empty, and they can send a message to your mobile. Dad loves that idea. He says he's going 6) __________ get one. 7) __________ show you the photos.

What about Saturday? 8) __________ you going to be at Matt's party? Let me know.

Ben

	A	B	C	D
1	we're	we won't	we'd	(D) we'll
2	will	won't	isn't	don't
3	it's	doesn't	it isn't	it won't
4	We	He	They	Them
5	aren't going to	won't	Will	do
6	to	won't	for	not
7	I'm not	I don't	I'm	I'll
8	Is	Will	Do	Are

Speak up

4 Work with a partner and discuss. What are your plans for tonight? Are you going to see friends? How much homework do you think you'll have? Will there be any good programmes on TV?

I'm going to watch a film at my friend's house.
I won't have any homework because it's Friday!

LISTENING

Power up

1 Work with a partner. Look at the picture and discuss the questions.

1 Do you think a robot vacuum cleaner …
- is noisy or quiet?
- has a cord and a plug?
- needs a person to use it?

2 Look at the photos in Exercise 3. With a partner, name the objects and discuss which things you have in your home.

Have you got hair straighteners?
No, but I've got a hairdryer.

Listen up

Exam

Are you listening for specific information? Before you listen, think about the names of the objects in the pictures.

3 3.2 **Listen and choose the correct answer A, B or C.**

1 Which does the woman like best?

2 What has a music player in it?

3 Which book is the girl going to read?

4 Which mobile ring tone does the girl choose?

5 What does the boy want?

Grammar XP

p. 136

someone, anyone, everyone, no one
something, anything, everything, nothing

Use these indefinite pronouns to talk about people: *someone, anyone, everyone, no one.*

***Someone** borrowed it yesterday.*
*Has **anyone** read it yet?*
***Everyone** likes the Baby Rap ringtone!*
***No one** has read it yet.*

Use these indefinite pronouns to talk about things: *something, anything, everything, nothing.*

*I'd like **something** funny.*
*Do you want **anything**?*
*It will tell us **everything** about the future of gadgets.*
*There's **nothing** in the fridge!*

We use *somebody/anybody* and *something/anything* in the same way as *some/any.*

4 Choose the correct word to complete the sentences.

1 Have you got *anything/nothing* to eat in your bag?
2 *Anyone/No one* in our family uses hair straighteners.
3 Is *someone/everyone* in our class going to go on the trip?
4 This is a great computer game. *Everything/Something* is really cool.
5 Where's the rest of our class? I can't see no one/anyone.
6 Do you want your present? I've got *something/everything* for you.
7 I'm sure *someone/anyone* knows the answer to this question.
8 We don't want to go to the cinema because there's *anything/nothing* on.

SPEAKING

Power up

1 Work with a partner. Talk about where you have seen robots.

films
toyshops
science laboratories
museums
the real world

2 Describe one robot you have seen. Could it do these things?

respond to instructions from a mobile phone
move to music tidy things record voices

3 3.3 Listen to a boy describing his robot. Which of the things in Exercise 2 can it do?

Speak up

4 Work with a partner. Look at the phrases for agreeing and disagreeing. Choose four phrases you can add to the Language XP box.

1 That's a good point.
2 You might be right.
3 Turn right.
4 I don't think so.
5 That's so funny.
6 I think so.

Language XP

Agreeing and disagreeing

I agree.	*I don't agree.*
I think that's right.	*I don't think that's right.*
Well, maybe …	*I'm not sure.*

5 Look at these robots. Choose one and describe it.

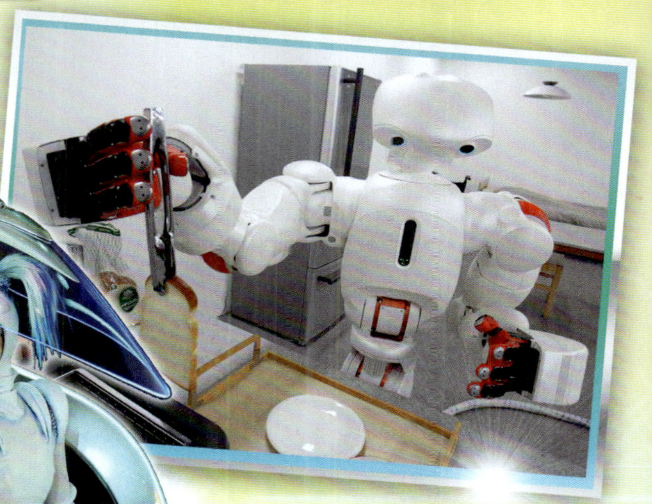

housework robot

transport robot

6 Work with a partner. Take it in turns to read your statements about the future of robots. Use the phrases in the Language XP box to agree or disagree with the statements. Do you think people will use these robots?

Scientists tell us about the future of robots …

Student A
They will make transport robots
These robots will look like chairs on wheels
People will sit on these robots
They will use them for short journeys

Student B
They will make housework robots
These robots will clean people's homes
They will carry things for us
They will bring us things we want

Skill

Are you taking turns with a partner? Listen to what they say, and then add your own view.

7 Work with a partner. Student A, look at page 130. Student B, look at page 142. Follow the instructions.

WRITING

Power up

1 Look at the technology word cloud. What other technology words can you add?

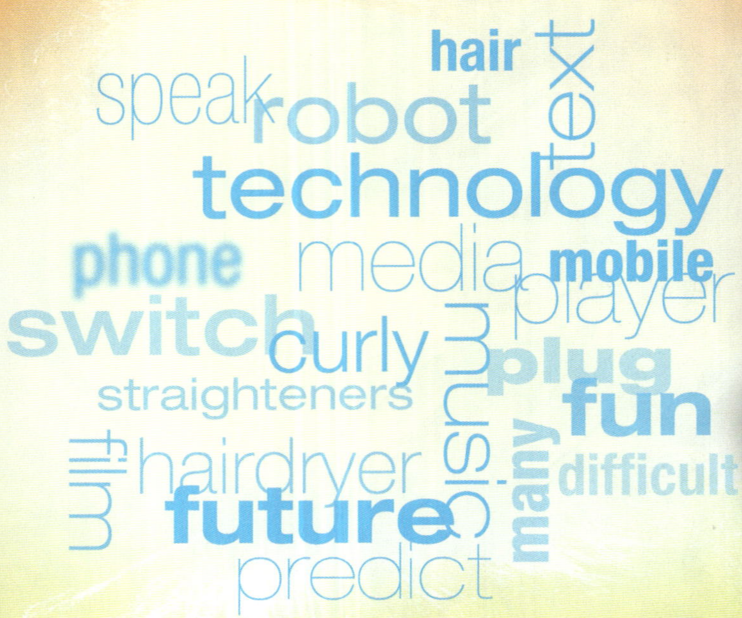

2 Read the notice and the two emails. Complete each space with the correct word.

– (no word) a an any some the

Severn Valley High School:

unplugged!

This year's 'Unplugged' day will be on 1) __________ Monday 15 January. Each student gives up 2) __________ gadget for the whole day.

What are YOU going to give up?

music player **mobile phone** **TV**
games console **computer or laptop**

Send us 3) __________ email. Explain the main reason for your decision. Predict how you will feel on the day.
We'll give 4) __________ free music vouchers for 5) __________ best email!
Send your ideas to the Technology Team

A

unplugged day

Dear technology team,

I'm going to give up watching TV for Unplugged Day. 6) __________ main reason for my decision is that I think it will be easy because I don't usually watch much TV anyway.
Another reason is that I won't spend 7) __________ time at home on Unplugged Day. I'll be at 8) __________ school until 3 p.m. and then I'll have football practice! In the evening, I'm going to play online games, so I won't miss TV at all.
Jason

B

give it up!

Dear technology team,
Everyone is giving up different things for Unplugged Day. Some of my friends will give up things that are easy, like TV.
Other people are going to give up their games consoles or mobiles. That will be more difficult than giving up TV because those things are more fun.
I'm going to give up my music player for one day because that's 9) __________ most difficult thing for me. I can't live without it, so it will be 10) __________ big challenge!
Best wishes,
Jade

3 **Which email in Exercise 2 gives one clear reason for a decision? Which email gives two reasons?**

4 **Choose the best answer.**

1 I'm going to watch X-Factor *so/because* it's my favourite programme.
2 I'm doing my homework on the laptop, *so/because* you can't play games on it.
3 We'll be away at the weekend, *so/because* I won't be able to come to the cinema.
4 He won't phone us *so/because* he can't get a mobile signal.
5 It's Jack's birthday, *so/because* we're going to go out for pizza.

Plan on

Language XP

Use *because* to give a reason for a decision.
Use *so* to give a result or next step.

5 **Ask and answer with a partner.**

1 What are you going to give up?
2 Will it be easier/more difficult than giving up TV/your mobile/your music player/your games console?
3 Why are you going to give up this thing?

6 **Complete the sentences for you.**

1 I'm going to give up …
2 It's easier/more difficult than giving up TV/my mobile/my music player/my games console.
3 I'm going to give up … because …

Write on

7 **Write an email to the technology team. Use the information in Exercise 6 to help you.**

Skill

When you've finished, read through your work. Check for simple errors, e.g. spelling, punctuation, correct use of articles (a/an/the).

Switch on

THE FUTURE IS HERE!

1 **Guess the answer. Then watch and check.**

Rebecca, Emma and Toby are talking about gadgets and technology in the future. In what order will they talk about these ideas?

A There won't be any shops on the high street.
B There won't be waitresses or waiters in restaurants.
C We will pay for everything electronically. We won't use money.

2 **Complete the sentences with these words.**

card cash online shopping
a robot ~~technology~~ tip

1 In the future you'll use __technology__ to order your food.
2 Maybe ________ will bring your food.
3 You don't have to ________ the computer.
4 We won't have ________ or coins on us any more.
5 You can tap your ________ and the money just goes.
6 There was a massive increase in ________ last year.

3 **Do you agree with the ideas in the video? Why/Why not? Do you think some of the ideas are true now?**

Project

4 **Work in small groups. Choose one of these ideas and make a poster called 'A look into the future'. Add pictures to support your ideas. Explain your poster to the class or make a video presentation.**

1 A look into the future!
2 Robots in the home.
3 Technology in schools.

We'll use robots to clean the house. They'll pick clothes up and put them in the washing machine.

04 Back to school

READING

Power up

1 **Where do you do these things? At home, at school or somewhere else?**

2 **Who knows more about these subjects and skills, students or teachers? Add three things to each list.**

fashion languages ~~science~~ ~~social networking sites~~

Students know more	Teachers know more
social networking sites	science

Read on

3 **Work with a partner. Look at the title of the article and photos on page 35. Answer the questions.**

1 Why has the man got a suitcase?
2 Who is teaching? What is the lesson?

4 **Read the article quickly and check your answers.**

5 **Read the article again. Choose the correct answer, A, B, C or D.**

	A	B	C	D
1	at	in	(C) on	to
2	his	their	our	your
3	under	in	on	outside
4	When	At	After	Next
5	there	here	it	where
6	Did	Was	Had	Could
7	stay	stop	finish	end
8	in	at	on	to
9	much	more	most	many
10	any	many	some	lots

Exam

When you've got your answers, read the text again with the words in the spaces. Do they sound correct?

6 **Find words in the article that mean the following.**

1 a piece of equipment that rings at the end of a lesson (Paragraph 1):
2 an ability to do something well (Paragraph 2):
3 something you get for doing well in a competition (Paragraph 2):
4 a person who tells you what work to do (Paragraph 3):
5 doing things that are silly or not useful (Paragraph 3):
6 sure that something is true (Paragraph 6):

Sum up

7 **Put the main events of the article in order. Use *First*, *Then*, *Next* and *Finally*.**

1 ____________, Mr Kershaw practised and revised.
2 ____________, Mr Kershaw learned ballet.
3 ____________, Ashley's teacher came to his house.
4 ____________, Ashley taught a scuba diving lesson.

Speak up

8 **Work with a partner and discuss. Was the weekend more difficult for Ashley or Mr Kershaw? Why? What skill would you like to teach your teacher?**

Pupil power!

Are students as clever as their teachers? Ashley and his teacher are going to find out.

1 Brrrring! The school bell was ringing at the end of another day. The teacher, Mr Kershaw, was giving the class their homework. It was the last lesson 1) ___on___ Friday afternoon, but Ashley wasn't happy. He was nervous. Why? Because it wasn't a normal weekend.

2 Mr Kershaw picked up a suitcase and went home – to Ashley's house! Actually, Ashley and Mr Kershaw were taking part in a TV series. In each programme, students taught 2) __________ teachers an unusual hobby, for example breakdancing, go-karting, rock climbing and ice skating. The poor teachers didn't know anything about these skills. They had one weekend to learn two new skills. Then. they had a test. So, what was the prize? An exciting adventure day for their whole class!

3 On Saturday morning, Mr Kershaw was sleeping when he heard a loud noise. Ashley was ringing a large bell 3) __________ the bedroom door. Mr Kershaw was too hungry to start lessons, so they had a big breakfast. After breakfast, Ashley explained his school rules carefully, 'No daydreaming. No mobile phones. No messing about.' 'You're the boss now,' said Mr Kershaw. 'Yeah, pupil power!' smiled Ashley happily.

"You're the boss now!"

4 4) __________, Ashley showed Mr Kershaw his curriculum and the timetable. There were only two subjects: scuba diving and ballet! Lesson one was ballet, but 5) __________ was no morning break. It was a long morning for the new ballet pupil, but he tried hard. 'I'm not a very stretchy person,' he explained. After the lunch break, the second lesson was scuba diving in a swimming pool. 6) __________ Mr Kershaw better at scuba diving than ballet? Yes!
Mr Kershaw was having fun. Scuba diving wasn't as difficult as ballet for Mr Kershaw, but in the evening Ashley gave him lots of homework. Mr Kershaw didn't 7) __________ it all because he was too tired!

5 On Sunday, Ashley taught Mr Kershaw more skills for both subjects. Mr Kershaw practised hard, and then 8) __________ the evening, he revised for his big test. On Monday morning, Mr Kershaw was 9) __________ nervous than Ashley. He wanted to pass, but could he do well enough? Would the test be too difficult?

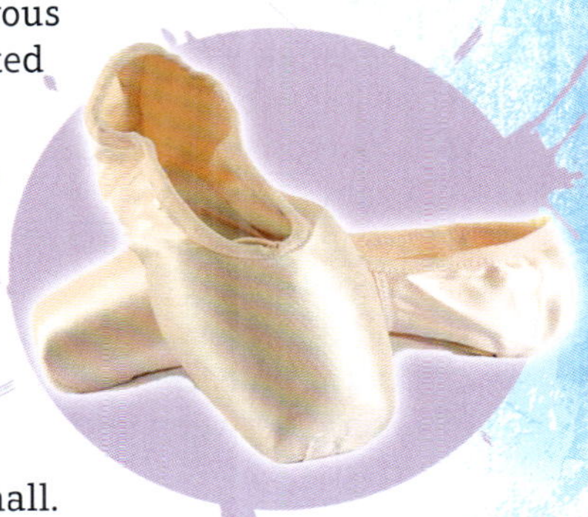

6 At school, he walked down the corridor and found 10) __________ of pupils in the school hall. When he took his ballet test they were all watching him. He danced slowly. An examiner marked his dancing. Could he get a good grade? And more importantly, did Mr Kershaw think Ashley was a good teacher? 'Definitely,' he answered. 'I'm very impressed.'

VOCABULARY

School and education

1 Match these nouns with the correct meanings (1–8).

break corridor curriculum examiner grade rule test timetable

1 the mark that a teacher gives for school work
2 a list of lessons and times for each day of the week
3 all the subjects students learn at school
4 a person who decides your mark in an exam
5 something you must or mustn't do at school
6 a long narrow area in a building, with rooms on each side
7 a time between lessons when you can talk to friends
8 a list of questions that check how much students know

2 4.1 Listen and check your answers.

3 Complete the sentences (1–5) with these verbs. Use the meanings and the article on page 35 to help you.

fail = to be unsuccessful in an exam
learn = to have lessons
pass = to be successful in an exam
practise = to do exercises
teach = to give lessons
revise = to study for a test/an exam

1 Ashley doesn't usually ___________ Mr Kershaw.
2 Ashley's class wants Mr Kershaw to ___________ his ballet exam, so that they can win a prize.
3 Mr Kershaw has to ___________ ballet and scuba diving in two days.
4 After he learns each new skill, Mr Kershaw must ___________ it.
5 Mr Kershaw must ___________ for his ballet exam because he doesn't want to ___________ .

4 Choose the correct words to complete the text.

I'm in an orchestra, and I'd like to 1) *learn/teach* my English teacher to play the violin. I'd be a good teacher, so she would 2) *learn/study* quickly. Music exams aren't easy, so a lot of students 3) *miss/fail*. In my opinion, you won't 4) *pass/take* your exam if you don't 5) *revise/practise* the violin every day.

Word XP

We use adverbs to say how we do something.
He explained carefully.
We form adverbs from adjectives. Add *-ly*.
*regular – regular**ly** slow – slow**ly***
For adjectives that end in *-y*, replace *-y* with *-ily*.
*easy – eas**ily** happy – happ**ily***
Some adjectives are irregular.
good – well
Some adjectives stay the same.
fast – fast high – high late – late long –long

5 Complete the second sentence so it means the same as the first. Use adverbs.

Top tips for learning a new skill

1 Do you want to be a quick learner?
learn quickly ? Write important words in colours.
2 Things are easy to remember if you draw doodles in your notebook!
You can ___________ if you draw doodles in your notebook!
3 If you want to be good at tests, try not to daydream.
If you want to do ___________ in tests, try not to daydream.
4 Your brain likes to get information 'little and often', so do regular revision.
Your brain likes to get information 'little and often', so ___________ .
5 Don't panic! Use careful planning. Don't panic! ___________

Game on

Work with a partner. Copy three sentences from the page, but change one word in one sentence. Then close your books. Swap sentences with a partner. Find and correct the mistake.

GRAMMAR

Grammar XP

p. 136

Making comparisons

Comparatives

Use *as* + adjective + *as* to compare two people or things that are equal.

*Are students **as clever as** their teachers?*

Use *not as* + adjective + *as* to compare two people or things that are not equal.

*Scuba diving **isn't as difficult** as ballet.*

We can also use adjective + *-er* + than or more + adjective + than to compare two people or things that are not equal.

*Was Mr Kershaw **better** at scuba diving **than** ballet?*

*Mr Kershaw was **more nervous than** Ashley.*

too/enough

Use *too* + adjective/adverb to mean 'more/less than necessary'.

*He didn't finish his homework because he was **too tired.***

Use adjective/adverb + *enough* to mean 'the right amount'.

*Could he do **well enough**?*

Use *not* + adjective/adverb + *enough* to mean 'not the right amount'.

*Mr Kershaw was **not stretchy enough**.*

1 Rewrite the sentences (1–6) so they have the same meaning. Use *not as … as*.

1 Climbing is more dangerous than football.
Football isn't as dangerous as climbing.
2 History is more useful than geography.
3 Singing is easier than playing a musical instrument.
4 Students are better at computer games than teachers.
5 Social networking sites are more interesting than fashion.
6 Ballet is safer than scuba diving.

2 Work with a partner. Do you agree or disagree with the statements in Exercise 1?

In my opinion, football isn't as exciting as basketball

I agree.

3 Choose the correct phrases.

1 Sam wants to be a comedian, but he is *too funny/not funny enough*.
2 Stop telling me what to do. You're *too bossy/not bossy enough*.
3 Irena never finishes her homework. She's *too lazy/not lazy enough*.
4 Stefan doesn't run marathons. He's *too fit/not fit enough*.
5 Sometimes we are *too noisy/not noisy enough*, and the teacher asks us to be quiet.
6 Are they *too clever/clever enough* to be on a TV quiz show?

4 Complete the article with these words and phrases.

as big as · enough · enough · happier · sunnier · too noisy · too white · ~~worst~~

CAN YOU LEARN BETTER IN THE RIGHT CLASSROOM?

New research shows that different classrooms can change the way we learn, and I agree. My 1) *worst* classroom was at my primary school. It was a new classroom, but it was too large and 2) ____________, so sometimes we couldn't hear our teacher. The walls were 3) ____________ and boring because there wasn't any colour. It wasn't warm 4) ____________ in winter, either. My favourite classroom is not 5) ____________ that primary school classroom, but it's quiet 6) ____________ for us to study. It looks 7) ____________, too because there's one yellow wall, and the windows are bigger. The students feel 8) ____________, and so I think we learn better in this room.

Write on

5 Compare your school with your home. Is it easier to revise at school or at home? Write three sentences.

The school library is quieter than my home …

LISTENING

Power up

1 **What do you usually do before going to school?**

do an exercise class
do last-minute homework
prepare a snack for school
pack my school bag
style my hair

2 **Do you find it difficult to get up early? Why/Why not?**

Listen up

3 4.2 **Listen to Amy and Max talking about a new activity at their school. Is the activity happening now or is it going to happen in the future?**

Exam

First, read the questions and the answers. Then, listen and choose the best answer for each question. Listen a second time and check your answers.

4 4.3 **Listen again. Choose the correct answer, A, B or C.**

1. How many gym classes are there?
   A three a week **B** one every day
   C two a week
2. When is the class?
   A after school **B** before school
   C after breakfast
3. Why is this type of class good for students?
   A It helps them to meet people.
   B It gets them out of bed early.
   C It helps their concentration at school.
4. How does Amy feel about the class?
   A She wants to do it.
   B She's nervous about it.
   C She doesn't like the idea.
5. What does Amy offer Max?
   A an alarm clock **B** a good breakfast
   C help with his exam
6. Where's Amy meeting her friend, Ben?
   A at her house **B** in the canteen
   C in the gym

Grammar XP

p. 123

Present continuous and present simple for future use
Use the present continuous for plans in the future.
I'm meeting Ben in the canteen in half an hour.
Use the present simple for schedules and timetables.
It starts next Monday.
shall
Use shall for suggestions and offers.
Shall we try it?

5 **Complete the article with the correct form of the verbs in brackets.**

Home | world | magazine | also in the news | editor's blog

GO | Status | Photo | Check In

Wake up, it's time for class!

How many times do you say to yourself, 'Tonight I 1) ___________ (go) to bed early'? You know your maths test 2) ___________ (be) at nine o'clock tomorrow and that you 3) ___________ (play) in a basketball match after school, but you still go to bed late. The result? You can't concentrate in class. However, some schools in Japan now have sleeping on the timetable! 'It's great,' says Asuka, a student, 'This morning, I 4) ___________ (practise) for the school play, then our teacher 5) ___________ (give) us a maths test . The lunch break 6) ___________ (start) at one o'clock and then everybody 7) ___________ (sleep) for fifteen minutes'.

Unlike · Comment 25 11

SPEAKING

Power up

1 Read the survey about how students concentrate. Do you think 1–6 are good ideas? Why/Why not?

According to a survey, students who regularly drink water find it easier to concentrate at school. From more than one hundred students aged 14–16, the students who drank water during the day did not need as many breaks at school. They had better concentration, and they got higher grades. However, the survey also discovered that some students find other, more interesting ways to help them concentrate.

1 eat apples
2 doodle
3 have a short sleep
4 chew chewing gum
5 stand on your head
6 turn off Facebook

2 What do you do to help you concentrate?

Speak up

3 4.4 Listen to Liam. What ideas does he mention from the survey in Exercise 1?

4 Read what Emily and James say about the survey. What are their preferences and what reasons do they give?

I'd rather doodle than stand on my head because it's more relaxing. Emily

Eating apples is a weird idea! I prefer chocolate. It isn't as healthy as apples, but I think it tastes better. James

Language XP

Explaining preferences
I prefer to + verb
I'd rather + verb …
Giving reasons
It's more … than.
I think it's/that's better/more useful than …

5 Work with a partner. Take it in turns to make questions using the prompts, and ask and answer the questions. Give reasons for your answers.

Student A

1 do homework in your bedroom/in the lounge?
Do you prefer to do your homework in your bedroom or in the lounge?
2 go home after school/go into town?
Would you rather go home after school or go into town?
3 have lessons in the morning/in the afternoon?
4 be in an English class/a maths class now?
5 have a short test at the end of every week/a long exam at the end of the term?

Student B

1 wear your own clothes/a uniform to school?
Would you rather wear your own clothes or a uniform to school?
2 speak English/write English in class?
Do you prefer to speak English or write English in class?
3 have more/less sport on your timetable?
4 talk to friends on Facebook/on the phone?
5 revise early for an exam/at the last minute?

Would you rather wear your own clothes or a uniform to school?

I'd rather wear my own clothes because uniforms are boring.

Skills

Are you comparing two ideas? Think of how they are different. Then, decide which you prefer.

6 What did you learn about your partner? Tell the class.

WRITING

Power up

1 Look at these notes and messages. Where would you read them?

MOBILE 10.16 96%

10.00 I'm leaving in five minutes.
10.15. Sorry! I'm leaving now!

When you finish your homework,
1: make your bed
2: walk the dog.

See you later. Mum

2 When did you last get a note or a message from someone?

3 Read the texts and answer the questions.

WELCOME PARTY FOR FRENCH EXCHANGE STUDENTS

When: Saturday 26 May. What time? 8 a.m.–12 p.m.

Come and meet new friends!

I'm really looking forward to coming to the UK. What are we doing on the first night? Our coach arrives at 5 p.m. Is that a good time for you? What do I need to bring?
See you soon!
Patricia

1 What's happening on 26 May?
2 Who is Patricia?
3 How many things does Patricia want to know? What are they?

4 Read the two replies to Patricia. What are the main differences between them?

A
Dear Patricia,
Thanks very much for your lovely card. The weather is beautiful in the UK at the moment, and I play tennis every day with my friends. Sometimes, we go to the café because they make fantastic sandwiches.
I can't wait for your visit to the UK. I've tidied my bedroom, so that there's room for all of your things. I'm glad you arrive on Saturday because we don't have school the next day. Five o'clock is a good time to arrive because we can eat before we go out. My friends are looking forward to seeing you.
I'm planning lots of nice things for your first visit to the UK. We can go shopping, and go to the new cinema. What's your favourite film?
Well, I have to go now because I've got to do my homework.
See you soon!

B
Hi Patricia,
5 p.m. is good for me. I can meet you when your coach arrives because my singing lesson finishes at 4.30 p.m. Can you bring your tennis racket, please?
Love

5 What information is missing from each reply in Exercise 4?

6 Write a reply to Patricia. Make sure you give Patricia all the information she needs.

Hi Patricia ...

Plan on

7 **What do exchange students do when they come to your school or town? Add two more ideas.**

visit the town
have a party

8 **Read a head teacher's note to students about the school exchange. What does he want students to do?**

Melton Secondary School

Dear students,
As you know, the French students arrive on 26 May. I'd like you all to write a card to your friend. Tell him/her what you are doing on their first day. Explain why you want to do it. Then suggest that you speak on the phone before he/she arrives.
Thanks very much. I think this will help the students feel at home.
Mr Bates

9 **Mr Bates wants students to write three things. Put them in the correct order.**

make a suggestion
talk about a plan
give an explanation

Write on

10 **Write a card to your friend in France. Do not write more than 45 words.**

Exam

There are three things you need to say. Make sure you give all the information.

Language XP

Starting your card
Hi …/Dear …
Ending your card
See you soon/Bye for now/Love
Talking about plans
We're having a party/We're going into town.
Giving an explanation
I think five o'clock is a good time, because/I think it's a good idea because …
Making a suggestion
Why don't you bring … ?/Why don't we … ?/Let's …

Switch on

PUPIL POWER!

1 **Guess the answers. Then watch and check.**

You're going to watch Ashley give his teacher Mr Kershaw, lessons in scuba diving and ballet.

1 Which place will we see?
A the sea **B** Ashley's bathroom
2 Will Mr Kershaw pass his ballet exam?
A yes **B** no

2 **Are the sentences (1–6) true (T) or false (F)?**

1 Ashley introduces his brother and sister.
2 If Mr Kershaw breaks the 'school rules', Ashley will pour water on him.
3 Mr Kershaw learns the five ballet positions.
4 When divers see a shark they must wave their hands.
5 Ashley's classmates are unhappy with the exam result.

3 **Do you think that Ashley was a good teacher? Why/Why not?**

Project

4 **Write your own video script for a short two-minute film or talk in which you teach a new skill.**

1 Decide on these things:
- What skill or hobby is your film or talk about?
- Who is the 'teacher' and who is the 'student'?
- What information will you give about this skill?
- What 'props' will you need (a skateboard? a karate kit? a basketball?)

2 Write your script or talk.
3 Act it out.

I'd like to teach you about …
I will show you how to …
It's quite easy/difficult.

Revision

VOCABULARY

1 Match the meanings (1–6) with these words.

air conditioning dishwasher fridge ~~iron~~ microwave speakers

1 something hot that you use to make clothes smooth and flat *iron*
2 a machine that cleans dirty plates, cups, spoons, etc.
3 You use this to keep the air in a building or car cool.
4 a machine that heats food quickly
5 a piece of kitchen equipment that keeps food and drinks cool
6 the part of a radio, computer or TV where the sound comes out

2 Complete the second sentence so that it means the same as the first. Use these verbs.

fail learn pass ~~practise~~ revise teach

1 When you're learning to play the piano you should do exercises every day.
When you're learning to play the piano you should *practise* every day.
2 Elizabeth can't go to the cinema; she's studying for an exam.
Elizabeth can't go to the cinema; she ______ .
3 Robert's brother is going to have driving lessons.
Robert's brother ______ to drive.
4 Alice was unsuccessful in her geography test.
Alice ______ her geography test.
5 Next year, Mr Wright is giving us maths lessons.
Next year, Mr Wright ______ us maths.
6 I think Paul and Rosie will be successful in their art exam.
I think Paul and Rosie will ______ their art exam.

3 Choose the correct phrases.

1 This is my favourite song. Can you *switch off/turn up* the music, please?
2 Do you want me to *pick up/plug in* your laptop? The battery's very low.
3 Can you *plug in/switch off* the iron when you finish using it, please?
4 Can you *pick up/turn down* your coat, please? You shouldn't leave it on the floor.
5 Can you *plug in/turn down* the radio, please? It's very loud, and I'm trying to work.
6 How do you *pick up/switch on* the washing machine? Is this the right button?

4 Choose the correct answer, A, B or C.

1 Languages are an essential part of the school ______ .
(A) curriculum B timetable C grade
2 The ______ told the students to open their exam papers.
A grade B rule C examiner
3 My sister is brilliant at maths. She always gets a good ______ in her exams.
A rule B test C grade
4 Your school ______ tells you when and where you have your lessons.
A examiner B timetable C rule
5 Students are not allowed to run in the ______ .
A corridor B grade C curriculum
6 I got eighteen out of twenty in my geography, ______ , so I was really pleased.
A test B grade C examiner
7 It's against the ______ to eat or drink in the classrooms.
A breaks B rules C tests
8 We have a lunch ______ at 1 p.m. every day.
A curriculum B timetable C break

5 Complete the text with adverbs made from the adjectives in brackets.

Sensible exam advice for students.

Revise 1) *well* (good) before your exam – don't leave it all until the night before! Revise 2) ______ (regular) and this will help you remember information better. Remember to read the questions 3) ______ (careful) before you try and answer them. You can make mistakes if you read too 4) ______ . (fast) It is also important to write 5) ______ . (clear) The examiner can't give you a mark if they can't read your writing! Look after your body, too. Go to sleep 6) ______ (early) the night before an exam, and have a good breakfast before you go to school. Do all these things, and I'm sure you'll be fine!

GRAMMAR

6 Choose the correct words/phrases.

1 I can't see *anyone/no one* in the gym. Do we have PE today?
2 Is there *everything/something* wrong with the computer? I can't switch it on.
3 There's *anything/nothing* in my school bag. It's empty.
4 I forgot *anything/everything* when the exam started. It was awful!
5 *Everyone/Everything* did well in the English test.
6 *Anyone/No one* told me we were in a different classroom for science today.
7 Do we need to bring *anything/nothing* to school tomorrow?
8 You can't speak to your teacher right now. She's talking to *anyone/someone*.

7 Write sentences. Use *too* or *enough* and the words in brackets.

1 Can you switch on the air conditioning, please? It's too hot. (it/hot)
2 Can you turn up the TV, please? __________ (it/loud)
3 I can't pick up this heavy box. __________ (I/strong)
4 I need to buy some hair straighteners. __________ (my hair/curly)
5 Can I use your laptop, please? __________ (my computer/slow)
6 This computer's very easy. __________ (it/difficult)

8 Complete the sentences with *'ll* or *'m going to*.

1 Oh no, I've forgotten my mobile! I 'll have to go back home and get it.
2 I __________ visit the science museum with school next week.
3 After school, I __________ play football with my friends.
4 Look at these speakers – they're great! I __________ ask the shop assistant how much they are.
5 Next week, I __________ buy some new hair straighteners with my birthday money.
6 I'm not sure if I have Tom's number. Just a minute, I __________ have a look on my phone.

9 Complete the second sentence so that means the same as the first. Use one word.

1 Rachel thinks maths is easier than chemistry.
Rachel thinks chemistry is not as easy as maths.
2 Our teacher isn't as strict as your teacher.
Your teacher is __________ than our teacher.
3 Emma gets better grades than Gina.
Gina's grades aren't as __________ as Emma's grades.
4 My school's bigger than yours.
Your school isn't __________ big as mine.
5 Our lunch break is longer than our morning break.
Our morning break isn't as __________ as our lunch break.
6 Kate is older than Tom.
Tom isn't as old __________ Kate.

10 Complete the conversation with the correct answer, A, B or C.

Chloe: Hi Ian. What 1) __________ you doing this evening?
Ian: Watching TV, Chloe. My mum's bought us a 3-D TV, and she 2) __________ it from the shop after work today.
Chloe: Wow! You're so lucky. I'd love one, but my dad says they're 3) __________ expensive.
Ian: Well, we 4) __________ a film on it this evening. Why don't you come and watch it with us? I've got a piano lesson first, but that 5) __________ at 7.30 p.m.
Chloe: Yeah, I'd love to, but I 6) __________ my mum first – I'm sure she'll say yes.
Ian: Great! See you later then.
Chloe: OK – oh, 7) __________ I bring some popcorn?
Ian: Good idea! See you later.

	A	B	C
1	**A** will	**B** are	**C** is
2	**A** 's getting	**B** shall get	**C** gets
3	**A** enough	**B** as	**C** too
4	**A** watch	**B** watching	**C** 're going to watch
5	**A** will finish	**B** finishes	**C** shall finish
6	**A** 'll ask	**B** ask	**C** 'm going to ask
7	**A** shall	**B** will	**C** do

05 Go for it!

READING

Power up

1 What sports can you do with this equipment?

board helmet goggles
racket wetsuit

2 When did you last buy any sports equipment? What was it?

Read on

3 Four teens want to try a new sport. Read their emails to a sports magazine. What sports do they mention?

A I like doing sport two or three times a week. I'm good at running and cycling, but I want to try something different. Learning a new sport with other people would be fun. **Sandra**

B I've just moved here and I want to get fit and have a laugh at the same time. I prefer to be outdoors and hate hot gyms. **Luke**

C I've done gymnastics since I was at primary school but now I'd like to try a team sport. I'm a strong swimmer, but I can only train one day a week. **Olivia**

D I love being outdoors even when the weather isn't very good. I've tried team sports, but I'm not very good! Water sports look fun, but I don't want to buy any expensive equipment. **Joseph**

A

4 Match these sports to the photos (A–F).

kickboxing kiteboarding
mud running sprint cycling
synchronised swimming
water polo

1 It's mad – its mud running!

Have you tried lots of sports, but can't find one you like? Obviously you haven't tried mud running. It's fast, it's cold, it's dirty, but it's FUN. Try it once and you will do it again! Find out what you can really achieve when you run through cold, muddy water in winter. Call now on …

C

3 Join a winning team – water polo

Can you catch a ball with one hand? Water polo is fast, hard and very tiring, but it's an exciting team sport. Our junior team has already won a national competition, and now we're looking for more talented teens who can score goals. We practise on Tuesdays. Call us soon.

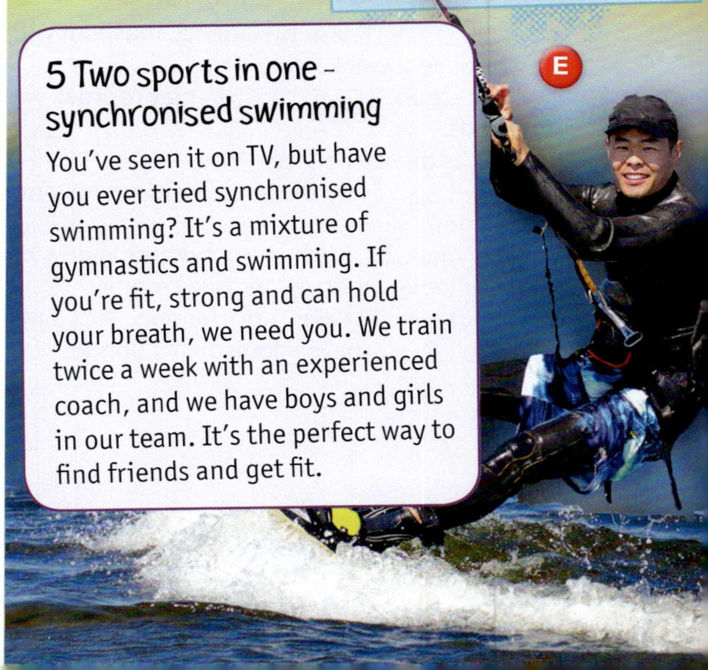

E

5 Two sports in one – synchronised swimming

You've seen it on TV, but have you ever tried synchronised swimming? It's a mixture of gymnastics and swimming. If you're fit, strong and can hold your breath, we need you. We train twice a week with an experienced coach, and we have boys and girls in our team. It's the perfect way to find friends and get fit.

FINDING THE RIGHT SPORT

B

2 Fast and fun – sprint cycling

You've always enjoyed cycling, but you haven't been in a race. Now is the time to join our sprint cycling club. It's for 13–17-year-olds, and all you need is your bike, a helmet and lots of energy. In our club, you will learn new skills on the track and the road, and you will train for racing competitions all over the country.

D

4 We've never said it's easy – kiteboarding

This sport is getting bigger and bigger, and a new club has opened near you. We've got all the equipment, including wetsuits, so you don't have to buy anything. Just come with lots of energy and enthusiasm. We meet every week, in good and bad weather. So, what are you waiting for?

F

6 Beginners welcome – kickboxing

Some people call it 'karate boxing'. Kickboxing is a fun and energetic contact sport. We've started a new course for all levels, from beginners to advanced. We meet in the sports centre twice a week, and can provide you with all the equipment you need. Come and find out more.

5 **Read the adverts (1–6). Decide which sport is the best for each teen in Exercise 3. Give two reasons for each answer.**

Exam

Are you matching information in different texts? Underline the parts that mean the same. Don't just match individual words.

6 **Find words in the adverts that mean the following.**

1. succeed in doing or getting something
2. become a member of a group
3. air that comes out of your lungs
4. a strong feeling of interest or excitement
5. for young people under a particular age

Sum up

7 **What do you remember about each sport in the adverts?**

Speak up

8 **Which sports in the adverts are fun/not fun? Why? Which of them can you do where you live?**

I don't think mud running is fun. It's cold and dirty. You can do synchronised swimming where I live. There are classes at the swimming pool.

SWITCH ON Just try it! page 51

VOCABULARY

Sport

1 Complete the notices with these words.

changing rooms coach court locker match prize race track

A Congratulations to Sophie Ennis who won first 1) ___________ in the junior judo competition.

B Please put your bags and football boots in a 2)__________, and leave your key with the PE teacher, Ms Bates.

C Patrick Headley won the 10 km 3)__________ on Saturday. He ran it in 45 minutes. Well done Patrick.

D Good at tennis? You could be a tennis 4) ___________ in our summer club. Two hours every day. Call 01974 988364.

E Tennis club rule: all players must wear tennis shoes on the 5) ___________, please.

F Football 6) ___________ against Horton High School on Saturday at seven o'clock. The coaches leave at 6.45 p.m.

G Running club – every Tuesday at the new 7)___________ in the park. All members can use the showers in the 8)___________ next to the park café.

2 Match these verbs with the underlined words and phrases.

beat compete hit kick score train win

1 Every year hundreds of students try to win against students from other countries. *compete*
2 How many goals did they get in the last half hour?
3 Jack moved the racket against the ball as hard as he could.
4 They've got lots of prizes because they are the best in every game.
5 In the last five minutes, Torres tried to put the ball in the net with his foot.
6 You can prepare for the competition with a coach at the swimming pool.
7 Spain did really well. They got more points than Italy. They won 3–1.

Word XP

Some nouns are the same as the verb.

score (v) – score (n), kick (v) – kick (n), race (v) – race (n)

Remember that some sound the same but the spelling is different.

practise (v) – practice (n)

3 Read the text. Choose the correct answer, A, B, C or D.

Italy versus Spain. What happened? Tell us now!
I watched the football 1) ___*match*___ last night between Italy and Spain. I couldn't believe the 2) ___________ was 4–0 to Spain. I wanted Italy to 3) ___________ because my dad is Italian, but it was a disaster. I think the team needs to 4) ___________ more because they aren't fast enough. The Spanish players work as a team and they're fast. They're also good because they 5) ___________ lots of goals. That's why nobody can 6) ___________ them at the moment!
Danielle

	A	B	C	D
1	competition	(B) match	play	race
2	goals	points	score	game
3	win	beat	play	train
4	train	hit	kick	win
5	win	hit	score	kick
6	race	beat	win	compete

Game on

Work with a partner. Explain a word on the page without saying it. See if your partner knows what it is.

A: *It's something you do in sport. You do it with your foot.*
B: *Kick!*

GRAMMAR

Grammar XP

p. 136

Present perfect simple
for something that happened in the past and that has a result in the present
*A new club **has opened** near you.*
for a situation or an experience in our lives that is still true now
***I've tried** lots of team sports, but I'm not very good.*
Present perfect simple with adverbs
Use *ever* and *never* for any time up to now.
*Have you **ever** tried synchronised swimming?*
*No, I've **never** tried it.*
Use *yet* for something we expect to happen.
*I haven't tried a swimming class **yet**.*
Use *just* for recent events.
*I've **just** moved here.*
Use *already* for something that has happened before now.
*Our team has **already** won a national competition.*
Remember we often use *for* and *since* with the present perfect.
*I haven't tried a new sport **for** years.*
*I've done gymnastics **since** I was at primary school.*

1 Complete the email with the correct form of the verbs in brackets. Use short forms where possible.

climbing wall

Hi Carl,
I 1) 've just had (just/have) a great day at a climbing wall. A new sports centre 2) ____________ (open), and there are some great activities. I 3) ____________ (never/ climb) a wall before, but it was brilliant. My friends and I 4) ____________ (always/do) a lot of sport, so I'm quite fit, but climbing was very different. I 5) ____________ (use) parts of my body that I 6) ____________ (never/use) before! I can't wait to go again. What about you? 7) ____________ you ____________ (ever/ try) climbing? Perhaps we can go together.
Love,
Nicole

2 Write the past participle form of these verbs.

buy cut do find have play see start watch win

3 5.1 Listen to six sentences. Which past participle do you hear in each sentence?

1 started

4 Complete the conversations (1–4) with the present perfect form of these verbs.

do live ~~swim~~ win

1 A: Have you ever swum in a river.
B: No, I haven't.
2 A: _________ you _________ a competition?
B: Yes, I _________.
3 A: _________ your family always _________ in this town?
B: No, they _________.
4 A: _________ you _________ any sport today?
B: No, I _________.

5 Complete the second sentence so it has the same meaning as the first.

1 This is the first time I've done kickboxing.
I _________ kickboxing before.
2 We arrived at the match a short time ago.
We _________ arrived at the match.
3 Patrick joined a different football club two years ago.
Patrick has been in a different football club _________ two years.
4 This isn't the first time I've tried mud running.
I _________ mud running before.
5 I will buy my new racket soon.
I _________ my new racket yet.
6 She became a swimming coach in July.
She has been a swimming coach _________ July.

Write on

6 Write the answers to these questions.

1 Who have you spoken to today?
2 What have/haven't you done today?
3 What has been the best/worst thing about today?

Exam

Listen to what both people are saying. Find words in the sentences that help you listen for the right information.

4 5.3 **Listen again and check your answers.**

Grammar XP

p. 137

Past simple
Use the past simple for an action that happened at a definite time or date in the past.
*A girl from my tennis class **texted** me a few minutes ago.*
*Emma **scored** the winning goal in the match last Saturday.*
Present perfect simple
Use the present perfect simple for a past action when we don't know the time or date of the action, or it isn't important.
*Three hundred people **have watched** it.*
*We**'ve won** all our games so far this year.*

LISTENING

Power up

1 **What can you see in the photo? Where are the people?**

2 **What do you know about freerunning? Would you like to try it? Why/Why not?**

Listen up

3 5.2 **Listen to Connor and Lucy talk about a video. Are the sentences (1–6) true (T) or false (F)?**

1 Lucy heard about the video from Connor. F
2 Connor isn't surprised that lots of people have seen the video.
3 The idea for the freerunning video came from Connor.
4 Lucy would like to try different sports at school.
5 Lucy doesn't like the idea of a freerunning class for beginners.
6 Connor's favourite part in the video is the music.

5 **Complete the sentences with the present perfect simple or past simple form of the verbs in brackets.**

1 I hope Nick wins the race. He has trained (train) really hard for it.
2 We ____________ (not win) the football match yesterday.
3 Lucy and Connor ____________ (start) a freerunning club. Shall we join?
4 Nicole's very fit. She ____________ (run) in a marathon at the weekend.
5 ____________ (you/watch) the swimming on TV last night?
6 I can't go cycling this afternoon. I ____________ (not finish) my homework yet.
7 This is a difficult race. ____________ (they/do) enough training for it?
8 Freerunning is very exciting. I ____________ (try) it last summer.

SPEAKING

Power up

1 **Is this statement true for you? Why/Why not?**

I enjoy watching sport but I don't enjoy doing it.

2 **Look at the photo and complete the notes.**

Place/weather: at home, in a house, on the sofa
People:
Objects/clothes:
Actions:
Feelings:

3 **Match the questions (1–6) with the answers (a–f).**

1 Who is in the photo?
2 Where are they?
3 What are they wearing?
4 What are they doing?
5 How are they feeling?
6 What do you think about this activity?

a They're all really happy and excited. I think they're enjoying the match. They are celebrating. They have their hands in the air. Perhaps their team has scored a goal.
b They're in a lounge. I can see a sofa. There's a white wall behind the sofa. It's bright in the room. I think it's sunny outside.
c I don't watch sport with my friends very often because I prefer doing sport.
d The boy on the left is quite smart. He's wearing a blue shirt and jeans. The other two boys are wearing T-shirts. One T-shirt is striped; it's red and black. The other one is green. I can also see some socks.
e It's a group of friends.
f They're watching sport on TV. It might be a football match because one boy is holding a football. They're eating popcorn.

4 **5.4 Listen to a girl describe the same photo. Find five things she doesn't mention from the answers (a–f) in Exercise 3.**

Language XP

Describing a photo
It's a photo of …/The photo shows …
On the left/On the right/At the back/At the front …
He/She/They look(s) …
When you aren't sure or don't know
It could/might be … Perhaps it's …/ Maybe it's … I can't remember what this is.

Speak up

5 **Work with a partner. Student A, look at page 130. Student B, look at page 142. Follow the instructions.**

Exam

Don't worry if you can't find the right words for everything in the photo. Just describe what you see, and keep talking!

6 **Work with a partner. Take it in turns to say what you thought about your partners' descriptions in Exercise 5.**

You used lots of interesting words.

You described their clothes well.

You didn't know the word for 'wetsuit', but I understood what you meant.

WRITING

Power up

1 **Look at the activities from the alternative Olympic Games in Wales. Have you tried them? Why/Why not?**

space hopper racing

mountain boarding

rock paper scissors competition

2 **Why do you think some people want to have an alternative Olympic Games?**

Language XP

Use these words to connect ideas

either … or	*I'll come on **either** Tuesday **or** Wednesday.*
as soon as	*I phoned him **as soon as** I heard the news.*
except	*Everyone wanted to go the match **except** Callum.*
so that	*I'm doing my homework now, **so that** I can go out later.*
although	*She's a good gymnast **although** she doesn't practise very often.*

3 **Complete the article with these words and phrases.**

although as soon as because except so that either … or

star letter

Sport – love it or hate it?

1 I've always enjoyed sport and done lots of different activities 1) __either__ at school __or__ at the sports centre. I've played basketball and football since primary school, and I've been in a football team for two years. I'm not the best player in the world,
2) ________ I have scored some great goals!
2 I haven't liked every sport that I've tried. One sport that I hate is running 3)________ it's so boring. Last year, I was in a race with some friends.
4) ________ the race started, it began to rain.
3 It was terrible, and I hated every minute of it. I don't want to run again, 5) ________ when I'm playing football of course!
Some people don't like doing sport, but they enjoy watching it. There are lots of exciting sports programmes on TV. My friends and I like watching extreme sports, like snowboarding or skydiving. I haven't tried an extreme sport yet. I've just bought a wetsuit 6) ________ I can start kite boarding. Perhaps you'll see me in the next Olympics!
Jessica, 16

4 **Complete the sentences (1–6) with a word or phrase in Exercise 3.**

1 All of the football players were happy with the score __except__ Sandra.
2 We're doing ________ hockey ________ volleyball today.
3 You can watch the match ________ you finish your dinner.
4 Luke's trained really hard ________ he wants to win the competition.
5 I've never liked doing sport, ________ I know it's good for me.
6 You should drink lots of water ________ your body is ready for the race.

Plan on

5 Read the article again. Match the ideas (a–c) to the information in the paragraphs.

Paragraph 1 ___b___
Paragraph 2 ________
Paragraph 3 ________

a Sports that Jessica hasn't enjoyed.
b Sports that Jessica has tried and liked.
c Sports that Jessica's watched and wants to try.

6 Read the advert and answer the questions.

Tell us about yourself! What sports or activities have you tried? What do you love 🙂 or hate 🙁? Is there a sport or activity that you've watched, but haven't tried yet? Write an article for our magazine called, 'I haven't tried it yet!' The winner wins the chance to try an exciting new activity with friends.

1 What does the advert invite students to write?
2 What's the prize?

7 Complete the notes with your ideas.

I've tried and I liked gymnastics
I've tried and I hated athletics
I've watched but I haven't tried kickboxing

8 Give more information for each sport or activity you wrote in Exercise 7.

Athletics – very hard
I didn't like athletics because it was very hard.

Write on

9 Write an article 'I haven't tried it yet!' Write about 120 words.

Exam

When you have your list of ideas, put them in the right order. Write three paragraphs.

Switch on

JUST TRY IT!

1 Guess the answers. Then watch and check.

Rebecca and Toby are talking about unusual sports and activities.

1 What has Rebecca tried?
  A underwater hockey **B** indoor skydiving
2 What does Toby want to do?
  A cheese rolling **B** wood chopping

2 Choose the correct answer A, B or C.

1 Would Rebecca try her unusual sport again?
  A Yes, definitely. **B** No, never.
  C She isn't sure.
2 How does Toby describe his unusual sport?
  A fun and dangerous **B** silly but safe
  C exciting and fast
3 When does Toby think he and Rebecca should try their sports?
  A the next day **B** on the same day
  C at the weekend

3 Which of the two sports or activities would you most like to try? Why?

Project

4 Work in pairs. Prepare an interview about an unusual sport or activity.

1 Decide on these things:
- What the unusual sport or activity is.
- Where you can do it.
- What you need for it.
- How it feels when you do it.

2 Write your interview.
3 Act it out or make a video to show the class.

What's your unusual sport or activity?
I'd like to talk about caving. There are lots of caves where I live. It's very exciting.

06 Getting on

READING

Power up

1 Match three of these feelings with the photos.

annoyed jealous excited bored surprised

2 Which feelings in Exercise 1 can you remember having when you were young? What happened?

Read on

3 Work with a partner. Talk about the article and photos on page 53.

1 Does the boy look happy? Why/why not?
2 What is the horse doing?
3 Have you ever … seen a horse? … ridden a horse?

4 Read the article quickly and check your answers to questions 1 and 2 in Exercise 3.

5 Read the article again. Are the sentences (1–10) true (T) or false (F)?

1 Kelly and Ryan are in a group of seven teenagers.
2 The course will teach them how to ride horses.
3 Wild horses sometimes run away or kick people.
4 You should move quickly to 'speak' to a horse.
5 It's difficult for horses to know how people are feeling.
6 It was easy for Kelly to control Teddy the horse.
7 Kelly wanted Teddy to move away from her.
8 Ryan made good friends with the horses.
9 Bernadette was unhappy with the teenagers' progress.
10 Through the course, the teenagers learned to think about other people.

Exam

Do you need to decide if a sentence is correct or incorrect? Check all the facts, e.g. Are they in a group? Are they all teenagers?

6 Find words in the article that mean the following.

1 the way that you act or behave: b __________
2 relaxed and not angry or upset: c __________
3 glass that you can see yourself in: m __________
4 not possible: i __________
5 always telling other people what to do, in a way that is annoying: b __________
6 behave towards other people in a particular way: t __________

Living

How to become … a horse whisperer

What do you do when you have problems? You might talk to your friends or family, but what happens if you're not getting on with them? When you fall out with people close to you, where can you go? One surprising answer might be … you can talk to a horse!

Bernadette Langfield owns a special centre for horses that have problems. Here, a group of seven teenagers will be able to learn about horse whispering. They are taking part in a course which will help the horses … and the people. Kelly Field and Ryan Houghton are part of the group. They have both had a difficult time at home and at school. As a result, they often feel annoyed or upset. The teenagers have two months to get to know the horses. Will they be able to deal with their own behaviour problems, too?

So, what happens when you meet a wild horse, face to face for the first time? These animals are big and nervous, so if you've never met a horse before, you could feel frightened. The horse might run away or, worse, it might kick you.

The best thing to do is to stay calm, as Kelly found out. Horse whispering is not really about speaking to the horse. You need to understand the horse's body language. Then you use your body language to 'speak' to the horse and show the horse that it can trust you. For example, you use calm, clear, body movements, but you can't be bossy.

Horses always understand people's feelings. 'Horses are like a mirror,' explains one horse trainer. 'They show you the same feeling that you show them.' Keeping calm is difficult for people like Kelly, who have a lot of problems in their lives.

On the first day, Kelly worked with a horse called Teddy. She had to make Teddy walk three steps – backwards! At first Kelly wasn't able to do it. She thought it was impossible. What could she do? Then, Kelly stayed still. She used clear hand signals and a firm voice. Teddy moved back. Success!

'How did you make him do that?' asked Bernadette.
'Because I wanted him to.'
'How impossible is it now?'
'Not impossible,' said Kelly

Ryan, too, enjoyed spending time with the horses. He fed them carrots and talked to them quietly. 'Some of these horses have had a hard time … I think we've got something in common.'

Slowly, the teenagers realised that they had to change their behaviour. Even Bernadette was surprised how much the teenagers learned: 'the change has been amazing.' So what lesson did they learn? Treat others as you want them to treat you.

Sum up

7 Think about the relationship between horses and people. Answer the questions.

1 What special skill do horses have which can help people?
2 What changes did Kelly make when was working with Teddy?
3 How did Ryan feel about horses?

Speak up

8 What do you think about the horse whisperer course? Would you like to try it? Why/Why not?

SWITCH ON Horse whisperers page 59

VOCABULARY

Friendship and feelings

1 Match these phrases (phr) and phrasal verbs (phr v) with the correct meanings (1–8).

have something in common
fall out with   get to know   get on with
have a hard time   spend time with
stay calm   deal with (a problem)

1 to be together (phr):
2 to become friends with (phr):
3 to share the same ideas or interests (phr v):
4 to have some difficult problems (phr):
5 to argue with a friend or someone you know (phr v):
6 to find a way to stop a problem (phr v):
7 to have a good relationship with (phr v):
8 to stop yourself getting upset or angry (phr):

2 Match the sentence halves.

1 My brother and I get
2 Harry sometimes falls
3 Anna's going to deal
4 I'd like to get to
5 If there's a fire, stay
6 My grandparents often spend
7 The students are having a hard
8 Steve and Paul haven't got
a know the new girl in our class.
b calm and leave the building.
c on really well with our cousins.
d time with us in the summer.
e time in a difficult maths test.
f out with his older sister.
g much in common.
h with her dog's bad behaviour.

3 6.1 Listen and check your answers.

4 Complete the sentences for you.

1 I don't want to fall out with …
2 It's hard to stay calm when …
3 After school, I enjoy spending time with …

Word XP

Adjectives + *-ed*/*-ing*
We use *-ed* endings to describe how people feel.
I'm amazed! She's surprised.
We use *-ing* endings to give an opinion of people, things or situations.
She's amazing! That's very surprising news.
Remember to say *I'm bored* not ~~*I'm boring*~~.

5 Choose the correct word to complete the messages.

messages

Emma > Joe
Guess what? We've got tickets for the One Direction concert! I was really 1) *annoyed/ annoying* yesterday because there weren't any tickets on the website. So my sister and I were VERY 2) *surprised/surprising* when my mum gave us two tickets. It's so 3) *excited/exciting*!!!

messages

Joe > Emma
I'm glad you've got tickets to see your favourite band. That's 4) *amazed/amazing.* ☺
I'm a bit 5) *bored/boring* at the moment. Are you 6) *interested/interesting* in going to the cinema on Saturday?

6 Complete the second sentence so that it means the same as the first. Use adjectives ending in *-ed* or *-ing*.

1 Yesterday, Niko watched the school football match, but he was bored.
Niko thought the school football match *was boring* .
2 My phone broke, which was really annoying.
I was ____________ because my phone broke.
3 The boat trip to the island will be really exciting.
We're really ____________ the boat trip to the island.
4 In Lucy's opinion, it's not a very interesting programme.
Lucy's not ____________ that programme.

Game on

Work with a partner. Choose a word.

with in get on time to have out

Your partner says phrases or phrasal verbs with this word.

GRAMMAR

Grammar XP

p. 137

Talking about ability and possibility

ability

Can has no future tense. Use *will be* able to to talk about ability in the future.

*They **can** understand horses. (present)*

*They **will be able to** understand horses.*

possibility

Use *can* to talk about possibility in the present.

*Where **can** you go?*

*You **can** talk to a horse!*

making a guess

Use *might* or *could* to make a guess about the present or future.

*The horse **might** kick you.*

*You **could** feel frightened.*

1 **Write sentences about the things that students will learn on the horse whisperer course in the article on page 53.**

1. understand horses √
2. talk to horses ×
3. ride a horse ×
4. control a horse √
5. control their feelings √

They will be able to understand horses.

2 **Look at these instructions from the horse centre. Write a sentence about what might happen in each case (1–5).**

1. Don't feed sweets to the horses. (get stomachache)
   The horses might get stomachache.
2. Be careful! Don't walk behind a horse. (kick)
3. Shut the gate. (run away)
4. Don't shout, and don't be bossy. (get annoyed)
5. Is your horse difficult to work with? (be tired)

3 **Choose the correct answers to complete the school web page.**

Welcome news and events academic

Woodstock Secondary School: *our Friend in Need system*

Your questions and answers

Q: What is the Friend in Need system?

A: Here at Woodstock School, we know students 1) *might/will be able* to have problems, so we have trained a group of Year 11 students to talk to younger students when they need help.

Q: Will I 2) *can/be able to* find a Friend in Need if I have a problem?

A: Yes, you 3) *can/could* recognise them from the blue badges they wear. They are always in the playground at break and at lunchtime.

Q: What kind of problems 4) *can/might* they help with?

A: Any kind of problem. You 5) *might/will be able* to be upset or angry, for example if you've had an argument with a friend. Sometimes students feel ill or they need to go home. Or you 6) *can/could* just want to chat!

If they can't find an answer straight away, a Friend in Need 7) *will be able to/could* take you to a teacher or the school nurse.

So don't be scared, just ask for help.

Write on

4 **Write three sentences about other problems students might have.**

Students might be worried about a test ...

LISTENING

Power up

1 Look at the questionnaire. What are the three most important qualities in a good friend?

What is the most important quality in a good friend? We want your opinions!

A good friend ...

1 has the same interests as you.
2 has the same sense of humour.
3 is relaxed, so you usually have a good time together.
4 is kind and patient and doesn't get annoyed .
5 is reliable – you can trust him/her.
6 is honest and tells the truth to you, but in a friendly way.
7 is generous and shares any good things he/she has.
8 is usually positive – life seems better when he/she is around.

2 Work with a partner. Put the sentences in the questionnaire in Exercise 1 in order (1 = very important).

Listen up

3 6.2 Listen to Lidia and Justyn talking about a website. What strange story do they read about?

Skill

Think about the relationship between people in a conversation. Are they chatting, agreeing, arguing or finding out information?

4 6.3 Listen again and choose the correct answer, A, B or C.

1 Why is Justyn looking at the website?
A Because there's an interesting questionnaire.
B Because it's his English homework.
C Because he likes reading funny stories.
2 How did the two animals become friends?
A The dog saw the orangutang and ran up to him.
B The zoo keepers introduced the animals.
C The orangutang wanted to get to know the dog.
3 What do Roscoe and Suryia often do when they spend time together?
A go for a swim
B play games
C go for a run
4 Why don't the two animals share everything?
A Because Roscoe isn't very generous.
B Because they don't always like the same things.
C Because Suryia sometimes gets annoyed with Roscoe.
5 What do Justyn and Lidia do when they read the questionnaire?
A They argue about it.
B They can't decide.
C They agree on an answer.

Grammar XP

p. 137

Zero conditional
Use *if/when* + present simple + present simple for something that always or usually happens.
*If a dog **sees** an orangutang, it usually **runs** away!*
First conditional
Use *if* + present simple + *will/might/could* for a possible action in the future.
*If you like animals, **you'll** love this story.*
*We **could** look at it together **if** you like.*
unless
Use *unless* for a negative meaning of *if not*.
*Suryia **doesn't** go anywhere **unless** Roscoe comes too!*

5 Choose the correct tense to complete each conditional sentence.

1 If you don't phone her, she is *upset/will be upset*
2 My parents' parties are boring because their friends never *dance/will dance*.
3 If I *clean/will clean* my room, my mum is always surprised.
4 I think *she's/she'll be* jealous if I talk to you all evening.
5 I'll be annoyed if he doesn't *come/won't come* home soon.

SPEAKING

Power up

1 **Describe the situation in the picture. What do you think they are saying/feeling?**

2 **In which situations do you say 'Sorry'? Is this important? Why/Why not?**

Speak up

3 **Complete the conversations with these words. Match the conversations (1–4) with the pictures (A–D).**

never mind ~~didn't mean to~~ really sorry won't happen again OK an accident

A

1

Teacher: Amanda! What time do you call this?
Girl: I'm sorry I'm late, Mrs Hall. I woke up late, but I 1) *didn't mean to.*
Teacher: OK, well, if you're late again I'll tell the head teacher.

B

2

Boy: Daisy! Why didn't you wait for me outside the shop?
Girl: Oh, sorry, Jack, I thought you left before me.
Boy: Oh well, 2) ____________ I found you anyway.

C

3

Girl: Hi Dad. Um, I've got something to tell you. I lost my trainers after the volleyball tournament.
Dad: You never take care of your things! If it happens again I won't buy a new pair.
Girl: It was 3) ____________ . It 4) ____________ .

D

4

Boy: Hello? Megan? I'm 5) ____________ . I forgot your birthday yesterday. Happy Birthday!
Girl: Thanks, George. That's 6) ____________ . It's nice of you to phone.
Boy: So, did you have a good day?

4 **6.4 Listen and check your answers.**

Language XP

Apologising and responding

I'm (very/really) sorry. *That's OK.*
It was an accident. *Never mind.*
I didn't mean to.
It won't happen again.

5 **Work with a partner. Choose and act out a conversation in Exercise 3.**

Skill

When you're taking part in a roleplay, imagine the situation is real. Make sure your voice goes up and down.

6 **Work with a partner. Student A, look at page 131. Student B, look at page 143. Follow the instructions.**

WRITING

Power up

1 **Which of these things make you feel most annoyed or upset?**

Someone borrows something, but doesn't ask you first.

Someone borrows something, but forgets to give it back to you.

You ask to borrow something from a friend, but they say, 'No'.

You borrow something from a friend, but they ask you to give it back the next day.

2 **What was the last thing you borrowed from a friend, or lent to a friend?**

a book or school book · a computer game · a piece of clothing · some money

3 **Read the email and answer the questions.**

Disk problem

Dear Uncle Frank,
It was good to see you and Auntie Lisa last weekend, and we had a lot of fun. Thanks for giving back my football game. I'm glad you enjoyed playing it on your Xbox!
There is a bit of a problem, though. When I opened the box last night the disk wasn't inside! I'm not annoyed, but I am a bit upset because it was my favourite game.
I'm not sure about the best way to deal with the problem. We might not see you for a long time now, so could you please post it to me? If you can send it soon I'll be very happy!
Thanks very much.
Love,
Alfie

1 What's the relationship between Frank and Alfie?
2 What's gone wrong?
3 What does Alfie ask Frank to do?

4 **Match these phrases with the meanings (1–5).**

by mistake · straight away · up to you · whatever you want · you prefer

1 you like that better
2 now, immediately
3 anything you want
4 your decision
5 accidentally

5 **Complete Frank's reply to Alfie with the phrases in the box in Exercise 4.**

I'm sorry!

Hi Alfie,
I'm really sorry about your football game. I left the disk in my Xbox 1)______________ . It was an accident.
If you like, I'll buy you a new game. I can order it online 2) ______________ , and you'll have it tomorrow. I'll keep the old game unless 3) ______________ to have it back.
Or, I can send the game back to you first thing tomorrow. How do you want to solve the problem?
It's 4)______________ . I'll do 5)______________ .
Lots of love from me and Auntie Lisa,
Frank

Plan on

6 Read the email. What does Antonio want?

> Hi!
>
> Message...
>
> I hope you enjoyed your time with us in London. Did you have a good journey home? There is a small problem. You might have my dictionary in your bag by mistake. Remember you borrowed it on the last night? I might be wrong, but I can't find it now.
>
> Can you tell me if you have it? Will you be able to post it to me? Thanks very much.
>
> Your friend,
>
> **Antonio**
>
> Preview Send

7 Which things (1–6) should you say to Antonio in your reply?

1 Give information about your holiday in London.
2 Say thanks to Antonio and his family.
3 Give information about your journey home.
4 List all the things you have in your bag.
5 Say whether you have the dictionary or not.
6 Say what you will do if you have the dictionary.

Exam

Are you replying to an email? Read it carefully, and make sure you understand what information is needed.

Write on

8 Write a short reply to Antonio. Write about 35–45 words. Include the correct information from Exercise 7. Explain that you have the dictionary and apologise. Use these ideas or one of your own to suggest a solution.

buy a new dictionary for Antonio   give it back when you visit   send some money   post the dictionary

Language XP

Suggesting alternatives

Or …
If you prefer + I can/I will
If you like + I can/I will
I can either … or …

Switch on

HORSE WHISPERERS

1 Guess the answer. Then watch and check.

You are going to see Ryan and Kelly at the centre for problem horses. Which of these things will you see?

A Ryan and Kelly taking school exams.
B Ryan feeding an apple to a horse.
C Kelly making a horse walk backwards.
D Ryan riding a horse.
E students cleaning the stables.
F a horse kicking Ryan.

2 Choose the correct answer A, B or C. Which places do you see these people? More than one answer may be possible.

1 Kelly **A** a classroom **B** a field **C** a stable
2 Ryan **A** a classroom **B** a field **C** a stable
3 Bernadette
A a classroom **B** a field **C** a stable
4 other students
A a classroom **B** a field **C** a stable

3 What changes do you notice in the students between the beginning of the video and at the end?

Project

4 Make a poster about an animal you'd like to 'whisper' to.

1 Find photos of the animal.
2 Write sentences.

I'd like to 'whisper' to a(n) … because …
I'd teach it to … and …
I think the experience might be …

VOCABULARY

1 Complete the sentences with the correct form of the verbs.

beat compete hit kick practise score ~~win~~

1 I hope our team ___wins___ the game!
2 Would you like to ____________ in the school gymnastics competition?
3 I can't ____________ the ball very hard. I've hurt my foot.
4 Ben always ____________ the most goals.
5 Emily is a great swimmer. She ____________ all the other girls in the competition last week.
6 Good footballers have to ____________ for hours every week.
7 The best tennis players can ____________ the ball very hard.

2 Match the meanings (1–8) with these words.

~~changing room~~ coach court locker match prize race track

1 a place where people can put on or take off sports clothes *changing room*
2 a type of path or road that is usually in a ring shape
3 something that the winner in a competition receives
4 a place where you play tennis or basketball
5 a person who teaches a sport
6 a small cupboard where you can leave your clothes
7 a game in which two people or teams play against each other
8 a competition to find the fastest person

3 Choose the correct words.

1 Daniel fell asleep on the sofa because the film was so *bored*/<u>*boring*</u>.
2 Victoria's really *excited/exciting* about the tennis match on Saturday.
3 Usain Bolt is an *amazed/amazing* runner.
4 I heard some very *surprised/surprising* news last night.
5 Simon's really *annoyed/annoying* because I broke his guitar.
6 I'm really *bored/boring*. Do you want to go to the park?

4 Complete the conversations with the correct phrases and phrasal verbs.

fall out with get on well with get to know ~~have a lot of things in common~~ spend a lot of time with stay calm

1 **A:** Do you and your brother ___have a lot of things in common___?
B: Yes. We both like the same kind of music and do the same sports.
2 **A:** What do you do in your free time?
B: Well, I ____________ my friends. We often play computer games.
3 **A:** Do you ____________ your parents?
B: Yes, most of the time! We only argue sometimes.
4 **A:** Why did Jane ____________ you?
B: Because I didn't want to go to a pop concert with her.
5 **A:** How do you feel when you lose a tennis match.
B: Angry! But you have to ____________ because it's part of the sport.
6 **A:** How did you ____________ , Stephen?
B: He was my next door neighbour when I first arrived in Manchester.

5 Complete the email with the correct words.

annoyed beat ~~out~~ prize race track wins

Hi Pippa,
I don't know what to do, and I need your advice! I've fallen 1) ___out___ with Sarah. She's 2) __________ because I 3) __________ her in the 200 metres 4) __________ at school yesterday. She always 5) __________ , and so she was really disappointed when she didn't get first 6) __________ this year. She didn't talk to me after we left the 7) __________ , and I haven't seen her since. What do you think I should do?
Love,
Beth

GRAMMAR

6 Choose the correct words.

1 If it rains, we usually *do/will do* gymnastics in the school hall.
2 William *is/will be* annoyed if his team loses the football match this afternoon.
3 I usually *enjoy/will enjoy* swimming if the water's warm.
4 If my brother dances at the party tomorrow, *I am/'ll be* very surprised.
5 Olivia always gets up early if she *has/will have* football practice.
6 My mum *is/will be* never happy if I come home late.

7 Complete the sentences with the past simple or present perfect simple form of the verbs in brackets.

1 Megan's excited about buying a skateboard. She *'s wanted* (want) one for a long time.
2 Leo ___________ (have) a hard time when he was at his old school.
3 I ___________ (see) Martin today. Do you know where he is?
4 Jake ___________ (fall) out with Imogen, and they're not talking to each other now.
5 We ___________ (be) bored yesterday because we didn't have anything to do.
6 I'm not going to enter the 100 m race. I ___________ (not do) enough training for it.

8 Put the words in the correct order to make sentences.

1 my friend Sam? / you / Have / met / ever
Have you ever met my friend Sam?
2 before./ never / I / done / mud running/ 've
3 yet. / her homework / finished / Charlotte / hasn't
4 Mr Travis / been/ two years. / our football coach / for/ has
5 the race. / already / They / finished / 've
6 My friend / told me / just / 's /about the party.
7 I was eleven. / 've / with this club / trained / since / I

9 Choose the correct answer.

1 Tom *can't/might* train on Tuesdays because he has piano lessons.
2 We're not sure yet, but we *might/will be able to* go on holiday to Turkey this year.
3 It's not possible today, but we *might not/'ll be able to* go kiteboarding tomorrow.
4 Don't feed the animals because they *could/will be able to* bite you.
5 *Can/Might* you go to the cinema at the weekend?

10 Complete the second sentence so that it means the same as the first.

1 I can't deal with your problem if you don't tell me about it.
I can't deal with your problem **unless** *you tell me* about it.
2 Unless he wins the competition, he won't be happy.
He'll be happy **if** ___________ the competition.
3 If it's a warm day, they'll go swimming.
They won't go swimming **unless** ___________ a warm day.
4 You won't get to know your neighbours if you don't speak to them.
You won't get to know your neighbours **unless** ___________ to them.
5 Harry won't be able to buy a phone unless he saves some money.
Harry won't be able to buy a phone **if** ___________ some money.
6 We can't go horse-riding if we don't wear helmets.
We can't go horse-riding **unless** ___________ helmets.

07 That's entertainment!

READING

Power up

1 **Do you have any musical events like these where you live? Do you think there are enough? Why/Why not?**

classical concerts
dance shows
jazz concerts
rock festivals
school musicals
singing competitions

2 **What musical instruments can you play or have you tried? What would you like to play? Talk about these instruments or others that you like.**

drums electric guitar
keyboard piano trumpet

Read on

3 **Look at the photos in the article and answer the questions.**

1. Who is in the photos?
2. What are they doing?
3. Where do you think they are?

4 **Read the article quickly. What does it tell you about the people in the photos?**

Two countries, one message.

Walk around the streets of Stirling in Scotland or Caracas in Venezuela and what type of music will you hear? Hip hop, Latin, folk? Yes, but you will also hear classical. A few years 1) ___ago___ only one school child in the Raploch area of Stirling was learning a musical instrument. Now, hundreds of children are 2) ___________ instruments, and in 2012 some of them performed live with Venezuela's famous Simón Bolívar Orchestra. 8,000 people were in the audience. So, how 3) ___________ the connection between Scotland and Venezuela happen, and why?

This musical adventure 4) ___________ in Caracas in 1975. The musician José Antonio Abreu wanted to offer free music lessons to children who lived in places where there weren't many after-school activities. His idea was simple. Give children classical music and they learn to work as a team, and they gain confidence. He knew that it would also help the community, so he began 'El Sistema', which means 'the system'. In the beginning, there 5) ___________ just eleven children. Since then, more than two million have taken part in the system.

One of those students is Genesis da Silva who dreams of being a great musician. 6) ___________ day after school, she spends five hours playing the clarinet before going home and practising more. She lives with her family and they all want her to do well. She says that the 7) ___________ important thing is to enjoy the music she says. Genesis is sure she can win a place in the system's Simón Bolívar Orchestra. After all her hard work, if she didn't get a place her family and friends would be very surprised.

Leswi Pantoja is a professional musician in the Simón Bolívar Orchestra and has known his musical friends 8) ___________ he was eleven years old. What would his life be like if he didn't have his music? It's hard to imagine. If he didn't play in the orchestra, he wouldn't have so many friends. 'We've grown 9) ___________ together as a family,' he says. Although Leswi grew up with Latin music and salsa, when he joined the system he learnt about classical music. Now he enjoys playing both.

After the success of the system in Venezuela, music teachers in Scotland were keen to see something similar, and in 2008 System Scotland began its own orchestra called The Big Noise. Schoolgirl Morgan is in the orchestra. She had learned to read music and plays many different kinds of instruments now. She loves the Big Noise and wants to keep on playing it in the future. The system has 10) ___________ children like Morgan the possibility to have dreams. They love being on stage, and the performance by Scottish schoolchildren and Venezuelan musicians showed that those dreams can come true.

Exam

When you are doing a gap-fill exercise, look at the words before and after the space. They will help you decide which word you need.

5 Read the article again and choose the correct answer, A, B, C or D.

	A	B	C	D
1	for	since	past	ago (circled)
2	making	having	playing	doing
3	did	was	has	will
4	started	based	introduced	opened
5	had	were	was	made
6	Some	Every	Both	All
7	more	such	too	most
8	as	when	for	since
9	up	into	out	off
10	made	given	sent	kept

6 Find words and phrases in the article that mean the following.

1. when you see or hear something at the same time that it happens (line 7)
2. the people who live in the same town or area (line 17)
3. a type of wind instrument (line 23)
4. doing an activity as a job (line 31)
5. to continue to do something (line 47)

Sum up

7 Work with a partner. Ask and answer the questions (1–3). Don't look at the text!

1. Where and why did the system start?
2. Why is the system important?
3. What do you remember about Genesis and Leswi?

Speak up

8 Are free music lessons after school a good idea? Why/Why not?

I think they're a good idea because they're often very expensive.

SWITCH ON We ❤ classical music page 69

VOCABULARY

Entertainment

1 **Label the picture with these words.**

audience choir costume exit
orchestra row stage

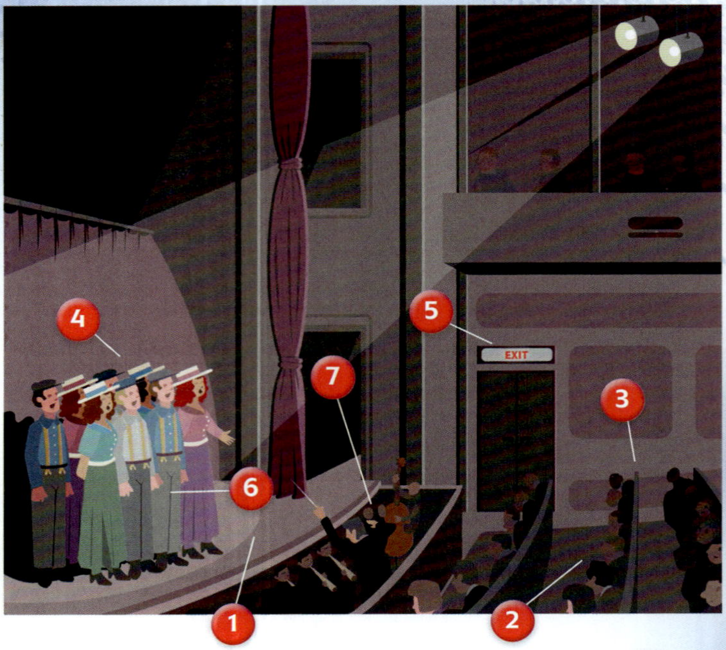

2 7.1 **Listen to the entertainment quiz. Answer with a word from Exercise 1.**

3 **Match the meanings (1–8) with these verbs.**

book clap entertain film interview
~~perform~~ record review

1 to do something in front of an audience, e.g. act, sing, dance *perform*
2 to write a report about something new, e.g. a book, a film, an album
3 to ask someone questions so that you can find out information
4 to do something that other people find interesting or funny
5 to make a film or moving picture
6 to put music, words or pictures on disk, so that people can listen to them or watch them
7 to arrange to have or do something at a time in the future
8 to hit your hands together several times to show you have enjoyed something

Word XP

When you learn a new verb, find other words that go with it.

record *a song/an album*
interview *an actor/a famous person*
perform *in a play/in a ballet/in a musical/on stage/in a TV show*
book *a ticket/seat*
film *a documentary/TV programme/scene*

4 7.2 **Listen to five situations. What is happening in each situation?**

1 *A woman is interviewing somebody about his writing.*

5 **Read the text. Choose the correct words.**

Welcome to your

What's on guide

– daily information on events in your area

Tonight, Harry Marley will 1) *entertain/perform* songs from his new album. Tickets only cost £5 so 2) *book/record* early as this is going to be popular.

Mollie Richards is 3) *interviewing/reviewing* Tyler Wilson about his new book for the Teen Literature festival. Admission is free.

The rock group, Dizzy, are recording their new 4) *album/play* at George Street studio. Listen to them on Radio Buzz at 6 p.m.

Would you like to be on a TV programme? ABC studio is 5) *entertaining/filming* in Newtown this evening. Call this number: 08944 84756.

The Urban Youth theatre is looking for talented teenagers to perform in an exciting new 6) *show/stage*. Come and meet us from 2–4 p.m. this afternoon.

Game on

Work with a partner. Choose a word from the page. Explain it to your partner, but don't say the word. You can say three things. Your partner tries to guess the word.

GRAMMAR

Grammar XP

Talking about imaginary situations and giving advice

Second conditional

for imaginary or unreal situations in the present

***If** he **didn't play** in the orchestra, he **wouldn't have** so many friends.*

for present or future situations that are possible, but not likely

*After all her hard work, **if** she **didn't get** a place, her family and friends **would be** very surprised.*

You can change the order of the *if* clause and the main clause.

*He **wouldn't have** so many friends **if** he **didn't play** in the orchestra.*

*What **would** he **do if** he **didn't have** music?*

Use *If I were you, I'd …* or *If I was you, I'd …* to give advice.

***If I were you, I'd** try a different instrument.*

1 7.3–4 **Listen. Now you say it!**

2 Choose the correct option.

1 If you came to South America, *you'd hear/'ll hear* lots of salsa.
2 If they *recorded/would record* a new album, their fans would buy it.
3 If Emily *is/were* in the band, she'd play drums.
4 You *aren't/wouldn't be* bored if you learnt to play an instrument.
5 He'd travel around Europe if he *would join/joined* the choir.

3 Complete the sentences (1–5) with the correct form of the verbs in brackets. Use the second conditional.

1 If I ___had___ (have) a better voice, I'd join a pop group.
2 If he ____________ (play) the violin badly, he wouldn't be in the orchestra.
3 We would go to the rock festival, if we ____________ (have) enough money.
4 The school choir would win the competition if it ____________ (practise) more.
5 If the DJ ____________ (not choose) such bad music, more people would dance.

4 Read the four notices or messages. Choose the correct answer, A, B or C.

> Skylight opera. – for one night only.
> Hurry! Only two tickets left!

1 The advert says …
A if you went to the theatre, you'd see *La Traviata*.
B if you want to see *La Traviata*, you should buy your tickets soon.
C if you liked opera, you wouldn't miss this performance.

> 14.32 PM
> I'll be at your house at seven. It starts at eight. If I were you, I'd have dinner before the concert. Edward

2 Edward is …
A offering to meet Phoebe at the concert.
B advising Phoebe to eat before the concert.
C telling Phoebe to change before the concert.

> Thanks for your invitation. I'd love to go, but I can't afford it this year. Ask Ben. He loves festivals.

3 Abigail says …
A Nicole and Ben would enjoy the festival.
B she would love to go to the festival with Ben.
C she would go to the festival if she had enough money.

> Are you coming to the play tonight? I don't feel so nervous when you're there. Jessica

4 What does Jessica think?
A She would prefer it if Charlie went.
B She would prefer it if Charlie didn't go.
C She would prefer Charlie to perform in the show.

Write on

5 Complete the sentences for you.

1 If I spoke perfect English, …
2 If my favourite pop group came to my school, …
3 I … if school closed early today.

LISTENING

Power up

1 **Read the news headline. Do you think this it's true? Why/Why not?**

CD sales are down, but digital downloads are up

2 **How do you find out about new music? Where do you buy your music?**

Listen up

3 7.5 **Listen to the conversations. Choose the correct answer, A, B or C.**

1 What type of music has the girl just bought?

A B C

2 What does the singer always wear?

A B C

3 What caused a problem at the festival?

A B C

4 How much did the boy pay for the CD?

A B C

5 Where did the boy buy his album?

A B C

6 Who helped the girl to download her new album??

A B C

4 7.6 **Listen again and check your answers.**

Exam

Take time to choose the answer. You might hear words that match the different pictures, but only one is correct.

Grammar XP

p. 138

Subject questions

In subject questions, the question word is the subject of the sentence. It is not followed by *do/does/did*.

***What** caused the fire at the theatre? **A lamp** caused the fire.*

***Who helped** Anna to download the album?*

***A friend** helped her*

Object questions

In object questions, the question word is the object of the verb. It is followed by do/does/did.

What did she download? She downloaded Lana del Rey's new album.

5 **Read the sentences and make questions.**

1 Will and Emily went to a music festival.
___Who___ went to a music festival?

2 Twenty thousand people downloaded the track.
__________ 20,000 people download?

3 The band arrived late for the concert.
__________ arrived late for the concert?

4 A fire started in the theatre.
__________ happened in the theatre?

5 He saw his friends from the orchestra in town.
__________ he see in the street?

6 Some famous people came out of the studio.
__________ came out of the studio?

SPEAKING

Power up

1 **Say what is happening in the photos. Use these phrases. Not all the phrases are needed.**

flash mob

live music in the street

music festival

singing competition

A

B

C

2 **Where do you go when you want to listen to music or hear live music?**

Speak up

3 7.7 **Listen to the conversation between Jacob and Kate. Which event in the photos in Exercise 1 do they talk about?**

4 7.8 **Listen again. Put the sentences in the order you hear them.**

If we went, we could be on TV.
Why don't we go to it? *1*
All right then.
I'm not really keen on dancing.

Language XP

Making suggestions
Why don't we/you …? What about/How about …? Let's do/go …
I think we should …
Saying *No* politely
I'm really sorry but … I'm afraid I can't because … I don't really like … It's a nice idea, but perhaps we could do it another day. I'm not very keen on …
Saying *Yes*
That sounds brilliant. What a great idea! OK/All right then.

5 **Work with a partner. Take it in turns to make suggestions and reply to your partner's suggestions.**

Student A
- go to a play
- watch a horror film
- download some new music

Student B
- go to a rock concert
- watch a comedian on TV
- join a choir

Let's go to a play.

What a great idea!

Skill

It's OK if you don't agree with your partner. You can say *No* to an idea, but be polite.

6 **Work with a partner. Choose one photo each from Exercise 1. Practise the conversation.**

Student A
Make a suggestion for this evening.
Agree with the suggestion.

Student B
Say *No* nicely, and make a suggestion.

7 **Work with a partner. Student A, look at page 131. Student B, look at page 143. Follow the instructions.**

WRITING

Power up

1 **Look at the photos (A–C). Match the photos with the comments (1–3).**

A

B

C

1 'An amazing TV show with great singing and dancing.'
2 'It's the best album they've made. Every track is brilliant.'
3 'One of the best films I've ever seen! Great music and fantastic costumes.'

2 **What's your favourite TV show ... ? music video ... ? film ... ? Why?**

3 **Read the concert review. Find words in the review that mean the following.**

1 a place where a public event happens
2 songs from an album
3 the feeling that an event or a place gives you
4 when a place is full of people
5 to have enough money to buy something
6 not happy because something wasn't as good as you wanted it to be

We asked you what concerts you've seen recently. Read our star review.

REVIEW

Last weekend, I went to a Florence and the Machine concert. The venue was the theatre and the concert lasted two hours. Lots of people my age were there.

The good thing about the concert was that Florence sang all my favourite tracks, including her last hit song 'Spectrum'. She also wore some amazing costumes. The best thing about the concert was the atmosphere because it was friendly and relaxed. Everybody in the audience was happy, although it was a bit crowded and there wasn't much room to dance. It was also boiling hot.

The only bad thing about the concert was the price of the tickets. They cost £60, and lots of people can't afford that. It's too expensive.

On the whole, I would recommend this band. If I were you, I'd book a ticket as soon as possible! You won't be disappointed.

4 **Find positive and negative adjectives in the review in Exercise 3.**

Positive: *good*   Negative:

5 **Read the review again. Put the questions in the order the information comes in the review.**

Do you think your friends would like it?
What was good about the concert?
What is the review of? *1*
What was bad about the concert?

Plan on

6 **You're going to write a review. Read the first part of the notice and choose what you want to write about.**

> **THAT'S ENTERTAINMENT!**
> SHOWS/FILMS/VIDEOS/ALBUMS/NEWS
> Have you watched a brilliant TV show recently, or discovered an amazing music video? Perhaps you've seen a fantastic film. We want to know ... read more

7 **Read the second part of the notice. Make notes for each question. Use the key words and phrases from Exercise 1, Exercise 3 and the Language XP box.**

> Tell us:
> What is your review of?
> Why is it/was it good? or Why is it/was it not so good?
> Would your friends like it?

Language XP

Saying something is/was good
The good thing about the concert/festival was the atmosphere.
The album/video is also good/amazing.
The best thing was the exciting story.
Saying something is/was bad
The sound wasn't so good.
The only bad thing about the show/video is the costumes.
The worst thing was the price of the tickets.
Making a recommendation
If you bought/watched/saw this, you'd love it.
On the whole, I would/can recommend this concert/album/show.

Write on

8 **Write a review of a TV show, music video or film. Write about 110 words.**

Skill

Are you writing a review? Give some good points and not so good points, and finish with your recommendation.

Switch on

WE ❤ CLASSICAL MUSIC

1 **Guess the answers. Then watch and check.**

You're going to watch a video of 'El Sistema' in Venezuela.

1. Is El Sistema for young children, older children or both?
2. Where do the students practise their music?

2 **Are the sentences (1–6) true (T) or false (F)?**

1. Music classes are the only after-school activity for the children.
2. The children practise seven days a week.
3. The girl with the necklace started playing the trumpet before the violin.
4. The system doesn't think pop music helps children as much as classical music.
5. 'El Sistema' has 166 orchestras for children and 216 for young people.
6. The 'Simon Bolivar' orchestra travels all over the world.

3 **Why do you think 'El Sistema' is so popular in Venezuela? Would it be a good idea where you live? Why/Why not?**

Project

4 **Work in small groups. Make a poster for a new music club in your school. Think of exciting reasons why students should join. Take it in turns to show your poster to the class and explain why your music club would be good.**

It's a great way to make new friends.
You can learn an instrument and gain confidence.

08 Going away

READING

Power up

1 **What's important to you when you go on holiday?**

activities travel people weather place

Read on

2 **Read the holiday wish lists. What do these people like and dislike?**

Holiday wish list

My favourite kind of holiday is a beach holiday; just swimming and relaxing in the sun. Unfortunately, my family and friends prefer something more sporty, with lots of exercise. Vicky, 14

My dad, mum and I enjoy sightseeing. We don't often go abroad because I suffer from travel sickness, and my mum hates flying – especially during take-off and landing. Adam, 15

My dream holiday is to get to know interesting people and to see different places. I'm lucky because I play a sport, which means I compete in other countries. Perfect! Stella, 15

My mum, my sister and I don't go away every year, but we like to stay somewhere nice with plenty of sunshine. We can't stand cold water or cold weather. Tony, 14

3 **Look at the travel photos. Which do you think are travel dreams or nightmares? Why?**

4 **Match the holiday wish lists in Exercise 2 for Vicky, Adam, Stella and Tony with the correct letter (1–6).**

5 **Look at the letters in the magazine article. Find words in the letters that mean the following.**

1 clean; without rubbish (Letter 1)
2 unluckily (Letter 3)
3 really good (Letter 2)
4 not calm (Letter 5)
5 sports competitions (Letter 4)
6 sports teacher (Letter 6)

Exam

In mixed texts, the information can be in any order. To find answers, you need to move around between the questions, personal information and short texts.

Letter 5
The worst holiday I've ever had was a trip to the beautiful seaside city of Barcelona. Unfortunately, there was a traffic jam on the motorway. The journey took five hours and we stopped five times because I felt ill. My dad is usually calm, but he was stressed that day.

Travel dreams v travel nightmares

This week in **fifty words ...**

We asked readers to tell us their holiday dreams and nightmares. As usual the prizes are:
£20 for the person who writes the prize letter
£10 for the first reader who correctly matches the four holiday wish lists to the correct letter.

Letter 1
My best holiday was a prize that Mum won in a TV competition. Our destination? The USA! We flew to Florida and checked in at a beach hotel. Before then, I hated water and couldn't swim, but the sea was so clear and warm that I learnt to swim.

Letter 2
Last year we flew to Poland, where I was born. We wanted to visit some cousins who live in Zakopane, a ski resort in the mountains. Unfortunately, there was a long delay at the border because of the snow, but we had a brilliant time with our cousins after that.

Letter 3
I'm from New Zealand, and I went to Australia last summer on a school trip. I was worried about dangerous spiders and snakes which live there. Instead we saw kangaroos jumping around and koalas with their cute babies. Unfortunately, a kangaroo kicked our teacher who had to go to hospital!

Letter 4
I play football and my team often travels around the country to take part in tournaments. It's not really a holiday, but it's fun. Last month we travelled across the border into Brazil. It was so exciting! The players we met were really friendly and one girl is my new e-friend.

Letter 6
I hate activity holidays and heights, so I wasn't looking forward to our adventure holiday. I wanted Dad to lose our passports! At the rope-climbing centre we had a friendly instructor who helped me to feel more confident. I completed a high rope course, and I felt really proud.

Sum up

6 Work with a partner. Match two letters in the magazine article in Exercise 5 to each of these points (1–3). Explain why they match.

1 The reader was worried before the holiday but enjoyed it in the end.
2 The reader learned a new skill.
3 The reader had travel problems.

Speak up

7 Work with a partner. Which trip is similar to/different from one of your holidays? Tell the class about it.

Holiday 4 is similar to my holiday last year. I played basketball for my school in Spain. It was great.

SWITCH ON Holiday survival tips page 77

VOCABULARY

Travel

1 8.1 **Listen to the words and definitions. Match the correct part of speech: noun (n), verb (v) or adverb (adv) with 1–12.**

1 abroad adv
2 border
3 check in
4 delay
5 destination
6 flight
7 land
8 motorway
9 passport
10 sightseeing
11 take off
12 traffic jam

2 Match the words in Exercise 1 with the correct heading.

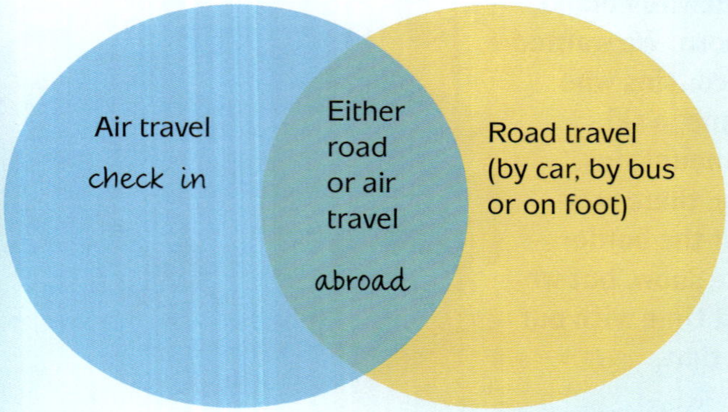

3 Look at these similar words and their definitions. Choose the correct words to complete the sentences (1–6).

travel (v): to make a journey
travel (n, uncountable): the general activity of travelling
journey (n, usually singular): the time when you are travelling from one place to another
trip (n): a short visit to a place, usually to go there and return home

1 We've just arrived home from Spain. We had a brilliant *travel/trip*.
2 I love *travel/travels*. I'd like to go around the world.
3 There was a long delay on the *journey/trip* back home.
4 Our *journey/travel* to Rome was fast because we went by plane.
5 My brother is going to *travel/trip* to Australia next year.
6 My mum is away on a two-day business *journey/trip* to New York.

Word XP

Verbs and nouns
Many nouns look the same as verbs. Some are very similar.

Verb	Noun
delay	*delay*
travel	*travel*
take off	*take-off*
check in	*check-in*

4 Complete the sentences with the correct form of the verbs from the Word XP box.

1 I was looking out of the window when the plane took off.
2 The traffic jam on the motorway d__________ us for about an hour.
3 When we got to the airport, there was a long queue at c__________ .
4 Our friends c__________ to the hotel yesterday.
5 My parents hate to t__________ in bad weather.

5 Complete Amir's travel story with these words.

abroad checked in check-in delay destination flight passports trip

This summer, we went on a 1) __________ to Turkey to visit Mum's family. Our 2) __________ was Bodrum. It was my first trip 3) __________ , and I was very excited. At the airport, we 4) __________ . Mum gave the 5) __________ to the assistant at the 6) __________ desk, but mine wasn't there. We searched for ten minutes, then I found it inside a magazine in my bag. Luckily, we didn't miss our 7) __________ because there was a two-hour 8) __________ .

Game on

Work with a partner. Write your answers for each question. You have two minutes. Can you name …

1 two popular tourist destinations near you?
2 a place to go sightseeing?
3 somewhere abroad?
4 a country or sea that is on the border of your country?
5 two reasons why people like/hate take-off and landing?
6 two things that can cause a travel delay?

Compare your ideas with the rest of the class. You get one point for each new idea.

GRAMMAR

Grammar XP

p. 123

Defining relative clauses
who/which/that as subject
Defining relative clauses tell us exactly which people, things or animals we are talking about.
*There is £20 for the person **who** writes the prize letter.*
Use *who* for people. Use *which* for things and animals.
*We went to visit some cousins **who** live in Zakopane.*
*I was worried about the spiders **which** live there.*
We can use *that* instead of *who* or *which*.
*We went to visit some cousins **that** live in Zakopane.*
*I was worried about the spiders **that** live there.*
***who/which/that* as object**
We can leave out *which/who/that* when it is the object of the verb, especially in speech and informal writing.
The players we met were really friendly.
*The players (**that/whichwho/which/that**) we met were really friendly.*

1 Choose the correct word to complete the sentences.

1. The pilot *who/which* flew our plane is my dad's cousin.
2. The flight *who/which* has just landed is from Ankara, Turkey.
3. Will the passenger *who/which* has lost a passport please go to the check-in desk?
4. There's a meeting after school for all the students *who/which* are going on the ski trip.

2 Rewrite the two sentences so they are one sentence. Use *that*.

1. Rio is a beautiful city. It's very popular with tourists.
   Rio is a beautiful city that's very popular with tourists.
2. Do you know the passenger? He spoke to you.
3. Here's the old castle. We visited it last summer.
4. Where are the beach towels? I left them here.

3 8.2 Listen and check your answers.

4 Which underlined nouns are the object of the verb? Complete the sentences with a relative pronoun. Write '–' if no pronoun is needed.

1. Snorkelling is a holiday activity *which/that* many tourists enjoy.
2. We loved the beach near Olu Deniz ____________ has sea turtles.
3. I'd like to go back to the place ____________ we saw yesterday.
4. We met some tourists ____________ showed us a good restaurant.
5. The flight ____________ we were waiting for was late because of fog.

5 Choose *who*, *which*, *that* or '–' to complete the article. More than one answer is usually possible.

Ready for a BIG adventure!

Flying is something 1) *which/that* – Kimberley Anyadike loves. Kimberley is a teenager 2) ____________ comes from California in the USA. When she was fifteen years old, Kimberley flew a small plane across the USA. She took off in California and landed in Virginia and then flew back home. The flight 3) ____________ she made took thirteen days. Kimberley learnt to fly when she was twelve. The plane 4)____________ she flew across the USA isn't her own, and her family isn't rich. It belongs to a plane museum 5) ____________ helps young pilots to learn about flying. Being away from home was difficult for Kimberley 6) ____________ missed her family. Another problem was the weather 7) ____________ was sometimes very stormy! There wasn't much time to sleep, 8) ____________ was also hard for Kimberley. So why did she do it? She said she wanted to inspire other kids to really believe in themselves.

Write on

6 Complete the sentences with information about you.

1. … is a friend who …
2. … is a place that …
3. … is a sport which …

LISTENING

Power up

1 Work with a partner. Read these real questions from tourists. Can you explain why they are silly?

At the airport

1 What time does the nine o'clock flight leave?
2 Why does the sign on the toilet say 'closed for cleaning'?
3 Do I have to use my real name on my airline ticket?

On a plane

4 Can we undo our seatbelts to go to the toilet?
5 Could you turn the engines down? They're too noisy.
6 It's hot in here. Could you open a window?

Listen up

2 8.3 Listen to a teacher talking to a group of students on a school trip. Write answers to these questions. Use words or numbers.

1 The teacher is going to give students information about what to do. What place does he mention?
2 How many students are on the trip?

3 8.4 Listen to the teacher giving more instructions to the students. Complete the notes with one or more words in each space.

Trip to 1) Madrid, Spain
Teachers: Mr Jones, Miss Harris, ~~Mr Hill~~, Mrs 2) ______
Staying at: Hotel 3) ______
Amount of money each student will need: 4) ______
Check-in desk: number four
Terminal: 5) ______
Flight number: Wings WI 6) ______
Sit next to teachers on plane? 7) ______

Exam

You must spell words correctly if they are very simple or when you hear the spelling.

Grammar XP

p. 138

Obligation and prohibition

must

We use *must* when we think it is important to do something. *Must* has no past or future tense.

*You **must** write that down carefully.*

*We use **mustn't** to mean, 'Don't do this!'*

*You **mustn't** leave your luggage anywhere.*

have to

We use have to/don't have to when something is/isn't necessary.

*You **have to** wear your seatbelt.* (= you must)

*You **don't have to** carry all your money.* (= it isn't necessary)

had to

Had to is the past tense of both *must* and *have to*.

*We **had to ask** another teacher to join us.*

will have to

Will have to is the future tense of both *must* and *have to*.

*You **will have to** talk to your leader if you have any problems.*

4 Choose the correct form of the verb.

1 I *mustn't/<u>won't have to</u>* buy any sunglasses. I've already got some.
2 James and Oliver *had to/must* get up early to catch their flight tomorrow.
3 We *must/mustn't* exchange some money today. We've only got £10.
4 You *don't have to/mustn't* come with me to the train station. I know the way.
5 Your suitcase is full already. You *must/mustn't* buy any more souvenirs.

5 Complete the second sentence so that it means the same as the first. In one question, more than one answer is possible.

1 Planning is important if you want a good holiday.
You ______ plan if you want a good holiday.
2 It isn't necessary to take lots of luggage.
You ______ take lots of luggage.
3 It was necessary to wait at the train station because of the snow.
We ______ wait at the train station because of the snow.
4 It's important not to forget your passport.
You ______ forget your passport.

SPEAKING

Power up

1 **How bad are the problems? Match the problems (A–F) with a number (1–3).**

1 = not too bad 2 = annoying 3 = a disaster - time to panic!

A You lose all your money

C Your phone battery dies

E You forget your ticket.

B You buy a great souvenir, but it breaks on the way home

D You can't see your family in a busy street.

F You have to share a bedroom with your cousins.

2 **Read the conversation about Jack's travel problem. Put Ruby's sentences (A–E) in the correct spaces (1–5) in the conversation.**

Jack: I was on a plane last year, when the captain made an important announcement.

Ruby: 1) ____________

Jack: The flight was from Brisbane to Sydney. The captain said, 'Ladies and gentlemen. Welcome on board. Today, we have a cargo of animals which is heading for Sydney Zoo. Don't worry, the animals are safely in the hold with the baggage. They can't escape.'

Ruby: 2) ____________

Jack: Yes, I think so. Half an hour later, there was another announcement: 'Ladies and gentlemen, please don't panic. Unfortunately, I have to inform you that one of the crocodiles we're carrying has escaped.'

Ruby: 3) ____________

Jack: I don't know. There were a few people who were scared of crocodiles. One lady screamed, but the flight attendants told her to stay calm.

Ruby: 4) ____________

Jack: Yes, she was OK, and they caught the crocodile when the plane landed.

Ruby: 5) ____________

Jack: No, the crocodile that escaped was only about sixty centimetres long – just a baby.

A Where were you going?
B So, was the lady OK? Did they catch the crocodile?
C Was anyone injured?
D Oh, were they in cages?
E Really? That was scary. How did that happen?

3 8.5 **Listen and check your answers.**

4 **Work with a partner. Decide whether you believe Jack's story. Why/Why not?**

Language XP

Helping someone express their ideas

Really? That's interesting/nice/awful/scary.
So, did you/they/anyone … ?
Was it a … ?
What happened then/next?
How did that happen?

5 **Work with a partner. Choose one of the problems in Exercise 1. Ask questions about your partner's problem and answer your partner's questions about your problem.**

A: *What happened?*
B: *I lost all my money.*

Skill

When you are talking to someone, show you are interested. If you need to interrupt, say Sorry to interrupt.

WRITING

Power up

1 **Work with a partner. Choose the holiday photo you like best. Take it in turns to describe it and explain the following.**

1 who is in the picture
2 where each person is standing
3 what they are doing, e.g. touching, hugging, picking up, leaning against
4 what it looks like

2 **Why do people take photos like the ones in Exercise 1? Have you got any similar holiday photos?**

3 **Read Bruno's blog. Find words and phrases in the blog that mean the following.**

1 my best advice
2 That's so boring!
3 all the time
4 all of them
5 a good plan

4 **Complete the sentences with words and phrases from Exercise 3.**

1 We visited five museums in one day. _Yawn!_
2 My brother plays on his Xbox ________ .
3 The hotel was full, but my dad had ________ – we slept in the car.
4 I bought three milkshakes, and I drank ________ .

I am Bruno

Top tips for a happy holiday

My parents are keen photographers who love taking photos of tourist attractions and scenery. Yawn!
Last year, we went to Salvador, which we all loved. But there was one problem that spoiled our fun. All day, every day Mum and Dad had their cameras ready and said things like, 'Stand here!', 'Don't move!' and 'SMILE!'
When we got home we had lots of photos, but my sister and I looked bored or annoyed in every single one.
That's when I had my bright idea for a better holiday. So what's my top tip? You don't have to let your parents take all the photos. Grab the camera or use your mobile and take some funny or unusual photos. What do you think of my plan? Let me know.
Bruno, Brazil

Like Comment 5 1

Switch on

Plan on

5 **Work with a partner. Which of these tips for a happy holiday do you think is best?**

1 Have you ever sat next to a crying baby on a bus or plane? It happened to me last year on a three-hour train journey to Madrid. My top tip is to take ear plugs or your music player. ALWAYS!

Like · Comment 12 3

2 You don't have to be embarrassed if you get travel sick. My top tip? Just take an airline sick bag with you when you travel. I never travel anywhere without one.

3 Last holiday, my dad dropped our camera in the sea. We lost all our holiday pictures. So my top tip is to take lots of photos – and upload them or make copies.

4 Are you going on a long journey? Will you have to sleep on the bus or in a hotel? My advice is to take the pillow from your bed. You can sleep anywhere and it will feel like home.

6 **What holiday tip(s) can you add to the blogs in Exercise 5?**

Skill

You can use questions in your blog to invite comments from your readers. In the real world you have to reply, too!

Write on

7 **Write a blog entry about something that happened on a holiday. Add your holiday tip(s). Invite readers to give their opinions.**

Language station

Inviting other people to give their opinions

Do you think that … ?
What do you think of this photo/idea/plan?
Let me know what you think.
Have you got any suggestions/good ideas?

HOLIDAY SURVIVAL TIPS

1 **Guess the answers. Then watch and check.**

Rebecca and Emma are talking about family holidays. Which of these tips will they mention?

- **A** Take your own sun cream.
- **B** Buy lots of souvenirs.
- **C** Don't play competitive sports.
- **D** Don't do karaoke.
- **E** Take a family photo.
- **F** Remember your sunglasses.
- **G** Offer to babysit.

2 **Are the sentences (1–6) true (T) or false (F)?**

1. Emma has just been on holiday.
2. The girls start with their most important tip.
3. Emma's first tip is about getting some free time.
4. Rebecca shows a family photo from when she was very young.
5. Emma's father doesn't mind losing.
6. Their final tip is about stopping their parents being embarrassing.

3 **Do you think any of their tips were useful? Why/Why not?**

Project

4 **Write your own video script for a short two-minute film in which you give your top five holiday tips.**

1. Decide on these things:
   - What your five top tips are.
   - What order you will present them in.
   - Who will present each tip.
   - What comments the other person/people will make.
2. Write your script.
3. Act it out.

Here are our top five tips for a great family holiday. First of all, ... / Then, ... / Next, ... / And finally, ...

VOCABULARY

1 Match the meanings (1–7) with these words.

audience choir costume ~~exit~~ orchestra row stage

1 the way out of a place *exit*
2 the clothes that an actor wears in a play or a film
3 the people who watch or listen to a performance
4 a large group of people who play musical instruments together
5 the place in a theatre where actors perform a play
6 a line of seats in a theatre, cinema, etc.
7 a group of people who sing together

2 Complete the sentences with these words/phrases.

're filming book clapped entertain interview ~~perform~~ record review

1 One day I want to *perform* in a play in front of a big audience.
2 Zak's a great singer. He's going to ____________ an album soon.
3 Can you go online and ____________ seats for the theatre tonight?
4 Sshh! They ____________ a wildlife documentary. We can watch it if we're quiet.
5 I want to be a music journalist, so that I can ____________ famous rock stars.
6 Charlie is very funny and can always ____________ friends with his jokes.
7 I enjoy writing, and often ____________ new films for the school magazine.
8 The audience loved the show and ____________ for a long time at the end.

3 Choose the correct words.

1 The train journey was terrible and it took five hours for us to reach our *destination/motorway*.
2 This year Emma's going *abroad/sightseeing* for the first time. She's never visited another country before.
3 The student's enjoyed the ski *trip/journey* and didn't want to come home.
4 They walked over the *border/check-in* between France and Spain during the night.
5 After the plane *landed/took off*, the air steward brought round food and a drink, and we watched a film.
6 We heard about the *flight/traffic jam* on the radio, so we chose a different road into town.

4 Choose the best answer A, B or C.

1 I had a fantastic holiday, but the ____________ home was long and very boring.
A trip **(B)** journey **C** travel
2 They couldn't ____________ their bags when they arrived because it was too early.
A take off **B** delay **C** check in
3 While we waiting for the concert to start, a girl came on stage and ____________ us with some jokes.
A performed **B** filmed **C** entertained
4 After watching the show, the ____________ clapped and shouted.
A audience **B** choir **C** orchestra
5 Can you tell me what time the ____________ to Madrid leaves, please?
A journey **B** flight **C** motorway
6 The planes couldn't ____________ from the airport because it was too foggy.
A take off **B** take-off **C** land

5 Complete the leaflet with the words.

book delay destination entertain flight ~~passport~~ row sightseeing travelling

Welcome to
Merlin Airlines!

Please be ready with your 1) *passport* and ticket when you hear your 2) ____________ number. Your boarding card shows a seat number. Passengers in 3) ____________ twenty-four have extra leg space. If there is a 4) ____________ of more than thirty minutes, all passengers receive a free meal. We like to 5) ____________ all our passengers on board, and offer a good choice of films. Merlin Airlines can also help you before you arrive at your 6) ____________ . If you would like to 7) ____________ theatre tickets or a 8) ____________ trip, please ask for details. We would like to thank you for 9) ____________ with Merlin Airlines.

GRAMMAR

6 Put the words in the correct order to make sentences.

1 were / If / you, / I'd /the tickets online./ I / book
If I were you, I'd book the tickets online.
2 they'd / joined the band, / If / see the world. / they
3 I / would / The journey / if / went by bus. / take ages
4 go sightseeing / I / you, / I'd / were / tomorrow. / If
5 write / more time. / if / had / I / more songs / I'd
6 would / if / Anna / she / love this musical / here. / were

7 Complete the questions with *What* or *Who*.

1 *What* did you say? I said something funny.
2 ___________ did he see at the concert? He saw his cousins.
3 ___________ did you hear? I heard a loud noise.
4 ___________ is meeting us? Jack is.
5 ___________ did she find? She found a cheap flight to New York.
6 ___________ broke on the stage? The guitar did.
7 ___________ is downloading a song? We're downloading a song.
8 ___________ performed well? Emily and Max did.

8 Choose the correct words.

1 Is that the girl *which*/*who* won the singing competition?
2 The person *that*/*which* I like watching most on stage is Beyoncé.
3 The performers *which*/*who* we saw at the festival were brilliant.
4 I'd like to find a flight *that*/*who* goes direct.
5 Do you know the name of the band *that*/*who* is on TV now.
6 There are some borders *which*/*who* are dangerous to cross.
7 That's the woman *which*/*who* we saw when we checked in.
8 The girl *which*/*who* I sat next to on the flight spoke Chinese.

9 Complete the sentences with the correct form of the verb in brackets.

1 You *don't have to* (not/have to) buy your tickets now. You can get them at the station.
2 The passengers were tired because they ___________ (have to) sleep in the airport last night.
3 It's a fantastic theatre. We ___________ (must) go there one day.
4 The motorway will be closed this evening, so we ___________ (have to) use the smaller roads.
5 We ___________ (must/not) forget our cameras when we go away at the weekend.
6 Olivia's in a choir, and she ___________ (have to) practise three times a week.
7 You can look at my costume for the play but you ___________ (must/not) laugh at it.
8 Maria wanted to go sightseeing, but first she ___________ (have to) unpack her bags.

10 Choose the correct word for each space.

Niall Horan, from the pop group *One Direction*, is a singer 1) ___________ has everything: millions of fans, lots of money and a close family in Ireland. It's a life 2) ___________ lots of talented teenagers would like to have. 3) ___________ really happens when a young teen suddenly become famous? For a start, they often 4) ___________ to travel a lot, and that can be difficult. 5) ___________ they weren't famous, they would probably see more of their families at home. School life also changes. Some teen pop stars 6) ___________ to go to school because they haven't got time. Perhaps that sounds fun, but 7) ___________ teaches them? Even pop stars know that they 8) ___________ get an education, so many of them travel around the world with a tutor. It isn't easy, but if you 9) ___________ these young stars a choice, they wouldn't change a thing.

	A	B	C	D
1	that	(B) who	which	where
2	that	what	who	then
3	Why	Who	What	How
4	had	will	must	have
5	If	Although	Because	So
6	don't have	didn't have	doesn't have	mustn't have
7	what	when	where	who
8	need	needn't	mustn't	must
9	make	gave	made	give

09 Weird and wonderful world

READING

Power up

1 Look at the photos. How weird or unusual are these hobbies?

collecting Pokémon

planking

beekeeping

2 Do you know somebody with a weird or unusual hobby? What's the most unusual hobby you've ever tried?

Read on

3 Read the first part of the article. What is Caroline's hobby?

astronomy   collecting telescopes   photography   playing a musical instrument

Supernova superstar!

Are you looking for a new hobby? Hobbies are a great way to chill out on your own or with friends. At Hobbynews, we've met teens who are passionate about what they do in their free time. How about Eliza Watkins who loves beekeeping? In last month's edition, she told us that her friends found her hobby weird. Does that matter to Eliza? No, not at all! She loves her hobby, and knows she's got talent. This month, we take a look at Caroline Moore. Her passion for studying the sky at night has made her a superstar in the world of astronomy. Here's her story.

Caroline was fourteen years old when she became the youngest person in the world to discover a supernova. Since the discovery, she's appeared on lots of TV shows, and even visited the White House. Caroline's really excited about her supernova, and never gets tired of talking about it and how she found it. On TV, she said that she felt important. So when did this unusual hobby begin?

Hobbynews

Exam

In a multiple-choice exercise, the wrong answers will have information that is similar to the text. Find the incorrect answers first.

Factfile:
What's a supernova?
It's a star that's dying. It's burning and exploding at a speed of 30,000 km/s.

When she was very young, Caroline was mad about science, but she didn't get her first telescope until she was ten. After that, she soon became hooked on the stars. In a TV interview she said that her dad was interested in the stars, too. One night, they stayed out in the freezing cold until one o'clock in the morning. Why? Because there was a cool object in the sky! Caroline enjoyed the hobby so much that she became a supernova hunter for a search team. She said that the team sent her pictures of the night sky and that she looked for changes. If something was different, there was a possibility it was a supernova.

One night, Caroline was studying some photos when she saw something unusual. She wasn't sure, but she thought it was a supernova, and she decided to tell the search team. When the phone rang later that night, Caroline was in bed. It was a friend from the search team. Caroline was grumpy, and didn't want to talk. 'What do you want?' she asked, 'I've got a big test tomorrow.' At first, her friend joked about the supernova. Then he told her that she was right. There was a supernova in the photo! Caroline couldn't believe it. She jumped up and down because she was so happy.

After finding the supernova, Caroline had a lot of publicity. She told one interviewer that she wanted to motivate other kids to try new things. She also said that we would see her back at the White House someday. So what about the future? Is astronomy a hobby for life? Of course it is, but Caroline also likes to find time for her other interests. She's into singing and she sings classical, jazz, Irish and folk music. We think she's amazing!

4 Read the rest of the article. Choose the correct answer, A, B, C or D.

1 What is the writer doing in the article?
  A encouraging people to look for supernovas
  B comparing different hobbies and interests
  C explaining why astronomy is important
  D showing that hobbies are a good thing
2 What does Caroline always like doing?
  A telling people about her supernova
  B talking about her visit to the White House
  C appearing on TV shows
  D helping people to understand astronomy
3 When did Caroline's interest in astronomy begin?
  A after she started doing science at school
  B when she was very young
  C after she got her first telescope
  D when she found an object in the sky
4 What did Caroline think when she heard there was a supernova?
  A her dad would be happy
  B she wasn't sure it was true
  C her friend at the search team was wrong
  D nobody would believe her
5 What's the best description of Caroline?
  A She shares her dad's interest and they are both famous in the world of astronomy.
  B She loves what she does and has a great future in astronomy.
  C She has more than one hobby and wants to encourage others to do something new.
  D She's always very busy and can't stop talking about her supernova.

5 Find words and phrases in the article that mean the following.

1 relax
2 producing heat and flames
3 when you like something a lot and can't stop doing it
4 quite angry because you are tired
5 make someone want to do something

Sum up

6 Work with a partner. Close your books and tell Caroline's story. First say what a supernova is, then talk about how Caroline found it.

Speak up

7 Work with a partner. Do you like watching the stars? Why/Why not?

I love watching the stars. The sky changes every night.

SWITCH ON Supernova, superstar page 87

VOCABULARY

Hobbies and interests

1 **Match the statements (1–9) with the activities (a–i).**

1 Let's paint it blue and grey. Then, we can put the windows in.
2 I'm trying to learn the drums because I want to be in a band.
3 I often play against my cousins, but my computer's broken at the moment.
4 It's very dark in here. You should use a flash for the picture.
5 I'm really into kickboxing. It's a fun way to exercise.
6 When I hang out with friends, we love making things like necklaces.
7 This year, we're doing a musical. You can join in if you want.
8 I've got hundreds of them, but this is my favourite. I got it on holiday last year.
9 That smells fantastic. Can we eat it now?

a collecting key rings
b cooking
c doing drama
d keeping fit
e making jewellery
f making models
g online gaming
h practising a musical instrument
i taking photos

2 9.1 **Listen. Which activities in Exercise 1 do you hear?**

3 **Match these nouns with the hobbies (1–3). There are two nouns for each hobby.**

battery glue ~~ingredients~~ paintbrush recipe zoom lens

1 cooking *ingredients*
2 photography
3 making models

4 **Match the definitions (1–6) with the words in the box in Exercise 3.**

1 instructions for how to cook something *recipe*
2 something that you use to join things together
3 a long, thin brush that you use to add colour to something
4 an object that provides power for a machine or piece of equipment
5 things that you use to make a particular type of food
6 a piece of curved glass or plastic that makes things look bigger

Word XP

You can use these phrases to talk about your hobbies and interests.

be into *photography/making models*
be mad about *cooking/keeping fit*
chill out *with friends/at home/at the beach*
hang out with *friends/other football fans/my cousins*
join in *the dancing/the fun*

5 **Read the blog. Choose the correct answer, A, B, C or D.**

Home Page | About Us | Services | Projects | FAQs | Contact Us

Welcome to hobbyblog!

Are you looking for a new hobby or do you just want to hang out 1) ______________ friends with the same interests? Perhaps you like 2) ______________ old comics or you're 3) ______________ making your own jewellery. We've got something for everyone at hobbyblog. This month, Jessica Danes is going to write on our blog. Jessica's 4) ______________ about making models, and she's going to do an online demonstration of a 3-D model. Why don't you 5) ______________ in the fun? All you need is some cardboard and a few 6) ______________ . What are you waiting for?

	A	B	C	D
1	A into	B in	C with	D about
2	A collecting	B making	C taking	D doing
3	A for	B in	C into	D about
4	A good	B bad	C into	D mad
5	A meet	B join	C hang	D chill
6	A paints	B glue	C battery	D ingredients

Game on

Work with a partner. Write down as many hobbies as you can. You have one minute. Who has the most?

GRAMMAR

Grammar XP

p. 139

Reported statements
The main verb usually goes back one tense into the past.
*'I **look** for changes in the pictures.'*
*Caroline said (that) she **looked** for changes.*
Other verbs change: *can-could, will-would*.
*She also said (that) we **would** see her back at the White House someday.*

Pronoun changes
Use personal pronouns, e.g. *I, you, mine* so that it's clear who or what they refer to.
'You're right, Caroline.'
*Liam told Caroline (that) **she** was right.*

Reporting verbs
Use *said (that)* or *told someone (that)*.
*She **said (that)** she felt important.*
*She **told one interviewer (that)** she wanted to motivate other kids to try new things.*
Remember that when we are talking, we often use reported speech without *that*.
She said (~~that~~) she was tired.

1 9.2–3 **Listen. Now you say it!**

2 **Daniel's invited friends from his drama group to his house after school. They've left messages on his phone. What did they say?**

iPod 3:45 PM

1 I can come after nine o'clock. Emily
Emily said she could come after nine o'clock.
2 I'll bring some snacks. Nathan
3 I can't come because I'm not feeling well. Jake
4 I love rehearsing after school! Chloe
5 I don't know my lines for the new play. Ben
6 We can try on the new costumes. Rachel

3 9.4 **Listen and check your answers.**

4 **Read Kate's Facebook post. What did she say? Write sentences.**

I'm having an amazing time at the hobby fair. There's so much to see. There are some good ideas for the school hobby club. I can't wait to tell you all about it! I'll post some photos of the collections of robots later.

Like · Comment 5 1

She said that she was having an amazing time at the hobby fair. She told us ...

5 **Complete the second sentence so that it means the same as the first.**

1. 'You can use the computer later,' Tom's mum said.
   Tom's mum said *(that) he could use* the computer later.
2. 'There's a photography competition,' the teacher said to us.
   The teacher told ______ a photography competition.
3. Ellie said, 'If you find some cardboard, you can make a model.'
   Ellie said that we could make a model if ______ some cardboard.
4. My dad said he would buy me a new computer game.
   My dad said, 'I ______ a new computer game'.
5. 'Online gaming is my favourite hobby,' she told us.
   She said that that online gaming ______ favourite hobby.
6. 'I'm making a necklace,' she said.
   She said that ______ a necklace.
7. 'We want to play the guitar,' the children said.
   The children said ______ to play the guitar.
8. 'I don't enjoy doing drama at school,' said Hayley.
   Hayley said that ______ doing drama at school.

Write on

6 **Work with a partner. Tell your partner the answers to these questions.**

1. Who was the first person you spoke to today? What did that person say?
2. What did you say in your last text message?

LISTENING

Power up

1 Match the numbers (1–4) with the words (a–d).

1 12 + 15 = 27
2 25%
3 12.5
4 3 x 4 = 12

a twelve point five
b three times four equals twelve
c twenty-five percent
d twelve plus fifteen equals twenty-seven

2 9.5–6 **Listen to these numbers. Listen again. Now you say it!**

12,000,000   10 x 10 = 100
1.5   999   4,576   70%

Listen up

3 9.7 **Listen to the first part of a radio show. What are you going to hear later in the show?**

some strange facts   the news
the weather report

4 9.8 **Listen to the second part of a radio show. Choose the correct answer, A, B or C.**

1 How many Pokémon objects does Lisa have?

A + 13,400   B + 13,500
C + 13,005

2 What did it take the man twenty years to make?

3 What did Sergey win a competition for?

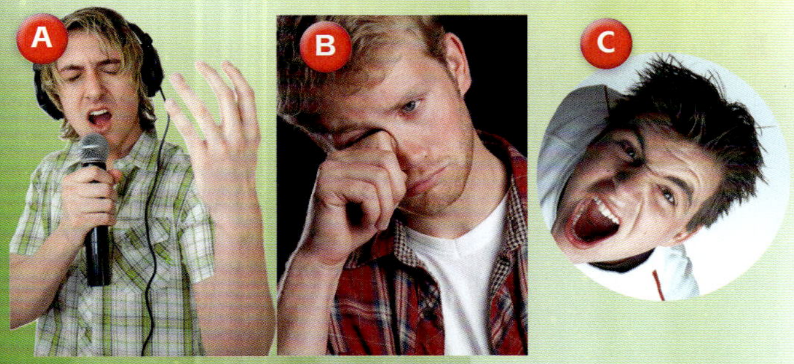

4 What was in the bag at the airport?

5 Where did the bull sleep for the night?

5 9.9 **Listen again and check your answers.**

Exam

Use the second listening to check your answers. Don't stop listening, even when you are sure you have the right answer.

Grammar XP

p. 139

used to

Use *used to* for actions that happened regularly in the past, but do not happen now.

*He **used to** scream as loud as an ambulance siren.*
*He **didn't use to** have any hobbies.*
***Did** he **use to** annoy the neighbours?*

6 9.10–11 **Listen. Now you say it!**

7 Complete the sentences with the correct form of *used to* and the verbs in brackets.

1 Jack doesn't run now, but he *used to run* (run)10 km every week.
2 When I was at primary school, I __________ (collect) cinema tickets.
3 Jack __________ (not have) a hobby when he was younger.
4 __________ (you/make) models of planes when you were young?

SPEAKING

Power up

1 What do you like/not like about strange facts? Give examples. Use these words

horrible interesting scary surprising unbelievable

Speak up

2 9.12 Listen and complete the conversation.

Amy: James, look at this article. It says that humans use their face to make 10,000 different expressions.
James: That's 1) amazing !
Amy: Yes, but 2) __________ it's true?
James: 3) I __________ . It also says the face has got forty-three muscles. Do you think 4) __________ ?
Amy: 5) I __________ . It's in the magazine, so it's probably right.
James: 6) I __________ , but you shouldn't always believe everything you read in magazines.
Amy: 7) __________ !

3 9.13 Listen again and check your answers.

4 Work with a partner. Read the first strange fact. Practise the conversation with your partner.

Do you think it's true?

Yes, it's right. I read about it online. It's weird isn't it?

It sounds very boring.

Yes, you're right. Extremely boring!

Skill

When you are trying to find out what your partner thinks, it's important to give your partner time to talk.

5 Work with a partner. Take it in turns to read a fact and find out what your partner thinks.

Believe it or not!

It took Leonardo da Vinci ten years to paint Mona Lisa's lips.

1 One guy in London likes to be on TV. When he sees a TV camera in a public place he tries to appear in the picture. He's often on TV … but always in the background.
2 Did you know, our eyes always stay the same size, but our noses and ears don't stop growing?
3 When you eat a piece of celery you burn more calories than you take in from the celery.
4 There's a woman who had a dream when she was fifteen about the number forty-three. Since her dream she's collected any object with the number forty-three on it.
5 How about this – it's impossible to sneeze with your eyes open. Is it true?
6 A cockroach can live for a week without its head. Ouch!
7 Does the zip on your trousers have YKK on it? About 90% of the world's zips are made by YKK in Japan.

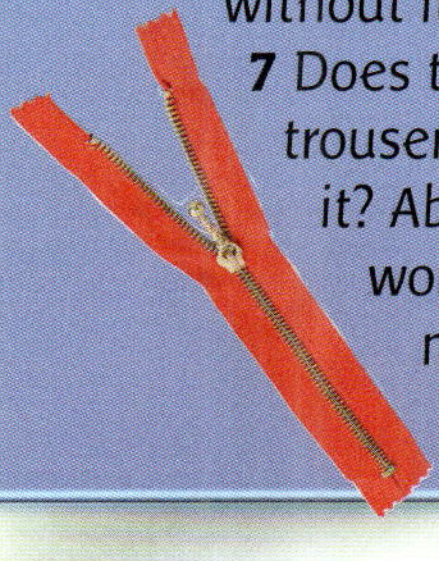

Language XP

Asking for an opinion
What do you think about … ?
Do you think it's/that's true/right/a good idea/a bad idea?
Why do you think that … ?
Expressing an opinion
I don't agree. I'm not sure. I suppose so.
Yes, I see what you mean but …
It's/That's amazing/weird/really crazy!

6 Tell the rest of the class what your partner said about the weird and wonderful facts.

Maria said the fact about the celery was interesting. She told me it was the same with cucumbers because the vegetables are just water.

WRITING

Power up

1 Everybody needs a hobby, including Hollywood stars. What hobbies do you think these celebrities have? (Check your answers at the bottom of the page.)

collecting insects

knitting

doing the Rubik's cube

online gaming

Russell Crowe

Mila Kunis

Justin Bieber

Exercise 1 answers: **A** Russell Crowe – knitting (He says it stops him feeling angry.) **B** Mila Kunis – online gaming (She loves *World of Warcraft*, but has to keep her name a secret because everyone wants to play with her.) **C** Justin Bieber – doing the Rubik's cube (He can do it in 1 m, 23 sec and there's a YouTube clip of it.)

2 Are you surprised by the hobbies that the celebrities in Exercise 1 have? Why/Why not?

3 Read the article about Johnny Depp. Find the adjectives and adverbs.

SEARCH GO

Celebhobbies

Do you know anybody who collects dolls? They can be new or old dolls. A surprising person with this hobby is Johnny Depp. He's got an unusual collection of Barbie dolls. He's also got dolls of Beyoncé and of the characters in *High School Musical*.

Johnny Depp is a fantastic actor. He's also a very funny pirate, and his *Pirates of The Caribbean* films have made him an international star. Johnny Depp doesn't have much free time. However, when he's not working, he likes having fun with his daughters and playing with the Barbie dolls. He once said that he liked using different voices with the dolls.

I think a good hobby is extremely important because it helps you to relax. Johnny Depp's hobby is brilliant because he spends time with his children and it's really good fun.

Language XP

Have you heard about … (a person, a hobby)?
A surprising/An interesting/An amazing person with this hobby is …
He/She once said that …
I think a good/interesting/weird hobby is …
X's hobby is great because it's …

Plan on

4 **Read the article again. In what paragraph (Paragraph 1, Paragraph 2 or Paragraph 3) does the writer do the following?**

1 say why they think that a good hobby is important
2 introduce the hobby
3 say why the person likes this hobby
4 introduce the person with the hobby
5 give more information about the person with the hobby
6 say why this hobby is good

5 **Read the advert. What are you going to write? What is it going to be about?**

Hobby news

Do you know someone with an exciting or interesting hobby? What is it and what's the hobby? Write an article for our magazine. We'll put the best ones in next week's issue.

four free magazines for the winning letter

6 **Think of a person you know with an exciting or interesting hobby. Make notes using the instructions (1–6) in Exercise 4.**

7 **What adjectives and adverbs can you use to describe the following?**

1 the person: *very funny, really interesting*
2 the hobby: *really exciting*

Write on

8 **Write an article for the magazine about a person you know with an exciting or interesting hobby. Write about 110–120 words.**

Skill

Do you want to know how to start an article? Use a question. This makes your reader interested at the beginning.

Switch on

SUPERNOVA, SUPERSTAR

1 **Guess the answers. Then watch and check.**

You're going to watch a video with young astronomer Caroline Moore. What are the endings to these questions?

A When did you first get interested …?
B What was the first thing that you saw …?
C Is it easy to …?
D When did you learn …?
E Why do you want to inspire …?
F Have you got any plans …?

2 **Are the sentences (1–8) true (T) or false (F)?**

1 Caroline's dad grew up in the city.
2 The first thing she saw through a telescope was the moon.
3 She discovered her first supernova in October 2008.
4 Caroline heard about the discovery at 11 p.m.
5 After the discovery, Caroline did interviews for radio and newspapers.
6 Caroline thinks everyone can enjoy science and astronomy.
7 It won't be easy for Caroline to decide what to do in the future.
8 Sometimes Caroline thinks she's got too many opportunities.

3 **Can someone like Caroline motivate other kids to try new things? Why/Why not?**

Project

4 **Work in small groups. Make a short play about Caroline. Choose one person to tell her story (narrator). Act the play out to your class and choose the best one.**

Scene 1: At home
Narrator: Caroline was ten years old when she got her first telescope.
Person 1: Happy Birthday, Caroline. I know you like watching the stars with me. I've bought you something special.
Caroline: Oh, thanks, Dad, it's perfect.

10 We can work it out!

READING

Power up

1 Match the jobs with the photos.

computer programmer

inventor

designer

hairdresser

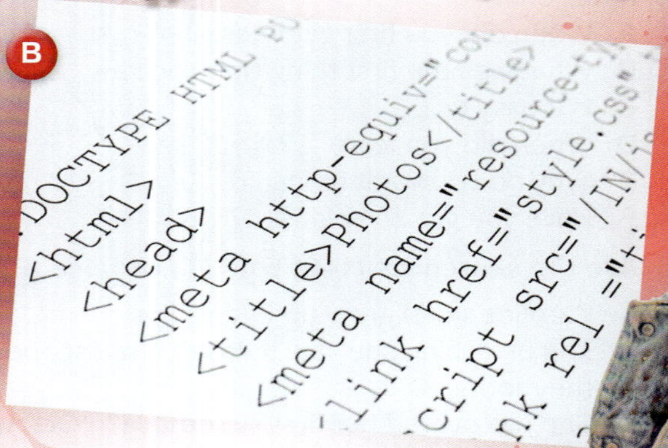

2 Can you think of four more jobs? What does each person create or do?

An artist creates a painting.

Read on

3 Work with a partner. Describe the products in the photos (A–B) on page 89.

4 Read the introduction to the article on page 89. What have Lily and Alex done? What do they want to do?

5 Read Lily's story and Alex's story. Are the sentences (1–10) true (T) or false (F)?

1 Lily has used two of her interests in her business. T
2 Young people never buy cheap sports clothes.
3 Lily has already designed sports clothes for big clubs.
4 Lily did some research into what sports people need.
5 The finished sports clothes are exactly right.
6 Alex designs computer games.
7 Alex's plan to make Richard notice him fails.
8 Alex is slow to make cards because he wants them to be good quality.
9 There are problems with Alex's new office equipment.
10 Alex's final decision is to continue his business.

6 Find words in the articles that mean the following.

1 organised ideas: p __________ (introduction)
2 the amount of money you pay for something: p __________ (Lily's story)
3 the design of a company name: l __________ (Lily's story)
4 possible to print from a computer: p __________ (Alex's story)
5 amazing; fantastic: a __________ (Alex's story)

Exam

You may not know some of the words or phrases in a reading text. Don't worry, you can still find the information you need to answer the questions.

Be your own **boss!**

What could you do with £100? Could you start running a small business? Businessman Richard Reed is looking for young people who have great business ideas. He gave £100 each to hundreds of young people, including Lily and Alex. He asked them to make more money. Now they have to tell Richard what they have done with his money. He wants them to explain their business plans, too. If they are good, they can have more money to improve their business. Both Lily and Alex would love to work for themselves, but what will Richard think?

Lily's story

Lily is a young designer who studied sportswear design at college. She loves designing clothes for young people and she enjoys doing sport. Lily has brought both of these skills together to create sports clothing for young people. Now Lily hopes to get some money, so she can make inexpensive clothes because a low price is important for most teenagers.

Lily has worked on football kits for teams like Bilbao and Manchester City. She has also made friends with some kickboxers and asked them what was important. 'Number one – being comfortable,' was the answer. Luckily, Richard loved Lily's designs and her business plan, so he gave her more money. Then Lily had to make clothes, organise a photographer and set up a website. 'Did I mention that I don't know how to run a business?' she laughed.

Lily had just six weeks to put together a new clothing collection, but she stayed calm under pressure. Unfortunately, when she picked up the clothes from the printing company, her logo wasn't quite straight. Lily wasn't happy, but there was no more time or money. It was time to show the clothes to Richard. What would he think?

Alex's story

Alex is a design student. He loves to make 3-D models and work with computers. His business idea brings together these two skills. What is it? A website which sells printable designs for 3-D birthday cards.

When Alex was waiting to meet Richard, he wasn't nervous. He was very creative and had a giant cardboard model to catch Richard's attention. It was the first thing Richard saw. 'That is awesome!' he said. Richard offered to help Alex, so Alex started to work on the new card designs. Progress was slow, but Alex wasn't impatient. Why? 'I want them to be perfect,' he said.

Alex used Richard's money to buy a new desk and computer. He stayed up all night to finish the designs, but suddenly his new computer stopped working. Would Alex lose all his designs? Finally, the computer started working again, but Alex wasn't sure about the future. He realised that it wasn't easy to create designs and run a business at the same time. Alex made a difficult decision. He explained to Richard that he wasn't interested in carrying on. He had enjoyed the challenge, but for him, making models was more fun than running a business.

Richard Reed

Sum up

7 Compare Lily and Alex. Think about the following.

1. what they studied at college
2. what their business idea is
3. any problems they have with their business

Speak up

8 What business would you set up on your own? Explain why you would/wouldn't enjoy it.

VOCABULARY

Skills for work

1 Match the phrases (1–10) with the correct meanings (a–j). Use the words in bold to help you.

1 enjoy a **challenge**
2 be a good **team player**
3 pick up new skills **quickly**
4 stay calm **under pressure**
5 speak **your** mind
6 be **creative**
7 always **do your best**
8 work **on your own**
9 **run** a business
10 **make** money

a to like doing **new, exciting things**
b to be relaxed **at a difficult time**
c to say exactly **what I think**
d to have a lot of **new ideas**
e to work **without any** help
f to learn **fast**
g to **manage** a company
h to **earn** money from working
i to work well **with other people**
j to always try to **do everything well**

2 Write a sentence about each person (1–6). Use some of the phrases in Exercise 1.

1 Claudia has a small company which fixes computers.
Claudia runs a business.
2 Eduardo always works well with other people at his parents' restaurant.
3 Carlos loves painting, and always has new ideas.
4 Emilio likes trying any new sports, even difficult ones!
5 Roberto learns fast.
6 Katerina and Marco always try to do everything well.

3 10.1 Listen and check your answers.

4 Work with a partner. Take it in turns to say two or three sentences about you.

Word XP

Do you want to make an adjective negative?
*tidy – **un**tidy*
*correct – **in**correct*
*polite – **im**polite*
If the adjective begins with *p*, you usually use *im-* (not *in-*) to make it negative.

5 Choose the correct negative prefix for each pair of words.

im- *in-* *un-*

1 usual/friendly
2 expensive/complete
3 patient/possible

6 Choose the correct words to complete the article.

A creative mind?

My sister Amelia's desk is really 1) *tidy/ untidy* – there are books and papers everywhere. It's annoying, and my mum gets very 2) *patient/ impatient*. Mum says, 'a messy desk means a messy mind,' but Amelia disagrees. She believes that a messy desk helps her to think.

Is Amelia's opinion 3) *correct/incorrect*? Researchers think it depends on your personality. For some creative people, it's 4) *possible/impossible* to work with a tidy desk. For example, famous scientist, Albert Einstein, had some of his most brilliant and 5) *usual/unusual* ideas when he was sitting at a messy desk.

Game on

Work with a partner. Say a word from the Word XP or Exercise 6. Your partner says the opposite word. They must make a sentence with this word.
A: *Possible.*
B: *Impossible. It's impossible to meet Albert Einstein.*

GRAMMAR

Grammar XP

p. 139

Talking about likes, dislikes and intentions

***to* + infinitive**

Use *to* + infinitive after some verbs: *agree, arrange, decide, hope, learn, promise, start, try, want.*

*Lily **hopes to get** some money.*

*Alex **started to work** on the new designs.*

You can put an object before the infinitive after some verbs: *ask, help, need, teach, want.*

*He **wants them to explain** their business plans.*

Use *to* + infinitive after some adjectives: *easy, happy, possible, important.*

*It's not **easy to create** designs and run a business.*

***-ing* form**

Use *-ing* after some verbs and phrases: *enjoy, finish, imagine, suggest, be good at.*

*She also **enjoys doing** sport.*

Use *-ing* after some phrases with prepositions: *bad/good at, interested in and after certain expressions: can't stand, don't mind.*

*He wasn't **interested in carrying on**.*

***I look forward to starting** the course.*

***to* + infinitive and *-ing* form**

Use *-ing* or *to* + infinitive after *like, love, prefer, start.* The meaning is the same.

*She **loves designing** clothes.*

*He **loves to make** 3-D models.*

Don't use *-ing* after ***would like/love/prefer.***
Use *to* + infinitive.

*Both Lily and Alex **would love to work** for themselves.*

1 Complete the sentences with the correct form of the verbs in brackets.

1 Are you good at staying (stay) calm under pressure?
2 I think it's important __________ (be) a good team player.
3 It's possible __________ (speak) your mind in our school.
4 We're interested in __________ (run) the school snack shop.
5 It's not easy __________ (learn) how to run a business.
6 I'm not bad at __________ (make) websites.

2 Complete the second sentence so that it means the same as the first.

1 I'm starting my own online magazine.
I've decided __________ my own online magazine.
2 We work well together as a team.
We're good __________ together as a team.
3 Do you think people can be both organised and creative?
Do you think it's possible __________ both organised and creative?
4 She always tries to do everything well.
She always wants __________ her best.

3 Complete the article with the correct forms of the verbs in brackets.

Young entrepreneurs win an award!

Are you interested in 1) running (run) a small business? Young Enterprise might be the answer. It's an organisation which teaches school pupils 2) __________ (become) entrepreneurs. How? Teams of pupils learn 3) __________ (work) together as a small company. Each team can decide their own name; for example Escape, MAD and Linx. Teamwork is important. Some people are good at 4) __________ (design) things, like the company logo, but other people like to 5) __________ (organise) things or make decisions. Teams 6) __________ (choose) or make products and sell them to family and friends, teachers or anyone who is interested. It's important 7) __________ (make) money because there's a prize for the most successful team each year.
Last Saturday, twelve teams of young entrepreneurs set up 'shops' in a shopping centre in Oxford. Lisa, sixteen, explained 'We don't mind 8) __________ (work) here. It's fun.' At about ten o'clock, customers began 9) __________ (arrive) and the teams were busy. At the end of a long day, Team Escape were very happy 10) __________ (win) an award for their shop.

Write on

4 Complete the sentences so they are true for you.

1 I'm good at …
2 I think it's important …
3 Tomorrow I'll start …

LISTENING

Power up

1 **Look at the photos. Which of these people helped to create the photos?**

artist
make-up artist
model photographer

2 **Work with a partner. What do you think each person did to create the photos in Exercise 1?**

follow instructions | make decisions | paint
sit or stand without moving
tell people what to do | use make-up

Exam

The first time you hear a conversation, listen for general understanding. The second time you hear it, listen for detailed meaning.

Listen up

3 10.2 **Listen to an interview with Kat Sykes, a young make-up artist. Choose the correct answer, A, B or C.**

1 What does Kat like about her job ?
 A working with paint
 B making people look interesting
 (C) creating interesting designs
2 What did Kat do to practise her skills?
 A She used her family as models and assistants.
 B She did lots of painting when she was a child.
 C She made hairstyles for her brother and sister.
3 At college, Kat …
 A did lots of experiments.
 B used real art to get ideas.
 C copied drawings from other artists.
4 In Kat's opinion, what is one of the good things about her job?
 A Make-up artists often become rich.
 B Make-up artists don't often have to change jobs.
 C Make-up artists can work with famous people.
5 Kat doesn't mind working for no money. Why?
 A She'll be able to get work more easily in future.
 B She doesn't need any money at the moment.
 C She wants to live in London, to be near friends.

4 10.3 **Listen again and check your answers.**

Grammar XP

p. 139

Indirect questions
For *wh-* questions, use a *wh-* word + sentence word order.
*Can you tell us **what** a make-up artist **does**?*
*Could you tell me **how** you **became** a make-up artist?*
*Can I ask **why** you**'re doing** that?*
For *Yes/No* questions use *if* + sentence word order.
*Do you know **if it's** easy to make money?*

5 **Put the words in the correct order to make sentences.**

1 what / Can I ask / you / doing? / are
 Can I ask what you are doing?
2 another job? / Do you know / you / find / will / if
3 worked here? / you / Could you tell us / how long / have
4 who / the / model / best / is? / Can you tell me
5 this / how / made / you / Can I ask / hairstyle?

SPEAKING

Power up

1 **What job are these people doing? Would you do this for no money?**

2 **Why do people do voluntary work?**

3 **Complete the conversation with one of these phrases.**

it looks like   long metal thing
red and yellow things   round your neck

Dina: Zach, is that you in the photo? With a red and purple thing 1) ___________ – is it a necklace?

Zach: Yes, that's me! That 'necklace' was my ID for the London Olympics. It was a summer job. I worked there for just ten days.

Dina: Brilliant! So did you make any money?

Zach: No, we didn't make any money. We were volunteers. More than 1,000 teenagers helped at the games.

Dina: So what are you doing in this photo? I'm not sure, but 2) ___________ you're fishing with a 3) ___________ !

Zach: Well, that 'long metal thing' is a remote control. I'm controlling a very small car, about 1 m long.

Dina: Oh, is that it? There are some strange 4) ___________ on top of the car.

Zach: Yeah, they were javelins. The car was carrying the javelins that the athletes throw.

Dina: Oh, I see. That's clever. Do you know what they did with the cars after the games?

Zach: I think they sold them. I'd love to have one!

4 10.4 **Listen and check your answers. What are the words for these things Dina was describing?**

1 the necklace
2 the long metal thing
3 the red and yellow things

Language XP

Dealing with unknown words

What's …   *that red and purple thing?*
the long, metal thing?
the thing round your neck?

It looks like a …

5 **Work with a partner. Student A, look at page 131. Student B, look at page 143. Follow the instructions.**

Skill

If you don't know a word, describe the size, colour and shape of an object. Describe the clothes, appearance or actions of a person.

WRITING

Power up

1 **Which job would you prefer to do? Why?**

2 **Which job would you hate to do? Why?**

3 **Read the advert. Answer the questions.**

1. Are the jobs paid or unpaid?
2. What are the main skills that everyone needs?
3. What are the other two skill areas you could work in?
4. What are they offering instead of money?

Summer spectacular stage show

We are looking for VOLUNTEERS to help with this year's show. We need 10–20 hours of your time in the summer. Are you good at working under pressure? Can you offer great customer service skills?

We are looking for people who have creative skills.

- artists and designers to create the stage costumes and scenery
- assistants to help with the lighting and sound
- actors, dancers and musicians for the smaller side shows

We are also looking for people who are good at organising and helping.

- ticket officers to check tickets at the entrance
- car park assistants to organise parking for visitors
- general assistants to sell programmes and show people around this huge event

Interested? Write a short application letter. We want you to tell us what job you are applying for. Explain what skills you have and why you would be good at that job. Tell us about any experience you have, too.

Successful applicants will get:

- **a special ID card and a VOLUNTEER T-shirt to keep**
- **free lunch and drinks each day**

4 **Read Edit's application email. Put the paragraphs (A–C) in order (1–3). Use the advert in Exercise 3 to help you.**

Volunteer work

Hi
I'd love to work as a volunteer!
A I have some experience, as last summer I worked at a children's sports camp. I organised team games and worked with the instructors to plan each day's activities.
B I'm a very organised person, and I'm also a good team player. I think both of those skills would be very useful.
C I'm interested in the job of General Assistant because I enjoy working with people and helping them.
Write soon!
Bye for now
Edit

Plan on

5 **Read Edit's email again. What is wrong with the words in red? Choose a phrase from the Language XP box to replace each word or phrase in red.**

Language XP

Starting and ending a formal letter
Dear Sir/Madam,
I am writing to apply for the job of …
I look forward to hearing from you soon.
Yours faithfully,

6 **Write out Edit's letter in the correct order with the correct words.**

Skill

Do you need to write an application letter? Check the advert, and include the information your reader needs.

Write on

7 **Write your own short application letter for a volunteer job.**

Switch on

BE YOUR OWN BOSS!

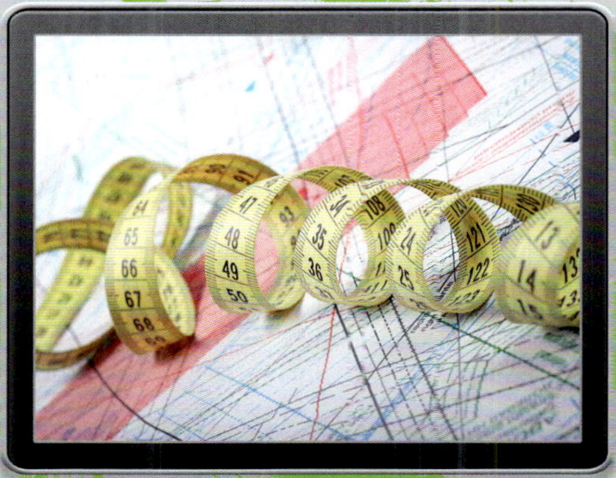

1 **Guess the answer. Then watch and check.**

You are going to see Alex and Lily working on their designs. Who has these things: Lily or Alex?

A one or two friends who help
B lots of friends who help
C black clothes
D white T-shirts
E a small tablet computer
F a large computer

2 **Choose the correct word to complete each sentence.**

1 Lily explains her *business model/clothing material* to Richard.
2 Lily has *plenty of time/not much time* to check the new sports clothes.
3 Richard likes the new designs and gives Lily more *time/money*.
4 Alex's giant model is a *green dinosaur/crocodile*.
5 Alex's friends think he's a(n) *robot/owl* because he doesn't sleep.
6 Alex's friends help him to make his new *models/desk*.

3 **What is your impression of each person now? Are they how you expected them to be?**

Project

4 **Write your own video script for a short two-minute film about a new design.**

1 Decide on these things:
- What is your design for? (Clothes? Gadgets? Models? Something else?)
- How will you show your design? (As a picture, photo or 3D model?)
- What information will you give about your design?

2 Write your script.
3 Act it out.

This is my design for a …
I think people will buy it because …

Revision

VOCABULARY

1 Match the words 1–7 with a–g.

1 making
2 keeping
3 practising
4 online
5 collecting
6 taking
7 doing

a a musical instrument
b key rings
c photos
d fit
e models
f drama
g gaming

2 Put the letters in brackets in the correct order.

1 Do you know a good ___recipe___ (creepi) for chocolate cake? I want to make one for my friends.
2 Let's make some __________ (trapsy). I've got flour, butter and water.
3 You need some new __________ (luge) to make a model. This one is dry and won't stick.
4 We need some __________ (siscross) to cut this material. We're making a costume for the play.
5 We didn't have all the __________ (greedstinin) to make pizza, so we're having a sandwich.
6 My new camera has a big, bright __________ (ecrens) that also works when it's sunny.

3 Choose the correct word.

1 I'm not doing anything this weekend. I just want to *chill out/join in* with friends at home.
2 Emma spoke to lots of people on her first day at school because she didn't want them to think that she was *unfriendly/untidy*.
3 The people at the bus stop were getting *impatient/impossible* because the bus was very late.
4 Ritzy is my favourite restaurant because the food is *incomplete/inexpensive* but good.
5 Will had a bad headache at the party and couldn't *hang out with/join in* the fun
6 Mum says my bedroom is *untidy/unusual* but your bedroom is worse. There are clothes everywhere.

4 Complete the sentences with the words.

a good team player do your best
make money run a business
~~stay calm under pressure~~ work on your own

1 Working in a busy office can be difficult and you have to know how to ___stay calm under pressure___.
2 My dad's got his own shop, but I don't want to __________. I'd rather work for someone else.
3 Olivia's __________, and always works well with other people.
4 In the summer I __________ because I help in my parent's shop. They don't pay much, but I enjoy it.
5 It's a difficult exam, but you can only __________.
6 I don't think you should __________. You hate it when you haven't got anybody to talk to.

5 Read the blog. Choose the correct answer, A, B, C or D.

Hobbies4jobs

Can a hobby become a job? Two years ago, Kate began 1) ___making___ jewellery. She was mad 2) __________ her hobby, and often 3) __________ photographs of her new designs and put them on the Internet. One day, a friend of her mum's saw one of Kate's necklaces. The friend 4) __________ a jewellery business, and offered Kate a job. She started to teach Kate about the business, and Kate 5) __________ up the new skills quickly. One day, a famous person from the royal family saw a photo of one of Kate's 6) __________, but popular necklaces. She bought it and wore it in public. The necklace became famous, and 7) __________ a lot of money for the company. Kate's very happy about her job, but has no idea what will happen next. 'It's 8) __________ to know,' she says, 'every day is different.' Has her life changed? 'Of course, but I still love hanging 9) __________ with my old school friends.'

	A	B	C	D
1	**A** modelling	**B** having	**C** doing	**(D)** making
2	**A** about	**B** into	**C** for	**D** in
3	**A** made	**B** caught	**C** took	**D** got
4	**A** enjoyed	**B** ran	**C** organised	**D** worked
5	**A** took	**B** picked	**C** held	**D** did
6	**A** inexpensive	**B** incorrect	**C** independent	**D** incomplete
7	**A** gained	**B** won	**C** enjoyed	**D** made
8	**A** impolite	**B** impossible	**C** impatient	**D** important
9	**A** onto	**B** in	**C** out	**D** into

GRAMMAR

6 Complete the sentences to make reported statements.

1 'I'm making a cake.'
He said that *he was making* a cake.
2 'I like keeping fit.'
Emily said that ___________ keeping fit.
3 'We can't practise the drums in the house.'
Dad said that ___________ practise the drums in the house.
4 'I will bring my camera.'
Sam said that he ___________ camera.'
5 'Online gaming is our favourite hobby.'
They said that online gaming ___________ favourite hobby.
6 'I want to make lots of money.'
She said that ___________ to make lots of money.
7 'I'll buy the ingredients for dinner.'
Liam said that ___________ buy the ingredients for dinner.
8 'I take funny photos of my friends.'
She said that she ___________ friends.

7 Complete the sentences with *use to* or *used to*.

1 He *used to* practise the violin every day.
2 Did you ___________ work on your own?
3 We didn't ___________ enjoy doing drama.
4 The boys ___________ collect models of trains.
5 I didn't ___________ take many photos.
6 Did he ___________ run a business?

8 Choose the correct answer.

1 Max has decided *starting/to start* a new hobby.
2 We can't imagine *making/to make* any money from our designs.
3 They can't stand *doing/to do* the same thing every day.
4 I promise *telling/to tell* you all about it.
5 Did you arrange *seeing/to see* Luke this evening?
6 I'm looking forward to *run/running* my own business.
7 Eliza doesn't want *doing/to do* drama today.
8 You're very good at *work/working* with other people.

9 Choose the correct ending for the questions.

1 Can you tell me what ...
(**A**) you do every day?
B do you do every day?
2 Do you know if ...
A is it easy to make pizza?
B it's easy to make pizza?
3 Can I ask you how ...
A you think of designs?
B do you think of designs?
4 Do you know if ...
A is there a zoom lens on this camera?
B there's a zoom lens on this camera?
5 Could you tell me how ...
A you trained for this job?
B did you train for this job?
6 Can you tell me what ...
A do I need to make a model of a plane?
B I need to make a model of a plane?

10 Complete the second sentence so that it means the same as the first. Use no more than three words.

1 Nathan said, 'I don't enjoy practising the guitar.'
Nathan said that he *didn't enjoy* practising the guitar.
2 When I was younger, I had lots of different hobbies.
When I was younger, I used ___________ lots of different hobbies.
3 Laura said, 'I'll bring a cake.'
Laura said that ___________ a cake.
4 My sister said that she loved making models.
My sister said, '___________ making models'.
5 The students work well on their own.
The students are good ___________ on their own.
6 Staying calm under pressure is difficult.
It isn't easy ___________ under pressure.
7 Did you enjoy cooking when you were a child?
Did you use ___________ cooking when you were a child?
8 Do you know if you can make money in this business?
Do you know if ___________ to make money in this business?

11 Our planet

READING

Power up

1 Which photo (A–C) is a documentary programme?

2 Describe a documentary programme you have watched recently. What was it about?

Read on

3 Read the first part of the review. What types of programmes does Raul normally watch?

Exam

Try to guess the word for each space before you look at the options.

4 Read the rest of the review. Choose the best word to complete each space.

	A	B	C	D
1	A until	B since	C while	D for
2	A wanted	B hoped	C used	D liked
3	A as	B who	C where	D if
4	A watched	B watching	C watch	D watches
5	A remember	B forget	C know	D think
6	A can	B must	C have to	D shall
7	A Past	B Ago	C Before	D Last
8	A a	B an	C there	D the
9	A for	B so	C because	D but
10	A in	B of	C with	D to

About me blog portfolio contact

Another world

Documentaries? No, thanks. That's my normal reaction. I love watching repeats of *The Simpsons* and *Friends*. But last week, 1) while I was channel-hopping, I discovered a programme that changed my mind.

Sea homes

Fabulous, blue-green sea, blue sky and tiny islands. The amazing scenery was like another world and I 2) __________ to be there, so I started watching. The narrator was talking about Bajau, in the Philippines, where many people live on boats or houses in the sea. Bajau children are taught to swim before they can walk. You know how most people get sea sick when they travel by boat? Well, 3) __________ the Bajau people walk on land, they feel 'land sick'!

What was it?

I looked up the programme in the TV guide. It was called *Human Planet*. The series shows the relationship between humans and some of the most amazing places on earth. Different places, such as deserts, jungles and mountains, we filmed for each programme. I decided to 4) __________ the next week's episode.

Raul's day

Fascinating facts

One reason I enjoyed the series was the interesting facts in each programme. For example, in Papua New Guinea, some homes are built in the jungle – thirty metres up a tree, so they are safe from wild animals. Everything is made of wood. Even babies and animals live in the tree houses. It looks scary to me, and it's a long way down if you 5) __________ something!

Humans and animals

The relationship between people and animals can be incredible, too. In Laguna, on the south coast of Brazil, local fishermen are helped by wild dolphins that chase fish towards their nets. The dolphins 6) __________ catch lots of fish, too, but it's an amazing example of teamwork.

An incredible journey

Fourteen-year-old Kusum and her brother Dolkar live in a tiny village in the Himalayan mountains, one hundred kilometres from their school. In winter, the snow is very deep on the roads, so they have to walk down a dangerous, frozen river to get to school. 7) __________ year, Kusum, Dolkar and their father were followed by the *Human Planet* team. In one valley, 8) __________ avalanche fell from the high, grey cliffs. Luckily it missed them. In another valley, the narrow path was covered in ice, and they nearly fell in the river. The journey took six days, but finally they arrived safely at school, ready for another term.

Personal favourite?

I love the sea, so I think the Bajau way of life is perfect. The weather is usually good 9) __________ the sea is calm and there aren't any big waves. Nohara was born on a boat, and she explains, 'I like to live on a boat because we go wherever we want.' I'd like that, too.

Recommendation?

If you're interested 10) __________ seeing how other people live around the world, watch *Human Planet* online, or get the DVD!

Raul, 14

5 **Find these words in the review. Match each word to the correct meaning (1–5).**

coast ice land net scenery

1 the natural things you see around you in the countryside
2 the dry part of the Earth where you walk; not water
3 the edge of a country next to the sea
4 something you use for catching fish
5 frozen water

Sum up

6 **What have you learned about these places? Think about people, homes and nature.**

Brazil Papua New Guinea The Himalayas The Philippines

Speak up

7 **Work with a partner. Which place do you think would be the most difficult to live in? Why?**

SWITCH ON Another world page 113

VOCABULARY

Natural world

1 🔊 11.1–2 **Look at the pictures. Listen. Now you say it!**

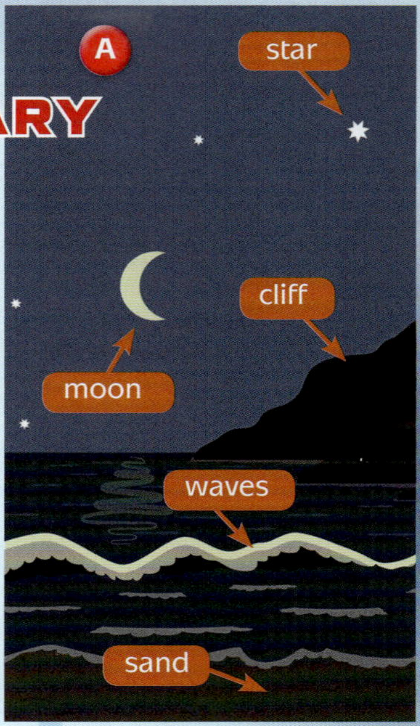

2 Put the words in the pictures in Exercise 1 with the correct group.

sky/weather water/snow/ice ground

3 Complete the sentences with a word in the pictures in Exercise 1.

Test your geography!

1 Farmers need good ____________ , sunshine and rain to grow plants for food.
2 Rain is important. Without it, soil becomes ____________ , and fields become deserts.
3 If you look at the cliffs on a beach, you see layers of soil and ____________ .
4 When snow melts on a mountain, it can fall in an ____________ .
5 ____________ is created when warm, wet air rises up and meets cool air.
6 A ____________ is an area of bad weather with clouds, rain and strong winds.
7 Stars create their own light, but light from the ____________ is reflected sunlight.
8 ____________ in the sea are bigger in stormy weather.

Word XP

We usually put an opinion adjective before a fact adjective: opinion + fact + noun.

dangerous, frozen river fabulous, blue-green sea

With two fact adjectives, we put size or age before colour: fact (size or age) + fact (colour) + noun.

high, grey cliffs

4 Choose fact adjective (FA) or opinion adjective (OA) for 1–9.

1	new	4	great	7	old
2	beautiful	5	scary	8	dangerous
3	high	6	horrible	9	huge

5 Choose the correct word order to complete the sentences.

1 There's a ____________ on the beach.
   A great, new café
   B café new, great
   C new, great café
2 A ____________ crashed down the mountain.
   A white, huge avalanche
   B huge, white avalanche
   C huge avalanche, white
3 They crossed the ____________ over the river.
   A high, scary bridge
   B high bridge, scary
   C scary, high bridge

Game on

In two teams, each person writes a quiz question for the other team. Use Exercise 5 as a model. Write about places near you. The other team guesses the correct answer, A, B or C.

GRAMMAR

Grammar XP

p. 140

Present simple and past simple passive

Use the present passive and the past passive to give more importance to the person or thing we talk about first.

*Everything **is made** of wood.*

*Different places **were filmed** for each programme.*

Use the passive in more formal writing, e.g. reports.

*Some homes **are built** thirty metres up a tree.*

Use *by* to say who or what does the action.

*The fishermen are helped **by** wild dolphins.*

Use the passive when we don't know, or can't say, who is doing the action.

*The narrow path **was covered** in ice.*

Some verbs can't be used in passive sentences: *go, come, happen, walk.*

1 **Look at the signs and leaflets. What do they say? Choose the best answer, A, B or C.**

CAUTION
Care is needed as the cliffs here are steep and dangerous.
You are warned to stay on the path for your own safety.

1 Who is the sign for?
A swimmers **B** walkers **C** drivers

Clearwater Beach
This beach is cleaned each evening.
Any lost property is taken to the hotel reception.

2 Who will clean the beach?
A visitors **B** the receptionist **C** we don't know

Visitors are asked
to use the right bins for recycling.

3 What must visitors do?
A recycle rubbish correctly
B use their own recycling bins
C ask about recycling

Turtle beach
This beach is used by nesting turtles. Please do not put sun umbrellas or other objects in the sand.

4 What mustn't visitors do?
A leave their sun umbrellas
B walk or sit near the turtle nests
C put things in the sand

2 11.3–4 **Listen. Now you say it!**

3 **Complete the fact file with the correct passive form of the verbs in brackets.**

1 Around 97% of all the water on Earth is *contained* (contain) in the oceans.
2 Over 70% of the world's surface area __________ (cover) by oceans and seas.
3 Too much fish __________ (eat) by humans, so many fish are endangered.
4 Over 90% of products which we sell to other countries __________ (carry) by ships.
5 Around half of all living things __________ (believe) to live in the oceans.
6 Most of the rubbish that __________ (find) on beaches is plastic.

4 **Complete the sentences with the present or past passive.**

1 In Papua New Guinea, women *created bridges from living trees*
Bridges in Papua New Guinea were created from living trees.
2 They didn't use metal, stones and concrete to make the bridges.
Metal, stones and concrete __________ .
3 They moved the branches carefully so that they didn't die.
The branches __________ .
4 At the side of the valleys, they made steps from more trees.
Steps __________
5 Now people use the bridges to cross the wide rivers.
Now the bridges __________ .

5 11.5 **Listen and check your answers.**

Write on

6 **Write a short report about some changes in your school. Use the past passive. Use these verbs for ideas.**

… was/were cleaned …
students were asked (not) to …
students were warned (not) to …

LISTENING

Power up

1 **Work with a partner. Match these words/sounds to the different opinions (1–3).**

Well ... Hmm.
Yes. Maybe.

1 you agree
2 you're not sure, but you're thinking about it
3 you disagree

2 11.6 **Listen to the sound of the phrases. Which phrases suggest agreement? Which phrases suggest that the speaker is not sure?**

Listen up

3 11.7 **Listen to Alexia and Jason talking about plans for their youth club. Are the sentences (1–6) true (T) or false (F)?**

1 Jason agrees with Alexia's argument about recycling.
2 Jason thinks Alexia's first idea is good.
3 Alexia thinks the Youth Club should buy the 'magazine seats'.
4 Alexia likes Jason's idea of buying batteries.
5 Jason likes Alexia's final suggestion of what to do.
6 Alexia wants to read an article in the newsletter before they go out.

4 **Which object (A–C) do they reject because they can make their own?**

Skill

Do you want to know if someone agrees or doesn't agree? Listen for phrases, e.g. *So do I. Neither do I.*

Grammar XP

p. 140

could
to make a suggestion from a number of possible ideas
*The Youth Club **could** buy rechargeable batteries.*
if you aren't sure the other person will agree
*We **could** get a pizza.*
should
to ask for advice
*Do you think I **should** change my idea? Yes, I think you **should**.*
to give strong advice, when you think something is a good or bad idea
*We **should** create a digital newsletter because it saves paper.*

5 **Choose the best word to complete each answer.**

1 **A:** I've just broken my mum's favourite plate. What shall I do?
B: I think you *could/should* tell her and say sorry.
2 **A:** What do you want to do this evening?
B: I don't mind. Maybe we *could/should* go to the cinema?
3 **A:** What shall I buy Eliza for her birthday?
B: You *could/should* get a nice box of chocolates.
4 **A:** I borrowed my brother's mobile without asking him.
B: Well, you *could/should* give it back straightaway.

6 **Work with a partner. Make suggestions for each situation (1–4). Use *could*, *should* or *shouldn't*.**

1 I can't decide which songs to download to my music player.
2 I've lost my new cap. I think it's at school.
3 We've got a maths test after lunch, but I haven't revised for it.
4 Let's choose a film to watch this evening. What would you like to watch?

SPEAKING

Power up

1 When and where do you drink the following? Why?

bottled water

tap water

2 Why is clean water important?

3 🔊 11.8 A group of students are explaining why they've made a giant sculpture. Listen and complete the conversation with these words.

after could neither should shouldn't so

Dan: Wow! I like your bottle sculpture. What's it for?
Anya: Well, we drink a lot of bottled water at school, but I think it's a problem for the environment.
Ben: 1) ___________ do I.
Carla: Why? I don't understand.
Teacher: 2) ___________ do I. Can you explain a bit more?
Anya: People 3) ___________ think about the rubbish that's produced and energy that's wasted when they drink bottled water.
Ben: We've …
Anya: So we …
Ben: Sorry, Anya Carry on.
Anya: No, 4) ___________ you.
Ben: We've made this giant bottle so that everyone thinks about the problem.
Carla: That's good, but what can we do?
Ben: Well, for a start, people 5) ___________ throw their bottles away. What do you think?
Teacher: I agree. We 6) ___________ put more recycling bins around the school, too. Do you agree?

4 Work with a partner. Explain why each missing word was used.

5 Work with a partner. Read about the problem. Look at the possible ways of making people think about the problem and decide which is best. Think about these things.

Cheap?	Expensive?	Will people see it?
Easy to understand?	Popular?	Will people take action?
	Will people remember it?	

Energy bills at your youth club are very high. You are on the committee. You need to make people think about the amount of electricity they use. Talk together about the different plans and then decide which would be best.

DESIGN/WEAR T-SHIRTS

wear/sell wristbands

make/design/put up posters

send emails

Language XP

Taking turns

After you. Carry on. Shall I go first? What do you think? So, do we/you agree?

Exam 💡

Do you need to agree on a decision with a partner? Don't rush! Discuss all the possibilities together first.

WRITING

Power up

1 **Exchange students are coming to your school. Think of one place in town and one place outside town that the students should definitely visit.**

a beach
a lake   a museum
a palace
some mountains

2 **Choose one of your suggestions and give more information. What could the students do there? Where could they eat or drink?**

3 **Work with a partner. Read Emel's description. Ask and answer the questions.**

1 What two places does she say tourists could visit?
2 What place should they visit?
3 What reasons does she give?

A place you should visit

If you are coming to Bodrum, there are many fascinating places you could visit. You could go to the castle, which was built more than six hundred years ago. Or, you could spend a day at the beach.

However, in my opinion you should definitely visit Kursunlu waterfall. It's in a scenic valley in a pine forest. This stunning waterfall is not often visited by tourists; mainly local people know about it. It's very peaceful, especially in springtime. Wild goats and deer are sometimes seen here, so have your camera ready because the deer are very shy. As it's also a perfect place for a picnic, pack some refreshing drinks and some lunch and set off. You'll love it!

Emel, 10th grade

4 **Find examples of passive tenses, adjectives and adverbs in Emel's description. Why does she use each one?**

Plan on

5 **Read the task your teacher has given the class and answer the questions.**

Do you think your writing should be …

1 very formal?
2 a mix of friendly and formal?
3 chatty and informal?

To: all students
Please could you write a description of a local place which our exchange students could visit with their teachers? Your description should include information about what they can see and do there. I will publish all the descriptions in a special booklet for them.
Thank you,
Mrs Jenkins

6 **Look at the photo. Write two or three sentences about it. Think about …**

1 some details about the place, e.g. Is it a natural place? Is it visited by many tourists? What wildlife is sometimes seen there?
2 why you are recommending this place.

Skill

Do you need to describe a place? Use interesting adjectives, e.g. fantastic, amazing.

Write on

7 **Write a description of a place. You can use the photo in Exercise 6, or choose somewhere in or near your home town.**

Language XP

Using a variety of adjectives before a noun

a fascinating/perfect place
a scenic/stunning waterfall/valley/river
peaceful/refreshing scenery

Switch on

ANOTHER WORLD

1 **Guess the answer. Then watch and check.**

You are going to see the Bajau people and Nohara. Which of these things will you see?

A a diver
B people swimming
C a plane
D a house boat
E a city
F sea houses

2 **Are the sentences (1–5) true (T) or false (F)?**

1 Most of the life on Earth is in the sea.
2 The diver usually dives for fun.
3 The level of water in the oceans is getting higher.
4 Nohara's family visit land to meet friends.
5 Some Bajau children can see better under water than in the air.
6 The diver is in the water for three minutes.

3 **What have you learned that was not in the reading text?**

Project

4 **Work with a partner. Write questions for a short quiz show about water or the sea. Video your quiz show or perform it for the class.**

1 Decide on these things:
- Where will you find your information? (online? in a book?)
- How many questions will you ask?
- Will you show pictures in your quiz?
- Will you give three possible answers for your questions?
- Who will ask the questions and who will answer them?

2 Write your quiz questions.
3 Act out your quiz show.

Where is ...?
Why do ...?
What kind of ...?

12 Something new!

READING

Power up

1 **Read the list of ten things to do this summer. Which ideas do you like? Why?**

Ten ideas for a summer to remember

1 write a song
2 learn first aid
3 send a message in a bottle
4 meet somebody famous
5 write a short story
6 be in a film as an extra
7 take a photo every day
8 make cakes
9 learn to juggle
10 try to win something

Read on

2 **Read the text quickly. Which sentence sums it up best?**

1 A travelling circus is a good way for teens to see the world.
2 Teens can learn lots of different skills with a travelling circus.

'We're not an average group of teenagers!'

1
Summer's on the way! Will you go away, or just hang out with friends at home? The choice is yours, but for some teenagers there is only one way to enjoy the summer – that's to try something new. This week, we've met some teenagers who did exactly that. They discovered new skills with a travelling circus.

2
Circus Smirkus was started by a former clown, Rob Mermin. Rob joined the circus when he was nineteen because his mum had told him to get a job. He loved it, and decided he wanted to offer other teenagers the same positive experience. Everyone in Circus Smirkus is between 14–19 years old. Each June, a new group of talented teenagers arrives at the blue and white tents on Rob's farm. Over the next three weeks, circus coaches create a show for them and they perform around the northeast of the USA. Can they turn these teens into circus artists? Of course they can, but it's often very challenging.

3
When Thula Martin was fourteen, she knew exactly what she wanted to do during the summer. She had seen a performance by Circus Smirkus, and she wanted to take part in it. For the next three summers, Thula performed as a contortionist and became famous for her very bendy back. However, travelling with the circus wasn't always easy. She said that life on the road was fun and exhausting, but at the end of the day, you just smile and pretend it's OK.

4
Two more performers are Book Kennison and Isabelle Schuster. Although Book is 1.90 metres tall and weighs 68 kilos, he's a juggler and a contortionist. He can squeeze his body through a tennis racket! Isabelle is from France, where her mum owns her own circus school. As a young child, Isabelle had watched her older sisters in the circus and was so jealous that she soon took up juggling and riding. She'd heard all about Circus Smirkus before she joined it. She spent two summers with them, and loved it.

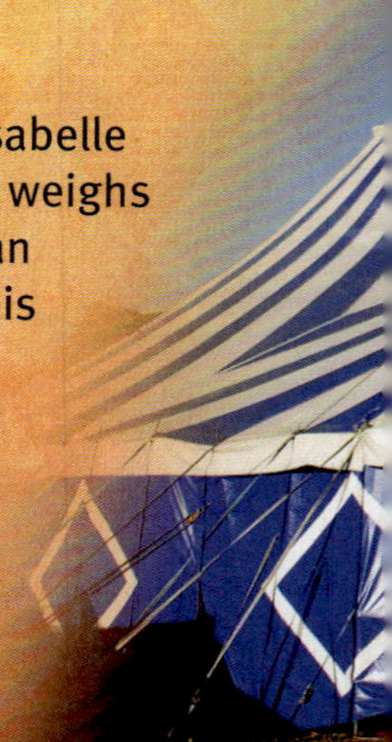

5
For teens like these, a few weeks with the circus is life-changing, and they meet others from all over the world with the same love of the circus. Circus life is also a chance to learn new skills – and not only circus skills. When they are touring, the teens learn to be independent. They help to cook and wash up. They also have to pack and unpack the props, clean up after the shows and sell snacks. Some teens admit that it's tough.

6
Before each show can take place, there's a lot to do. Many of the teenagers' parents help to paint faces, collect tickets and show people to their seats. The show isn't always perfect, but the audience claps loudly. It's like the best summer camp in the world, but with a lot of make-up. Bravo Circus Smirkus!

Exam

Do you need to understand the writer's purpose? The first question often asks about this. Make sure you know what the words mean, e.g. describe, explain, compare, advise, persuade, argue.

3 Read the article again. Choose the correct answer, A, B, C or D.

1 What is the writer doing in the text?
A persuading more teenagers to join a travelling circus
B advising teenagers to do something new this summer
C explaining how a travelling circus can be good for teenagers
D comparing different summer activities

2 Why did Rob Mermin start Circus Smirkus?
A So that other teenagers could do what he did.
B Because he needed a job.
C Because he loved his job with a circus.
D So that he could offer teenagers jobs.

3 When did Thula decide she wanted to join the circus?
A when the summer holidays started
B before she saw Circus Smirkus
C after she saw Circus Smirkus
D when she left school

4 Why did Isabelle learn to juggle and ride?
A She wanted to do what her sisters could do.
B She liked learning new things.
C Her sisters wanted her to do it.
D She wanted to make her sisters jealous.

5 Why is circus life difficult for the teenagers?
A Because they travel and perform a lot.
B Because they are learning to do things on their own.
C Because they don't know anybody.
D Because they have to wash up and clean.

4 Find words in the article that mean the following.

1 a decision to choose between two or more things (Paragraph 1)
2 having an ability to do something well (Paragraph 2)
3 moves easily because it's soft and flexible (Paragraph 3)
4 push something into or through a small space (Paragraph 4)
5 the ability to do things well often because you have practised a lot (Paragraph 5)
6 coloured creams that you put on your face for a show or to look good (Paragraph 6)

Sum up

5 What do you know about the history of Circus Smirkus? Who is Circus Smirkus for and where do they train and perform? What do you know about Thula, Book and Isabelle?

Speak up

6 Work with a partner. Take it in turns to ask and answer the questions.

1 Do you like the idea of learning something new during the summer? Why/Why not?
2 What can you learn where you live?

Challenge Toby! page 113

VOCABULARY

Describing experiences

1 Describe the situations (1–9). Use these words.

challenging embarrassing exhausting ~~fun~~ life-changing motivating positive relaxing tough

1 We enjoyed the circus show. *It was fun.*
2 Practising circus skills can be very tiring.
3 Learning a new skill is often difficult but good fun.
4 Everybody said it was a very good experience.
5 After the brilliant dance class, we all wanted to improve.
6 Daniel thought the exam was very difficult.
7 We had a quiet night with friends and didn't worry about anything.
8 The course gave the teens new skills, so that they could do something different.
9 The girl was going to collect her prize on stage when she fell. Everyone was watching.

2 Are the words in the box in Exercise 1 positive or negative? Why? Give reasons.

3 12.1 Listen to Sam talk about his summer. Which adjectives in Exercise 1 describe his experience? Why?

4 Match the sentence halves.

1 If you want to do something positive,
2 James and I thought it was fun,
3 After a relaxing day,
4 Learning a new language is challenging
5 Oliver thinks the climbing course is tough,
6 The trip was a life-changing experience,

a and they've decided to go and live there.
b and doesn't want to do it anymore.
c but the other students didn't enjoy it.
d I'm ready to go out now.
e when it's got a different alphabet.
f start a new hobby.

5 Match the meanings (1–8) with these phrasal verbs.

find out give up keep on sort out take part in take place ~~take up~~ turn into

1 to start doing a new job or hobby *take up*
2 to continue doing something
3 to become something different
4 to be involved in an event or activity
5 to stop doing something
6 to happen
7 to deal with or organise something
8 to discover

Language XP

Do you want to remember phrasal verbs? Try learning them in pairs!

By preposition
*sort **out** → find **out***
By verb
***take** place → **take** part in*
By opposites
*take **up** → give **up***

6 Rewrite the sentences. Use phrasal verbs from Exercise 5 to replace the words in bold.

1 Alice **stopped doing** yoga because it was boring.
Alice gave up yoga because it was boring.
2 We're trying to **discover** when the course starts.
3 The summer festival always **happens** on my birthday.
4 Nathan **continued** talking during the class.
5 The rain **became** snow that evening.
6 I don't want to **be involved in** the circus anymore.
7 This summer I'm going to **start** cooking.
8 Chloe decided to **organise** her notes before she went into class.

Game on

Work with a partner. Take it in turns to see how many words or phrases you can remember from the page. You have thirty seconds. You get one point for each word/phrase. Who wins?

GRAMMAR

Grammar XP

p. 141

Ordering events in the past

Past perfect simple

Use the past perfect simple when you are talking about an action that happened in an earlier past.

As a young child, Isabelle had watched her older sisters in the circus.

Past perfect simple and past simple

Use the past perfect and past simple in the same sentence to show that one action happened before another action.

*She **had seen** a performance and she **wanted** to take part in it.*

Past ----------|-------------|---------- Now (1: *had seen a performance*; 2: *wanted to take part*)

We often use adverbs of time and linking words: *after, before, when, just, never, ever* with the past perfect.

*He **joined** a circus **after** his mum **had told** him to get a job.*

1 12.2–3 Listen. Now you say it!

2 Complete the text with the correct past perfect simple form of the verbs in brackets.

Sam 1) had planned (plan) his party well. He 2) ____________ (invite) all of his friends. His dad 3) ____________ (make) pizza for everyone and Sam 4) ____________ (buy) a cake. He 5) ____________ (choose) some great music but nobody was there. Why? Because Sam 6) ____________ (not given) them the right date!

3 Choose the action that happened first.

1 The clown had changed his clothes when I saw him.
2 They had just finished packing their bags when the taxi arrived.
3 Keira called for Joseph, but he had already left.
4 I cleaned the kitchen after I had prepared the food.
5 Phoebe fell asleep after they had eaten dinner.
6 They had forgotten their tickets, so they couldn't see the show.

4 Complete the sentences with the correct form of the verbs in brackets.

1 Maria 1) had found (find) a job with a circus, when I last 2) ____________ (see) her.
2 When I 3) ____________ (speak) to him, he 4) ____________ (just/arrive) home from summer camp.
3 The performers 5) ____________ (be) worried because they 6) ____________ (not/practise) enough for the show.
4 The show 7) ____________ (just/start) when there 8) ____________ (be) a problem with the lights.

5 Read the blog. Choose the correct answer, A, B, C or D.

Summerfestivalblog

My friends and I 1) ____________ to go to Latitude after we'd read a review about it. We wanted to do something different, and we 2) ____________ a festival before. We booked our tickets online, and downloaded a list of things to take that the organisers 3) ____________ on the website. My rucksack 4) ____________ really heavy because my mum had given me lots of food! We travelled with hundreds of other teenagers who 5) ____________ tickets for the festival. At the campsite, it took ages to put up our tent because we 6) ____________ the instructions. It was exhausting! At last, we were ready. There were poetry classes, art exhibitions, dance demonstrations and lots more. Finally we 7) ____________ at the stage where my favourite singer had 8) ____________ started her performance. She was amazing!

	A	B	C
1	A have decided	B decided	C were deciding
2	A hadn't tried	B didn't try	C tried
3	A put	B had put	C have put
4	A was	B has been	C were
5	A have bought	B had bought	C bought
6	A didn't pack	B haven't packed	C hadn't packed
7	A have arrived	B arrived	C had arrived
8	A ever	B never	C already

Write on

6 Complete the sentences.

1 I had just finished my homework when …
2 The film had started before we …
3 When you called yesterday evening, we had …
4 I had just … when you …

LISTENING

Power up

1 Read the comments. Match the comments to the photos.

B

A
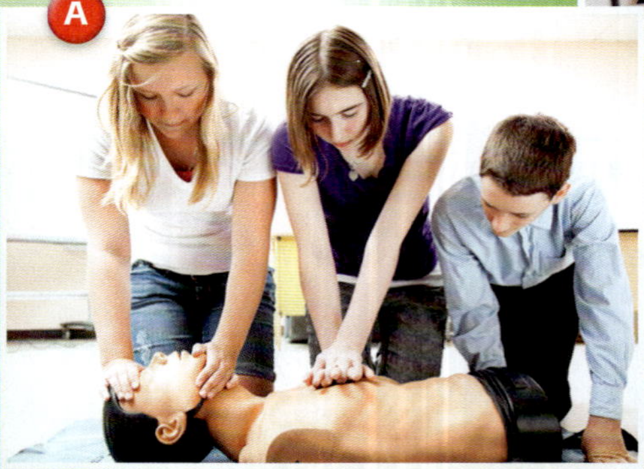

C
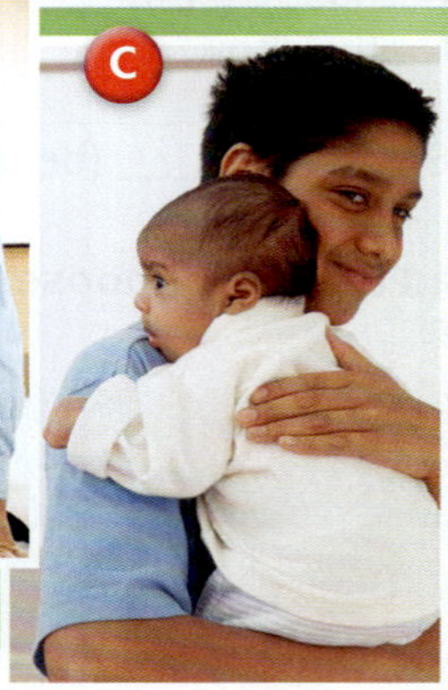

1 I found the course challenging because it's a different way of communicating. I've learned a lot and I don't want to give up because my brother is deaf.
Maria

2 We learned a lot, but it was a bit embarrassing because we had to act. I was helping a person who had broken their leg, but I started laughing.
Josh

3 It was really tough, especially when they were crying or hungry. You have to think what you can do to make them happy and comfortable.
Ben

2 Which activities in Exercise 1 would you like to try? Why?

Listen up

3 12.4 Listen to the first part of a radio interview. Answer the questions.

1 What's the weather like?
2 What are we going to hear about?
3 When will it happen?

4 12.5 Listen to the second part of the interview and complete the information.

THE BEST EVENT OF THE SUMMER

Summer skills fair at Northwood Park

Date: 1) *15 August*
Time: from 2) ___________ until *8.30p.m.*
Learn something new!
Classes in 3) *first aid, hairdressing and* ___________
New this year: two levels of first aid – basic and 4) ___________
Evening concert with The Gorillaz – tickets are 5) £ ___________
For more information and your chance to win free tickets, send your name and address to Fizz Radio, 6) ___________, London.

Exam

Are you listening for information about times, dates and prices? You will hear different numbers, but only one will be correct.

5 12.6 Listen again and check your answers.

Grammar XP

p. 141

have/get something done
Use *have/get* something done when someone else does a job for you.
You can have your hair styled. (someone else styled their hair)
Use *by* someone to say exactly who does the job for you.
The winners get their photo taken ***by*** *a professional photographer.*

6 Complete the sentences with the correct present form of *have/get* and the past participle of the verbs in brackets.

1 Louis *is having* his hair coloured red for the party. (colour)
2 Where can I ___________ these posters for the fair ___________? (print)
3 Gemma isn't here. She ___________ her photo ___________ for the school magazine. (take)
4 He usually ___________ his hair ___________ by the same hairdresser. (cut)

SPEAKING

Power up

1 **Work with a partner. Look at the words. Take it in turns to talk about the topics. Say at least two things about each topic.**

films home
my personality
my town school
the planet

2 **Which topic did you find most difficult to talk about? Why? What can you do to say more?**

Speak up

3 12.7 **Listen to four people. Which topic in Exercise 1 is each person talking about?**

4 **Work with a partner. Take it in turns to ask and answer questions. Give reasons for your answers.**

Student A
What did you do last summer? Did you enjoy it?
What's your favourite food?
Where are you going at the weekend?

Student B
Who did you see last weekend?
Where do you go after school?
What are you going to do this evening?

Skill

Show that you understand the different tenses by using a variety of present, past and future forms correctly.

5 **Work with a partner. Read the rules. Play the game.**

- Each player starts the game with ten points.
- Take it in turns to talk about each topic for thirty seconds.
- If you talk without stopping, you win two extra points.
- If you stop or repeat a sentence, you lose two points.
- The person with the most points is the winner.

A: FINISH	*B: FINISH*
4 family	*4 future plans*
3 hobbies	*3 sports*
2 skills	*2 holidays*
1 music	*1 school*
A: START	*B START*

Language XP

Talking about experiences
It was challenging, but I loved every minute of it.
I didn't think I could do it because it was so tough.
Talking about situations now
I try to revise early for my exams.
I usually do sport three times a week because I love keeping fit.
Talking about future plans
I'm going to do a first aid course in the summer.

WRITING

Power up

1 **Read the magazine survey. Choose the answers that are true for you.**

My perfect day...

1 I wake up at ...
A 7 a.m. (I like to start things early.)
B 9 a.m. (It's later than a school day.)
C lunchtime. (I need to sleep!)

2 The weather is ...
A sunny. (Yah! Let's go out.)
B cloudy. (Good, it isn't too hot.)
C wet and cold. (Brilliant! I can stay in and watch a film.)

3 I spend the day with ...
A friends. (Of course!)
B family and friends. (I love being with lots of people.)
C on my own. (It's relaxing!)

4 I get a nice surprise and it's ...
A a present. (a big one)
B a big cake. (chocolate!)
C a party invitation. (for tonight)

5 The day ends with ...
A a book and bed.
B a good film and a pizza.
C a party that finishes very late!

2 **Compare your results with the rest of the class. Which answers are the most popular?**

3 **Complete the story with these words.**

~~a day trip~~ delicious discovered do something different nervous steep the view very hungry

A perfect day!

A Last summer, I went on 1) __a day trip__ to the amazing Parque de Catacumba in Rio de Janeiro. My friends and I had arranged the trip because we wanted to 2) ________ and get away from the city.

B The first thing we did at the park was eat because we were 3) ________. We had taken a 4) ________ picnic with pizza slices and soft drinks. After that, we tried zip wiring, which I hadn't done before. I was 5) ________, but I loved it. Then we went to an open air art gallery. When we had done that, we walked up a very long, 6) ________ path through the trees, so that we could take photos of 7) ________. It was exhausting!

C After a long day, we decided to go home because were very tired. However, when we got to the bottom, I 8) ________ that I had left my camera at the top!

4 **Read the story in Exercise 3 again. Match the events (1–4) with the correct paragraph (A–C).**

1 what happened at the end of the day
2 what they did first
3 what other activities they did
4 when they arranged the trip A

5 **Does the story in Exercise 3 have a good or bad ending?**

Plan on

6 **Look at the poster. What do you have to do for the competition?**

> Have you had, 'A day with a difference' recently? Write a true story. Who were you with? Where did you go and what did you do? Your story could win two free tickets to a theme park!

7 **What makes a day with a difference? Add more ideas.**

good friends
fun things to do

8 **Read the questions (1–6) and make notes.**

1 When did the story take place?
last month/on my birthday
2 Where did you go and why?
3 Who were you with?
4 What did you do first?
5 What other things did you do?
6 What happened at the end of the day?

Language XP

Ordering events

Last summer/winter/March/month
At the weekend/On Tuesday/On my birthday
The first thing we did was …
After that …
When we had done/finished/seen that …
After a long/tiring/brilliant day …

Write on

9 **Write a true story called 'A day with a difference'. Use your ideas and notes from Exercises 6 and 7 and the Language XP box to help you. Write about 100 words.**

Skill

Do you want your story to be the best? Make sure that your story has a clear beginning, middle and end.

Switch on

CHALLENGE TOBY!

1 **Guess the answers. Then watch and check.**

Toby has an unusual challenge. Which words are correct?

- **A** Toby's challenge is to *wash/plait* Rebecca's hair.
- **B** He's got *five/three* minutes for the challenge.
- **C** Toby *enjoys/doesn't* enjoy the challenge.
- **D** Toby *passes/fails* the challenge.

2 **Who says the following: Rebecca (R), Toby (T) or Emma (E)?**

1 *Are you ready? Go!* R
2 Cross that over to the middle.
3 Very tricky.
4 You know the basics.
5 Your side is obviously a little bit better.
6 You could style everyone's hair at school.
7 OK. I haven't got a rubber band.
8 How can we conclude?

3 **Do you think Toby did well? Was it a good challenge? Why/Why not?**

Project

4 **Work in pairs. Take it in turns to complete your partner's challenge.**

1 Decide on these things:
- What the challenge is for your partner.
- What instructions you can give to your partner.
- How long you will give for the challenge.
- If your partner has passed or failed the challenge.

2 Act out your challenge.

Your challenge today is to …!
You're going to …
You've got … minute(s).

Revision

VOCABULARY

1 Read the meanings and write the word.

1 when there is wind and rain and sometimes snow *storm*
2 a large ball of gas in the sky, that is burning
3 the large white object that shines in the sky at night
4 a high piece of land that is very steep and usually next to the sea
5 a white or grey shape in the sky that is made of water
6 a large piece of stone
7 a track that you can walk along
8 small pieces of rocks that you find in the desert or on the beach

2 Put the words in the correct order. Use a comma where necessary.

1 had / exhausting / an / hot / the / day / at / They / beach.
They had an exhausting hot day at the beach.
2 walked / hot We / across / sand. / the / black
3 blue / at / Look / the / sky. / beautiful
4 appear. / Big / clouds / started / grey / to
5 They / amazing / an / waterfall. / high / found
6 looking / rock. / for / We're / small / a / pink

3 Make phrasal verbs and complete the sentences.

~~find~~ give keep sort take take take part
turn in into on ~~out~~ out place up up

1 You can *find out* more about our first aid classes on our website.
2 Emily decided to ____________ her piano lessons because she didn't have enough time.
3 You need to ____________ practising if you want to join the orchestra.
4 I'm going to ____________ all of my books before school starts again.
5 Where is the race going to ____________ ?
6 I want to ____________ photography, but first I have to buy a better camera.
7 About ninety people ____________ the show every year.
8 Can a hobby ever ____________ a job? Write and tell us your story.

4 Choose the correct word.

1 You should *keep on/take part in* learning sign language. You're very good at it.
2 Jack's football match was *exhausting/embarrassing*, and he was too tired to go out that evening.
3 The students haven't climbed a high mountain before, so it's a *relaxing/tough* day for them.
4 A concert is *taking place/taking up* in the town square tonight. Let's go!
5 Living in another country is a *positive/tough* experience and I'm enjoying every minute of it.
6 After a difficult day, Sam had a *motivating/relaxing* evening lying on the sofa watching his favourite film.
7 Let's go online and *find out/sort out* where the nearest nature park is. We could go at the weekend.
8 This birthday party is *giving up/turning into* a complete disaster.

5 Complete the post with the words.

big, white challenging ~~exhausting~~ positive
relaxing sort out turn into waterfall

Hello from Mexico!

Hello from the Tamul river in Mexico! We have just arrived after an 1) *exhausting* , six-hour hike from our last camp site. When we got here, we had to 2) ____________ the tents and the food. It took ages to organise everything. There are a lot of 3) ____________ rocks around the river, and I can hear the sound of the water as it falls from the famous Tamul 4) ____________ . Tomorrow we're going out in a boat, but I've heard that it's very 5) ____________ because the water moves very quickly. The weather's a bit cold and windy, but hopefully it won't 6) ____________ a storm. We're all tired, so we're having a 7) ____________ evening around the camp fire. I'll post some photos soon of this fantastic trip. I think this is the most 8) ____________ thing I've ever done, and I can't wait to tell you more about it.

GRAMMAR

6 Complete the passive sentences using the verbs in brackets and the tense given.

1 The evening meals were prepared (prepare) on the campsite. (past simple)
2 The documentary ____________ (film) in South America. (past simple)
3 The beaches ____________ (clean) every day in summer. (present simple)
4 A large star ____________ (discover) by a fourteen-year-old girl. (past simple)
5 How many animals ____________ (use) in the TV programme? (past simple)
6 Their circus costumes ____________ (make) by their parents. (present simple)

7 Read the sentences. Are they suggestions (S), asking for advice (A) or giving strong advice (SA)?

1 You should do more exercise. A
2 We could go by train.
3 You shouldn't use you camera in here.
4 You should look at the map before you go.
5 They could talk to their teacher.
6 Dan could go to bed earlier.
7 What should I say to him?
8 Anna and Nick should read this article.

8 Complete the sentences with the correct form of the past perfect.

1 They had put up (put up) their tents when the rain started.
2 Finally, we found the waterfall that everybody ____________ (tell) us about.
3 They got lost because Alex ____________ (not bring) the map.
4 After I ____________ (finish) the pizza, I put the box in the recycling bin.
5 Louisa ____________ (not have) time to see Tom before he went on holiday.
6 They had to leave the village because the storm ____________ (destroy) their houses.
7 I couldn't believe what I ____________ (hear) on the news.
8 The farmer wasn't happy with the rubbish the tourists ____________ (leave) on his land.

9 Put the words in the sentences in the correct order.

1 The / are / week. / emptied / every / recycling bins
The recycling bins are emptied every week.
2 is / The / waterfall / hundreds of tourists / visited / by / day. / every
3 enjoyed / are / adults and children. / by / The songs
4 summer. / The / every / show / is / day / in / performed
5 The / camp / food / is / around / fire. / eaten / the
6 cleaned / The / is / at / the / the / end / day. / beach / of

10 Complete the second sentence so that it means the same as the first. Use no more than three words.

1 Millions of people around the world watch the show.
The show is watched by millions of people around the world.
2 The price of the ticket doesn't include a drink.
A drink ____________ in the price of the ticket.
3 The teacher advised her students to watch the news every day.
The teacher said, 'You ____________ the news every day.'
4 They prepared the meals in the huge kitchen.
The meals ____________ in the huge kitchen.
5 'I suggest that we take the shorter path,' she said.
'We ____________ the shorter path,' she suggested.
6 They took the photo and then they left.
They left after they ____________ the photo.

11 Choose the correct answer, A, B, C or D.

1 Elena didn't understand how she ____________ lost the others.
A have **B** did **C** was **D** had
2 I don't think that you ____________ go out on your own.
A could **B** must **C** should **D** shouldn't
3 How many children ____________ at this school?
A are **B** is **C** be **D** aren't
4 After they had watched the stars, they ____________ inside.
A gone **B** went **C** was **D** were
5 Yesterday's avalanche ____________ caused by a change in temperature.
A were **B** is **C** was **D** are

Speaking ✎ Writing

Unit 1

SPEAKING

Talking about personal information

1 **Work with a partner. Take it in turns to ask for and give the information to complete the application form. Spell any difficult words. Check that the information is correct.**

School Film Club
Application form

First name: ______________
Surname: ______________
Age: ______________
Email address: ______________

What type of films do you like?

☐ horror films ☐ comedies ☐ science fiction films
☐ action films ☐ animated films ☐ other

What is the name of your favourite film?
Who is your favourite actor?

2 **Work with a partner. Take it in turns to ask each other the questions. When you answer a question remember to give examples and reasons.**

1 What's your favourite school subject?
2 Can you tell me about your family?
3 What's your favourite food? Is there anything you don't like?
4 What sports do you like?
5 What do you enjoy doing at weekends?
6 What kind of music do you like?

Language XP

Giving reasons and examples

My favourite food is spaghetti. My mum's from Rome so we eat a lot of Italian food.
I really like maths. One reason is that I'm really good at it, but I also think it's an interesting subject.

If you don't understand what someone has said, ask them to repeat it.

WRITING

A personal profile

Plan

- What is the profile for? (a competition entry, a school website, etc.)
- What kind of information should you include? (name, age, nationality, hobbies, interests, etc.)
- Make a list of the key facts about yourself and put them in order.
- Try and find something extra to say about why you are different or interesting.

Write

- Give information about where you live.
  I live in the south of Spain.
  We live in the centre of the city.
  I live on a farm in the country.
  My country is quite small, but very beautiful.
- Give information about your hobbies and interests.
  I'm really keen on skateboarding.
  I love horses and go horse-riding every weekend.
  I enjoy skiing, but I'm not very good!
  We live near the sea so I often go to the beach, and I love swimming.
- Add extra information that makes you different or special.
  I live in a really lively place.
  I'm confident and friendly and love meeting new people.
  I'm really sporty and have lots of unusual hobbies.
  Choose me because I love telling funny jokes.

Check

- Are the facts about yourself clear?
- Is your profile interesting?
- Does your profile include words like *very* and *quite* to make adjectives stronger or less strong?
- Do you join sentences with *and*, *but*, *or*, *because*, and *so?*

Extra

Write a personal profile for a competition to win an activity holiday.

Unit 2

SPEAKING

Talking on the phone

1 Put the lines of this telephone conversation in the correct order (1–7).

Yes. Hi, Jonathan! Are you ... [voice is difficult to hear]
Yes, I can hear you now. What did you say before?
Yes, that would be great!
Sorry Rachel. I can't hear you. Can you speak louder?
Do you want to go to the cinema this evening?
Is that Rachel?
Hang on, Jonathan. I'll turn the radio down. Is that better?

2 Work with a partner. Choose a reason for phoning and a problem. Take it in turns to phone each other.

Reason for phoning
to arrange to meet in town
to invite your friend to your birthday party
to ask for help with your homework

Problem
you don't have a signal
there's too much noise

It's a good idea to repeat the information someone gives you on the telephone. This will help you check that you have understood correctly.

Language XP

Asking who's calling
Is that ... ?
Saying who's calling
It's ...
Asking someone to wait
Just a second/Just a minute/Hang on.
Saying when there's a problem
Sorry, I can't hear you. I haven't got a signal.
Asking someone to talk louder or repeat
Can you speak/talk louder please?

WRITING

A short story

Plan

- Decide what type of story you want to write. (a funny story, a romantic story, etc.)
- Who's going to read the story? (your teacher, magazine readers, online readers, etc.)
- Make a list of the main ideas for your story: When did it happen? Where did it happen? Who was there? What was the main action? What happened in the end?

Write

- Remember to say when the story happened and where you were.
  Last summer, when I was on holiday in Tunisia ...
  I was at my friend's house last Monday, when ...
  Yesterday, I was walking home from school ...
- Give information about who was there when the story happened.
  I was with my two cousins, Jack and Chloe ...
  My friend's mum and sister were having dinner with us ...
  We met some more friends from school at the beach ...
- Write what happened. Use the correct order.
  We were having a great time. At the end of the afternoon, we all got out of the sea. Then, we noticed our towels and bags weren't there ...
- Make sure the end of your story is clear.
  In the end, we all laughed.
  We'll never forget that day!

Check

- Is it clear when and where the story happened and who was there?
- Does the story have a clear beginning, middle and end?
- Is your story interesting?

Extra

Write a funny story for a travel website. Begin with:
A funny thing happened to me on holiday ...

Unit 3

SPEAKING

Agreeing and disagreeing

1 Complete the conversation with the correct words.

agree might point so sure

Anna: Do you think in 2050 fewer people will own cars?
Leo: I'm not 1) ______________ . More and more people want cars.
Anna: I 2) ______________ , but maybe it will become too expensive.
Leo: You have a 3) ______________ . The cost of petrol will probably be very high in 2050.
Anna: Yes, I think 4) ______________ , but the cars in the future might not need petrol.
Leo: Yes, you 5) ______________ be right.

2 Work with a partner. Use the phrases in the Language XP box to agree or disagree with these statements.

In the year 2050 ...
... there will be no paper books, only e-books.
... houses will be more environmentally friendly in the future.
... children in [name of your country] will learn Chinese at school.
... people will be healthier and fitter.
... most people won't travel abroad for their holidays.

Language XP

Agreeing and disagreeing

I agree.	*I think so.*
I think that's right.	*I don't agree.*
Well, maybe ...	*I don't think that's right.*
That's a good point.	*I'm not sure.*
You might be right.	*I don't think so.*

When you are talking to someone, remember to make eye contact. Make your voice go up and down to show interest in what your partner is saying.

WRITING

An email about plans

Plan

- Think of the person you are writing to. (a friend, a magazine, somebody you don't know, etc.)
- How should you start and finish the email?
- Make a list of the things that you want to tell the person.

Write

- Start your email correctly.
  Dear Technology Team,
  Dear Dan,
  Hi Jane,
- Say what your email is about.
  I'm going to give up my Xbox.
- Give a reason.
  I love playing computer games, so it's going to be a real challenge.
  - Describe how you will feel.
  I'm going to feel really bored without my Xbox, but I think I'll enjoy doing something different in the evening.
- Finish your email with the correct ending.
  Best wishes,
  Mark

Check

- Does your email say what you're planning to do and why?
- Do you use adjectives to predict how you'll feel?
- Do you use words like *and*, *but* and *so* to make your sentences longer?

Extra

Write an email to your teacher about your plans to not use electricity for a day. Say why you are doing it and predict how you will feel.

Unit 4

SPEAKING

Explaining preferences

1 Choose the sentences (a–d) that explain the preferences (1–4).

1 I prefer to study in the morning.
2 I'd rather learn physics than history.
3 I prefer to watch films at home.
4 I prefer to walk to school.

a It's more relaxing than going to the cinema.
b I think it's healthier than going by car.
c I think it's better than the afternoon.
d I think science is more useful.

2 Make questions using the words in brackets.

1 go to a big school/small school (rather)
Would you rather go to a big school or a small school?
2 have lunch at home/in the school canteen (prefer)
Do you prefer to have lunch at home or in the school canteen?
3 borrow a book from the library/read an e-book on your phone (rather)
4 have an art lesson/a sports lesson (rather)
5 do your homework with music on/in silence (prefer)
6 revise with friends/on your own (prefer)

3 Work with a partner. Take it in turns to ask and answer the questions in Exercise 2. Give a reason for your answer.

Language station

Explaining preferences

I prefer to + verb … *I'd rather + verb …*

Giving reasons

It's more … than … *I think it's/that's better/ more useful than …*

Always give a reason for preferring something. You can make your answers longer and more interesting by giving examples.

WRITING

A card (about plans)

Plan

- Think about how to start and end your card in a friendly way.
- Make notes of what you want to say in your card. (plans for activities, suggestions about what to bring, etc.)
- Do not include information that is not important.

Write

- Start your card in a friendly way.
  Hi Alma,
  Dear Yan,
- Talk about your plans.
  We're going to have a picnic.
  We're going to watch a film at the cinema.
- Give an explanation.
  I think three o'clock is a good time because the shops will still be open.
- Make a suggestion.
  Why don't you bring a swimsuit?
  Let's go swimming if we have enough time.
  Why don't we go for a pizza before the film starts?

Check

- Does your card begin and end correctly?
- Have you explained your plans and given clear explanations and suggestions?

Extra

Write a card to a friend coming to visit you. Explain what you plan to do and make suggestions about what your friend should bring and why.

Unit 5

SPEAKING

Describing pictures 1

1 Work with a partner. Student A, look at photo A. Student B, look at photo B.

A

B

2 Take it in turns to describe your photo. Use the questions below to help you.

1 Who is in the photo?
2 Where are they?
3 What are they wearing?
4 What are they doing?
5 How are they feeling?
6 What do you think about this activity?

Language XP

It's a photo of …/The photo shows …
On the left/On the right/At the back/At the front …
He/She/They look(s) …
When you aren't sure or don't know
It could/might be …
Perhaps it's …/Maybe it's …
I can't remember what this is.

Remember don't just describe what you can see. Think about how the people in the photo are feeling.

WRITING

An article

Plan

- What is the topic of your article and who is it for? (other students, parents, etc.)
- Think of a good title for your article.
- Make a list of all the key points you want to include in your article and organise them into paragraphs.

Write

- Make sure the first sentence of each paragraph introduces the topic.
  I have tried lots of different hobbies, and I've enjoyed most of them.
- Give examples to support what you say.
  Next month, I'm going to join a dance class.
- Make sure your article has a clear ending.
  Maybe you'll see my artwork in a gallery!

Check

- Is your article interesting for the person who is reading it?
- Are your ideas clearly organised?
- Have you used the connecting words and phrases, e.g. except, although, so that, and either … or?
- Does your article have a good first and last sentence?

Extra

Interview your partner to find out which hobbies they have tried and haven't tried. Use this information to write an article about your partner.

Unit 6

SPEAKING

Apologising and responding

1 Match the problems (a–d) with the correct conversations.

a borrow something without asking
b lose something
c miss a meeting
d break something

1
Boy: I'm really sorry, Mum, it was an accident.
Mum: OK, Joe, but next time don't leave your glass on the floor.

2
Dad: Oh, Natalie! What have you done with your keys? How are you going to get into the house after school now?
Girl: Sorry, Dad. I didn't mean to lose them. I put them in my pocket yesterday, but they're not there now.

3
Boy: Sorry I wasn't at football practice yesterday, Mr Stokes. I completely forgot about it.
Teacher: Never mind, just make sure you write it in your school diary for next week.

4
Dan: Where's my laptop? I need it for my homework.
Leah: Sorry, Dan. I've got it. Don't be angry with me!
Dan: You should ask first. It's my laptop.
Leah: Yes, OK. It won't happen again.

2 Work with a partner. Choose one of the problems from Exercise 1 and roleplay a short conversation.

Language XP

Apologising and responding

I'm (very/really) sorry.	*That's OK.*
It was an accident.	*Never mind.*
I didn't mean to.	
It won't happen again.	

Try to put real feeling into what you are saying, e.g. when you apologise, make your partner believe you are really sorry.

WRITING

An email (dealing with a problem)

Plan

- Who are you writing to? (a friend, somebody in your family, etc.)
- What is your reason for writing? (to explain that you have found/forgotten something, etc.)
- What information do you need to include in your email?

Write

- Start your email in a friendly way.
  It was great seeing you last week.
  Thank you for taking me to London on Saturday. I had a great time.
  I had a good journey back from your house yesterday.
- Include all the necessary information in your email.
  I think I left my phone at your house.
  There's a small problem. I can't find my dictionary.
  I'm sorry, I put your e-book in my bag by accident.
- Ask for or suggest action in a polite way
  I'm not sure about the best way to deal with the problem. Could you post my book to me, please?
  How do you want to solve the problem?
  It's up to you. I can buy you some new headphones online if you like.
- Finish the email in a friendly way.
  Thank you very much. Your friend, Carlos
  Thank you. Love, Alice

Check

- Have you included all the necessary information in your email?
- Is it clear what you want the other person to do?
- Is your email friendly and polite?

Extra

Write an email to a friend who has left their phone at your house.

Unit 7

SPEAKING

Making and responding to suggestions

1 Work with a partner. Read the list of things that are happening this week. Choose three things that interest you.

Your What's on guide … something for everyone!

It's back! Your favourite singing competition on TV – starts this Friday.
Come to a free, classical concert in the park.
Listen to an interview on the radio with local pop band Fizz.
Make your own crazy costume and come to a fancy dress party this Friday at Mega sports club.
Enjoy ballet at the theatre with international dancers.
School choirs from around the world perform at Hatton School. Saturday night only.
The mystery writer, George Dutton, will talk at Foundation book shop. Come and find out why teens love his books.

2 Work with a partner. Practise the conversation.

Anna: Look at this Max. George Dutton is going to be at the Foundation book shop. Let's go and meet him.
Max: It's a nice idea, but I've got a singing lesson that day.
Anna: Oh, what about the fancy dress party this Friday?
Max: Yes, that sounds fantastic. Why don't we go together?
Anna: Great.

After you say Yes to a suggestion, you can often make another suggestion, e.g. Why don't we go together?/Let's go together.

3 Take it in turns to make suggestions and respond.

Language XP

Making suggestions
Why don't we/you … ?
What about …
Let's do/go …
Saying No politely
I'm really sorry, but …
It's a nice idea, but …
Saying Yes
That sounds fantastic. When can we go?
What a brilliant idea!

WRITING

A review

Plan

- Decide what you are going to review. (a film, an album, an event, etc.)
- Think about who your review is for. (a magazine, a blog, etc.)
- Use adjectives that make your review interesting and lively.
- Write four paragraphs.

Write

- Say what you are reviewing and give some general information.
  I've just bought the new Taylor Swift album.
  Last week, I was at a rock festival.
  It's a new action film with Matt Damon.
  It was at the Park Lane theatre.
- Describe what is/was good about it.
  The good thing about the film was that it was exciting.
  The best thing was the atmosphere.
- Describe what isn't/wasn't good about it.
  The only bad thing about the album is the price.
  The worst thing is the venue because it's small.
- Give your opinion and say if you recommend it or not.
  If you watched/saw/bought this, you'd enjoy it.
  This album is boring, so I wouldn't recommend it.

Check

- Is it clear at the beginning what your review is about?
- Does your review have four paragraphs?
- Does it sound enthusiastic with lots of adjectives?

Extra

Write a review of a film, an album or an event.

Unit 8

SPEAKING

Helping someone express their ideas

1 Things sometimes go wrong on school trips. Which ideas are the most/least common?

1 You don't hear the alarm clock, and you get up late.
2 The coach breaks down.
3 You're going abroad, but you leave your passport at home.
4 You're in a long traffic jam.
5 You're sick, or one of your friends is sick.
6 You forget your phone or money.
7 You get lost.
8 It rains all day.

2 Think about a school trip you have had recently. You are going to tell your partner about the trip. Use the questions to help you decide what to say.

1 When was it?
About a month ago, we went to …
2 Where did you go?
3 Who were you with?
4 What did you do?
5 What happened?
5 What happened in the end?

3 Work with a partner. Take it in turns to tell each other about the trip. When you are listening, show your partner that you are interested. Don't interrupt, but ask lots of questions and let your partner know what you think.

There was a delay at the airport and we had to wait five hours.

Really? That's awful!

Language XP

Helping someone express their ideas

Really? That's interesting/nice/awful/scary.
So, did you/they/anyone … ?
Was it a … ?
What happened then/next?
How did that happen?

WRITING

A blog

Plan

- Decide who you are writing for (people your own age, older/younger readers, etc.).
- Think about what you are going to write about (something that happened on a journey/on holiday/on a school trip, etc.).
- Write in a friendly style.
- Ask your reader questions, and invite them to comment.

Write

- Start your blog with a question that interests your reader.
  Have you ever missed your train/arrived late at the airport/got stuck in a traffic jam?
- Say what happened to you and when.
  Last year, I was on holiday with my parents. When we arrived at the hotel, …
  Last summer, I went to London to do a language course. One day, I …
- Describe how you felt.
  It was so embarrassing.
  It was brilliant/fantastic/awful.
- Give your tip for a good holiday.
  What's my top tip? Take your camera./Take your own food./Don't arrive late!
  The best thing to do is take your camera/take your own food/arrive early.

Check

- Do you give your reader lots of interesting information?
- Does you blog sound friendly?
- Have you asked your readers questions?

Extra

Write a blog about a recent holiday or school trip.

Unit 9

SPEAKING

Asking for and expressing an opinion

1 **Read the comments. Do you agree with them? Why/Why not?**

Online gaming is bad for your health.
Doing drama is a waste of time at school.
Schools should offer keep fit classes every day.
The best chefs are men.
Making jewellery is only for girls.

2 **Read the conversation. Who thinks doing drama is a good idea: Nathan, Amy or Liam?**

Nathan: What do you think about doing drama at school, Amy?
Amy: I'm not sure. Sometimes I think that it's a waste of time. I prefer doing sport.
Nathan: What about you Liam?
Liam: I don't agree. I think drama is brilliant. You make lots of friends, and it gives you confidence.
Nathan: Yes, you're right.

3 **Work with a partner or in small groups. Find out what each person thinks about the comments in Exercise 1.**

Language XP

Asking for an opinion
What about you?
What do you think about … ?
Do you think it's/that's true/right/good idea/a bad idea?
Do you think that … is bad for your health/boring/a waste of time?
Expressing an opinion
I don't agree.
I'm not sure./I don't really know because I don't do it./I haven't tried it.
You're right./It's right.

You don't always have to have a strong opinion about something. Sometimes it's fine to say I'm not sure or I don't really know. However, it's good to explain why.

WRITING

An article

Plan

- Decide who or what you are going to write about.
- Find out interesting information about that person/activity.
- Make notes and organise your ideas.

Write

- Start your article with a question that attracts your reader.
  Have you heard of Nick Jonas?
  Have you heard about a hobby called Extreme Ironing?
- Introduce the person/activity you are writing about.
  Nick Jonas is an actor and a singer. He …
  Extreme Ironing is a hobby that people do in strange places.
- Give the main information about that person/activity.
  Nick loves writing songs.
  He plays in a band with his brothers.
  It's a hobby that you can do anywhere.
  It doesn't cost anything.
- Finish with your opinion about this person/activity.
  I think he/she's amazing because he/she's does lots of things.
  Extreme ironing is great because it's very funny.

Check

- Is your article interesting and informative?
- Does your article include interesting adjectives and adverbs.
- Is the main information in the middle of your article?

Extra

Write an article about a person or an activity.

Unit 10

SPEAKING

Describing pictures 2

1 **Work with a partner. Student A, look at Photo A. Student B, look at Photo B.**

A

B

2 **Take it in turns to describe your photo. Think about these things.**

actions clothes colours physical description place unusual objects

Language XP

Dealing with unknown words

What's … *that long, metal thing?*
the white thing behind the girls with a window?
the thing on her head?

It looks like a …
You use it for cooking/repairing things.

If you don't know the word for an object or the name of a person, don't stop talking. Think of other things to say about it. What does the object/person look like or what does the object/person do?

WRITING

A formal letter

Plan

- Make sure you understand why you are writing the letter.
- Make notes of what you want to say, and organise your notes.
- Be polite, but clear.

Write

- Start your letter.
  Dear Sir/Madam,
- Say why you are writing.
  I'm writing to apply for the job of …
  I'm writing about … which I saw online/in the newspaper.
- Give information about yourself.
  I'm organised/polite/confident.
  I'm good at working in a team.
  I have some/lots of experience with children.
- End your letter.
  I look forward to hearing from you soon.
  I hope to hear from you soon.
  Yours faithfully,
  [your name]

Check

- Does your letter begin and end correctly?
- Have you explained why you are writing?
- Have you included useful information about yourself?

Extra

Write an application letter for a volunteer job at your local museum.

Unit 11

SPEAKING

Taking turns

1 **Look at the posters about how your school can help the environment. Which idea do you prefer? Why?**

2 **Work with a partner. Think of reasons for (√) and against (×) each action.**

1 No plastic bags
√ ___________
× *you have to put dirty football boots in a plastic bag*

2 Recycle clothes
√ *you can make money from old clothes* × ___________

3 **Work with a partner. Take it in turns to talk about the actions in Exercise 2. Decide which one is the best for your school. Use your ideas from Exercise 2.**

Language XP

Taking turns
Why don't I/you start? *Shall I begin?* *Carry on.*
Do you think that's right? *So, do we/you agree?*

If you need to agree on a decision with a partner, make sure you discuss all the ideas for and against each action.

WRITING

A description of a place

Plan

- Think of a place you know well and like.
- Write down special words that describe the place, e.g. scenic, peaceful, refreshing.
- Think about what your reader will find interesting.

Write

- What place are you describing?
  ... is a town/a city/a small village in ...
  It's near the mountains/the sea.
- Give more information about the place.
  It's got a beautiful beach/a lovely river/an amazing volcano.
  There are lots of animals/tourists/old buildings.
  It's an exciting place.
- Say when it's a good time to see the place and why.
  You should see the town in spring when it isn't too busy.
  The best time to visit is winter because it usually snows and it's beautiful.

Check

- Is it clear what you are describing?
- Is your description interesting?
- Does your description sound enthusiastic?

Extra

Write a description of a place you enjoy visiting.

Unit 12

SPEAKING

Talking about different topics

1 Choose three of these topics.

A perfect day is … At the weekend …
This summer … My worst holiday was …
The last film I saw was … When I'm twenty …

2 Complete the conversations with these questions.

Who are you going with?
Where do you go?
What are you going to do there?
What do you usually do?

1

A: A perfect day is with friends.
B: *What do you usually do?*
A: We hang out and chat.
B: 1) ___________ ?
A: We often go to the shopping centre, or to the park.

2

A: This summer, I'm going to New York.
B: 2) ___________ ?
A: I'm going alone.
B: 3) ___________ ?
A: I'm going to stay with my aunt and uncle.

3 Work with a partner. Take it in turns to talk about the topics you chose in Exercise 1. Ask and answer questions to get more information.

Language XP

Talking about past experiences
It was tough, but I enjoyed it.
I had a good time, and it was very motivating.
Talking about situations now
I like meeting friends after school.
I live with my family, and we're very noisy.
Talking about future plans
I'm going to study science in the future.

Don't forget to use different tenses when you talk, and show that you can use them correctly.

WRITING

A story

Plan

- Decide what happens in your story.
- Make notes, and put the events in order.
- Think of a clear beginning, middle and end.
- Use words to describe the experiences, feelings and places.

Write

- Start the story. Say when it happened.
  One day last year, …
  It was the day of my birthday party/of my exam results, …
  Two years ago, …
- Describe where the story happened and who was there.
  I was on a train with some friends.
  My cousins and I were walking through a shopping centre.
  A group of friends were going on a school trip to a museum.
- Put the main events in the correct order.
  The first thing we did was …
  After that, …/Then, …
  When we had finished that, we …
- Describe what happened at the end.
  At the end of the evening/After a long day, …
  Unfortunately/Fortunately, …
  We/I discovered that we/I had …
- Give your story a title.
  A disaster!
  An unforgettable adventure
  A funny day!

Check

- Are the events in the correct order?
- Is it clear who is in the story and what happened?
- Have you got a good, strong ending?

Extra

Write a short story.

Vocabulary file

01

PERSONAL INFORMATION

bossy (adj)
calm (adj)
clever (adj)
confident (adj)
funny (adj)
lazy (adj)
lively (adj)
noisy (adj)
rude (adj)
serious (adj)
shy (adj)
sporty (adj)

ADJECTIVE PHRASES

bad at …
bored with …
brilliant at …
excited about …
fed up with …
frightened of …
good at …
interested in …
terrible at …

02

LANGUAGE AND COMMUNICATION

explain (v)
mean (v)
pronounce (v)
repeat (v)
say (v)
speak (v)
translate (v)
understand (v)

03

TECHNOLOGY AROUND THE HOME

3-D TV (n)
air conditioning (n)
dishwasher (n)
fridge (n)
hair straighteners (n)
hairdryer (n)
headphones (n)
iron (n)
microwave (n)
plug (n)
speakers (n)
washing machine (n)

PHRASAL VERBS

pick up
plug in
switch off
switch on
turn down
turn up

04

SCHOOL AND EDUCATION

break (n)
carefully (adv)
corridor (n)
curriculum (n)
early (adj)/(adv)
easily (adv)
examiner (n)
fail (v)
fast (adj)/(adv)
grade (n)
happily (adv)
hard (adj)/(adv)
high (adj)/(adv)
late (adj)/(adv)
learn (v)
long (adj)/(adv)
low (adj)/(adv)
near (adj)/(adv)
pass (v)
practise (v)
regularly (adv)
revise (v)
rule (n)
slowly (adv)
teach (v)
test (n)
timetable (n)
well (adv)

05

SPORT

beat (n)
changing rooms (n)
coach (n)
compete (n)
court (n)
hit (v)
kick (n)/(v)
locker (n)
match (n)
practice (n)
practise (v)
prize (n)
race (n)/(v)
score (n)/(v)
track (n)
train (v)
win (v)

06

FRIENDSHIP AND FEELINGS

amazed (adj)
amazing (adj)
bored (adj)
boring (adj)
surprised (adj)
surprising (adj)

COLLOCATIONS

deal with
fall out with
get on with
get to know
have a hard time
have something in common
spend time with
stay calm

07
ENTERTAINMENT

audience (n)
book (v)
choir (n)
clap (v)
costume (n)
entertain (v)
exit (n)
film (v)
interview (v)
orchestra (n)
perform (v)
record (v)
review (v)
row (n)
stage (n)

COLLOCATIONS

book a ticket/seat
film a documentary/a TV programme/a scene
interview an actor/a famous person
perform in a play/a ballet/a musical/a TV show
perform on stage
record a song/an album

08
TRAVEL

abroad (adv)
border (n)
check in (v)
check-in (n)
delay (n)/(v)
destination (n)
flight (n)
journey (n)
land (v)
motorway (n)
passport (n)
sightseeing (n)
take off (v)
take-off (n)
traffic jam (n)
travel (n)/(v)
trip (n)

09
HOBBIES AND INTERESTS

battery (n)
collecting key rings (n)
cooking (n)
doing drama (n)
glue (n)
ingredients (n)
keeping fit (n)
making jewellery (n)
making models (n)
online gaming (n)
paintbrush (n)
practising a musical instrument (n)
recipe (n)
taking photos (n)
zoom lens (n)

COLLOCATIONS

be into photography/making models
be mad about cooking/keeping fit
chill out with friends/at home/at the beach
hang out with friends/other football fans/my cousins
join in the dancing/the fun

10
SKILLS FOR WORK

impatient (adj)
impossible (adj)
impolite (adj)
incomplete (adj)
incorrect (adj)
inexpensive (adj)
unfriendly (adj)
untidy (adj)
unusual (adj)

COLLOCATIONS

always do (my/you/his/her/their) best
be a good team player
be creative
enjoy a challenge
make money
pick up new skills quickly
run a business
speak (my/you/his/her/their) mind
stay calm under pressure
work on (my/you/his/her/their) own

11
NATURAL WORLD

avalanche (n)
cliff (n)
cloud (n)
mist (n)
moon (n)
path (n)
rock (n)
sand (n)
soil (n)
star (n)
storm (n)
sunshine (n)
waterfall (n)
wave (n)

12
DESCRIBING EXPERIENCES

challenging (adj)
embarrassing (adj)
exhausting (adj)
fun (adj)
life-changing (adj)
motivating (adj)
positive (adj)
relaxing (adj)
tough (adj)

PHRASAL VERBS

find out
give up
keep on
sort out
take part in
take place
take up
turn into

STUDENT A

Unit 1

You and Student B are going to ask and answer questions to complete a form.

1 Ask Student B for the information to complete the form.
2 Imagine you are your favourite actor or pop star. Answer Student B's questions.

Interview with a star!

First name:
Surname:
Nickname:
Town/city:
Famous for:

Unit 3

Take it in turns to read one statement about the future and discuss it with Student B.

Your statements:

1 No one will have a TV in their house.

2 We won't use pens or write on paper.

3 Children won't go to school. They will have online lessons from their home.

Unit 5

Take it in turns to talk about a photo. Look at Photo A. Use these questions to help you prepare what to say.

1 Who is in the photo?
2 Where are they?
3 What are they wearing?
4 What are they doing?
5 How are they feeling?
6 What do you think about this activity?

A

You begin. Talk about Photo A.

Now listen to Student B. Do they talk about these things?

activity clothes feelings
person/people place

Unit 6

You borrowed Student B's camera for a school trip yesterday. You've left it at home. Say sorry and explain why. Suggest a solution to the problem.

I've got something to tell you. I didn't mean to, but …

Now listen to Student B. They went to the cinema last night and didn't invite you. Listen to what they say and respond.

Unit 7

You're deciding what to do at the weekend with Student B. Use this information.

You want to:
watch a film with friends on Friday
play tennis on Saturday
practise with your rock band
buy a present for a friend's birthday

You don't want to:
stay out late
watch football on TV on Sunday

Take it in turns to make suggestions and respond. Find two things that you can do together. You begin.

Let's watch a film with friends on Friday.

Unit 10

Take it in turns to talk about a photo. Remember to describe the clothes, appearance or actions of the people. If you don't know the name of something, try to describe the size, colour and shape of it. You begin.

A

Verb list

VERB	PAST SIMPLE	PAST PARTICIPLE
be	was/were	been
become	became	become
begin	began	begun
bring	brought	brought
build	built	built
buy	bought	bought
catch	caught	caught
choose	chose	chosen
come	came	come
cost	cost	cost
cut	cut	cut
do	did	done
draw	drew	drawn
drink	drank	drunk
drive	drove	driven
eat	ate	eaten
fall	fell	fallen
feed	fed	fed
feel	felt	felt
fight	fought	fought
find	found	found
fly	flew	flown
forget	forgot	forgotten
get	got	got
give	gave	given
go	went	gone/been
have	had	had
hear	heard	heard
keep	kept	kept
know	knew	known
learn	learned/learnt	learned/learnt
leave	left	left
let	let	let
lose	lost	lost

VERB	PAST SIMPLE	PAST PARTICIPLE
make	made	made
mean	meant	meant
meet	met	met
pay	paid	paid
put	put	put
read	read	read
ride	rode	ridden
ring	rang	rung
run	ran	run
say	said	said
see	saw	seen
sell	sold	sold
send	sent	sent
show	showed	shown
shut	shut	shut
sit	sat	sat
sleep	slept	slept
speak	spoke	spoken
spend	spent	spent
stand	stood	stood
steal	stole	stolen
swim	swam	swum
take	took	taken
teach	taught	taught
tell	told	told
think	thought	thought
understand	understood	understood
wake	woke	woken
wear	wore	worn
win	won	won
write	wrote	written

Unit 1

Present simple

Positive

I/We/You/They	dance.
He/She/It	dance**s**.

Negative

I/We/You/They	**don't** dance.
He/She/It	**doesn't** dance.

Questions

Do	I/we/you/they	dance?
Does	he/she/it	

Short answers

Yes,	I/we/you/they	**do**.
	he/she/it	**does**.
No,	I/we/you/they	**don't**.
	he/she/it	**doesn't**.

We use the present simple to talk about:

- permanent states
  *She **lives** in Spain.*
- habits or repeated actions
  *He **sees** his friends most weekends.*

Present continuous

Positive

I	**'m**	work**ing**.
He/She/It	**'s**	
We/You/They	**'re**	

Negative

I	**'m not**	work**ing**.
He/She/It	**isn't**	
We/You/They	**aren't**	

Questions

Am	I	work**ing**?
Is	he/she/it	
Are	we/you/they	

Short answers

Yes,	I	**am**.
	he/she/it	**is**.
	we/you/they	**are**.
No,	I	**'m not**.
	he/she/it	**isn't**.
	we/you/they	**aren't**.

Look at the spelling changes:
put – pu**tt**ing, tak**e** – tak**ing**
We use the present continuous to talk about:

- actions that are happening now.
  *She**'s talking** to the teacher.*
- actions that are happening around now.
  *We**'re studying** ancient Greece at school.*

State verbs

We don't usually use state verbs in the continuous form. State verbs describe states not actions:

- verbs of being and owning, e.g. *be, have, own*
- verbs of feeling or wanting, e.g. *hate, like, love, need, prefer, want, wish*
- verbs of thinking, e.g. *agree, believe, know, remember, think, understand*
- verbs that describe the senses, e.g. *feel, hear, smell, see, taste*

We use some state verbs in the continuous form when we describe actions.
*We**'re having** lunch at the moment. (having = eating)*
*I**'m thinking** about my answer. (thinking = considering)*
*I**'m seeing** my friend tonight. (seeing = meeting)*

Time expressions and adverbs of frequency

We use adverbs of frequency to say how often something happens.

100% ↑ always
usually
frequently/often
sometimes/occasionally
rarely/hardly ever
0% never

Adverbs of frequency come before main verbs, but after the verb *be*.
*I **never** go swimming in the winter.*
*Mark is **always** happy.*

Other time expressions usually go at the end of a sentence.
*We go to the cinema **twice a month**.*

Unit 2

Past simple

The verb *be*

Positive

I/He/She/It	**was**.
We/You/They	**were**.

Negative

I/He/She/It	**wasn't**.
We/You/They	**weren't**.

Questions

Was	I/he/she/it	the best?
Were	we/you/they	helpful?

Short answers

Yes,	I/he/she/it	**was**.
	we/you/they	**were**.
No,	I/he/she/it	**wasn't**.
	we/you/they	**weren't**.

Regular and irregular verbs

Positive

I/He/She/It/We/You/They	**helped** at the event.
I/He/She/It/We/You/They	**went** to the event.

Negative

I/He/She/It/We/You/They	**didn't help** at the event.
I/He/She/It/We/You/They	**didn't go** to the event.

Questions

Did	I/he/she/it/we/you/they	**help** at the event?
Did	I/he/she/it/we/you/they	**go** to the event?

Short answers

Yes,	I/he/she/it/we/you/they	**did**.
No,	I/he/she/it/we/you/they	**didn't**.

Look at the spelling changes:
help – help**ed**, practis**e** – practis**ed**, stud**y** – stud**ied**, cho**p** – cho**pped**

We use the past simple to talk about:

- an action that started and finished in the past.
  *Lisa **finished** the game.*
- one completed past action after another.
  *They **went** home and **had** a drink and a snack.*
- a past habit or regular past event.
  *Tom and Rachel **swam** in the sea every day on holiday.*

Past continuous

Positive

I/He/She/It	**was**	wait**ing**.
We/You/They	**were**	

Negative

I/He/She/It	**wasn't**	wait**ing**.
We/You/They	**weren't**	

Questions

Was	I/he/she/it	waiting?
Were	we/you/they	

Short answers

Yes,	I/he/she/it	**was.**
	we/you/they	**were.**
No,	I/he/she/it	**wasn't.**
	we/you/they	**weren't.**

We use the past continuous to:

- talk about an action in progress in the past.
  *I **was playing** on my computer.*
  *We **were eating** our lunch.*
- set the scene in a story.
  *It **was raining**.*
  *They **were watching** TV.*

We use the past simple for an action that interrupts another action in progress in the past (past continuous).
*Ellen **was studying** in Rome when she **met** Marco.*

We can use *while* instead of *when*, but we put *while* before the past continuous verb.
*Dan found his watch **while** he **was tidying** his room.*

Unit 3

will

Positive

I/He/She/It/We/You/They	**will**	win.

Negative

I/He/She/It/We/You/They	**won't**	win.

Questions

Will	I/he/she/it/we/you/they	win?

Short answers

Yes,	I/he/she/it/we/you/they	**will.**
No,	I/he/she/it/we/you/they	**won't.**

We use *will*:

- to talk about things we think are going to happen, based on our personal opinion.
  *Perhaps we **will use** e-books for all our studies in the future.*
- to make offers.
  *I'**ll help** you with your homework.*
- for unplanned decisions that we make at the time we are speaking.
  *I feel tired. I think I'**ll go** home now.*

going to

Positive

I	**'m (am)**	**going to**	leave.
He/She/It	**'s (is)**		
We/You/They	**'re (are)**		

Negative

I	**'m (am) not**	**going to**	leave.
He/She/It	**isn't (is not)**		
We/You/They	**aren't (are not)**		

Questions

Am	I	**going to**	leave?
Is	he/she/it		
Are	we/you/they		

Short answers

Yes,	I	**am.**
	he/she/it	**is.**
	we/you/they	**are.**
No,	I	**'m not.**
	he/she/it	**isn't.**
	we/you/they	**aren't.**

We use *going to* to talk about:

- plans.
  *I'**m going to visit** my friend in Turkey in June.*
- things that we expect to happen because of something we know now.
  *It's **going to rain** soon. (There are big grey clouds.)*

Indefinite pronouns

For people:	someone	anyone	everyone	no one
For things:	something	anything	everything	nothing

We use indefinite pronouns to talk about a person or a thing when we don't know who/what it is, or it is not important.

We use *something* and *someone* in positive sentences.
I can smell ***something*** *nice.*
I can see ***someone*** *at the window.*

We use *anything* and *anyone* in negative sentences and questions.
Karen doesn't know ***anyone*** *here.*
Do you want ***anything*** *from the shops?*

We use *everything* and *everyone* in positive and negative sentences, and in questions.
Everyone *is in the kitchen.*
Have you got ***everything*** *for the picnic?*

We use *nothing* and *no one* in positive sentences to mean 'not anything' and 'not anyone'.
There's ***nothing*** *in my bag.*
No one *is sitting in this seat.*

For people, we can also use *somebody, anybody, everybody* and *nobody.*

Unit 4

Comparative and superlative adjectives

Use *as* + adjective + *as* to compare two people or things that are equal.
Kirsty is ***as tall as*** *her sister.*

Use *not as* + adjective + *as* to compare two people or things that are not equal.
*Football is**n't as** dangerous **as** skiing.*

We can also use adjective *-er* + *than* or *more* + adjective + *than* to compare two people or things that are not equal.
Did Alex get a ***better*** *mark in maths* ***than*** *Sophie?*
I was ***more tired than*** *you after the tennis match.*

Type of adjective	Comparative/Superlative
most one syllable	+ *-er* → *fast**er**/* + *-est* → *the fast**est***
one syllable ending in *-e*	+ *-r* → *nice**r**/* + *-st* → *the nice**st***
one syllable ending in one vowel and one consonant	double the consonant + *-er* → *big**ger**/* double the consonant + *-est* → *the big**gest***
one or two syllables ending in *-y*	change *-y* to *-ier* → *happ**ier**/* take away *-y* and + *-iest* → *the happ**iest***
two or more syllables	*more* + adjective → ***more*** *interested/* *the most* + adjective → *the* ***most*** *interesting*
irregular, e.g. *good, bad, far*	*better, worse, further/farther/ the best, the worst, the farthest/ the furthest*

To compare three or more things, use superlatives with *the -est/the most.*
This is ***the best*** *book I've ever read.*

too/enough

Use *too* + adjective/adverb to mean 'more than necessary'.
*He didn't buy the black jeans because they were t**oo expensive.***
Use adjective/adverb + ***enough*** to mean 'the right amount'.
Is the music ***loud enough****?*
Use ***not*** + adjective/adverb + ***enough*** to mean 'less than necessary'.
*James wasn'**t old enough** to watch the horror film at the cinema.*

Present continuous and present simple for future use

Use the present continuous for plans in the future.
I'm playing *in a football match on Saturday.*
Use the present simple for schedules and timetables
The film ***finishes*** *at 9.30 p.m.*

shall

We use *shall* for suggestions and offers.
Shall *I bring some crisps for the picnic?*
What ***shall*** *we do after school today?*

Unit 5

Present perfect simple

Positive

I/We/You/They	**'ve (have)**	**finished.**
He/She/It	**'s (has)**	

Negative

I/We/You/They	**haven't (have not)**	**finished.**
He/She/It	**hasn't (has not)**	

Questions

Have	I/we/you/they	**finished?**
Has	he/she/it	

Short answers

Yes,	I/we/you/they	**have.**
	he/she/it	**has.**
No,	I/we/you/they	**haven't.**
	he/she/it	**hasn't.**

We use the present perfect simple to talk about:
- something that happened in the past that has a result in the present.
  Robert ***has bought*** *some new trainers.*
- for a situation or an experience in our lives that is still true now.
  I've lived *in this street all my life.*

Present perfect simple with adverbs

We use *ever* in questions and statements to talk about whether an event or experience has/hasn't happened at some point in the past.
Have *you* ***ever*** *lived in the USA?*

We use *never* to talk about something that hasn't happened.
I've never *eaten Japanese food.*

Use *yet* for something we expect to happen.
I ***haven't*** *finished my homework* ***yet****.*

Use *just* for recent events.
I've just *had a text from my friend.*

Use *already* for something that has happened before now.
*We're not hungry because we****'ve already*** *had lunch.*

Remember that we often use *for* and *since* with the present perfect.
I haven't heard *this song* ***for*** *years.* (a period of time)
I've known *Samantha* ***since*** *I was seven.* (a specific time in the past)

Past simple and present perfect simple

Use the past simple for an action that happened at a definite time or date in the past.
I ***joined*** *a chess club a few weeks ago.*

Use the present perfect simple for a past action when we don't know the time or date of the action, or it isn't important.
*We****'ve visited*** *this town before.*

Unit 6

Ability

Positive

I/He/She/It/We/You/They	**can**	**play.**

Negative

I/He/She/It/We/You/They	**can't**	**win.**

Questions

Can	I/he/she/it/we/you/they	**play?**

Short answers

Yes,	I/he/she/it/ we/you/they	**can.**
No,		**can't.**

Can has no future tense. We use *will be able to* to talk about ability in the future.
They ***can watch*** *TV now they have finished their homework. (present)*
They ***will be able to watch*** *TV after they finish their homework. (future)*

Possibility

We use *can* to talk about possibility in the present.
*Where **can** I sit?*
*You **can** do lots of different activities at the sports centre.*

Making a guess

We use *might* or *could* to make a guess about the present or the future.
*You **might** find skateboarding difficult.*
*This horse **could** be too big for you.*

Zero conditional

If clause	main clause
If/When **+ present tense**	**main verb + present tense**
When I **do** my homework quickly,	I often **make** mistakes.

We use *if/when* + present simple + present simple for something that always or usually happens.
***If/when** my cat **sees** a dog, it **runs** away.*
*I **don't go** to school **if/when** I **feel** ill.*

First conditional

If clause	main clause
If **+ present tense**	**will/could/might + infinitive**
If you **like** romantic stories,	you'**ll enjoy** this film.

We use *if* + present simple + *will/might/could* for a possible action in the future.
***If** you **don't understand** your homework, Mark **could help** you with it.*
***If** I **have** time at the weekend, I **might tidy** my room.*

unless

We can use *unless* instead of *if … not*.

*I can't help you **if** you **don't tell** me your problem.*
*I can't help you **unless** you **tell** me your problem.*

***If** he **doesn't pass** his exam, Tom won't be happy.*
***Unless** he **passes** his exam, Tom won't be happy.*

Unit 7

Second conditional

If clause	main clause
If **+ past simple**	***would*** **+ infinitive**
If I became a singer,	I would travel around the world.

We use the second conditional to talk about:

- imaginary or unreal situations in the present.
  ***If** I **were** a good singer, I **would be** in a famous pop group.*
- present or future situations that are possible, but not likely.
  ***If** I **won** lots of money, I'**d buy** more musical instruments for my school.*
- for giving advice.
  ***If** I **were** you, I'**d have** extra music lessons.*

Subject questions

***Who called** you?*
***What happened** at the party?*

When *who* or *what* is the subject of the question, there is no auxiliary verb and the word order is the same as the statement.
***Who** called you? **Sam** called you.* (*Sam* is the subject)

Object questions

***Who did** you **call**?*
***What did** you **watch**?*

When *who* or *what* is the object of the question, we use an auxiliary verb before the subject.
***What did** you **watch**? I watched **a concert**.* (*a concert* is the object)

Unit 8

Defining relative clauses

That's the girl	**who/that**	wants to be a pilot.
The train	**which/that**	leaves in ten minutes is full.

We use defining relative clauses to describe exactly which people, things or animals we mean.
We use:

- *who* or *that* for people.
- *which* or *that* for things/animals.

Defining relative clauses can give us information about the subject or the object of the main clause. We often use them to join two sentences.

***A girl** found my passport.* (a girl is the subject)
She was very nice.
*The girl **who found** my passport was very nice.*

I met a girl yesterday. (a girl is the object)
She speaks four languages.
*The girl **who I met** yesterday speaks four languages.*

We can leave out the relative pronoun when it is the object of the relative clause.
*The girl **I met** yesterday speaks four languages.*

We don't use commas in defining relative clauses.

must/have to/had to/will have to

Present

must	*I **must** get a new passport.* *You **mustn't** use a mobile phone on the plane.*
have to	*We **have to** collect the tickets from the station.* *They **don't have to** leave now.* *It **has to** stay here.* *She **doesn't have to** stay here.* ***Do** we **have to** go now?* ***Does** he **have to** be here?*

Past

had to	*I was late so I **had to** run to the bus stop.* *We **didn't have to** walk because the bus came.* ***Did** you **have to** buy another ticket?*

Future

will have to	*We'll **have to** go home soon.* *You **won't have to** talk to him again.* ***Will** she **have to** find a different flight?*

We use *must* when we think it is very important or necessary to do something.
*I **must** buy a new bag for the journey.*

We use *mustn't* + infinitive when it's important or necessary not to do something, or when something is prohibited.
*You **mustn't** tell him about the party.*

We use *have to* + infinitive to talk about something that is important or necessary, often because it's a general rule.
*All passengers **have to** show their passports before they get on the plane.*

We use *don't have to* + infinitive to talk about something that isn't necessary, or when there is no obligation
*You **don't have to** sit there if you don't want to.*

We use *had to* to talk about obligation in the past.
*I **had to** buy another ticket.*

We use *will have to* to talk about obligation in the future.
*You'**ll have to** take the bus to the airport.*

Unit 9

Reported speech

Direct speech	Reported speech
'I **study** photos of the sky.'	Liam said (that) he **studied** photos of the sky.
'I **can** see it.'	Elena said (that) she **could** see it.
'I **will** do it again.'	Nathan said (that) he **would** do it again.

We use reported speech to tell somebody else what a person said.
*Max said (that) he **looked** at the stars every night.*
In reported speech:

- the main verb usually moves back one tense into the past.
  *She said, 'I **want** to be a dancer.'*
  *She said (that) she **wanted** to be a dancer.*
- *can* changes to *could* and *will* changes to *would*.
  He said, 'I'll bring a cake.'
  *He said (that) he **would** bring a cake.*

We change subject pronouns, e.g. *I, you, he, she*, possessive pronouns, e.g. *mine, yours, his, hers* and possessive adjectives, e.g. *my, your, his, her*, so that it's clear who or what they refer to.
*Sandra said, '**My** hobby is collecting shells.'*
*Sandra said (that) **her** hobby was collecting shells.*

We use *say* when reporting what somebody has said.
Luke said, 'I don't do drama in the summer.'
*Luke **said** (that) he didn't do drama in the summer.*

We can use *tell* when we know who somebody is talking to.
Luke told Anna, 'I love making models.'
*Luke **told** Anna (that) he loved making models.*

Grammar file

used to

Positive

I/You/He/She/It/ We/They/You	**used to**	collect comics.

Negative

I/You/He/She/It/We/ They/You	**didn't use to**	have any hobbies.

Questions

Did	I/you/he/she/it/ we/they/you	**use to**	have any hobbies?

We use *used to* + infinitive to talk about something that happened regularly in the past, but does not happen now.
*He **used to** enjoy drama at school, but he doesn't do it now.*
*I **didn't use to** watch horror films, but I like them now.*
*You speak French well. **Did** you **use to** live in France?*

Unit 10

to + infinitive and the *-ing* form

We use *to* + infinitive:

- after certain verbs: *agree, allow, arrange, ask, choose, decide, forget, help, hope, learn, offer, plan, prepare, promise, start, try, want.*
  *Chloe **hopes to work** with children this summer.*
  *Jack **wanted to work** in his mum's café.*

We can put an object:

- before the infinitive after some verbs: *ask, help, need, teach, want.*
  *I asked **Paul** to leave a message.*
  *We helped **them** to find a volunteer job.*
- after some adjectives: *easy, difficult, happy, important, possible.*
  *It's **important to find** a job that you like.*

We use the *-ing* form:

- after some verbs: *begin, continue, enjoy, finish, hate, like, love, imagine, practise, remember, start, stop, suggest.*
  *I **enjoyed working** in the summer.*
  *George **loves running** the family business.*
- after some phrases with prepositions: *bad/good at, bored with, interested in, tired of.*
  *He's **interested in learning** new skills.*
- after certain expressions: *can't stand, don't mind, look forward to.*
  *Olivia **can't stand working** on her own.*

We don't use the *-ing* form after *would like/would love/would prefer.*

We can use the *-ing* form or *to* + infinitive after *like, love, prefer, start.* The meaning is the same.
*I **like working** with my dad.*
*I **like to work** with my dad.*

Indirect questions

Direct question	Indirect question
'**What is** a supernova?'	'Could you tell me **what** a supernova **is**?'

In indirect questions with *is/are*, the verb comes after the subject.

Direct question	Indirect question
'**Where do** you **work**?'	'Can you tell us **where** you **work**?'
'**Why do** you **enjoy** your job?'	'Can I ask **why** you **enjoy** your job?'

Indirect questions don't use the auxiliary verbs *do/does/did.*

Indirect questions + *if*

Direct question	Indirect question
'**Is it** a difficult job?'	'Do you know **if it's** a difficult job?'
'**Are they** happy?'	'Do you know **if they are** happy?'

We use *if* when the direct questions is a *Yes* or *No* question.
We use indirect questions in more formal or polite situations.

Unit 11

Present simple passive

subject + ***be***	+ past participle + ***(by)***
am/is/are *am not/isn't/aren't*	*built, cleaned, destroyed, done, found, used,* etc.

*The river **is cleaned** every year.*

Past simple passive

subject + ***be***	+ past participle + ***(by)***
was/were *wasn't/weren't*	*built, cleaned, destroyed, done, found, used,* etc.

*The trees **were destroyed by** the fire.*

We use the present simple passive or past simple passive:

- when the action is more important than the person.
  *The old clothes **are recycled**.*
- in more formal writing, e.g. a report.
  *The waterfall **is visited** by hundreds of people every day.*
- when we don't know, or can't say, who does or did the action.
  *The film **was watched** around the world.*
- When we know who does or did the action, we use *by*.
  *The island was discovered **by** a famous scientist.*

Some verbs aren't used in passive sentences, e.g. *come, go, happen, walk.*

could/should

We use *could* + infinitive:

- to make a suggestion when different options are possible.
  *We **could go** by train to the beach.*
- to make a suggestion when you aren't sure the other person will agree.
  *We **could swim** across the river.*

We use *should* + infinitive to ask for advice.
*Do you think I **should try** something different?*
***Should** I **try** something different?*

We use *should/shouldn't* + infinitive to give strong advice, when you think something is a good or bad idea.
*You **shouldn't go** camping without warm clothes.*

Unit 12

Past perfect simple

Positive

I/You/He/She/It/We/They/You	**'d (had)**	**finished**.

Negative

I/You/He/She/It/We/They/You	**hadn't (had not)**	**finished**.

Questions

Had	I/you/he/she/it/we/they/you	**finished?**

Short answers

Yes,	I/you/he/she/it/we/they/you	**had**.
No,		**hadn't**.

We use the past perfect simple to talk about something that was completed in an earlier past.
*He **had made** all the food for the party.*

We use the past perfect simple with the past simple to show that one action happened before another in the past. The past perfect simple describes the first action, and the past simple describes the second action.

past ______________ x ______________ x ____________ now

*The party **had finished*** — *when Ben **arrived**.*

(First, the party finished. Then, Ben arrived.)
We can also say: *When Ben **arrived**, the party **had finished**.*
We use many of the same **time expressions** that with use with the past perfect simple: *after, by, before, ever, just, never, until, when.*

***After** they **had seen** the concert, they **went** to bed.*

have/get something *done*

have/get	+ **object**	+ **past participle**
		cut, made, repaired, taken, etc.

*I **have** my hair **cut** at Headlines.*
*We **get** our photos **taken** at school today.*

We use *have/get* something *done* when somebody else is doing something for us. We often use *get something done* when we are talking.

Pairwork file

STUDENT B

Unit 1

You and Student A are going to ask and answer questions to complete a form.

1 Imagine you are your favourite actor or pop star. Answer Student A's questions.
2 Ask Student A for the information to complete the form.

Interview with a star!

First name:
Surname:
Nickname:
Town/city:
Famous for:

Unit 3

Take it in turns to read one statement about the future and discuss it with Student A.

Your statements:

1 There won't be any cinemas.

2 Every family will have a robot.

3 All restaurants will have a place to plug in your headphones.

Unit 5

Take it in turns to talk about a photo. Look at Photo B. Use these questions to help you prepare what to say.

1 Who is in the photo?
2 Where are they?
3 What are they wearing?
4 What are they doing?
5 How are they feeling?
6 What do you think about this activity?

Student A begins. Listen to Student A. Do they talk about these things?

activity clothes feelings person/people place

Now talk about Photo B.

Unit 6

Listen to Student A. They borrowed your camera for a school trip yesterday, but they've left it at home. You need it now. Explain why you need it.

I need it for my art homework.

Now tell Student A that you went to the cinema last night, but didn't invite them. Explain that you phoned them, but they weren't at home.

I'm really sorry …

Unit 7

You're deciding what to do at the weekend with Student A. Use this information.

You want to:
go out on Friday
play tennis
practise with your rock band
watch football on TV on Sunday

You don't want to:
stay at home on Friday
go shopping

Take it in turns to make suggestions and respond. Find two things that you can do together. Student A begins. Listen and respond.

It's a nice idea, but perhaps we could watch a film on Sunday. What about going out on Friday?

Unit 10

Take it in turns to talk about a photo. Remember to describe the clothes, appearance or actions of the people. If you don't know the name of something, try to describe the size, colour and shape of it. Student A begins.

Pearson Education Limited
Edinburgh Gate
Harlow
Essex CM20 2JE
England
and Associated Companies throughout the world.

www.pearsonelt.com

© Pearson Education Limited 2014

The right of Carolyn Barraclough and Suzanne Gaynor to be identified as authors of this Work has been asserted by them in accordance with the Copyright, Designs and Patents Act 1988.

All rights reserved; no part of this publication may be reproduced, stored in a retrieval system, or transmitted in any form or by any means, electronic, mechanical, photocopying, recording, or otherwise without the prior written permission of the Publishers

First published 2014
Seventh impression 2018

ISBN: 978-1-4479-6192-5 (Student's Book with MultiROM)
ISBN: 978-1-4479-6193-2 (Student's Book with MyEnglishLab)

Set in 10pt Mixage ITC Std
Printed by Neografia, Slovakia

Acknowledgements
The publishers and author would like to thank the following people for their feedback and comments during the development of the material:

Elif Berk, Turkey; Alan Del Castillo Castellanos, Mexico; Dilek Kokler, Turkey; Trevor Lewis, The Netherlands; Nancy Ramirez, Mexico; Jacqueline Van Mil-Walker, The Netherlands

The publisher would like to thank the following for their kind permission to reproduce their photographs:

(Key: b-bottom; c-centre; l-left; r-right; t-top)

Alamy Images: Adrian Sherratt 50cl, Blend Images 34t/1b, Craig Joiner Photography 90cr, David Pearson 76cl, Derek Traskinv Ltd 71b, E. Westmacott 68tc, geodigital 30bl/3 (5a), Geoffrey Robinson 143br, Moodboard 26cl, Rebecca Wright 142bc, Stuart Pearce 112br, Dimitar Todorov 87; **Bridgeman Art Library Ltd:** De Agostini Picture Library 92, Self portrait by Henri Gaudier -Brzeska 1913 / Southampton Art Gallery, Hampshire, UK 92 (a); **Corbis:** Andrew Fox 130bc, Antenna / Fstop 68cl, Bloomimage 48tl, Franz-Peter Tschauner 45br/4f, I Love Images 52bl/1c, Issei Kato / Reuters 31tr/5, James L. Amos 88tr/1a, Laurence Mouton / PhotoAlto 22tr, 55tr, Ocean 66l/3 (1c), Raymond Patrick / National Geographic Society 17bl, Splash News 56tl; **Creatas:** 26cr; **DK Images:** Ruth Jenkinson 110tl/1c, William Shaw 9cr; **Fotolia.com:** araraadt 84tr/5b, Avava 11cl, contrastwerkstatt 59, David Hughes 8cl, Dmitry Vereshchagin 66l/3 (2b), Elnur 66l/3 (2c), emicristea 8bl, F / 2.8 by ARC 84bl/4 (2c), Farah-Diba 53br, Gina Smith 88c/1c, goodluz 17cr, 125tl, Grasko 88cr/1d, hotshotsworldwide 71tl, hurricane 12cl, Indigofish 44l/3b, industrieblick 45cl/4c, Ivonne Wierink 26b, Jelena Ivanovic 85br/5, Jorg Hackerman 70cl, Kayann 70br, lassedesignen 28cl, Lisa F. Young 110tl/1a, lunamarina 19tr, makuromi 89l, Nikolai Sorokin 88cl/1b, noomhh 50bl, nyul 70bc, paolese 106-107b, raywoo 30bl/3 (3c), Riccardo Piccinni 76tr, ronstik 95, Sabphoto 53tr, Ian Scott 41, Sto 35t, stockyimages 6tr, tomispin 30bl/3 (5b), wavebreakmediamicro 26t, Werner Fellman 30bl/3 (2a), wolfelarry 30bl/3 (1a), Zap Ichigo 7tr; **Getty Images:** AFP 9tr, 69, Alexander Hassenstein 93br, Timothy Allen 98-99, 99tr, Bloomberg 45t/4b, Dave Etheridge-Barnes 50tl, Dave Kotinsky 73c, Felix Rioux / Lonely Planet Images 80tl, Getty Images for Fox 68tl, Glow Images 14cr, Jack Hollingsworth / Photodisc 49cl, Jeff J Mitchell 63bl, 131br, Koichi Kamoshida 31c/5, Michael Steele 93cr, Paul Lewis / AFP 93tl, Reinhard Dirscheri / Waterframe RM 104-105br, Sarah Salmela 106bl, Washington Post 38br; **Imagestate Media:** John Foxx Collection 84bl/4 (3c); **Masterfile UK Ltd:** 110tl/1b; nisyndication.com: Richard Morrison 62t; **Andrew Oliver:** 32-33t, 32-33c, 33b, 33bl, 37br, 40c, 41cl, 58b; **Pearson Education Ltd:** 15, 30bl/3 (3a), 30bl/3 (3b), 33, 51, 77, 113, Gareth Boden 12c, 34t/1a, 66l/3 (6c), Jon Barlow 13tc, Jules Selmes 13tr, MindStudio 44l/3A, Sophie Bluy 11cr; **Photolibrary.com:** Mike Kemp / Rubberball 20br; **Rex Features:** 89r, Keystone USA / Zuma 80cl, Sipa Press 80c; **Shutterstock.com:** Ammit Jack 120tl/1a, Andreas Gradin 84tr/4b, Anneka 106tr, Andrey Bayda 23, Debbie Wong 14t, Denis Radovanovic 44cr/4d, Efired 105, Elena Dijour 67bc, Featureflash 86c, Gemenacom 126c, IgorXIII 71tr, Lilu2005 67cl, Patryk Kosminder 29tr, pjhpix 67t, Royster 35b, Ryanking999 66l/3 (2a), s_bukley 86tr, 86cl, 86bc, S1001 30bl/3 (1c), 30bl/3 (1b), Sakala 44tr/4a, Tumar 98tl/1a; **Kat Sykes:** 92 (c); **The Kobal Collection:** New Line Cinema 68bl; **Veer/Corbis:** Alexander Podshivalov 44bl/4e, Andreas Karelias 70bl, Artur Gabrysiak 66l/3 (1a), chrupka 84tr/5a, cynoclub 84tr/4c, Deklofenak 120cl, edbockstock 80bl, elenathewise 14c, Eugeny Kostsov 84tr/5c, Garry 85bl, geotrac 30bl/3 (4c), graja 30bl/3 (4c), Hit Toon 98tl/1b, homestudio 84bl/4 (2b), jgroupstudios 85cr/5, jirkaejc 26tl, Johan Swanepoel 98tl/1c, jspm 14tr/1, keeweeboy 84bl/4 (3b), kingjon 28bc/D, Lars Hallstrom 44l/3d, leaf 14tr/2, leonido 28tr/B, leungchopan 8tl, Mangostock 125cl, Mikhail Dudarev 30bl/3 (4b), Monkey Business Images 34t/1c, 52cl/1b, 66l/3 (6a), 70c, nickp37 6tl, 34t/1d, olly 52tl/1a, Pakhnyushchyy Vitaliy 26bl, 84bl/4 (2a), Patrick Lane 8tr, 44l/3c, Paul Inkles 84bl/4 (3a), PeJo29 86tc, piai 30bl/3 (2c), Piotr Pawinski 28l/C, popovaphoto 85t, PT Images 66l/3 (6b), robertsrob 30bl/3 (2b), Rui Vale de Sousa 30bl/3 (5c), Salladart 8-9bc, shell114 28br/E, Sheval 28tl/A, stevanovicigor 86tl, Svetlana Gryankina 66l/3 (1b), VadiCo 84tr/4a, vkraskouski 6tc

We are grateful to the following for permission to reproduce copyright material:

Text
Extract Unit 7.6 after Olympic festival 2012: Little voice in the Big Noise orchestra - audio slideshow, *The Guardian*, http://www.guardian.co.uk/music/audioslideshow/2012/jun/20/olympic-2012-big-noise-orchestra-audio-slideshow, With kind permission of Guardian News and Media Ltd 2012; Interview on page 92 adapted from Kat Sykes author interview, With kind permission from Kat Sykes

Cover images: *Front:* **Fotolia.com:** Alexander Yakovlev

All other images © Pearson Education

Every effort has been made to trace the copyright holders and we apologise in advance for any unintentional omissions. We would be pleased to insert the appropriate acknowledgement in any subsequent edition of this publication.

NATIONAL GEOGRAPHIC LEARNING | CENGAGE Learning

Life

5

CB080296

Paul Dummett
John Hughes
Helen Stephenson

NATIONAL GEOGRAPHIC LEARNING | CENGAGE Learning

Life Level 5 Student Book

Paul Dummett

John Hughes

Helen Stephenson

Publisher: Sherrise Roehr

Executive Editor: Sarah T. Kenney

Editorial Assistant: Patricia Giunta

Director of Global Marketing: Ian Martin

Senior Product Marketing Manager: Caitlin Thomas

Director of Content and Media Production: Michael Burggren

Production Manager: Daisy Sosa

Senior Print Buyer: Mary Beth Hennebury

Cover Designers: Scott Baker and Alex Dull

Cover Image: © Steve Bloom Images / Alamy

Compositor: MPS Limited

Cover Image

A male panther chameleon stalking prey in beach-side vegetation, Bay of Antongil, Masoala Peninsula National Park, Madagascar.

© 2015 National Geographic Learning, a part of Cengage Learning

ALL RIGHTS RESERVED. No part of this work covered by the copyright herein may be reproduced, transmitted, stored, or used in any form or by any means graphic, electronic, or mechanical, including but not limited to photocopying, recording, scanning, digitizing, taping, Web distribution, information networks, or information storage and retrieval systems, except as permitted under Section 107 or 108 of the 1976 United States Copyright Act, or applicable copyright law of another jurisdiction, without the prior written permission of the publisher.

For permission to use material from this text or product, submit all requests online at **www.cengage.com/permissions**
Further permissions questions can be emailed to **permissionrequest@cengage.com**

Student Book
ISBN-13: 978-1-305-25630-9

Student Book + CD-ROM
ISBN-13: 978-1-305-25634-7

Student Book + Online Workbook
ISBN-13: 978-1-305-26039-9

National Geographic Learning/Cengage Learning
20 Channel Center Street
Boston, MA 02210
USA

Cengage Learning is a leading provider of customized learning solutions with office locations around the globe, including Singapore, the United Kingdom, Australia, Mexico, Brazil, and Japan.

Cengage Learning products are represented in Canada by Nelson Education, Ltd.

Visit National Geographic Learning online at **ngl.cengage.com**
Visit our corporate website at **www.cengage.com**

Printed in the United States of America
6 7 8 9 10 21 20 19 18

UNIT 1
RELATIONSHIPS
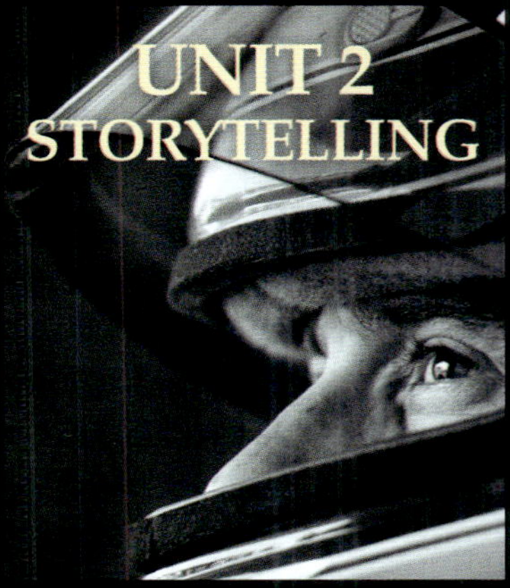
UNIT 2
STORYTELLING

UNIT 3
SCIENCE AND TECHNOLOGY

UNIT 4
ART AND CREATIVITY

UNIT 5
DEVELOPMENT

UNIT 6
ALTERNATIVE TRAVEL

UNIT 7
NATURAL RESOURCES

UNIT 8
THE NEWS

UNIT 9
TALENTED PEOPLE

UNIT 10
CUSTOMS AND BEHAVIOR

UNIT 11
KNOWLEDGE AND LEARNING

UNIT 12
THE ECONOMY

Contents

LISTENING	READING	CRITICAL THINKING	SPEAKING	WRITING
part of a radio show about animal friendships	an article about changing attitudes in China an article about immigrant families in New York	identifying the main theme	your friends the generation gap family influences	text type: an informal email (1) writing skill: greetings and endings
an interview with a film critic	a true story about dangerous animals an article about the brothers Grimm	close reading	the movie of the book a famous writer or filmmaker narrow escapes storytelling	text type: a story writing skill: using descriptive words
a presentation about overpopulation	an article about augmented reality an article about appropriate technology	balancing arguments	global problems overpopulation information age predictions technological solutions	text type: short email requests writing skill: being polite
part of a radio show about what's on in Melbourne an artist's opinion about what art is	an article about unusual street art an article about the origins of rap	analyzing contrasts	participation in the arts an art competition music and values	text type: an online review writing skill: personalizing your writing
an interview with a reporter about social development in southern India	an article about urban development in Dubai an article about a hydroelectric dam in Laos	fact or opinion	changes in your town a happy society sensitive development evaluating a development project	text type: an opinion essay writing skill: linking words
an interview about volunteer vacations	a blog about vacations at home part of a travel magazine article on unusual hotels	claims and justifications	local knowledge planning a staycation opinions about travel ideas for an unusual hotel	text type: a letter of complaint writing skill: formal language

LISTENING	READING	CRITICAL THINKING	SPEAKING	WRITING
four people talking about saving water	an article about Ecuador's plan to protect resources an article about Madagascar's unique ecology	emotive language	how we use water conservation wishes	text type: a letter to the editor writing skill: giving vivid examples
four feel-good news stories	an article about an iconic image an article about the power of the press	different perspectives	the ethics of taking photographs feel-good news stories reputations	text type: minutes from a meeting writing skill: impersonal language
an interview about Emerging Explorers	an article about an extraordinary career an article about a woman who was king	weighing the evidence	a career path personal qualities women at work	text type: an online profile writing skill: writing in note form
part of a radio show about a tribe with an unusual diet	an article about the "tiger mother" approach to parenting an article about body language	sources	typical behavior food and eating habits customs in your country wedding traditions	text type: an informal email (2) writing skill: elision in informal writing
a talk by a psychologist on memory	an article about an ethnobotanist an article about a parrot	reinforcing ideas	acquiring knowledge memory tests why you forgot types of learners	text type: an email about a misunderstanding writing skill: linking contrasting ideas
an interview with the author of *The Servant Economy*	an article about Norway's riches an article about an alternative economic model	signposts to key information	the economy in your country getting things done gift giving and exchange	text type: a report writing skill: subheadings and bullet points

Life around the world

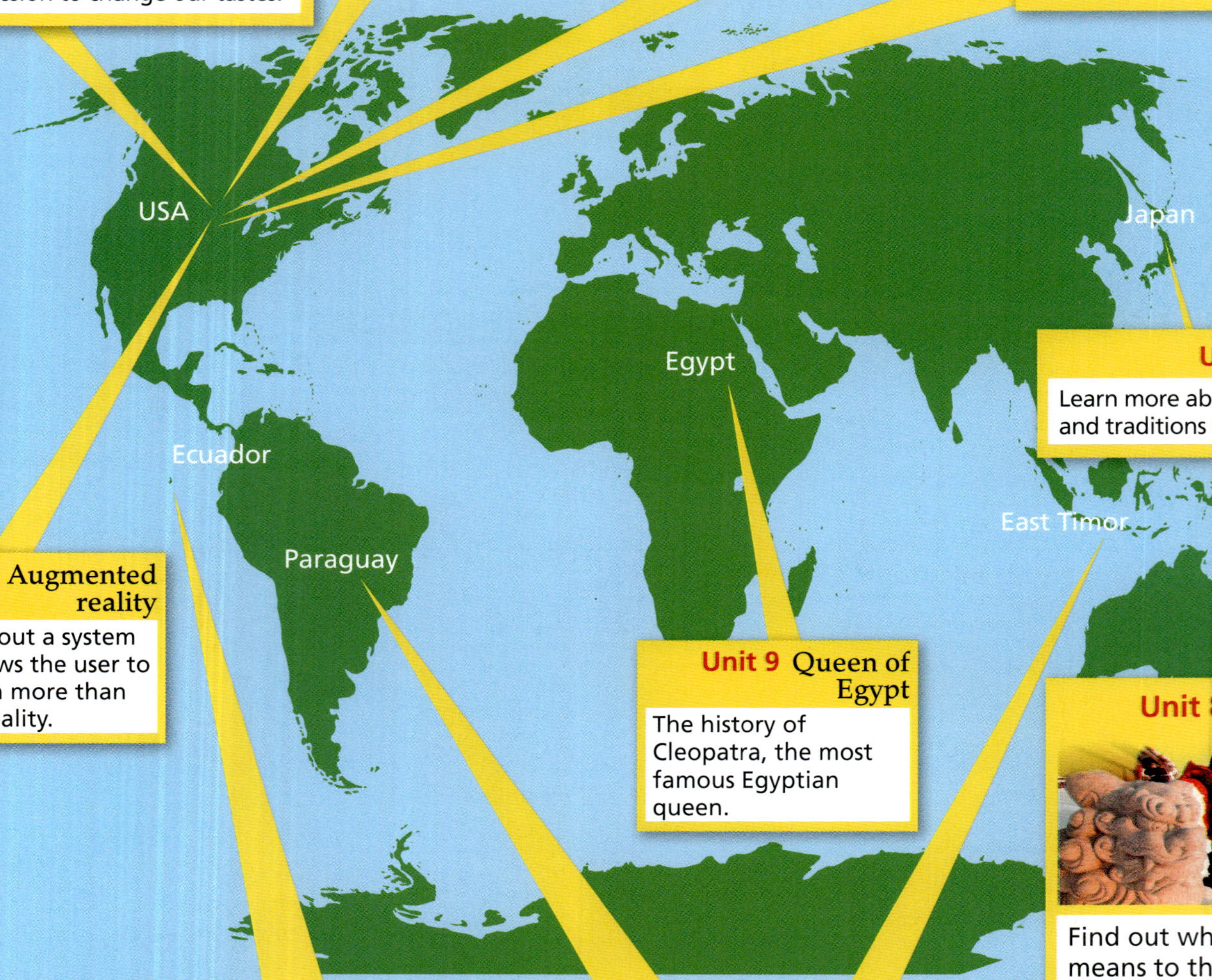

Unit 10 Eating insects

Discover why eating insects could be good for you, and why one man is on a mission to change our tastes.

Unit 1 Immigration

The history of immigration in the United States.

Unit 2 History of film

A history of film, from its early beginnings in the 19th century to the Hollywood blockbusters of today.

Unit 4 Urban art

Discover the world of graffiti and innovative music.

Unit 5 Aquarium on Wheels

A special aquarium that gives its student teachers lessons in life.

Unit 12 Japan

Learn more about the history and traditions of Japan.

Unit 3 Augmented reality

Learn about a system that allows the user to see much more than simple reality.

Unit 9 Queen of Egypt

The history of Cleopatra, the most famous Egyptian queen.

Unit 8 Mount Fuji

Find out what Mount Fuji means to the Japanese.

Unit 7 Galapagos energy

Find out about the impact of humans and tourism on the Galapagos Islands.

Unit 11 Paraguay shaman

Find out why it's essential to record plants from the rain forests of Paraguay before they disappear.

Unit 6 East Timor

The slow process of creating a new tourist destination.

Unit 1 Relationships

A baby camel gets a hug in Jordan.

FEATURES

1 Work in pairs. Look at the photo and the caption. Choose the phrase you think best describes the photo.

a faithful companion	blood relatives
an old friend	a passing acquaintance
mutual respect	a strong bond
true friends	an odd couple

2 Look at these English sayings about relationships. What do they mean? Do you have a similar saying in your language?

1 Blood is thicker than water.
2 A friend in need is a friend indeed.
3 Like father, like son.
4 No man is an island.

3 Think of a person (a) you have been meaning to contact for a long time and (b) you have shared a travel experience with. Tell your partner about these people.

1a Unlikely friends

Image by Stevi Calandra for the National Geographic Channel

Listening

1 Work in pairs. Look at the photo. Discuss the questions.

1 What are the two animals in the photo?
2 Are they normally pets, wild animals, or something else?
3 What does the photo suggest about these animals' characters?

2 🔊 **1** Now listen to part of a radio show about an unlikely friendship between these two animals. What things do they do together to enjoy each other's company?

3 🔊 **1** Listen again and choose the right word to complete each statement.

1 Cooperation between different species is not ______ .
a natural b easy c usual
2 Dogs are usually ______ apes.
a friendly toward b afraid of c aggressive toward
3 This particular dog and orangutan behave like ______ .
a old friends b children c people
4 Their behavior has attracted the interest of a lot of ______ .
a TV viewers b scientists c psychologists
5 Orangutans are very ______ creatures.
a physical b naughty c kind
6 Their relationship is based on their need to ______ .
a share new experiences b hunt together c be social

4 Do you believe animals can have friendships? Or do they form relationships only for practical reasons? Do you know other examples of sociable animals? Discuss.

Grammar present tenses review

PRESENT TENSES REVIEW

Simple present
Suriya lives with his keepers.

Present continuous
The two animals are fulfilling a basic social need in each other.

Present perfect
Suriya has understood that the dog is very hungry.

Present perfect continuous
They have been doing this every day.

For more information and practice, see page 156.

5 Look at the grammar box. Match the tenses (1–4) with their uses (a–d).

1 simple present
2 present continuous
3 present perfect
4 present perfect continuous

a highlights a recent activity
b describes a situation in progress or happening around now
c describes a permanent / usual situation
d highlights the present result of a recent action

6 Choose the correct tense to complete this paragraph about animal friendships.

A number of recent videos on YouTube showing unlikely animal friends [1] *have started / have been starting* a debate about animal friendships. Lately many people [2] *have discussed / have been discussing* a particularly moving film which shows a dog making friends with an elephant. Elephants often [3] *show / are showing* concern for their social group, but there is one extraordinary scene where the elephant becomes distressed when the dog gets injured. The dog [4] *has recovered / has been recovering* now and the two animals have been inseparable. The question scientists [5] *ask / are asking* is: is such behavior normal, or do we just want it to be? Some say it happens when animals [6] *have lived / have been living* close to humans. No one [7] *has provided / has been providing* a definite answer, but it seems some animals are just naturally sociable. Others, like giant pandas, [8] *live / are living* more independent and solitary lives.

7 Work in pairs. Explain to each other the use of the verb forms in bold in sentences 1–10 using a–d from Exercise 5.

1 We're not close friends—we**'re** just **studying** French at the same evening class.
This sentence describes a situation in progress.
2 I **live** with Sarah, but each of us **has** our own group of friends that we hang out with.
3 Olivia and I went on a trip to Peru together ten years ago and we**'ve kept in touch** with each other ever since.
4 I wouldn't say we were friends really. We**'ve met** a couple of times at parties.
5 Oh, **do you know** Arun? He's a good friend of mine too. We should all meet up some time.
6 Jacob **always hangs around** when he's bored, but he **never comes over** when he has something better to do.
7 Kate **has always stood by** me in hard times. If ever I'm in trouble, I **know** I can rely on her for help.
8 Cho and I **have been teaching** at the same school for years. We get along well, even though we **never really see** each other socially. I think I've been over to his house once.
9 Kuma and I **have known** each other since we were in school. It doesn't matter if we **haven't seen** each other for a while; we just seem to pick up where we left off.
10 Jessica and I want a medieval-style wedding. Themed weddings **are becoming** very fashionable.

Vocabulary friends: nouns and phrasal verbs

8 Work in pairs. What type of friend or person is each person talking about in Exercise 7? Match each sentence with a person from the box.

acquaintance	fair-weather friend
fellow student	roommate
girlfriend	mutual friend
old friend	travel companion
true friend	colleague

9 Find the following phrasal verbs in the sentences in Exercise 7. Which ones contain two prepositions instead of one? Discuss what each verb means.

- 1 verb with *get*
- 1 verb with *stand*
- 2 verbs with *hang*
- 2 verbs with *over*
- 2 verbs with *up*

10 Choose the correct phrasal verbs to complete these sentences.

1 We come from different backgrounds but we ______ really well.
2 We don't have to do anything special, like going to a show. It would just be nice to ______ together.
3 Why don't you ______ to my house for supper tonight?
4 Some friends are great just to have a good time with, but real friends are the ones who ______ you when you're in trouble.
5 I'm busy at 6:00 but we could ______ later, if you like. Say, 8:30?

Speaking

11 Work in pairs. Think about three of your friends. What kind of friends are they? Choose from the types in Exercise 8. Think also about how often you see these people and what things you do together. Discuss if your friendships are similar in any way.

1b A confused generation

Reading

1 Work in pairs. Look at the photo accompanying the article below. Discuss the questions.

1 What does it show?
2 What do you think is the matter?
3 Is this situation familiar to you?

2 Discuss what effects you think China's recent economic boom has had on the attitudes of the younger and older generations.

3 Read the article and compare your answers.

4 Find examples of the following to show how attitudes are changing in China.

- language use
- caring for the old
- the relationship between parents and children
- shopping
- knowledge of the world

5 Do Bella's parents seem to accept the changes that are happening in China or not? Do you think the changes are difficult for Bella too? Why? / Why not?

Grammar the passive voice

6 Work in pairs. Look at the examples of passive verbs (1–6). Then look at uses of the passive (a–d). Which are true and which are false?

1 Bella is the name that she **has been given** by her English teacher.
2 But at the same time, these new values **are** also **being questioned**.
3 **Have** our lives **been made** richer?
4 **Is** Chinese culture **being supplanted**?
5 When they go shopping Bella makes sure that the "right" Western brands **are selected**.
6 "Our advice **is not listened to** and **not wanted**," her mother says.

a The person doing the action—the agent—is not the main focus of the sentence.
b We use *from* to introduce the agent.
c The agent is often unimportant or unknown—it is the action that interests us.
d The passive is often used because we want to start a sentence with something that has already been mentioned.

Change brings problems. Bella lives with her parents in a brand new apartment in Shanghai. Her real name is Zhou Jiaying; Bella is the name that she has been given by her English teacher. Her parents are representative of a confused generation in a confused time. In modern Chinese society, different ideologies are fighting against each other. Enormous material benefits have been brought by China's economic boom, but the debate is not about these; it's about family life and values. Old values—the respect of family and the older generations—are being replaced by new ones which place money as the critical measurement of one's position in society. But at the same time, these new values are also being questioned. Have our lives been made richer by all our new possessions? Is Chinese culture being replaced? As in all changing societies, people are trying to find the right balance between the new and the old.

Recently, Bella's family put their grandfather into a nursing home. It was a painful decision. In traditional China, caring for aged parents has always been an unavoidable duty, but times are changing. Bella's ambition? "I want one day to put my parents in the best nursing home"—the best that money can buy, she means.

"When she told us that," Bella's father says, "I thought, Is it selfish to think she will be a dutiful and caring daughter and look after us? We don't want to be a burden to her when we get old. This is something my daughter has taught us. Once it was parents who taught children, but now we learn from them." The family can buy many more things these days, and when they go shopping, Bella makes sure that the "right" Western brands are selected. (Pizza Hut is her favorite restaurant.) She also teaches her parents the latest slang.

Her parents want to be supportive, but they no longer help with Bella's homework; in spoken English, she has surpassed them. She has already learned much more about the outside world than they have. "Our advice is not listened to and not wanted," her mother says. "When she was little, she agreed with all my opinions. Now she sits there without saying anything, but I know she doesn't agree with me." Bella glares, but says nothing. "I suppose our child-raising has been a failure." In China there is no concept of the rebellious teenager.

▶ THE PASSIVE VOICE

Simple present passive
I am given, you/we/they are given, he/she/it is given

Present continuous passive
I am being given, you/we/they are being given, he/she/it is being given

Present perfect passive
I/you/we/they have been given, he/she/it has been given

For more information and practice, see page 157.

7 Look at the grammar box. Transform the sentences from active to passive where appropriate. Check your answers with your teacher.

There are many children like Bella in China. They [1] **admire** Western brands. Their parents [2] **have spoiled** them a little, perhaps. Often these children [3] **receive** a better education than their parents. Their parents [4] **send** them to private schools and they [5] **encourage** them to go to college. In China, the new economy [6] **is raising** everyone's hopes.

▶ WORDBUILDING forming adjectives from nouns

There are various endings in English: *-ful*, *-ish*, *-ent*, *-ious*, *-ive*, used to form adjectives from nouns.
support → supportive, rebel → rebellious

8 Complete the sentences with the correct passive form.

1. A lot of changes .... (introduce) in China.
2. As a result, the average Chinese person .... (give) a better standard of living.
3. Couples .... (allow) to have only one child.
4. A lot of money .... (invest) in each child's future.
5. But changes in this policy .... (discuss).
6. The government .... (become) concerned by the growing number of people over 60.

9 Complete the sentences by putting the verb in the correct tense and the active or passive voice. More than one answer may be possible.

1. Children .... (grow) up much too quickly today. Girls of twelve *dress* (dress) as if they are eighteen.
2. We .... (leave) behind by all the new technology they use.
3. They .... (probably / work) harder than us, but they .... (not / have) so much fun.
4. They .... (live) longer and longer and we .... (expect) to look after them. It's not fair.
5. Our parents aren't so different from us: they .... (listen) to the same music, for example.
6. In recent years respect, old values like respect for wisdom and knowledge .... (replace) by respect for money.
7. I rebelled against my parents. My children feel that they .... (expect) to rebel, but in fact they have nothing to complain about or rebel against.
8. We .... (often / criticize) for being selfish and having no moral values, but that's our parents' fault: we .... (spoil) by them.

Speaking

10 Work in groups. Discuss whether it was a young person or an older person that said each of the items in Exercise 9. Which of the statements do you agree with?

11 Do you think the gap between your generation and your parents' generation is greater than the one between your generation and the next generation?

1c Bloodlines

Reading

1 Work in pairs. Why do people emigrate? What difficulties do people face in a new country? Compare your ideas with another pair.

2 Read the article about immigrants in New York. Answer the questions. Then compare your answers with your partner.

1. What is special about the area of Queens?
2. What do Richard and Tanja's families have in common?
3. How are their stories different?

3 Are the sentences true (T) or false (F) according to the article?

1. Immigrants in Queens feel attached to their new country.
2. People are much more interested in learning about distant ancestors than recent generations.
3. Years after immigrating to America, Tomas met his brother in New York by accident.
4. Richard's grandmother has kept the family history alive.
5. Tanja's mother wasn't able to balance work with looking after her children's education.
6. Tanja and her sister have chosen similar careers to their parents'.

4 Look at the article and choose the correct explanation for each phrase.

1 *a melting pot* (paragraph 1)
  a a place of conflict
  b a place where all mix together
  c a place which attracts

2 *their ancestral roots* (para 2)
  a where their family came from originally
  b how they got to America
  c their parents' character

3 *one recurring theme* (para 3)
  a a sad fact
  b a common story
  c an unusual quality

4 *seeking his fortune* (para 4)
  a hoping to get lucky
  b looking for the right job
  c looking for a way to get rich

5 *a must* (para 5)
  a a good thing
  b a right
  c a necessity

Critical thinking identifying the main idea

5 Work in pairs. This article deals with different aspects of emigration. Identify the themes in each of the first three paragraphs. Compare your answers with another pair to check you have identified the same themes.

6 Which themes do the personal accounts of the immigrants pick up on? Which are not really mentioned again?

7 What is the main idea, or message, of the article? Did other pairs reach the same conclusion?

Speaking

8 Look at these phrases describing family characteristics or traits and discuss what they mean.

"He was clearly something of a free spirit."
"My parents have a strong work ethic."
"We've both inherited that desire to get ahead."

9 Look at the questions below and write down your answers. Then ask your partner about their answers. Does family have a similarly strong influence in your lives?

HOW DOES FAMILY SHAPE YOU?

Are you a close family? How much time do you spend with family:
- out of a sense of duty?
- because you choose to?

Is family a consideration for you in choosing where to live?

How conscious are you of your family's history?

Is there a strong family trait? Have you inherited it?

Is there a head of the family? How important is it to have this person's approval?

Is there someone in the family you particularly admire? Why?

Has your family influenced the career path that you have chosen?

When seeking advice, are you more likely to turn to friends or family?

How important is it to you that your family approves of your partner?

Would you say your family members have the same attitude toward:
- money?
- bringing up children?

Blood lines

America is well-known for being a melting pot of different ethnic groups and cultures, but nowhere is this diversity more pronounced than in Queens, New York. Here, second-generation Puerto Ricans live alongside third-generation Greeks and first-generation Koreans, all united by a common feeling of pride in their American identity.

However, they are also proud and curious about their ancestral roots. National Geographic's Genographic Project, also known as the Human Family Tree, set out to trace the origins and common ancestry of the community's immigrants by examining their genetic makeup using a simple DNA test. The study was well supported by local residents, but often what interested them more was something which intrigues us all: the history of our *recent* ancestry. In other words, how their ancestors arrived in America, and what brought them here in the first place.

One recurring theme among immigrants seems to be the hard work and sacrifices that went into building a new life, and how their descendants now feel a duty to honor that effort by working hard too. Here are two Queens residents' stories.

Richard, 38

My great-grandfather Tomas came to America from Poland when he was fifteen. His mother had died, and his father remarried so he could care for his seven children. Tomas didn't like his stepmother, so he ran away to Belgium, where he boarded a ship to America—without a ticket. He was clearly something of a free spirit. Arriving in America with nothing, he got a job on the railroads in California. Then one day he saw an announcement in a newspaper that was read by immigrants. It was from his brother in New York who was also seeking his fortune in America and was looking for him. Tomas got in touch and they had an emotional reunion in New York, where Tomas subsequently settled. This is the story that my grandmother has passed down to us, to my parents, and all my aunts and uncles. She is an amazing woman and the head of the family, I suppose; the one who holds us all together. She's actually quite forgetful now, but she never forgets family details. What that has meant is that all of us have a strong family bond and a strong sense of belonging to a group that has struggled and fought together to succeed here.

Tanja, 29

I'm a first-generation American. Both my parents came here from Jamaica, where getting a good education is a must. My mother always says that people may take everything away from you, but they can never take away your education. My father was a nurse in Jamaica, but he had an ambition to be a doctor in the US; when he first came here, he studied during the day and worked at night. My parents have a strong work ethic. My mom has always worked as a nurse, but at the same time has always been very involved in our lives, helping with our studies and following our careers with interest. Both my sister and I have followed them into the medical profession, and now I'm working as a doctor at Mount Sinai hospital in Queens. I don't know if that kind of dedication is genetic or just something that you learn from your parents, but that desire to get ahead … we've certainly both inherited it. The great thing about America is that it gives you the opportunity to live those dreams too.

1d A face from the past

Real life meeting people you know

1 Work in pairs. Discuss the questions.

1 When was the last time you bumped into someone that you hadn't seen for a while?
2 What did you talk about?
3 Had he / she changed a lot?

2 2 Listen to the conversation between two people who meet by accident in the street. Answer the questions.

1 What have they been doing since they last met?
2 What future arrangement do they make?

3 2 Look at the box, listen again, and mark the expressions the speakers use.

4 Match each situation (1–6) with an expression.

1 Greta expresses surprise at meeting Tan
2 Greta asks Tan for his news
3 what Tan says about Greta's appearance
4 how Greta describes her business
5 what Greta says about Amanda, their other friend
6 how Greta says she can't carry on the conversation

MEETING PEOPLE YOU KNOW

Imagine meeting / bumping into / seeing you here!
What a (nice) surprise!

How are things?
What have you been up to?
How's everything going?

Busy as ever.
I've been completely swamped.
It has its ups and downs.

You're looking well.
It obviously suits you.

Do you see much of Amanda?
How's Amanda doing?
She was asking about you the other day.

Give her my regards.
Say hello to her from me.

Well, I should probably go and…
Sorry, I've got to run. / I'm in a bit of a hurry.
I don't mean to be rude, but I need to…
It was really nice seeing you. / Great to see you.
Good luck with…

5 Pronunciation expressive intonation

a 3 Emotion (surprise, excitement) is often conveyed by expressive or exaggerated intonation. Flat intonation often suggests a lack of emotion or interest. Listen for these phrases and mark if the intonation is expressive (E) or flat (F).

		E	F
1	Imagine bumping into you here.	☐	☐
2	I had a contract with the consulate.	☐	☐
3	Is it going OK?	☐	☐
4	Do you see much of her?	☐	☐
5	We still get together now and then.	☐	☐
6	I'm only back for a week.	☐	☐

b Work in groups. Choose a phrase from the box and say it either with expressive intonation or with flat intonation. Ask the others in the group to say which intonation you used.

6 Imagine you are in a large mall during your lunch break. Walk around and "bump into" people you know. Find out what each person has been doing and make a future plan. Then move on until you bump into someone else. Use the box to help you.

1e News from home

Writing an informal email (1)

1 How often do you send news to friends and family? Do you communicate by letter, email, or text message?

2 Read the email below from Ben to his friend. Where is Ben and what is he doing there? How would you summarize each paragraph?

> Hey Mark,
>
> How's it going? I've been meaning to write for a while, but my work takes up a lot of my time. Please don't think it's because I haven't been thinking about you all—I have, and I'm getting pretty homesick. But I have to remind myself why I am here: to get established as a freelance journalist and photographer.
>
> I'm now in Sri Lanka visiting some tea plantations and talking to people about how their lives have changed in the last 20 years or so. The countryside here is amazing, so lush and green, you wouldn't believe it. I'm trying to get an interview with one of the plantation owners so I can make it into a magazine feature. Fingers crossed!
>
> My plan is to stay here until the end of September and then get a plane back home and see if I can find someone to publish this stuff. It would be great to get together with you then. How is everyone? Is Mei still working for that horrible real estate agent? Say hi to everyone for me. I'll write again soon.
>
> Talk to you soon!
>
> Ben

3 What features of the language in this letter tell you that it is in an informal style?

4 Writing skill greetings and endings

Which of these phrases for greeting and ending would be appropriate in an informal email?

All my love	Best	Dear Mr. Franks
Dear Sir or Madam	Hello	Hi John
Kind regards	Hey	Regards
Thanks	Love	Warm regards
Sincerely	Yours	Yours faithfully

5 Word focus *get*

a The verb *get* is often used in spoken or informal written English. Find five phrases or sentences in the letter where it is used. What does it mean in each case? Think of a synonym for *get* in each case.

b Read the sentences. Match the uses of *get* to a word with a similar meaning in the box.

be (in passive sentences) catch persuade reach receive

1. Did you get my last letter?
2. I got a virus which kept me in bed for weeks.
3. We got delayed for four hours at the border.
4. I'm going to try to get him to come with me.
5. I'll call you when I get to Buenos Aires.

c Write three sentences of your own with *get* giving recent news about yourself. Work in small groups and read them to each other.

6 Imagine you have been away from home for some time. Write an email (200 words) to a friend or family member asking them for news from home and giving them your news. Try to use *get* at least twice.

7 Work in pairs. Exchange letters. Check for the following:

- Is the use of tenses correct?
- Is the style not too formal?
- Did they use the correct greeting and ending?

1f Immigration

Video

Fleeing economic and political hardships, many millions left their homelands in Europe and Asia in search of a better life.

Before you watch

1 In groups, discuss the questions.

1 Where are the people in the photo?
2 What do you think they are doing?
3 What does the caption tell us about the people?

2 Work in pairs. Write down five images you think you will see in the video.

An immigration officer checking the documents of a person arriving in the US by boat.

While you watch

3 Watch the video and check your ideas from Exercise 2.

4 Watch the first part of the video (to 02:30). Find and underline eleven errors and correct them below.

Immigrants have come to the United States since the early 17th century. Europeans settled mainly in the western half of the country, immigrants from Asia and Mexico in the east and northwest. Between 1892 and 1954, Ellis Island in Los Angeles Harbor admitted 17 million immigrants. In 1907, as many as 11,000 people a week were processed. Today, four out of every five Americans can trace part of their family history directly back to Ellis Island. Many of these immigrants settled on the Upper East Side of Manhattan. Large families often lived in just two rooms. On the West Coast, families arrived at Devil Island, where conditions were more relaxed for Asians.

1 ....
2 ....
3 ....
4 ....
5 ....
6 ....
7 ....
8 ....
9 ....
10 ....
11 ....

5 Watch the second part of the video (02:31 to the end). Answer these questions.

1 How many legal immigrants arrive in the US each year?
....
2 What particular challenge is there along the US–Mexico border?
....
3 What have immigrants brought to the US?
....
4 How is the US economy affected by immigration?
....
5 What do immigrants usually share with people already living in the US?
....
6 How does this help the immigrants?
....

After you watch

6 Roleplay arriving at Ellis Island

Work in pairs.

Student A: You are an immigrant arriving at Ellis Island. Prepare the information below.

Student B: You are an immigration officer at Ellis Island. Read the information below and prepare questions to ask Student A.

- where you come from
- your journey
- why you want to come to the US

Act out the interview, then change roles and act out the interview again.

7 Lavinia Limon says, "We're in a much better position because we have maintained our immigration flows." What do you think she means? Do you agree with her?

8 Work in groups and discuss these questions.

1 What kind of problems do you think immigrants faced when they arrived in the United States in the 1920s?
2 Do you think immigrants face similar problems today?
3 Do you think immigrants should try to keep the customs and values of their home countries, or adopt those of their new country?

contend with (v) /kən'tend wɪð/ deal with a difficult situation
discrimination (n) /dɪsˌkrɪmə'neɪʃən/ treating a group of people in an unfair way
diverse (adj) /dɪ'vɜrs/ varied
flee (v) /fli/ escape from
hardship (n) /'hɑrdʃɪp/ something that makes life difficult
harsh (adj) /hɑrʃ/ extremely difficult to live in
leap (n) /lip/ jump
partition (v) /pɑr'tɪʃən/ divide
shore (n) /ʃɔr/ coast
tenement (n) /'tenəmənt/ a large building divided into apartments in a poor area of a city

UNIT 1 REVIEW

Grammar

1 Read the article below about families. Answer the questions.

1 What is the difference between a nuclear and an extended family?
2 What are the benefits of an extended family?

2 Underline the best option to complete the text. Then check your answers with your partner.

3 Work in pairs. Make a list of other advantages and disadvantages of living in an extended family. Then compare your answers with another pair.

When talking about family, a distinction [1] *is making / is made* between extended and nuclear families. The nuclear family includes only parents and children. The extended family is everyone who [2] *is related / has been related* by blood and by marriage: aunts, uncles, grandparents, nieces, nephews, in-laws, etc. In the West, the importance of extended family [3] *has decreased / has been decreased* greatly in the last 50 years. But the extended family has many economic benefits. Grandparents [4] *help / are helped* with childcare, and in turn they [5] *are looked after / have been looked after* when they are old. Also, when domestic chores [6] *are sharing / are shared* by many, living costs decrease. But in recent years, young people [7] *are choosing / have been choosing* to live in nuclear families so the economics [8] *have changed / have been changing*. The older generation say that traditional family values [9] *are losing / are being lost*; but the more serious economic issue is that everyone's support network [10] *has been taking / has been taken* away.

I CAN	
use present tenses	☐
talk about events in present time using active and passive forms	☐

Vocabulary

4 Read each definition and then put in the correct word.

1 Someone who is also studying, like you = a ______ student
2 Someone you go on a trip with = a ______ companion
3 Someone who you can really depend on = a ______ friend
4 Someone you and another friend both know = a ______ friend
5 Someone you share an apartment with = a ______
6 Someone you know who is not really a friend = an ______
7 Someone you are related to by birth = a ______ relative

5 Work in pairs. Give details about one of the people in Exercise 4:

- who you hang out with regularly
- who you haven't kept in touch with
- whose house you go over to regularly

I CAN	
describe different types of friends and acquaintances	☐
use phrasal verbs that describe relationships	☐

Real life

6 Put the sentences below in the right order to complete the conversation between Katia (K) and Julio (J).

K: Hello Julio. Imagine bumping into you here. *1*
K: Great. Well, I should probably go. I need to get to the bank.
K: Of course I will. We should get together some time.
K: You know—busy as ever.
K: You too. Good luck with the work in New York.
K: Not bad, thanks. What have you been up to?
K: Really? That's sounds exciting. You're looking well.
J: Thanks. You too. How's David doing these days?
J: Well, tell him I say hi.
J: Yes, that would be nice. I'll get in touch when I'm back next month.
J: Well, it was great seeing you.
J: I've been working in New York for the past month.
J: Oh hello, Katia. What a nice surprise! How are things?

7 Work in pairs. Imagine you meet each other in the street by accident. Act out a similar conversation.

I CAN	
have a conversation with someone I haven't seen for some time	☐

Speaking

8 Work in pairs. Tell each other about a relationship with a family member or friend that is important in your life.

Unit 2 Storytelling

Race car driver Ayrton Senna at his last race, Imola, Italy, 1994
Photograph by Dario Mitidieri

FEATURES

1 Work in pairs. Look at the photo and the caption. What do you know about race car drivers? Answer the questions.

1 What facts about a race car driver's life do you think would make a good movie?
2 Which would interest you more, a biography of Senna or a movie about his life? Why?

2 Match these adjective to their opposites.

accurate	unfair
fair	impartial
objective	biased
partial	misleading
sympathetic	subjective
truthful	critical

3 Match the adjectives (1–5) with the genres (a–e).

1 sentimental, touching
2 creepy, scary
3 fast-moving, gripping
4 original, thought-provoking
5 powerful, authentic

a thriller
b historical drama
c science fiction
d romantic comedy
e horror

4 Describe to your partner a book you have enjoyed recently. Would you like to see the movie or read the book your partner has described?

2a From page to screen

Vocabulary books and movies

1 Work in pairs. Look at the photo below. What kind of movie do you think this was a location for?

2 Do the words in the box relate to books, movies, or both? Put them into three categories.

audience	author	best seller
blockbuster	box office	cast
chapter	characters	director
location	plot	portrayal
producer	publisher	readers
scene	screenwriter	script
setting	storyline	theme
trilogy		

3 Match words from the books list and the movies list to make pairs of words that are related. What is the difference between the words in each pair? Compare your list with others.

Example:

author and screenwriter—the author is the writer of a book, a screenwriter writes the script of a movie

WORDBUILDING synonyms

Synonyms are words which are close in meaning but not exactly the same, or the same in meaning but different in use: *storyline* and *plot*

Speaking and listening

4 Work in pairs. Ask each other the questions.

1 Do you like to see movie adaptations of books you have read?
2 Do you sometimes read a book because you saw the movie?

5 **4** What do you think is the secret of making a good movie adaptation of a book? Tell your partner if you agree with a, b, or c. Then listen to an interview with a film critic and say which answer he gives.

a to remain completely faithful to the details of the story and the characters in the book
b to remain faithful to the spirit and main themes of the book
c to create a story that works on film, even if it is not faithful to the book

6 4 Answer the questions. Then listen again and check.

1 What do people generally think are the ingredients for a box office success?
2 What does the critic say about the success of movie adaptations of books?
3 What are *Sense and Sensibility* and *The Shining* examples of, according to the critic?
4 To what does the critic compare making a good movie from a book?
5 What is the central theme of *The Lord of the Rings*?
6 Why was it difficult to reproduce the world J.R.R. Tolkien created?
7 How did director Peter Jackson compensate for leaving out elements of Tolkien's story?

7 Work in groups. Discuss the questions.

1 Have you seen any good movie adaptations of books? And any bad ones?
2 What made them good or bad?
3 Were the reasons similar to the ones described by the critic?

Grammar simple past and present perfect

8 Work in pairs. Match each sentence (1–5) to one of the uses of the simple past and present perfect (a–e).

1 Some film adaptations **have worked**, others **have flopped**.
2 "What is the secret?" That **was** the question I **put** to him earlier.
3 He **has followed** the progress of many book-to-film adaptations in his time.
4 The author, Tolkien, **created** a magical world.
5 It **has become** one of the most successful movies of all time.

a When the action is clearly linked to a specific time in the past, we use the simple past.
b When the experience is more important than the time, and the time is not stated, we use the present perfect.
c We use the present perfect to talk about people's life experiences.
d If the person is dead, we use the simple past to talk about their lives.
e When we talk about a period of time that is not finished (over the past few weeks, this year), we use the present perfect even if the action itself is finished.

SIMPLE PAST and PRESENT PERFECT

Simple past
I visited / He visited...
I didn't visit...
Did you visit... ?

Present perfect
I have visited / She has visited...
I have not visited...
Have you visited... ?

For more information and practice, see page 158.

9 Look at the grammar box. Then choose the best option to complete the sentences.

1 I first .... (read) *The Hobbit* when I was twelve years old. What about you?
No, I .... (never / read) *The Hobbit*, but I know a guy who .... (read) it 24 times. He never gets tired of it.
2 There .... (be) a lot of movie adaptations of Stephen King's books over the years.
Yes, I know. There .... (be) a great adaptation of *The Green Mile* a few years ago.
3 .... you ever .... (write) a play or a screenplay?
No, but my great grandfather .... (write) a play for radio.
4 .... you .... (see) *2001: A Space Odyssey* on TV last night?
No, but I .... (see) it before.

Writing and speaking

10 Think about a living writer or filmmaker. Make notes about their life and work. Use the chart to help you. Then describe this person's work to your partner. Ask questions about the person your partner chose.

What is the person's name?	
Where is he/she from?	
Is he/she an author, screenwriter, or other?	
What are three famous works from this person?	
What style of movie or book does he/she make?	
What is your favorite example of this person's work?	
Why?	

2b A close shave

Reading

1 Work in pairs. Discuss how you would react if faced with the following dangerous situations. What do you think would be the right thing to do?

- a snake hissing at you
- a shark swimming near you
- a bear approaching when you are having a picnic

2 Have you had any "close shaves" with dangerous animals? What happened? Tell the class.

3 Read the story below about three encounters two National Geographic reporters had with rhinos on the same day. What did the rhinos do in each case and how did the people react?

4 Look at the eight highlighted verbs in the article and guess their meaning from the context. Check your answers in a dictionary.

5 What effect does the use of these verbs have on the story?

A CLOSE SHAVE

KAZIRANGA NATIONAL PARK in India is home to two of the world's most endangered species: the tiger and the single-horned rhino. Photographer Steve Winter and writer Douglas Chadwick had only been working there a few days when they had a very close shave with some rhinos.

They were driving into the park to start filming when their guide stopped the jeep to move a turtle from the middle of the road just ahead of them. Winter, Chadwick, and their guard got out to **stretch** their legs and watch. But when Chadwick turned to look up the road, he saw something terrible: a rhino charging at them!

Rhinos can **sprint** more than 25 miles an hour, so there was no time to **leap** back in the car. Instinctively, the guard fired a shot into the ground just in front of the rhino. The crack of the rifle and the dirt that the bullet kicked up was enough to distract their attacker and it **veered** off into the grass seconds before reaching them.

Shaken, but relieved the incident had not been worse, they drove on. As they were entering the forest area, three young rhinos entered the road in front of them. The jeep stopped hurriedly, but this time the animals seemed uninterested and disappeared into the forest. Just then, however, the mother of the three, who had been keeping an eye on her young, came crashing through the trees. No time to shoot this time. The female rhino **slammed** into the side of the jeep and started to **wrestle** it off the road. Indian rhinos don't use their horns in a fight; instead they bite and this female's teeth were **gouging** deep into the side of the jeep.

The guide had laid down a rule for his guests at Kaziranga: no one was allowed to be scared. But his guests were breaking the rule, praying the driver could get them out of there. With the engine screaming, at last the vehicle **skidded** free. Even then the rhino came after them and it was only 500 feet later that she gave up the chase.

Grammar past tenses review

6 Look at the grammar box. Match the tenses (1–4) with their uses (a–d). Then find other examples of the tenses in the article.

1 past continuous
2 simple past
3 past perfect
4 past perfect continuous

a to describe the main events in sequence
b to refer to an action that happened earlier but not in the main sequence of events
c to describe a (background) event in progress around the time of the main event
d to describe an action in progress before or up to the main event(s) in the past

> **PAST TENSES REVIEW**
>
> **Past continuous**
> *They were driving into the park to start filming when their guide stopped the jeep.*
>
> **Simple past**
> *Winter, Chadwick, and their guard got out to stretch their legs and watch.*
>
> **Past perfect**
> *Shaken, but relieved the incident had not been worse, they drove on.*
>
> **Past perfect continuous**
> *Winter and Chadwick had only been working there a few days when they had a very close shave.*
>
> For more information and practice, see page 158.

7 Complete the summary of Winter and Chadwick's story using the past tense of the verbs given. Use contracted forms where possible.

Steve Winter and Douglas Chadwick, who [1] .... (work) in Kaziranga National Park, [2] .... (have) three close encounters with rhinos all on the same day. Before entering the park, their guide [3] .... (tell) them not to be afraid, so they [4] .... (be / not) especially worried, but clearly the incidents [5] .... (shock) them. They [6] .... (know) that filming in the park was dangerous work, but they [7] .... (not / expect) to meet danger so soon or so frequently. But it [8] .... (not / keep) them from carrying on!

8 **Pronunciation contracted negative forms**

5 Listen and repeat these sentences after the speaker. Pay attention to the negative contractions.

1 I *haven't* been to India.	5 I *hadn't* noticed.
2 It *isn't* far.	6 They *weren't* late.
3 You *aren't* allowed.	7 She *hasn't* called.
4 It *doesn't* matter.	8 We *didn't* care.

9 Complete these reports of lucky escapes by putting each verb in the most appropriate past tense. Use contracted forms where possible. Check your answers with your teacher.

THE NEAR MISS

I [1] .... (mountain bike) with a friend in Wales and we [2] .... (just / finish) a long off-road climb out of the Dysynni Valley. It [3] .... (rain) earlier but now the sun [4] .... (shine) and we [5] .... (feel) pretty warm. Since the rest of the route was downhill on paved roads, I [6] .... (take) off my bike helmet and [7] .... (set) off. Suddenly the road [8] .... (become) very steep and the bike [9] .... (pick) up speed quickly. There was a turn ahead in the road and I knew I was going to crash. The bike [10] .... (go) straight into a wall, but luckily I...

THE UNEXPECTED

Mr. Charles Everson and his wife Linda [11] .... (drive) home from a friend's house one Sunday when a cow [12] .... (fall) from the sky and [13] .... (land) on the hood of their van. The cow, which [14] .... (escape) from a breeding farm, [15] .... (graze) too close to the edge of a cliff next to the road and [16] .... (slip) and plunged 200 feet. When the emergency crew [17] .... (arrive) at the scene they ..

10 In pairs, complete the last sentence of each story. Then get together with another pair and share your endings.

When the emergency crew arrived at the scene, they had to call a vet to take care of the cow!

Speaking

11 Prepare a description of a time that you had a near miss or lucky escape. Choose one of the following themes and use each tense at least once. Then tell your story to your partner. When you come near the end, stop and ask your partner what they think happened next.

- escaping injury or physical accident
- a scary incident when something unexpected happened
- getting away with something you did wrong
- seeing something dangerous happen and trying to help

2c Once upon a time...

Reading

1 Work in pairs. What were your favorite stories as a child? Tell your partner what they were about and why you still remember them.

2 Look at these titles of fairy tales by the brothers Grimm. Discuss the questions.

Cinderella	The Elves and the Shoemaker
Snow White	Little Red Riding Hood
Sleeping Beauty	The Frog Prince

1 Which of these fairy tales is depicted in the photo on page 27?
2 Which are well known in your country?
3 What is the name for them in your language? Is the name similar or very different?

3 Where did the stories in Exercise 2 come from originally and what did the brothers Grimm do to them? Read the article and find out.

4 Look back at the article and find significant (or surprising) facts about the following:

1 the popularity of the Grimms' fairy tales now
2 how popular they were at the time
3 Germany at the time the brothers were writing
4 *Little Red Riding Hood* and *Snow White*
5 the attitude of parents to the stories

5 The writer uses various words and expressions associated with fairy tales. Find and match them with the definitions below.

1 a long time ago (para 1)
2 the opposite of *a hero* (para 1)
3 clever and knowledgeable (para 1)
4 distant countries (para 1)
5 the lesson to be learned (para 5)
6 a woman (often bad) who does magic (para 6)
7 the opposite of *kind* (para 6)
8 for the rest of time (para 7)

Critical thinking close reading

6 What conclusions can you draw about the brothers Grimm from reading this article? According to the text, are these statements true (T) or false (F)? Or is there not enough information (N) to say?

1 They were very motivated young men.
2 They had an academic interest in the stories.
3 Their aim was to write down stories that had previously been told orally.
4 They were interested in the stories themselves, not the social message behind them.
5 Wilhelm disliked their cruelty and violence.
6 In the end, the stories reached the mass audience that the brothers had wished them to.

7 Work in pairs. Summarize the brothers Grimms' achievement, according to the writer.

Word focus *keep*

8 Work in pairs. In the article, find three phrases with the word *keep*. Discuss what each one means. Then do the same with the phrases below.

1 Please **keep an eye on** the time. We shouldn't leave any later than ten thirty.
2 Try to **keep your chin up**. I'm sure things will get better.
3 I wouldn't tell him your news just yet, if I were you. He's not very good at **keeping a secret**.
4 Technology is moving so fast these days. It's difficult to **keep track** of all the changes.
5 Sorry, I don't want to **keep** you. I just need to ask you a quick question.
6 I always think it's a good idea to **keep a diary** that you can look back on later.

Writing and speaking

9 Think of a traditional story or fairy tale you know well. Make notes on the main elements of the story. Use a dictionary if necessary.

10 Work in pairs. Tell each other your story as you remember it, or tell the same story but in a modern setting. When you have heard each other's stories, change partners and tell your new partner the story you were told.

Once upon a time...

Once upon a time there lived in Germany two brothers who loved a good story—one with magic and danger, royalty and villains. At school they met a wise man who led them to a treasure—a library of old books with tales more enchanting than any they had ever heard. Inspired, the brothers began collecting their own stories, listening to the folktales people told them. Soon they produced their own treasure—a book of fairy tales that would charm millions in faraway lands for generations to come.

The brothers Grimm, Jacob and Wilhelm, named their story collection *Children's and Household Tales* and published it in Germany in 1812. The collection, which has been translated into more than 160 languages, from Inupiat in the Arctic to Swahili in Africa, is a publishing phenomenon that competes with the Bible. The stories and their characters have appeared in theater, opera, comic books, movies, paintings, rock music, advertising, and even fashion. The Japanese have built two theme parks devoted to the tales, and in the United States, the Grimms' collection helped launch Disney as an entertainment giant.

Such fame would have shocked the humble Grimms. During their lifetimes, the book sold few copies in Germany. The early editions were not even aimed at children. They had no illustrations, and scholarly footnotes took up almost as much space as the tales themselves. Jacob and Wilhelm Grimm viewed themselves as patriotic students of folklore. They began their work at a time when Germany had been occupied by the French under Napoleon. The new rulers suppressed local culture. As young scholars, the brothers Grimm began work on the fairy tale collection in order to save the endangered oral storytelling tradition of Germany.

Long before the Grimms' time, storytelling thrived in inns, barns, and peasant homes. During winter nights, as they sat spinning wool, women kept each other company and entertained each other with tales of adventure, romance, and magic. Altogether, 40 such storytellers delivered tales to the Grimms, many of them coming to their house in Kassel. One of them, "Marie," was credited with narrating many of the most famous tales: *Little Red Riding Hood, Snow White,* and *Sleeping Beauty*. But these were not from the German oral tradition. Marie had had French nannies who retold stories that they themselves had read in a collection written by Charles Perrault in 1697, *Tales of My Mother Goose*.

Although the brothers implied that they were just recording the tales, Wilhelm polished and reshaped them up to the final edition of 1857. In an effort to make them more acceptable to children and their parents, he stressed the moral of each tale, and emphasized gender roles. According to the Grimms, the collection served as "a manual of manners." To this day, parents read them to their children because they approve of the lessons in the stories: keep your promises, don't talk to strangers, work hard, obey your parents.

Yet despite Wilhelm's polish, the coarse medieval core of the stories remained untouched. The cruel treatment of children (like Hansel and Gretel, who are put in a cage and fattened for eating), the violent punishments handed out to the villains (like Snow White's evil stepmother, who in the original story is forced to dance in red-hot iron shoes until she falls down dead), are too much for some parents.

So what accounts for their popularity? Some have suggested it is because the characters are always striving for happiness. But the truth probably lies in their origin. The Grimms' tales were born out of a storytelling tradition without boundaries of age or culture. The brothers' skill was to translate these into a universal style of writing that seems to mirror whatever moods or interests we bring to our reading of them. And so it was that the Grimms' fairy tales lived happily ever after.

coarseness (n) /ˈkɔrsnɪs/ being rough and down-to-earth; a lack of sophistication or refinement
folklore (n) /ˈfoʊkˌlɔr/ the traditional songs, stories, proverbs, legends of a society
nanny (n) /ˈnæni/ a woman paid to look after young children
spin (v) /spɪn/ to make natural fiber (like wool) into thread

2d What a disaster!

Real life reacting to stories

1 Work in pairs. What kind of things do you find often go wrong day-to-day: computers, transport, things in the house, forgetting things?

2 6 Look at these extracts from six personal accounts of things that went wrong. Discuss what you think happened next. Then listen and check.

1 The bus broke down on the highway so we were all left stranded until help could arrive.
2 My pants got caught on the door handle and as I walked away they tore.
3 I bent the key trying to force it into the lock and when I tried to straighten it, it snapped.
4 The elevator got stuck between floors twenty-five stories up.
5 The tires on my bicycle were badly worn and when I hit a bump in the road one of them burst.
6 My computer froze while I was working.

3 6 Look at the responses below. Tell your partner which ones were used in each of the conversations in Exercise 2. Then listen again and check your answers.

REACTING TO STORIES

Sympathizing when something bad has happened
Oh, that's awful.
How embarrassing!
What a disaster!
Oh, that's really awkward.
Poor you!
What a nightmare!
Really? That's odd.
Really? How strange!

Commenting on a good outcome to a bad situation
Phew!
That must have been a relief.
That was clever.
That was good thinking.
That was lucky.
That was a stroke of luck.

Talking about similar experiences
I can sympathize with that.
Yeah, I think I would have done the same thing.
Yeah, something like that happened to me once.
Yeah, I once had the same experience…

4 Pronunciation linking and assimilation

a 7 Listen to these short responses. Notice how the underlined sounds are either linked (as in *been a*) or assimilated (as in *what did*, where the *t* of *what* disappears and is replaced by the *d* of *did*). Repeat each phrase.

That must have been a relief.

So what did you do?

b 8 Work in pairs. Underline the sounds in these sentences that you think are linked or assimilated. Then listen and check. Practice saying the sentences.

Linked
1 What a nightmare!
2 Oh, that's awful.
3 How embarrassing!
4 Really? That's odd.

Assimilated
5 That was good thinking.
6 Something like that happened to me.

5 Work in groups. Choose two of the following topics each and prepare to tell a short story about something that happened to you. Those listening to the story should react.

- a time you were lost or stranded
- something embarrassing that happened to you
- a minor accident you had
- a computer problem
- a situation when someone you were with panicked
- a situation where something broke or got stuck

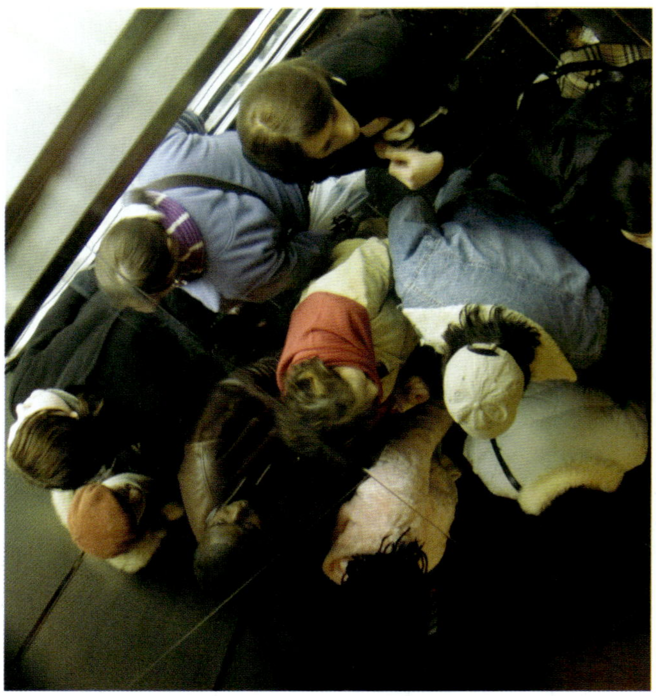

2e A real-life drama

Writing a story

1 Read the opening paragraph from a story about two men walking in the Amazon rain forest in Peru. Answer the questions.

1 What happened to Rowan?
2 How are the two characters feeling?

2 Work in pairs. Identify the events in the story. Put them in chronological order.

> "I can't move," cried Rowan, "my foot's caught in something – it's really painful!" Chris knew that Rowan was struggling. He had been moaning all day about his sore feet and they had only covered a mile in the last half hour. Chris was tired too from trudging through the thick jungle, but was eager to get back to the camp before it got dark. They weren't carrying many supplies with them and neither had eaten anything for at least three hours. "It's probably just a thorn bush or something," he said encouragingly, walking back slowly to see what the problem was. "Reach down and try to free your foot." But as he got nearer, he could see that it wasn't a bush that had caught Rowan but a metal animal trap which had clamped itself firmly to his right ankle.

3 Why does the writer choose to start the story at the point when Rowan cries out?

4 Writing skill using descriptive words

a Look at the highlighted expressions in the story. Which describe movement and which a way of speaking? Discuss the exact meaning of each expression.

b Look at the words in bold in these sentences. Try to work out their meaning from the context. Then check in a dictionary to see if you were right.

Speaking

1 "Help," she **screamed**, "that man took my wallet."
2 Jin could tell Ping was unhappy because she kept **muttering** under her breath.
3 He **mumbled** something about it being unfair, but I couldn't catch his exact words.
4 "OK, let's try your way then," she **said wearily**. She had lost the energy to argue anymore.
5 "I'll go first," he **said bravely**, but he was scared.

Moving

6 We **edged** our way along the narrow path, conscious of the steep drop to our left.
7 When he heard the car arrive, he **leapt** to his feet and ran to the door.
8 She **stumbled** on a rock and almost fell, but then regained her balance.
9 We **walked briskly** for the next hour but then slowed to our usual pace.
10 She **turned apprehensively** towards the door, as heavy footsteps approached.

c Do you know any other verbs that describe a particular way of speaking or moving? Tell the class.

5 Write the ending of the story (at least five sentences). Try to use some descriptive verbs and adverbs, but don't overuse them!

6 Exchange your ending with your partner. Did he or she:

- use the different past tenses correctly?
- include some descriptive verbs and adverbs?

7 Now read other students' stories. Decide which ending you like best.

2f History of film

Video

Inventors realized they could create the illusion of motion by presenting a quick succession of pictures.

Before you watch

1 Work in groups. Look at the photo and discuss the questions.

1 What do you think the man in the photo is doing?
2 When do you think the photo was taken?
3 Why do you think the photo is made up of several images?

2 You are going to watch a video about the history of film. Mark the things and people you think you will see in the video.

an old film projector	an Oscar statue
a documentary filmmaker	an earthquake
a scene from a melodrama	Charlie Chaplin
a scene from an animated movie	the Arctic
actors arriving at an awards ceremony	

While you watch

3 Watch the video and check your answers from Exercise 2. Which other early actor is mentioned in the video?

4 Watch the first part of the video (to 01:36). Number the events in the order they happened.

a The projector was developed.
b People watched movies in arcades.
c Hollywood became the center of the studio system.
d Melodramas became popular.
e Actors became part of a new American aristocracy.
f Edison and Dickson invented the kinetoscope.

5 Watch the second part of the video (01:37 to the end). Answer the questions.

1 What have movies allowed us to do outside of Hollywood?

....

2 Name three events that the video shows being covered by early newsmen.

....
....
....

3 Name two unusual activities you see as examples of how documentary filmmakers have used the camera in new ways.

....
....

4 How have studio blockbusters influenced documentaries?

....
....
....

6 Watch the video again. Complete the phrases with the missing time expressions.

1 ...., movies have captured the imagination of audiences all over the world.
2 ...., inventors realized they could create the illusion of motion.
3 ...., projection allowed large audiences to view the spectacle at the theater.
4 ...., the emerging movie studio system was centered in Hollywood, California.
5 ...., newsmen carried cameras looking for history in the making.
6 .... documentary filmmakers have learned to borrow from the studio blockbusters.

After you watch

7 Roleplay an interview with an actor or actress

Work in pairs.

Student A: Imagine you are a famous Hollywood actor or actress. Choose who you want to be. Read the information below and make notes.

Student B: You are going to interview a famous Hollywood actor or actress. Read the information below and prepare questions.

- background
- career to date (movies and other work)
- how Hollywood has changed over the years

Act out the interview, then change roles. Student B should choose a different actor or actress.

8 Work in groups and discuss these questions.

1 What kind of movies do you prefer watching?
2 Do you enjoy watching documentaries? Why?
3 How important is the movie industry in your country?

arcade (n) /ɑr'keɪd/ a passage with a roof and stores on both sides
entrancing (adj) /en'trænsɪŋ/ fascinating
flickering (adj) /'flɪkərɪŋ/ quick-moving and not very clear
landmark (n) /'lænd,mɑrk/ an important historical moment
loop (n) /lup/ a circle
melodrama (n) /'melə,drɑmə/ an old style of drama that has exaggerated emotion and action
nickelodeon (n) /,nɪkə'loʊdiən/ an old type of movie theater
peep (v) /pip/ look at something through narrowed eyes
projection (n) /prə'dʒekʃən/ putting an image on a screen
Tinseltown (n) /'tɪnsəl,taʊn/ another name for Hollywood
train (v) /treɪn/ point a camera lens at something
vaudeville (n) /'vɔd,vɪl/ a type of variety show

UNIT 2 REVIEW

Grammar

1 Complete the story below about a narrow escape. Put each verb into the correct tense: present perfect, simple past, past continuous, past perfect, or past perfect continuous.

I [1] ________ (film) lions a lot—ever since I was 25 years old—and I [2] ________ (never / have) serious problems with them. Strangely, I [3] ________ (feel) most at danger when lions [4] ________ (want) to play. I remember an expedition a few years ago in Tanzania. I [5] ________ (sit) in my tent reading just after sunset. One of our guides [6] ________ (call) out "Lion!" That [7] ________ (not / be) particularly unusual, so I [8] ________ (not / take) much notice. But when the guide [9] ________ (call) out again, I looked out and saw that two lions [10] ________ (slowly / approach) our camp. We [11] ________ (park) our car some distance away and it was too far to reach. So I [12] ________ (run) back to the tent and quickly [13] ________ (zip) it up. I could hear a lot of noise coming from the kitchen, so I [14] ________ (assume) the guides [15] ________ (go) back there to make noise to scare the lions off. I [16] ________ (wait), and when the noise [17] ________ (die) down, I [18] ________ (look) out again. The two guides [19] ________ (lock) themselves in the car. The lions were gone, but where they [20] ________ (play) in the kitchen, there was an incredible mess.

2 Work in pairs. Answer these questions.

1 Where did the filmmaker hide from the lions?
2 What did he think the guides had done to save the situation?
3 What had actually happened?

I CAN	
talk about past experience	☐
use narrative tenses to tell a story	☐

Vocabulary

3 Choose the correct words.

1 A documentary should be *biased / impartial* and factually *accurate / authentic*.
2 The *author / publisher* of a book must make sure the *characters / cast* are believable.
3 I'm reading a thriller. The *script / plot* is very *gripping / touching*.
4 The movie gives the *audience / cast* a very realistic *scene / portrayal* of life in the nineteenth century.
5 The movie was a *bestseller / blockbuster* based on a science fiction book with some very *thought-provoking / sympathetic* ideas.

4 Work in pairs. Describe a movie based on a book you have read. Was it a successful adaptation? How faithful was it to the book?

I CAN	
describe movies and books	☐
talk about the different elements of a movie or book	☐

Real life

5 Match the piece of news (1–6) with a response (a–f).

1 My pen leaked and ink got all over my jacket and my shirt, but it came out in the wash.
2 The garden was OK because we had asked a neighbor to water it while we were away.
3 When I got home at midnight all the lights in the house were on, but no one was there.
4 I went all the way downtown to get my new passport, only to find the office is closed on Mondays.
5 He asked me for my honest opinion, so I gave it.
6 The car I had hit was my boss's!

a Poor you!
b Yes, I think I would have done the same thing.
c Really? That's odd.
d That must have been a relief.
e How embarrassing!
f That was good thinking.

6 Work in pairs. Tell each other about something bad (embarrassing, annoying, a narrow escape) that happened to you recently.

I CAN	
react to stories in a natural way	☐

Speaking

7 Work in small groups. Use the first and last lines below to make your own fairy tale. When you are ready, each person should tell the story to a member of another group.

"There were once two neighbors, one very lazy and the other very hard-working...

...And so it was that these two, who had been enemies for so long, became the greatest of friends."

Unit 3 Science and technology

Hands-free! The screen is in the glasses and you can text using thought-power alone.

FEATURES

1 How much do you depend on technology in your day-to-day life and work? What happens if you lose your phone or your computer crashes?

2 Work in pairs. Look at the photo and read the caption. Now look at the words below. In which area(s) is the technological breakthrough in the photo? Which area will give rise to the main breakthrough of the next 50 years?

artificial intelligence	communications	energy use
medicine	space exploration	transportation

3 In pairs, discuss these predictions about the future. Do you think they are justified? Why? Which do you think will come true?

1 I expect that most of my generation will live to be around 100 years old.
2 I think in the future people will interact with intelligent machines even more than they do now.
3 I don't think global warming is going to be the problem that everyone says it is.

3a Is technology the answer?

Kolkata's streets crammed with vendors, pedestrians, and taxis

Speaking

1 Work in groups. Look at the photo. Which problems does the photo illustrate?

congestion	epidemic
overpopulation	pollution
poverty	starvation

2 Which of these problems could have a technological solution?

Listening

3 9 Read the opinions (1–3). Then listen to the presentation about overpopulation. Match the opinion with the people (a–c).

1 Whenever the population is too big, a disaster reduces it.
2 Many people will die because there will not be enough food.
3 Science and technology will find a solution.

a the speaker
b Thomas Malthus
c Paul Ehrlich

4 9 Listen again. Are the sentences true (T) or false (F)?

1 The speaker has some ideas for action which can immediately solve the problem of overpopulation.
2 Paul Ehrlich thought that we should control the number of babies being born.
3 There will be 7 billion people in the world by the middle of the century.
4 Nanotechnology has saved the world from mass starvation.
5 Earth does not have space for 9 billion people.
6 The growth in the "global middle class" will put big pressure on resources.
7 According to the speaker, people are basically lazy.

5 What is the meaning of each underlined prefix in these words from the speech? Match the prefix (1–6) to the meaning (a–f).

1 biofuels	a very small
2 nanotechnology	b very big
3 megacities	c extremely
4 microphone	d of life or living things
5 semi-retired	e half
6 ultracautious	f $\times 10^{-9}$

WORDBUILDING prefixes

There are many prefixes in English taken from Latin and Greek, each of which have a particular meaning: *microphone*, *megacity*

6 Do you share the speaker's faith in science and technology? Why?

Grammar future forms review

> **FUTURE FORMS REVIEW**
>
> ***will***
> *One moment, I'll just adjust my microphone.*
> *It will be a bad thing for the planet if all those people start eating meat and driving big cars.*
> *The population will probably peak at around 9 billion by the middle of the century.*
> ***going to***
> *I'm not going to speak for too long.*
> *Those of you who have come here looking for answers are going to be disappointed.*
> ***about to***
> *Science is about to step in again with nanotechnology solutions.*
> **Present continuous**
> *I'm speaking to a government committee tomorrow.*
> **Simple present**
> *France is the world's favorite vacation destination*
>
> For more information and practice, see page 159.

7 Look at the grammar box. Match the verb forms (1–5) with their uses (a–i). Some verb forms have more than one use.

1 *will*
2 *going to*
3 *about to*
4 present continuous
5 simple present

a a scheduled event
b a future event in an *if* or *when* clause
c a prediction
d a confident prediction based on present information
e a decision made at the time of speaking
f an intention or previously made decision
g a formal arrangement
h a simple statement of fact
i an event in the immediate future

8 Underline the correct future forms in this presentation. Sometimes there is more than one possibility.

"I think [1] *we wait* / *<u>we'll wait</u>* a few moments until everyone [2] *arrives* / *will arrive*… OK, [3] *I am beginning* / *I'll begin* now. Hello everyone and thank you for coming to hear my presentation about appropriate technology. I am [4] *about to* / *going to* speak for about 30 minutes and then I [5] *will take* / *am taking* your questions. If there [6] *is* / *is going to be* anything that you don't understand, please ask me then, rather than during the presentation. My colleague, Liesel Babel, [7] *talks* / *is talking* this afternoon in the green seminar room, if people would like to learn more about appropriate technology. I think her session [8] *starts* / *is starting* at two o'clock. She [9] *is speaking* / *will speak* about her experiences in the field, working on various development projects in Africa. OK, [10] *I am going to show* / *I'll show* you a short video now…"

9 Complete the news headlines using an appropriate future form. Check your answers with your teacher.

1 World leaders .... (meet) in Geneva tomorrow to discuss the issue of overpopulation.
2 In the next few weeks, the government .... (introduce) a fee for each child that couples have after their first two children.
3 Scientists say that space colonies .... (be) the only solution for overpopulation in the near future.
4 Doctors have said that in the future they .... (not / spend) so much effort keeping the old alive.
5 The government .... (launch) a new education program later today to encourage women to have fewer children.
6 People .... (have to) change their lifestyles if they .... (want) the world's resources to support the growing population in the coming years.

10 Work in pairs. Underline all the time expressions in the sentences in Exercise 9. Then put them in order of the nearest to the most distant future. Compare your answers with another pair.

1 .... *later today* ....
2 ....
3 ....
4 ....
5 ....
6 ....

Speaking

11 Work in groups. Decide which of the ideas in Exercise 9, or one of your own, are the best course of action for dealing with overpopulation. Then explain your plan and the reasons for it to the class.

3b Revealed world

Speaking

1 Work in pairs. What information (news, travel advice, maps) do you get through printed media and what through digital media?

WORDBUILDING compound nouns (noun + noun)

We can use two nouns together to mean one thing.
information overload, computer graphics

Reading

2 Work in pairs. Look at the picture and the labels. Which information would you find useful or interesting if you were a visitor in Washington, DC? What other information might you want?

3 Read the article about augmented reality and complete the table.

Other terms for augmented reality:	1 *AR* 2
Examples of augmented reality already in use:	3 *restaurant menus and prices* 4
Devices we will use to see the augmented reality world:	5 6
Future applications for augmented reality technology:	7 *3-D repair instructions* 8

REVEALED WORLD

By Tim Folger

The regular world presented to us by our five senses—you could call it reality 1.0—is not always the most user-friendly of places. We get lost in unfamiliar cities; we meet people whose language we don't understand. So why not try the improved version: augmented reality (AR) or reality 2.0? AR technology superimposes computer-generated information on the real world, via a cell phone camera or special video glasses.

Early forms of AR are already here. With the right downloads, smart phones can deliver information about nearby ATMs and restaurants and other points of interest. Not only can you see that there's a Chinese restaurant on the next block, you can read the menu and prices, read reviews, and even find out how busy it is at the time.

This is where the next revolution in computing will take place: not in ever-more-sophisticated virtual-reality games, but rather in the interface between the real world and the information brought to us via the Internet. Imagine bubbles floating before your eyes, filled with cool information about anything and everything that you see in front of you. Information overload? Maybe not.

Let's jump ahead ten years. People trying to fix their cars won't be looking at online repair manuals or books; they will be wearing a device that projects animated 3-D computer graphics onto the equipment under repair, labeling parts and giving step-by-step guidance. Such technology is already being used by the US Marines.

Today's window into the AR world can be a smart phone or special video glasses that look like wraparound sunglasses. But in ten years' time, cell phones and video glasses will have been replaced by contact lenses etched with tiny LEDs which display text and images at a readable distance in front of the eye. A deaf person wearing these inconspicuous lenses will be able to see a real-time transcript of what people are saying as they speak.

The question is: while we are all absorbed in our new AR worlds, how will we be interacting with each other?

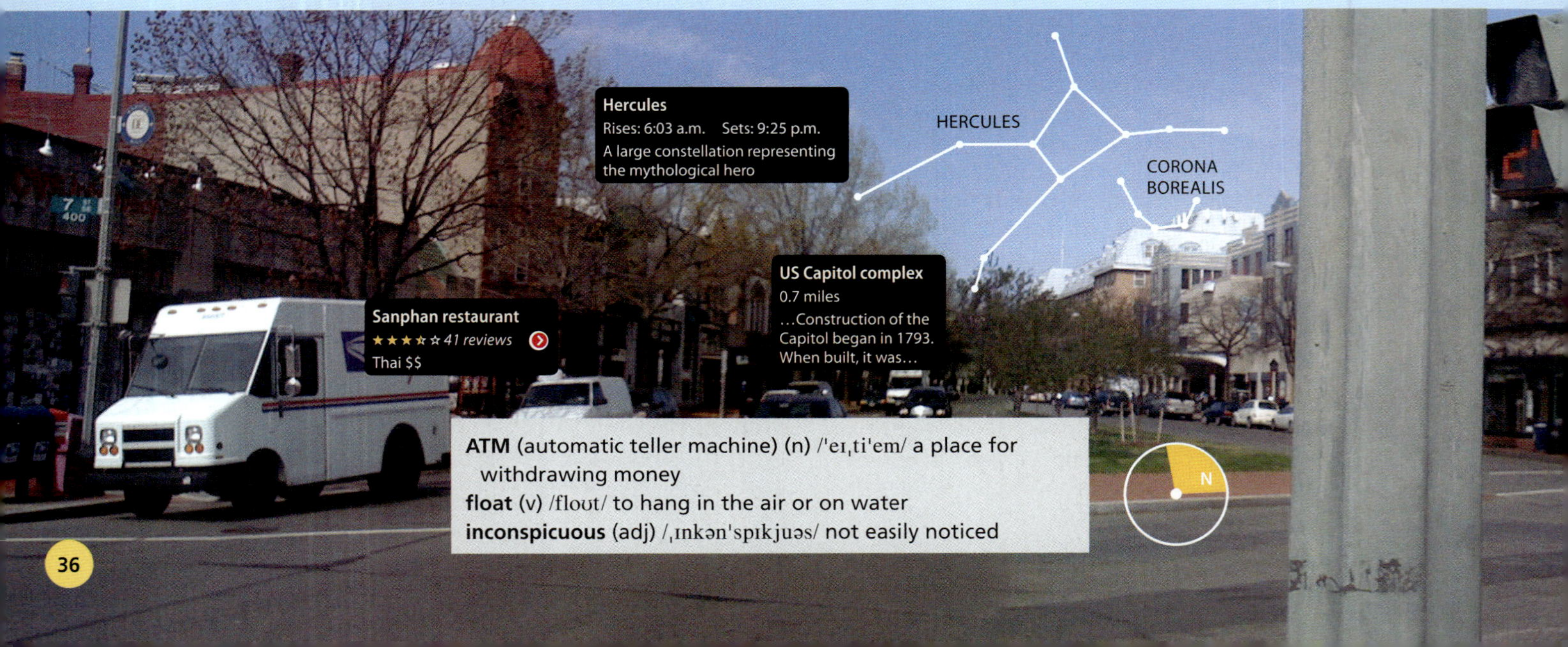

ATM (automatic teller machine) (n) /ˈeɪˌtiˈem/ a place for withdrawing money
float (v) /floʊt/ to hang in the air or on water
inconspicuous (adj) /ˌɪnkənˈspɪkjuəs/ not easily noticed

4 As a class, discuss the questions.

1 Which of the AR applications described in the article do you think will be really useful?
2 Can you think of any other applications?
3 What do you think is the answer to the author's final question?

Grammar future continuous and future perfect

5 Look at the sentences (a–e) and the verbs in bold. Which sentences describe:

1 an action in progress some time in the future?
2 an action completed before a certain point of time in the future?

a A few years from now, the quantity of information available **will have increased** enormously.
b Ten years from now, people trying to fix their cars **won't be looking** at repair manuals.
c They **will be wearing** a device that projects animated 3-D computer graphics onto the equipment under repair.
d In ten years' time this device **will have been replaced** by contact lenses etched with LEDs.
e But in our new AR worlds, how **will we be interacting** with each other?

FUTURE CONTINUOUS and FUTURE PERFECT

Future continuous
We will be using...
We won't (will not) be using...
Will we be using...?
Future perfect
We will have used...
We won't (will not) have used...
Will we have used...?

For more information and practice, see page 160.

6 Look at the grammar box. Complete the predictions (1–10) by putting the verb in the future continuous or future perfect.
Ten years from now:

1 very few people in the developed world .... (use) credit cards because cell phone payment .... (replace) them.
2 people .... (sit) in front of traditional computers much less than they do now.
3 data security .... (become) a huge issue because mobile devices will store so much personal information.
4 advertisers .... (put) their ads on mobile devices instead of in traditional media like TV, magazines, etc.
5 we .... (get) used to ads which target us directly with personalized messages.
6 body sensors connected to our mobile devices .... (provide) us with real-time information about our health.
7 the problem of short battery life .... (disappear) because phones and mobile devices .... (use) more sophisticated power sources, like kinetic energy.
8 cell phones .... (become) very sophisticated, so that in addition to using them as a calendar, address book, and music player, you .... (also / use) them as your secretary, accountant, and lawyer.
9 everyone .... (use) universal translators in their cell phones, which will make language learning less necessary.
10 it is unlikely that we .... (find) a way to use technology to know exactly where people are, because legally it is so difficult.

Speaking

7 Work in groups. Discuss the predictions for mobile technology in Exercise 6 and decide which ones you think will come true and which not. Then make two more predictions of your own.

3c One size doesn't fit all

Reading

1 What does the term "one size fits all" mean about a product? What products could it be applied to?

2 Read the article once quickly. Are the facts about appropriate technology true (T) or false (F)?

1 It's simple technology.
2 It's used in developing countries.
3 It improves people's lives.

3 Find a phrase in the article that defines what "appropriate technology" means these days. What does the author say about this?

4 Work in pairs. Discuss what each of these devices is and what it's an example of according to the author.

a central heating system	a solar-powered lamp
a device for shelling corn	a water purifier
a sewing machine	an efficient stove

5 Look at these phrases in bold from the article. Then choose the correct definition of the sentence.

1 in a way that **empowered** them (para 1)
gave them more *energy* / *control*
2 **intermediate** technology solutions (para 2)
temporary / *not too complicated* solutions
3 **has its place** in the developed world (para 3)
can also *be useful* / *be found* in
4 a way to **harness** the energy (para 4)
a way to *convert* / *make use* of the energy
5 they **valued** the time (para 5)
they *appreciated* / *calculated* the time
6 **gas-guzzling** cars (para 6)
cars that consume *a lot of gas* / *little gas*

Critical thinking balancing arguments

6 What are the potential risks and benefits associated with appropriate technology? Find the arguments in the article and make notes.

7 Work in pairs. Compare your answers. Is the author in favor of appropriate technology or not?

Vocabulary useful devices

8 Complete the definitions with these adjectives.

appropriate	easy	efficient	long-term
renewable	useful	old	

1 It's a very **neat** solution: both clever and *appropriate* .
2 It's a **time-consuming process**. We need to find a solution that's more ________ .
3 We don't just want a **quick fix**; we want a ________ solution.
4 It's a **handy gadget**, much more ________ than an average penknife.
5 It's not **cutting-edge technology**, but often the ________ ways are the best.
6 It's essentially a **labor-saving device**; it makes cutting up wood very ________ .
7 It's an **environmentally-friendly product** because it's made from ________ materials.

9 Work in pairs. Tell your partner about your favorite device or gadget using one of the expressions in Exercise 8.

Speaking

10 Work in pairs. Complete the sentences (1–8) using these phrases. What is each product?

6 hours	about 4 pounds
6 people	light and a little heat
only $3.10	put up in a few minutes
solar power	strong nylon

Product 1
1 It can hold up to…
2 It's made of…
3 It can be…
4 It weighs…

Product 2
5 It runs on…
6 It lasts up to…
7 It costs…
8 It provides…

11 Work in groups. You are going to take part in a competition: "Best appropriate technology product of the year." Your group will have to present one of the products shown below. Look at the instructions on page 153.

one size doesn't fit all

Even if the term "appropriate technology" is a relatively new one, the concept certainly isn't. In the 1930s, Mahatma Gandhi claimed that the advanced technology used by Western industrialized nations did not represent the right route to progress for his homeland, India. His favorite machines were the sewing machine, a device invented "out of love," he said, and the bicycle, which he rode all his life. He wanted the poor villagers of India to use technology that empowered them and helped them to become self-reliant.

This was also the philosophy promoted by E. F. Schumacher in his famous 1970s book *Small Is Beautiful*, which called for "intermediate technology" solutions. Do not start with technology and see what it can do for people, he argued. Instead, "find out what people are doing and then help them to do it better." According to Schumacher, it did not matter whether the technological answers to people's needs were simple or sophisticated. What was important was that solutions were long-term, practical, and, above all, firmly in the hands of the users.

More recently, the term "appropriate technology" has come to mean not just technology which is suited to the needs and capabilities of the user, but technology that takes particular account of environmental, ethical, and cultural considerations. That is clearly a much more difficult thing to achieve. Often it is found in rural communities in developing or less industrialized countries. For example, solar-powered lamps that bring light to areas with no electricity and water purifiers that work simply by the action of sucking through a straw. But the principle of appropriate technology does not only apply to developing countries. It also has its place in the developed world.

For example, a Swedish state-owned company has found a way to harness the energy produced by the 250,000 bodies rushing through Stockholm's central train station each day. The body heat is absorbed by the building's ventilation system, then used to warm up water that is pumped through pipes over to the new office building nearby. It's old technology, a system of pipes, water, and pumps, but used in a new way. It is expected to bring down central heating costs in the building by up to 20 percent.

Wherever it is deployed, there is no guarantee, however, that appropriate technology will in fact be appropriate. After some visiting engineers observed how labor-intensive and slow it was for the women of a Guatemalan village to shell corn by hand, they designed a simple mechanical device to do the job more quickly. The new device certainly saved time, but after a few weeks the women returned to the old manual method. Why? Because they valued the time that hand-shelling gave them to chat and exchange news.

In another case, in Malawi, a local entrepreneur was encouraged to manufacture super-efficient wood-burning stoves to sell to local villagers. Burning wood in an open fire, which is traditional in the developing world, is responsible for 10–20 percent of all global CO_2 emissions, so this seemed to be an excellent scheme. However, the entrepreneur was so successful that he bought himself a whole fleet of gas-guzzling cars. "We haven't worked out the CO_2 implications of that yet," said a spokesman for the organization that promoted the scheme.

3d Computer problems

Real life asking for and offering technical help

1 Work in pairs. Ask and answer the questions.

1 How are your computer skills?
2 Can you use the following applications proficiently?

- a search engine (like Google)
- spreadsheets (like Microsoft Excel)
- a presentation slide show (like PowerPoint)
- photo editing (like Photoshop)
- word processing (like Microsoft Word)

2 Where do you turn for computer help? Do people turn to you?

3 **10** Listen to a conversation about a computer problem. What is Ben trying to do? What two possible solutions does Sophie propose?

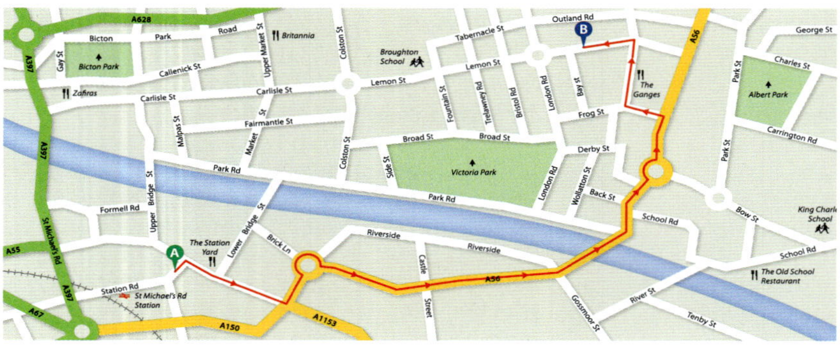

4 **10** Listen again and complete sentences 1–10.

ASKING FOR AND OFFERING TECHNICAL HELP

Person in need of help	Helper
Can you give me a hand? I'm having trouble [1] ………… .	OK. What do you want to do exactly?
I'm trying to [2] ………… .	You could just [3] ………… .
The trouble is [4] ………… .	Let me take a look.
What should I do then?	There are two possibilities. You can either [5] ………… or…
What does that involve?	I'll show you. Just [6] ………… . That should do the trick.
I see, but [7] ………… . What else do you suggest?	Have you tried [8] ………… ? If you do a search, you might [9] ………… .
OK I'll give that a try.	Feel free to [10] ………… .

5 **Pronunciation** stress in two-syllable verbs

a **11** Work in pairs. Listen for these phrases and note how the stress in the two-syllable verbs falls on the second syllable. Then practice saying them.

What do you suggest?
What does that involve?
It won't allow me to copy it.
First select the picture,…
What are you trying to achieve?
What solution do you propose?
Did you attach the document?

b Think of two more two-syllable verbs. Put them into a phrase or sentence. Then tell another pair your words.

6 Choose one of the tasks below or think of a technical problem that you have had. Then roleplay a conversation similar to the one in Exercise 4. Use the box to help you. Begin like this:

Can you help me? I'm trying to edit this photo.

I'll try. What do you want to do exactly?

- editing a photo of a person (to leave only the head and shoulders)
- sorting a list of names (members of a club you are the secretary of) alphabetically from A–Z
- adding your comments to someone else's document (a report written by a colleague)
- making your presentation slides more interesting (they are just plain text for now)
- searching the Internet to get the right information (such as up-to-date news about smart technology)

3e A technical problem

Writing short email requests

1 Match the emails (1–4) with the correct reply (A–D) below. Answer the questions.

1 What is the relationship between the correspondents in each case?
2 What help is offered in response to each request?

2 Writing skill being polite

a How polite you are depends on your relationship to your correspondent and on what you are asking for. Underline the phrases used to make polite requests in emails 1–4 and the polite forms used to apologize in emails A–D.

b Now answer the questions.

1 What word is used for more formal requests?
2 What is the difference between *can you* and *could you*?
3 Is *would you mind* more or less direct than *could you please*?
4 What is a more formal way of saying *I'm sorry*?

3 Word focus *out of*

a Work in pairs. Circle the expressions with *out of* in the emails and discuss what you think they mean. Then compare your answers with another pair.

b Complete these other expressions with *out of* using the words given.

blue   date   hands   luck   order   time

1 I've done all I can to get them to change their decision. It's out of my ________ now.
2 She is still in shock after losing her job; the news came out of the ________.
3 I'm afraid that printer is out of ________. You'll have to use the one in the next office.
4 This information is out of ________. It has last year's numbers on it, not this year's
5 I'm sorry we are out of ________. Let's continue the discussion tomorrow.
6 You're out of ________, I'm afraid. We sold the last one an hour ago.

4 Look at the following situation and write a short email requesting help.

You buy two cartridges for your printer online, but when they arrive you notice that the expiration date on them has already passed. Write and ask for replacements to be sent.

5 Exchange emails with your partner. Use these questions to check your partner's email. Then write a reply.

- Are the situation and the action demanded clear?
- Is the email in the right tone (formal or informal) and polite in its request?

1 Three months ago I bought one of your X3000 digital cameras from a store that has since gone out of business. The camera is fine but I cannot find the user manual. Could you please tell me where I can find one? I've looked on the Internet, but without success. Thank you.

2 I bought a printer at your store only five weeks ago and the pages are coming out very light. I am very disappointed and would like to return it and get a new one. Can you please tell me how?

3 Thanks a lot for the advice with the car, Jim. I changed the air filter and it's running much better now. Just out of curiosity, do you happen to know anything else I could do to improve its performance? Let me know!

4 Would you mind stopping by and having a look at my bike sometime? It's making a strange noise. I'd be really grateful. Please don't go out of your way, though. Anytime in the next week is fine.

A Sorry, I'd love to help, but I'm going on vacation tomorrow for three weeks. Why not take it to Cycle Surgery on Main Street? They know their stuff.

B I am sorry, but an exchange is out of the question. It is too long after the original purchase date. However, from what you say, it may be that it is just out of ink. Please check the ink cartridges. If that does not work, contact our technical team for further advice.

C I'm afraid I'm out of my depth there. Try looking at the discussion boards on the Internet for your particular model. I'm sure someone'll know.

D I regret to say that we only supply user manuals with the equipment at the time of purchase. However, you can download one using the link below.

3f Augmented reality

Video

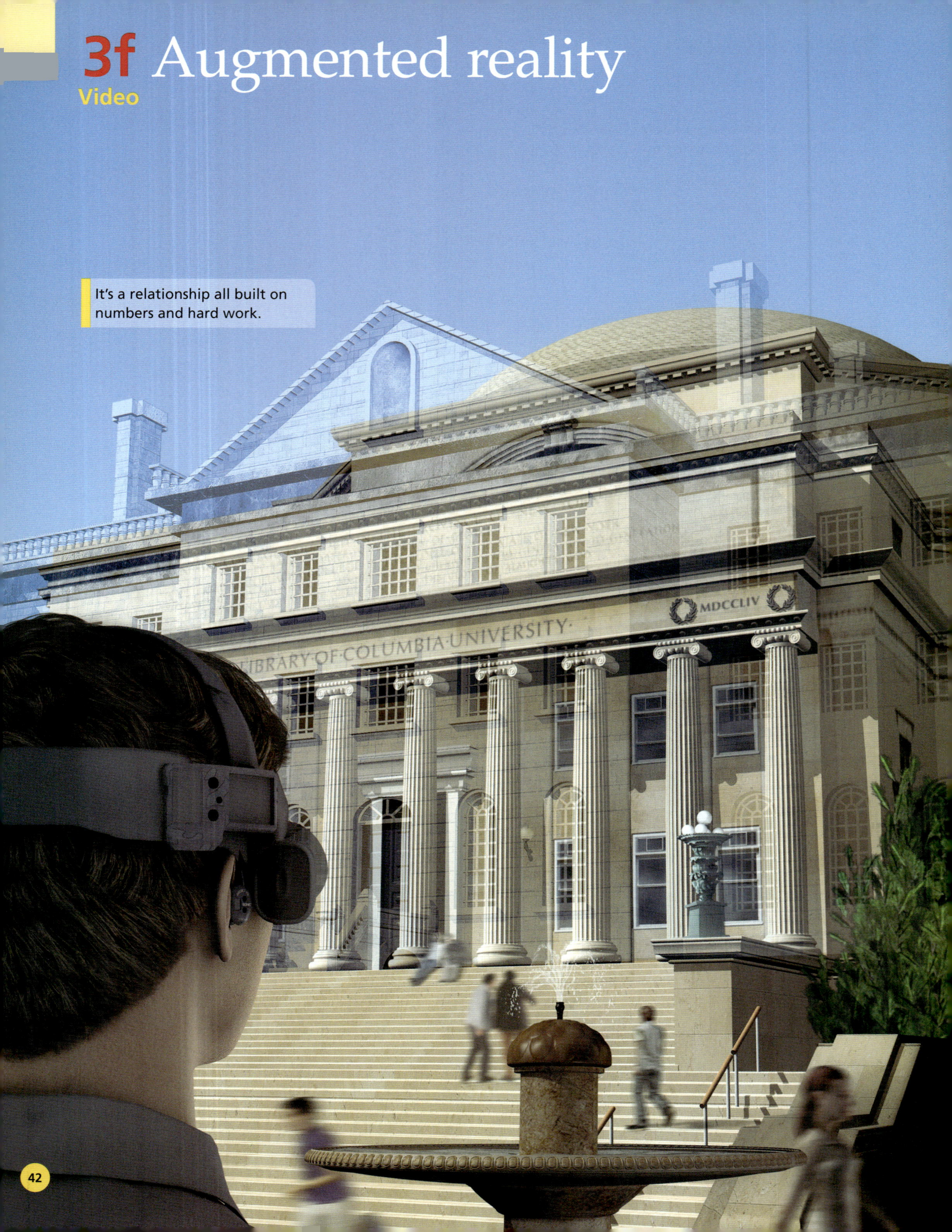

It's a relationship all built on numbers and hard work.

Before you watch

1 Work in groups. Look at the picture and discuss the questions.

1 What do you know about augmented reality?
2 Where do you think the man in the picture is?
3 What is he wearing? Why?
4 What do you think the caption means?

2 How do you think a headset like this could be used? Work in pairs and write down three things you think you could use it for.

While you watch

3 Watch the video and check your ideas from Exercise 2. Which three groups of people does the video say could benefit from this technology?

4 Watch the video again and correct these sentences.

1 Professor Feiner is working with a group of biology students.

....

2 The team wants to develop a virtual world that is separate from the physical world.

....

3 The virtual world can provide extra information about what you feel.

....

4 A global positioning system allows the team to use the equipment in the laboratory.

....

5 The system wouldn't be very useful for people to find their way around places they don't know well.

....

6 Professor Feiner developed the technology because he has a bad sense of smell.

....

5 Watch the video again and answer the questions.

1 What is the Columbia University program trying to do?

....

2 How could these people use this technology?
a firefighters ....
b pilots ....
c tourists ....

3 What do you think a "situated documentary" is?

....

4 What would visitors to the campus "see" in addition to the library?

....

After you watch

6 **Roleplay an interview with Professor Feiner**

Work in pairs. Use the information in the list.

Student A: Imagine you are a reporter for the Columbia University newspaper. Prepare a list of questions to ask Professor Feiner.

Student B: Imagine you are Professor Feiner. You are going to be interviewed for the Columbia University newspaper. Think about what you are going to say to the reporter.

- when you started the project
- how many students work with you
- what the technology could be used for
- what you have to do in the laboratory
- why you decided to do research on augmented reality
- how you think the technology could be advanced in the future

Act out the interview. Then change roles and act out the interview again.

7 Work in pairs and discuss these questions.

1 Have you ever seen or used any of the following devices?

- simulators for learning to drive
- night vision glasses for seeing in the dark
- billboard ads that speak to pedestrians
- Wii™ games
- T-shirts with moving images

2 How useful do you think they are?
3 What are the advantages and disadvantages of augmented reality technology?

asylum (n) /ə'saɪləm/ a hospital for mentally ill patients
blueprints (n) /'blu,prɪnts/ building plans
cockpit (n) /'kɑk,pɪt/ place in an airplane where the pilot sits
handheld (adj) /'hænd,held/ carried in the hand
obscure (v) /əb'skjʊr/ hide
overlay (v) /,oʊvər'leɪ/ show on top of
prototype (n) /'proʊtə,taɪp/ an experimental working model
superimpose (v) /,supərɪm'poʊz/ put one image on top of another
surroundings (n) /sə'raʊndɪŋz/ the area around something or someone

UNIT 3 REVIEW

Grammar

1 Work in pairs. Name at least three of the global problems mentioned in the unit.

2 Look at the photo. What global problems could these windmills be the answer to?

3 Read the text and answer the questions.

1 What is the problem the author mentions?
2 What should be our target if we want to solve the problem?
3 How can we achieve this target?
4 Why are windmills not a solution?

4 Choose the correct option.

Reducing CO_2 emissions is perhaps the world's biggest problem. If we [1] *won't reduce / don't reduce* our emissions to almost zero, global temperatures [2] *will continue / are continuing* to rise. At the current rate, temperatures [3] *will be increasing / will have increased* by three or four degrees by 2050.

CO_2 emissions [4] *will come / are about to come* down if one of three things [5] *happens / will happen*. First, if we change our lifestyles and stop using electricity; second, if the gadgets we use don't need energy; or third, if we find a way to generate electricity without producing CO_2.

Well, people [6] *are not stopping / are not going to stop* using electricity. If anything, in 30 years' time, they [7] *will be using / will have used* more. Perhaps in the future, gadgets [8] *will consume / will be consuming* less energy, but certainly not zero energy.

That leaves only one possibility. Scientists [9] *are having / will have* to find a way to generate CO_2-free electricity. Wind and solar power are only intermittent energy sources. What miracle invention [10] *will be generating / will have generated* our electricity in 2050? No one knows, but the miracle will need to happen soon.

I CAN	
talk about future events, intentions, and arrangements using a variety of future forms	☐
make predictions using the future continuous and future perfect	☐

Vocabulary

5 Read the definitions. Complete the words. The first letter has been given for you.

1 too much information = information o________
2 a big advance in science = a technological b________
3 technology suited to its context = a________ technology
4 a clever answer to a problem = a n________ solution
5 a useful device = a h________ gadget
6 a fast, easy solution to a problem = a quick f________

6 Work in small groups and answer these questions.

1 Which of these problems do you think technology will solve? Why?

epidemics   overpopulation   pollution   starvation

2 In what area will new technology most change people's lives in the next 50 years?

I CAN	
talk about global problems and solutions	☐
talk about new technology: devices and gadgets	☐

Real life

7 Match each statement or question (1–5) with the correct response (a–e).

1 Can you give me a hand?
2 What do you want to do exactly?
3 If you restart the computer, that should do the trick.
4 What else do you suggest?
5 The trouble is the computer won't allow me to copy it.

a Have you tried looking for another type of map?
b Thanks. I'll give that a try.
c Sure. I'll be with you in a second.
d Let me have a look.
e I'm trying to paste this map into a document.

8 Work in pairs. Act out a conversation asking for help with a computer problem.

I CAN	
ask for and give technical help	☐
talk about computing tasks	☐

Speaking

9 Work in pairs. Tell each other your predictions for your life (education, job, where you will live, travel, relationships, etc.). Use the future continuous and future perfect to talk about:

- a year from now
- three years from now
- ten years from now

10 Change partners and tell each other your original partner's predictions.

Unit 4 Art and creativity

A juggler in Scotland performs at dusk.
Photograph by Emanuele Picchirallo

FEATURES

1 Work in pairs. Match the performers with what and where they perform. How many combinations can you make?

Example:

a dance company + a performance + a theater

Who: a band, a comedian, a dance company, a circus act, a drama company, an orchestra, an artist

What: a gig, a show, an exhibition, a classical concert, a play, a musical, a performance

Where: a concert hall, a live music venue, a theater, a gallery, a club, the street

2 Look at the photo and caption. Which words from Exercise 1 can describe what is happening? Have you seen anything like this in your country?

3 What's your favorite type of performance? What performance do you dislike? Tell a partner.

4a All about Melbourne

Listening

1 Work in pairs. Ask and answer the questions.

1 What art forms are popular in your city or country: theater, dance, music, movies, art (like painting and sculpture)?
2 Which of the arts have you practiced yourself?
3 Which of the arts do you follow?
4 Can you describe an exhibition or a performance that you've enjoyed recently?

2 Discuss what type of activities and opportunities Australia offers visitors and tourists.

3 **12** Listen to part of *The Travel Show*, a weekly radio program, about Melbourne, and answer the questions.

1 What is the essential difference between Melbourne and Sydney?
2 What does Melbourne offer visitors?
3 What does it offer local people? What do they enjoy in their free time?

4 **12** Listen again and mark the statements true (T) or false (F).

1 Melbourne has great weather and many places of natural beauty.
2 It is known as Australia's architectural capital.
3 The arts are enjoyed by a small number of art lovers.
4 The summer is a good time for festivals.
5 Melbourne's Formula One motor race and tennis tournament are world famous.
6 Not many visitors know about the local sports.

5 Would you like to visit Melbourne after hearing this guide? What would you do there?

Grammar expressions of quantity

6 Turn to the audioscript on page 176. Find the examples of the items below. Make a note of which expressions have *of* after them and which don't. Then compare your list with your partner.

- expressions in the script that mean "many or much"
- expressions that mean "not many or much"
- expressions that mean "some"

> **EXPRESSIONS OF QUANTITY**
>
> **+ plural count noun**
> *(not) many, (a) few, a (small) number of, several*
> **+ noncount noun**
> *(not) much, (a) little (of), a/an (large) amount of*
> **+ plural count or noncount noun**
> *a lot of, lots of, plenty of, loads of, lack of, (almost) no, (not/hardly) any, some, enough*
>
> For more information and practice, see page 161.

7 Look at the grammar box. Then read the pairs of sentences and answer the questions.

1 Which expression means "some" and which means "only a small number of"?
   a **Few** people will be familiar with it.
   b Melbourne may have **a few** gray days.
2 Can you use the same expression in both sentences?
   a In fact there are **hardly any** forms of artistic expression that are not represented.
   b In fact there are **almost no** forms of artistic expression that are not represented.
3 Which expression is used more often in affirmative sentences?
   a **Lots of** people around the world know the Australian Formula One Grand Prix.
   b But there **aren't many** people who know Australian Rules football.
4 Which expression is used with count nouns?
   a Art enjoys **an enormous amount of** support.
   b There are **a huge number of** smaller art spaces and venues.
5 Which expression is used in negative sentences?
   a There is **a lot of** information on what to do in Melbourne on the website.
   b There **isn't much** information about where to eat on the website.

8 Choose the correct option to complete each sentence.

1 A visit to the opera can cost *much / a lot of* money.
2 A reasonable *number / amount* of the winter festivals are free.
3 There is almost *no / any* rain in Melbourne at Christmastime.
4 There are *few / a few* tickets for the Australian Open Tennis available at the gate.
5 We saw *several / some* interesting street art at the Sweet Streets festival.
6 *Almost / Hardly* anyone attended the play.
7 Visitors show *a little / little* interest in dance.
8 There aren't as *many / much* differences between Melbourne and Sydney as people say.

9 Pronunciation weak form: *of*

a 13 Listen and note how *of* is pronounced in these phrases.

> a huge amount of support
> a huge number of galleries
> a lack of natural attractions
> a lot of information
> lots of people

b Work in pairs. Practice saying these phrases where *of* is a weak form.

> as a matter of fact
> first of all
> in spite of that
> instead of me
> just the two of us
> most of the time
> of course
> that's nice of you

10 Work in pairs. Look at the charts on page 153 showing the results of a survey on Australians' participation in the arts. Complete the sentences using one word to describe what they show.

1 Overall quite a *lot* of Australians take an interest in the arts, but only a .... participate creatively.
2 It seems that .... of Australians read literature and a surprising .... of them also write creatively.
3 There is certainly .... lack of interest in the visual arts, with almost half of the population being involved in some way.
4 .... attend concerts or musicals and .... anyone did not listen to music at all.
5 The main reason for not participating is not having .... time. But the .... of money it costs to be involved and a .... of opportunities are also important factors.

Speaking

11 Work in groups. Research your classmates' participation in the arts and then report your findings. Follow these steps:

- Each group must research ONE of the following: visual arts and crafts, theater and dance, reading and writing, music.
- Make a list of four or five questions to find out how people participate (creatively or receptively) and reasons for non-participation.
- Go around the class asking and answering questions.
- Come back to your group and share your results. Make conclusions, using expressions of quantity.
- Present your findings to the class.

4b Reverse graffiti

Listening

1 🔊 **14** Look at the statements about art. Do you agree with any of them? Listen to an artist's opinion and write down what he says about each one.

1. Art should be pleasing to the viewer.
2. Art should involve effort on the part of the artist.
3. Art should involve technical skill.
4. Art should have a social message or make a political point.

2 🔊 **14** Listen again. What are the roles of an artist and a viewer according to the speaker?

3 Work in pairs. Discuss what each of these types of artwork is.

graffiti landscape sculpture sketch

▶ WORDBUILDING suffixes

Some noun suffixes have no clear meaning (*-ment, -tion*). Others like *-scape* have a particular meaning: *cityscape, landscape, seascape, moonscape*

REVERSE GRAFFITI

When is cleaning walls a crime? When you're doing it to create art, obviously. A number of street artists around the world have started expressing themselves through a practice known as reverse graffiti. Inspired by the "clean me" messages that you see written on the back of some trucks, they find dirty surfaces and inscribe them with images or messages using cleaning brushes or pressure hoses. Either way, it's the same principle: the image is made by cleaning away the dirt.

Each artist has an individual style, but all artists share a common aim: to draw attention to pollution in our cities. The UK's Paul Curtis, better known as Moose, operates around Leeds and has been commissioned by a number of companies to make reverse graffiti ads.

Brazilian artist Alexandre Orion turned one of São Paulo's traffic tunnels into an amazing mural by scraping away the dirt. Made up of a series of white skulls, the mural reminds drivers of the effect their pollution is having on the planet. "Every driver sits in the comfort of a car, but they don't give any consideration to the price their comfort has for the environment and consequently for themselves," says Orion.

The anti-pollution message of the reverse graffiti artists confuses city authorities since the main argument against graffiti is that it spoils the appearance of both public and private property. This was what Leeds City Council said about Moose's work: "Leeds residents want to live in clean and attractive neighborhoods. We view this kind of advertising as environmental damage and will take strong action against any advertisers carrying out such campaigns." It seems that no action was taken against the advertisers—no fines or any other punishment—but Moose himself was ordered to clean up his act. Was he supposed to make all the property he had cleaned dirty again?

As for Orion, the authorities were annoyed but could find nothing to charge him with. They had no other option but to clean the tunnel—but only the parts Orion had already cleaned. The artist merely continued his campaign on the other side. The city officials then decided to take drastic action. They not only cleaned the whole tunnel but also every other tunnel in São Paulo.

Reading

4 What do you think about graffiti in cities? Do you think it improves or spoils the appearance of the urban landscape?

5 What do you think *reverse graffiti* is? Read the article and check.

6 Use the information in the article to complete these sentences. Use one word per space.

1 Reverse graffiti works by cleaning away the .... on walls.
2 The aim of the reverse graffiti artists is to highlight the problem of ....
3 Some reverse graffiti artists are paid to make images that act as ....
4 Orion made his message for ....
5 The local authorities in Leeds were .... by this new type of graffiti.
6 In São Paulo, the response of the authorities was to .... every tunnel.

7 Work in pairs. Discuss the questions.

1 Do you like this kind of graffiti?
2 If you were a city authority, how would you deal with reverse graffiti in your city?

Grammar determiners

8 Work in pairs. Look at the highlighted words in the article and decide if the nouns that come after each are singular, plural, or noncount.

▶ DETERMINERS
each, every, either, the whole + singular noun
all, both + plural noun
any, no + singular or plural noun
all, any, no + noncount noun
For more information and practice, see page 161.

9 Look at the grammar box. Answer the questions.

1 Which determiner emphasizes the individual?
a **Every** artist has an individual style.
b **Each** artist has an individual style.
c **All** artists have an individual style.

2 Which determiner(s) talk about two things?
a **Every** way, it's the same principle.
b **Either** way, it's the same principle.
c **Both** ways, it's the same principle.

3 Which sentence(s) about the action taken against advertisers are negative?
a They took **no** action against them.
b They didn't take **any** action against them.
c Did they take **any** action against them?

10 Choose the correct option. Sometimes there is more than one possibility.

Every / all / each child is an artist. The problem is how to remain an artist once he grows up. *Pablo Picasso, artist*

Every / all / each art is an imitation of nature. *Seneca, philosopher and writer*

Drawing is the honesty of the art. There is *any / no* possibility of cheating. It is either good or bad. *Salvador Dali, artist*

As an artist you want it *both / either / every* ways. You want it to have an immediate impact, and deep meaning as well. *Damien Hirst, artist*

Some days I produce something, other days nothing. *Each / Every / Either* way, I feel it's time well spent. *Anonymous, artist*

Science and art belong to *all / the whole / every* world, and before them vanish the barriers of nationality. *Goethe, writer*

Let *each / every / all* man exercise the art he knows. *Aristophanes, dramatist*

Do not fear mistakes; there aren't *no / any*. *Miles Davis, musician*

11 Discuss the quotations. How do they fit with the definitions of art that you discussed earlier?

12 Complete the rules for an art prize with a determiner.

1 .... candidates are chosen for an exhibition they have given in the last year.
2 Candidates are nominated by the public or by the jury. .... way, the jury has the final say in the four who are shortlisted.
3 The aim of the prize is to celebrate .... innovation and young talent.
4 .... candidate is invited to display examples of their work at the exhibition.
5 .... artist over 50 years can enter.
6 The artists can use .... medium they like.
7 The winner receives $25,000. .... other shortlisted candidates get $5,000.

Speaking

13 Your city would like to commission a piece of art that would (a) improve the appearance of the downtown area; (b) be fun; and (c) attract visitors. Work in small groups and:

- discuss what you want and who should make it
- make a list of rules for the competition

14 Exchange your rules with another group. Then submit an idea for piece of art to be evaluated

4c Hip-hop planet

Reading

1 Work in pairs. Look at the different music genres in the box. Discuss the questions.

1 How often do you listen to each type of music?
2 When you listen, do you pay much attention to the lyrics?
3 Do you identify strongly with this type of music?

blues	classical
country	hip-hop
jazz	pop
reggae	rock
soul	traditional / folk

2 Discuss what themes or attitudes you associate with hip-hop and rap music. Who do you think listens to this music? Then read the article and compare your answers with what the author says.

3 Read the article again quickly. Answer the questions.

1 What was the theme of the first rap song the author heard?
2 Aside from music, what are other artistic expressions of hip-hop culture?
3 What do the DJs do to create hip-hop's individual sound?
4 What is the appeal of hip-hop to middle-class children?
5 Why does Assane say that rap belongs to his country?
6 What does the author not like about hip-hop music?

4 Explain these phrases.

1 It sounded like a broken record (para 1)
2 the way you step over a crack in the pavement (para 2)
3 life on the other side of the tracks (para 4)
4 its macho pose (para 6)
5 the empty moral cupboard that we have left our children (para 7)

Critical thinking analyzing contrasts

5 This article is all about what hip-hop is and isn't. Find and underline sentences that tell you:

1 a what the author thought of rap music 26 years ago
b what he thinks now
2 a the environment in which rap music originated
b where it thrives now
3 a the message conveyed by the early rappers
b the message conveyed by successful hip-hop artists now
4 a that hip-hop culture can seem selfish
b that this selfishness in young people is not their fault

6 Work in pairs. Compare your answers, then write a short summary of the values of hip-hop culture, according to the author. Do you agree with him?

Word focus *cool*

7 *Cool* has a few meanings in English: (1) not warm; (2) stylish and fashionable; (3) calm; (4) OK. Which meaning does it have in the article (para 5) and in sentences 1–6?

1 I don't know what I've done to offend Liz. She was really **cool with** me when I spoke to her earlier.
2 It's not **cool** to arrive early at a party like that.
3 Jaime **lost his cool** completely when his computer froze.
4 That's a really **cool** jacket. Where did you get it?
5 I think she did very well to **keep her cool** with that customer. I would have gotten very angry with them.
6 Wait for the frying pan to **cool down** before you add more oil.

Speaking

8 Work in pairs. Look at the lyrics below. What themes and attitudes to life can you identify in each genre?

Country song

When you ain't got a friend to lean on
There are folks you can depend on
Home, that's where you turn to
Family won't turn their back on you
Yeah, it's all right there in your own backyard
They'll be waitin' when times are hard

Rock song

Ooh, be true to yourself
Don't let anyone put you down
If you feel you're getting tied
Then ride right on out of town
Don't be nobody's slave
Live your life—that's what I say

9 Look at the genres in Exercise 1 and discuss the questions.

1 What values does each genre project?
2 Do you have to believe these values to like the music?

HIP-HOP PLANET

BY JAMES MCBRIDE

I first heard rap in 1980, at a party in Harlem. It sounded like a broken record. It was a version of an old hit record called *Good Times*, the same four bars looped over and over. On top of this loop, a kid chanted a rhyme about how he was the best disc jockey in the world. It was called *Rapper's Delight*. I thought it was the most ridiculous thing I'd ever heard.

For the next 26 years, I avoided rap music the way you step over a crack in the pavement. I heard it booming out of cars and alleyways from Paris to Abidjan, but I never listened. In doing so, I missed the most important cultural event in my lifetime. No American music has exploded across the world with such force since swing jazz in the 1930s. This defiant culture of song, graffiti, and dance, collectively known as hip-hop, has permeated almost every society.

Hip-hop began in the mid-1970s, in an almost bankrupt New York City. The bored kids of the South Bronx and Harlem came up with a new entertainment. This is how it worked: one guy, the DJ, played records on two turntables. Another guy—or girl—served as master of ceremonies, or MC. The DJs learned to move the record back and forth under the needle to create a *scratch*, or to drop the needle on the record and play *a break* over and over to keep people dancing. The MCs rapped over the music to keep the party going. One MC sought to out-talk the other. Dance styles were created. Graffiti artists also emphasized the *I* because the music was all about identity: I am the best.

Initially, hip-hop artists produced socially-conscious songs that described life on the other side of the tracks, where people are denied the same opportunities as the rich. Grandmaster Flash's 1982 hit *The Message* is a perfect example. It describes a child who is born and raised in the ghetto, hating the world for his situation and all the things he cannot have.

These days most commercial rappers in America brag about their lives of crime and what fame and money have brought them, among which women seem to be just another material possession. For those from poor backgrounds, the life of a successful rapper has become an aspiration; for richer suburban kids, it is a symbol of something cool.

In poor urban communities around the globe, rap music is a universal expression of outrage at the injustice of the distribution of wealth. Its macho pose has been borrowed from commercial hip-hop in the US, but for most, the music represents an old dream: a better life. "We want money to help our parents," Assane, a nineteen-year-old budding DJ from Dakar in Senegal, tells me. "We watch our mothers boil water to cook and have nothing to put in the pot. Rap doesn't belong to American culture," he says. "It belongs here. It has always existed here, because of our pain and our hardships and our suffering."

That is why, after 26 years, I have come to embrace this music I tried so hard to ignore. Much of hip-hop, particularly the commercial side, I hate. Yet I love the good of it. Even if some of it embraces violence, hip-hop is a music that exposes the empty moral cupboard that we have left our children. They can hear it and understand it. The question is: can we?

brag (v) /bræg/ speak proudly about your achievements
defiant (adj) /dɪˈfaɪənt/ challenging or opposing another's authority
looped (adj) /luːpt/ repeated without a break
out-talk (v) /ˌaʊt ˈtɔːk/ talk longer or better than another

4d Personal tastes

Real life describing likes and dislikes

1 Do you like musicals? Which ones have you seen? Did you see them live or on film? Tell your partner.

2 15 Listen to a conversation in which Tomas and Jae talk about the musical *The Lion King*. Put a check (✓) next to the items they both like and an ✗ next to those they don't.

ticket prices	☐	the music	☐
Disney comic characters	☐	the visual effects	☐
Elton John	☐	this production	☐
musicals in general	☐		

3 15 Look at the box. Tell your partner which of the phrases Tomas used to express each like and dislike. Then listen again and check.

DESCRIBING LIKES AND DISLIKES

Likes	Dislikes
I love…	I can't stand…
I'm a big fan of…	I'm not generally a fan of…
I'm really into…	I'm not very big on…
It is very inspiring.	…doesn't really do anything for me
It sounds right up my alley.	I never feel particularly/ especially inspired by…
I could watch / read / listen to… all day.	It doesn't really sound like my kind of thing.
	…really gets on my nerves
	I get a little tired of…

4 Work in pairs. Look at these sentences and say which words most naturally go in each space.

1 I'm not ______ big on romantic comedies.
2 I get ______ tired of reality TV shows.
3 I never feel ______ inspired by science fiction books.
4 I'm not ______ a fan of musicals.
5 Rap doesn't ______ do anything for me.
6 I'm afraid opera gets on my ______ .

5 Work in pairs. Tell each other about something (a type of music, characters in a book or a movie, a particular ad) that you dislike. Use the phrases in Exercise 3 to help you. Do you share each other's dislikes?

6 Now work in groups. Each of you think of a musical, play, movie, concert, TV show, or exhibition you enjoyed recently. Describe it to the group and compare and discuss your likes and dislikes. Use the box to help you.

I'm a big fan of Star Trek and I loved the last movie!

Really? I can't stand science fiction!

4e You have to see this

Writing an online review

1 Read the online review of an exhibition by a recent visitor to London. Would you follow the recommendation? Why?

2 Answer the questions. Then compare your answers in pairs.

1. How are the following themes organized in the review? Put them in order (1–5).
   - the recommendation
   - an introduction
   - the content of the exhibition
   - the occasion of the visit
   - where and when it is on
2. What information about the event does she include?
3. Is the tone of the review personal or impersonal?

3 Writing skill personalizing your writing

a Work in pairs. Look at the following features of personal and impersonal writing. Then find examples of the personal tone in the review.

Personal tone

- use pronouns
- use active verbs
- use contracted forms
- use phrasal verbs
- add personal details
- use conversational linking phrases (like *what's more*)
- share your feelings

Impersonal tone

- use pronouns
- use passive verbs
- use uncontracted forms
- use formal verbs
- avoids personal information
- use formal linking phrases (like *furthermore*)
- be objective in your judgments

http://www.travelreviews.com

I find that it's always worth checking out the parks when you visit a foreign city. Besides providing a welcome break, they can contain some interesting surprises. Last week, exhausted from visiting two museums and too tired even to think about shopping anymore, my friend and I took a walk in Kensington Gardens. I was so glad we did, because otherwise we'd have missed Anish Kapoor's mirror sculptures.

There are four of them, and rather than looking out of place as so many modern sculptures can, these really complemented their surroundings.

Sky Mirror, as its name suggests, is placed at an angle to reflect the changing sky. Another, Red Mirror, is also directed at the sky but has a red tint. The one I liked best was the C-Curve, a convex mirror that makes you see everything upside down. It was so funny to watch dogs and children approach it, trying to figure out what they were looking at.

The secret of this exhibition's success is that it makes you appreciate what is already a lovely park even more. It will be on display until March 30th. I'd definitely recommend taking the time to go and see it for yourself if you're in London. What's more, it's free!

4 Write a brief, personalized review of something for a website. Then exchange your review with another person in the class.

5 Read your partner's review. Check that it:

- makes you want to go and see this event.
- includes all the items described in Exercise 2 in their correct order.
- feels friendly and personal.
- includes features from Exercise 3.

4f Urban art

Video

Urban art is all about innovation.

Before you watch

1 Work in groups. Look at the photo and discuss the questions.

1 Where are the people?
2 What is unusual about the exhibition?
3 What do you know about graffiti?

2 Aside from graffiti, what other kinds of urban art can you think of? What kinds of art do you think you are going to see in this video?

While you watch

3 Watch the video and check your answers from Exercise 2.

4 Watch the video again and put these things in the order you first see them.

a a painting of a Japanese woman
b a train
c an art gallery
d a CD cover
e a shopping cart
f paint cans
g a trumpet

5 Mark whether each statement is true about Nick Posada (P) or Jafar Barron (B).

a He is a trumpeter.
b He is a graffiti artist.
c He grew up in a Philadelphia neighborhood.
d He has a record deal.
e He grew up in Washington, DC.
f His parents are jazz musicians.
g His first exhibition was in Georgetown.
h He plays in clubs where he grew up.

6 Answer the questions.

1 In what ways is urban art about innovation? Give three examples.

....

2 Why is Nick Posada disappointed when he visits the wall of fame?

....

3 What does Nick think real graffiti artists know?

....

4 Why does Chris Murray like graffiti art?

....

5 What is Jafar Barron's music a mix of?

....

6 What does Jafar think are his influences?

....

7 Use these words and phrases to complete what Don Kimes says about urban art (03:20 to 03:36).

authentic	boundaries	come from
emerge	envelope	one more step
to the edge		

It's about sort of taking what it is that you [1] ...., what you [2] .... from, what's [3] .... for you and pushing it [4] .... of its [5] ...., to the edge of its [6] ...., its limits and taking [7] ....

After you watch

8 Roleplay interviewing an urban artist

Work in pairs.

Student A: Imagine you are an urban artist. Choose a medium (visual or sound). Invent information about the following:

- your life (for example, where you grew up, what your parents do, where you live now)
- your art (for example, what you do, why you do it, what your inspiration is)
- your aspirations (for example, what you would like to happen, where you see your work in five years' time)

Student B: Imagine you are a local reporter. Interview the urban artist about his or her life, art, and aspirations.

Act out the interview, then change roles and act out the conversation again. Student B should choose a different medium.

9 Work in groups and discuss these questions.

1 What type of art do you like?
2 Does the type of art you like differ from art in your parents' generation? How?
3 Is innovation in art a good thing?

authentic (adj) /ɔ'θentɪk/ genuine, real
caution (v) /'kɔʃən/ warn someone about a problem or danger
collector (n) /kə'lektər/ a person who buys art
exposure (n) /ɪks'poʊʒər/ giving someone a particular experience
highlight (v) /'haɪˌlaɪt/ draw people's attention to something
innovative (adj) /'ɪnəˌveɪtɪv/ new and original
inventive (adj) /ɪn'ventɪv/ creative
uninhibited (adj) /ˌʌnɪn'hɪbɪtɪd/ saying and doing anything you want
vilify (v) /'vɪləˌfaɪ/ say bad things about someone or something

UNIT 4 REVIEW

Grammar

1 Work in pairs. What art festivals are famous in your country? What happens at them?

2 Read the article. What is the Edinburgh Fringe Festival famous for?

3 Choose the correct option to complete the article. Sometimes more than one option is correct.

The Edinburgh Fringe Festival is the world's largest art festival. It takes place [1] *all / every / each* year in August and for the [2] *all / every / whole* month the city is taken over by actors, street performers, comedians, artists, and musicians. There is [3] *some / little / enough* variety to please everyone. The festival attracts a huge [4] *number / amount / lack* of visitors from all over the world. There are over 2,000 different shows and the tickets don't cost [5] *a lot / much / plenty*, but since most people try to see [6] *a lot / many / plenty* of shows, the costs can add up.

[7] *Few / Little / A few* artists just come to perform for the fun of it, but in [8] *many / enough / plenty* cases they are young performers hoping to be discovered. The festival is perhaps best known for its comedy, and has launched the careers of [9] *some / several / any* notable comedians. But the festival is [10] *no / any / not any* respecter of reputations. [11] *All / Both / Either* unknown and well-known artists compete for attention and [12] *all / each / every* have an equal chance of success or failure.

I CAN	
use expressions of quantity	☐
use determiners	☐

Vocabulary

4 Put these words into three categories: music, art, and theater (four words per category).

a band	a gig	a musical
a play	a show	a sketch
an installation	drama company	folk
landscape	lyrics	sculpture

5 Work in small groups. Answer the questions.

1 Do you have a favorite work of art? What art or copies of art (e.g. prints, posters) do you have at home? Describe them and why you chose them.
2 What was the most memorable concert you ever saw?
3 How often do you go to the theater? What is the best thing you have seen there?

I CAN	
describe different art forms, performers, and venues	☐
talk about different kinds of art	☐

Real life

6 Put these phrases (a–f) into two groups: like and dislike.

a I can't stand…
b I'm not very big on…
c …don't really do anything for me.
d I'm a big fan of…
e …get on my nerves.
f I'm really into…

7 Work in groups. Use the phrases in Exercise 6 to tell each other about the kind of TV shows that you like and dislike.

I CAN	
describe my personal tastes in the arts	☐

Speaking

8 Work in groups. Tell each other about the arts in your city or country:

- how many people do what
- how expensive each activity is (for example, whether museums are free)
- how the government views the arts

Unit 5 Development

A minimalist beach chalet under construction on the Persian Gulf
Photograph by George Steinmetz

FEATURES

1 Work in pairs. Look at the photo and the six types of development in the box. What kind of development is represented here?

economic	personal	product
social	sustainable	urban

2 Match the examples of development below with the types of development in Exercise 1.

a new housing project	a new university
a new railway line	a zero-energy house
a new smart phone	learning a language

3 Describe examples of two types of development from your own experience. Were they positive?

I took a public speaking course. I don't really need it for my work, but I just thought it would be good for my own personal development. It was a really interesting experience; it gave me a lot of confidence.

5a From reality to fantasy

Reading

1 Work in pairs. The photo was taken in Dubai. Discuss the questions.

1 Where was it taken from?
2 What can you see below?
3 What do you know about Dubai? For example, where it is, its famous landmarks, who goes there?

2 Read the article and answer the questions.

1 How has Dubai changed in 50 years?
2 According to the author, what are the attractions for visitors and residents?
3 What do other countries feel about this change?

3 Would you like to visit Dubai? Why?

FROM REALITY TO FANTASY

There once was a sheikh with big dreams. His land was a sleepy village occupied by pearl divers, fishermen, and traders who docked their boats along a small creek. It was here that Sheikh Rashid bin Saeed al Maktoum imagined creating a gateway to the world. It was a dream he could not afford to realize. So in 1959, he asked a neighbor to lend him many millions of dollars. He made the creek wider, built roads, schools, and homes. With his young son Mohammed by his side, he walked along the empty waterfront and painted his dream with words. And some years later, it was as he had said: he built it, and they came.

Then it was his son's turn to carry on developing his father's vision. Sheikh Mohammed bin Rashid al Maktoum transformed Dubai into an air-conditioned fantasy world of 1.5 million people. No project seemed to be too ambitious for him. He built the world's tallest skyscraper (the 2,717-foot Burj Khalifa), the world's biggest shopping mall, and the world's largest highway intersection. He helped little Dubai become the shopping capital of the Middle East. In the last five years, it has attracted more tourists than India. Its most famous landmark, the Palm Jumeirah, an artificial island built in the shape of a palm tree, provides vacation villas for the rich and famous.

But the financial crisis of 2008 made people think again and Dubai failed to sell many of its new luxury apartments. Up to then, property in Dubai had been increasing in value and it had been easy to get people to invest. These days, investors risk losing money.

The rest of the world looks on with a mixture of wonder and suspicion. Is this a capitalist model worth copying, or has Dubai abandoned its heritage and become the Las Vegas of the Middle East?

creek (n) /krik/ a small stream that flows into a river (often they dry up in summer)
dock (v) /dɑk/ to "park" a boat in a harbor or port
pearl (n) /pɜrl/ a round white jewel made by oysters

Grammar verb + infinitive or *-ing*

4 Complete the sentences from the article.

1 Sheikh Rashid imagined ________ a gateway to the world.
2 It was a dream Sheikh Rashid could not afford ________.
3 In 1959, he asked ________ him some money.
4 He helped ________ the shopping capital of the Middle East.

5 Read the article again quickly and find:

1 two more verbs followed by the *-ing* form
2 two more verbs followed by infinitive
3 one more verb followed by somebody + infinitive
4 one more verb followed by the base form

VERB + INFINITIVE	VERB + *-ING*
Verb + infinitive *He couldn't afford to build a new harbor.* **Verb + someone + infinitive** *He asked a friend to lend him some money.* **Verb + someone + base form** *He helped Dubai become a great city.*	**Verb + *-ing*** *He imagined building an amazing city.*

For more information and practice, see page 162.

6 Fill in the blanks with the right form.

1 The population of Dubai grew from half a million in 1990 to 1.5 million in 2008 and has kept on ________ (grow) to this day.
2 Sheikh al Maktoum decided ________ (make) Dubai the region's most important financial center.
3 Attracting foreign banks and companies involved ________ (reduce) taxes for companies and individuals.
4 The expansion of the airport allowed ________ (Dubai / become) the fourth busiest international airport in the world.
5 If you enjoy ________ (shop), Dubai has over 70 shopping malls to choose from.
6 By planting 10,000 trees each year for the past four years, the city planners have managed ________ (create) many green spaces.
7 The banking crisis made ________ (construction / slow) down.
8 But it seems that Dubai can't help ________ (build) more property and tourist attractions.

Vocabulary

7 Work in pairs. Make urban features by combining words in A and B.

A

green	high-rise
leisure	luxury
highway	pedestrian
shopping	waterfront

B

apartment	building
center	development
overpass	mall
spaces	zone

8 Complete the sentences with the correct forms of the verbs below. Then check your answers with your teacher.

convert	redevelop
demolish	ruin
modernize	transform

1 In the 1960s the local authority decided to ________ the area as a shopping district.
2 This involved ________ all the houses and making way for huge parking lots.
3 Even the residents seemed to accept that the area had to be ________.
4 If you proposed ________ houses into stores on such a big scale today, I don't think you would be allowed to do it.
5 The result was that they ________ the city's character.
6 Now, 50 years later, the local authorities want to ________ it into a mixed area again.

9 Replace the underlined words in the questions (1–6) with words from Exercise 8 that mean the same thing.

1 Have any old factories been <u>turned into</u> apartments or houses?
2 Is there an area of the town that has been <u>changed completely</u> in your lifetime?
3 Is there an area of the town that has been <u>damaged</u> by new development?
4 Do you have a transportation system that needs to be <u>brought up to date</u>?
5 What buildings were you sorry to see <u>knocked down</u>?
6 Is there a run-down area of the city that you would like to see <u>rebuilt</u>? How?

Speaking

10 Work in pairs. Ask and answer the questions in Exercise 9 about your own town.

5b The Kerala model

Listening

1 Look at the two photos taken in the Indian state of Kerala. Which of these adjectives could you use to describe each place shown?

exotic	fertile	gorgeous	hectic
prosperous	remarkable	tranquil	

2 16 Listen to an interview. What is surprising about the level of social development in Kerala?

3 16 Listen again. Are the sentences true (T) or false (F)?

1 The journalist went to Kerala to write an article.
2 Kerala has a lot of people in a small area.
3 One of the signs of Kerala's social development is the high level of education.
4 Women have a superior social position to men.
5 People in Trivandrum are too busy to be involved in politics.
6 One of the secrets of Kerala's success is the open-minded attitude of its people.

4 Convert these definitions to adjectives. Check your answers in the audioscript on page 177.

Having…
1 a good rate of literacy = *literate*
2 a good standard of living = ...-................
3 a good education = ...-................
4 good health = ...
5 a high level of culture = ...
6 strong interest in politics = ...
7 tolerance of differences = ...

> **WORDBUILDING adverb + adjective**
> Adverbs and adjectives can be combined to describe people and things.
> *politically engaged, highly cultured*

5 Work in pairs. Answer the questions.

1 What do you think is the main reason for Kerala's success as a society?
2 Could this kind of society work anywhere?

6 Pronunciation: rhyming words

a 17 Work in pairs. Words that rhyme end with the same sound. Match the words (1–8) with the word that rhymes (a–h). Then listen and practice saying them.

1	state	a	faced
2	low	b	plane
3	head	c	opt
4	course	d	though
5	main	e	weight
6	stopped	f	force
7	none	g	fun
8	waste	h	said

b Look at these words. Can you think of a word that rhymes with each?

break foot height signed walk word

Grammar: verbs with *-ing* and infinitive

7 Match each verb in bold to the correct meaning (a or b).

1 Have you **tried visiting** India?
2 I'm **trying to show** how remarkable Kerala is.
a attempting something
b experimenting with something

3 I was meaning to **go on to tour** other parts.
4 The students **went on protesting** for four days.
a continuing an action
b a change of situation

5 It was **meant to be** a vacation.
6 Usually that would **mean** people **having** a fairly poor quality of life.
a describing intentions
b describing what is involved

7 I don't **regret changing** my plans.
8 No land is wasted, which I **regret to say** is not always the case in some developing countries.
a apologizing for what you are about to say
b saying you are sorry about a past event

9 **I remember going** there in the 1990s.
10 Please **remember to send** me a copy.
a describing memories
b talking about things that need to be done

11 We **stopped to visit** an Indian journalist I know.
12 Keralites never **stop debating**.
a ending something
b the reason for stopping

> **VERBS WITH *-ING* AND INFINITIVE**
>
> **Verbs with two meanings**
> *remember, go on, stop, mean, try, regret* + *-ing* and infinitive
>
> **Verbs with no change in meaning**
> *prefer, continue, hate, like, love, start* + *-ing* and infinitive
>
> For more information and practice, see page 163.

8 Look at the grammar box. Then choose the correct form.

1 No one knows how long Kerala will be able to go on *to maintain / maintaining* this model society.
2 This is the journalist's impression of Kerala. You would have to try *to live / living* there yourself to see if it was the reality.
3 I regret *to tell / telling* you that getting there by plane is really expensive.
4 If you stopped *to see / seeing* some other places in India on the way, it would make it more worthwhile.
5 But that would also mean *to plan / planning* your trip more carefully.
6 The interviewer remembers *to visit / visiting* beautiful beaches and lagoons.

9 Complete the interview using the correct form of the verbs in parentheses.

Interview

WHAT INTERESTED YOU IN KERALA IN THE FIRST PLACE?

Well, I remember [1] .... (read) an interesting article about it about 15 years ago and I meant [2] .... (visit) and see for myself, but I only managed to go last year.

AND WHAT DID YOU FIND? WAS IT THE PERFECT MODEL THAT MANY PEOPLE HAVE SAID IT IS?

I think what they have achieved is amazing. The government implemented a number of measures to try [3] .... (improve) people's quality of life and on the whole, they have succeeded.

FOR EXAMPLE?

The most important is land reforms. In the 1960s, they stopped [4] .... (allow) landlords to charge rent to tenant farmers. This meant [5] .... (give) the land back to the people, mostly peasants, who worked on it.

SO POOR PEOPLE BENEFITTED?

Certainly. At the same time, the government also started [6] .... (invest) heavily in education, so poor people not only became better off, they also became better educated.

AND WHAT ARE THE NEGATIVE EFFECTS OF ALL THIS? THERE MUST BE SOME.

No system is perfect, I regret [7] .... (say). The problem in Kerala is that the economy is still largely based on agriculture. And someone who leaves school with a good education probably doesn't want to go on [8] .... (work) in the fields. So even though they prefer [9] .... (live) in Kerala, they often move to another more industrially developed state in India, or even abroad, to get a decent job.

Speaking

10 Work in pairs. Ask and answer the questions on page 155 to find out how happy your society is. Then compare your answer with another pair. Were people's answers very different? If so, why?

5c Sustainable development?

Reading

1 Work in pairs. Look at the photo on page 63 of the Mekong River in Laos before a hydroelectric dam project. How do you think the dam affected the lives of the people living near the river?

2 Read the article quickly and check your answers from Exercise 1. In what other ways did the dam affect people's lives?

3 Answer the questions based on the article.

1 Who helped to finance the project?
2 Why was this surprising?
3 How much electricity will it generate?
4 Who will use the electricity?
5 How many local people are affected?
6 What will happen to the local people?
7 Who says life is better now for local people?
8 Why do environmentalists think life for local people could get worse?

4 Complete the statements based on the article.

1 The dam flooded a big area and created a huge ________ . (para 1)
2 The World Bank would like the project to be a ________ that everyone can admire. (para 2)
3 The people from the flooded area should have better ________ in the future. (para 5)
4 Without their farmland, locals will have to find new ways to ________ a ________ . (para 5)
5 The people now have ________ that they didn't have before, like electricity, sanitation, and clean water. (para 8)
6 Changing the environment so dramatically has a big effect on the local ________ and ________ . (para 10)

Vocabulary *re-*

5 Underline all the words in the article beginning with *re-*. Then circle the verbs that mean "to do something again." Form nouns from them.

> **WORDBUILDING prefix *re-* with verbs and nouns**
>
> verb: *redevelop*
> noun: *redevelopment*

Critical thinking fact or opinion

6 Work in pairs. This article contains a mixture of facts and opinions about the benefits of the Nam Theun 2 hydroelectric dam. List the facts and opinions about the project's impact on the:

- local economy
- local people
- environment

7 Look back at the article. What told you when an opinion was being given rather than a fact? Tell your partner.

8 Compare your answers with another pair. Do you think that the dam has brought more benefits than disadvantages to Laos?

Word focus *pick*

9 Work in pairs. Find two phrases in the article using the word *pick* and discuss what they mean. Then do the same for the phrases in bold below.

1 I think it's easy to **pick holes** in the World Bank plan, but at least they are trying to do the right thing.
2 Can I **pick your brain** for a moment? I'm not sure my facts are right.
3 Sales of electricity to Thailand were slow at first but they**'re picking up** now.
4 He feels that he **is being picked on** by everybody.
5 I asked him to **pick me up** from the airport.
6 We offer a range of services—you can **pick and choose** what you want.

Speaking

10 Work in pairs. What is the impact on people and the environment in the following development projects? How do you deal with this sensitively? Discuss and make lists.

- helping a city damaged by a hurricane
- building a high-speed railway line between two cities
- moving people from a poor and depressed area in a city to a new town

Kai Kensavaong will never again walk along the muddy lanes of Sop On, the village in southern Laos where she was born. Her old home now lies at the bottom of a reservoir created to feed a hydroelectric power plant, the first to be funded by the World Bank for over twenty years. "I'll never forget that place," says the 41-year-old villager. "It was my home. I picked my first bamboo stalks there."

The World Bank stopped financing hydropower projects in developing countries twenty years ago because of criticism that such projects were harming local communities and the environment. But Nam Theun 2—a 127-foot-high (39 m) dam on the Mekong River that generates over 1,000 megawatts of electricity—is the showpiece for the bank's new policy of supporting sustainable hydropower projects. For Laos, it is part of a longer-term strategy to revitalize the economy and become the battery of Southeast Asia.

The bank says that lessons have been learned from projects in the sixties and seventies, when people were forced to resettle and whole areas of forest or agricultural land were flooded. When it comes to clean energy, the bank thinks hydropower is the best option, offering the best solution to the 1.5 billion people without access to electricity.

In 2010, Nam Theun 2 brought $5.6 million in sales of electricity, and it is estimated that during the next 25 years it will generate around $2 billion in revenue to Laos, one of Asia's poorest countries, since most of the electricity will be exported to its power-hungry neighbor, Thailand. The government has promised that this money will be spent on reducing poverty and renewing and improving the country's infrastructure.

Seventeen villages in the flooded area have now been rebuilt and the 6,200 people, mostly farmers, who lived in them have been retrained to make a living from the reservoir. The power company has promised to double their living standards within five years. According to the World Bank, 87 percent of those resettled believe life is much better than before, since they now have electricity, sanitation, clean water, new roads, and greater access to schools and health care.

"In the old village, things just weren't convenient," said Tiea, 25, one of the relocated villagers. "It wasn't a pretty place, the houses weren't very nice, and we didn't have power. In the new village, we have electricity, we can see better."

But the old criticisms remain. Environmental and human rights groups warn that the dam will have a negative impact on water quality and fish, and that the local people who were relocated after the area was flooded may not be able to support themselves economically in the future.

"People are happy with these new amenities, but the real problem is how to restore sustainable livelihoods for communities who used to rely on the natural resources—forests, fish, and grazing lands for their animals—now that they've lost these," says Ikuko Matsumoto, program director for the environmental group, International Rivers.

In addition to the 6,200 villagers already rehoused, activists also point out that there are over 110,000 people in riverside villages downstream from the dam whose lives will have to change because of the new river ecosystem. They claim that these people will have to deal with issues like flooding, decline of the fish population and poor water quality. How quickly they will pick up new skills is uncertain.

But the World Bank says it is responsive to these problems. A 1,500-square-mile (4,100 km) protected area has been established around the dam to safeguard flora and fauna. It admits, though, that rebuilding the lives of the villagers is not a short-term process, and that everyone is trying to learn and readjust as they go along.

SUSTAINABLE DEVELOPMENT?

5d Evaluating a project

Real life making decisions

1 Work in pairs. What kind of development would most improve your town? Choose three items and number them (1–3) in order of importance.

a new arts center (theater, music, film, fine art)
a new rec (recreation) center
a new shopping mall
better local stores
better public transportation
fewer cars (pedestrian zones, bike trails)
more (affordable) housing
more green spaces

2 18 Listen to a meeting of some bank employees who are discussing a project they have funded and complete the notes.

1 Amount of loan	The bank lent the local government $ ....
2 Purpose of loan	To help redevelop a .... in the city.
3 Aims of project	To give local residents a nicer park and some .... facilities.
4 Progress so far	They have cleaned the area up, planted .... , laid new .... They have also built the .... and the children's ....
5 Other work	They have built a .... and bought a sculpture for $ ....
6 Needs	A new loan of $250,000 to complete the .... courts and .... course.

3 18 What do the bank employees decide to do about the new loan? Do they all agree?

4 18 Complete the sentences in the box with the phrases the speakers use to give their opinions and to agree and disagree. Then listen again and check.

MAKING DECISIONS

What do you think we should do?
What's your view / opinion?
If you [1] .... , that's completely wrong.
Personally, I think that's absurd.
I don't think we [2] .... give them another cent.
I find it amazing / ridiculous that he said that.
I think we should / we ought to give them the benefit of the doubt.
[3] .... be too hasty. / We shouldn't be too hasty.
We need [4] .... whether they are in the spirit of the original aims of the project.
That really [5] .... the opinion of the local residents.
The [6] .... see it, it's probably a good thing.
I'd [7] .... with that.
That's right.
I agree.
Is everyone OK / happy with that?
Exactly.
Are we all [8] .... ?
That [9] .... to me.

Speaking

5 Work in pairs. Read the report on page 153 about another project which the bank is financing and consider these points.

- name of project
- date started
- original goals
- action taken and money spent
- results (positive and negative)
- next steps and money needed

Decide together if you think the bank should lend more money for this project. Discuss your decision with another pair and try to come to an agreement with them.

5e Big cities, big problems

Writing an opinion essay

1 Work in pairs. Why do you think people want to live in big cities? Make a list of the reasons. Do you think their lives are better there?

2 The chart shows the percentage of the world's population living in cities. What problems do you think this creates?

3 Look at the title of the opinion essay and then read the answer. What is the opinion of the writer?

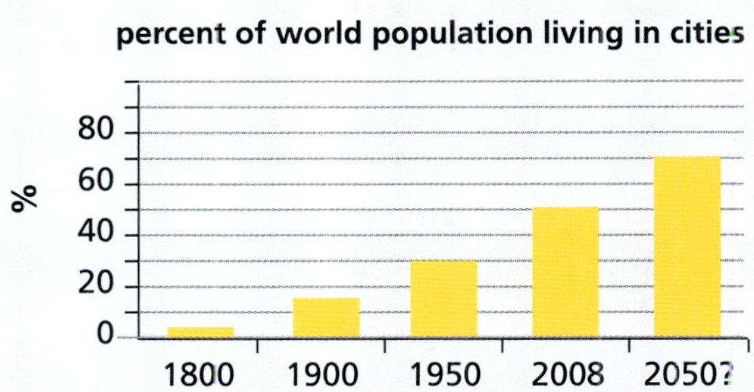

Our cities have become too big. The problems they create outweigh the benefits.

In 1800, only two percent of the world's population lived in cities. Over the last 20 years, more and more people have moved to cities looking for work and a better life. As a result, more than half the world's population now live in cities and that number is expected to grow. Cities are monuments to the amazing organizing abilities of human beings. However, in some cases, they also have many social, economic, and environmental problems. The question is: do the problems they create outweigh their benefits?

Cities exist because they are more convenient places to live. Jobs, schools, and hospitals are all close to home. There is a wide choice of people to socialize with and good choices for entertainment.

On the other hand, there also seems to be more crime, more poverty, and more pollution, often in a particular area, making things even worse. But this is not so surprising, if you think about it. The same problems exist in the countryside or in smaller towns, but they are not so concentrated. Because of this, they are noticed less.

As long as the population of cities does not grow more quickly than the services available to it, cities can solve a lot of our problems. They keep the population from spreading into the countryside. In addition, they provide jobs and a more interesting life. The problem with cities is not how big they are, but how well managed they are.

4 Does this opinion essay follow the standard format?

Introduction → Arguments for → Arguments against → Conclusion

5 An introduction can take different forms. Which of these does the writer use?

- a dramatic example of the problem
- a story about the problem from the writer's own experience
- statistics that illustrate the seriousness of the problem
- a quote from someone famous about the topic

6 Writing skill linking words

a Look at the linking phrases below. Then underline other examples of each type in the essay. Compare your answers with your partner.

Adding an argument	Introducing a contrasting fact	Explaining the consequences
Furthermore,	Then again,	Consequently,

b Complete the sentences with a linking phrase.

1 Certain cities in the world have become especially popular. ______, we have seen the emergence of megacities with over ten million inhabitants.
2 A lot of people find a better standard of living in big cities. ______, you can also find very poor people living in them.
3 ______ to being convenient for people, cities are also convenient for business.

7 Write an opinion essay about the statement below. Then compare your answer with your partner. Did you use the same arguments?

In our modern lifestyles, we have lost our sense of community. We need to return to a simpler way of life.

8 Read your partner's essay and check the following:

- Do you find the arguments convincing?
- Is it organized in clear paragraphs?
- Does it follow the format suggested in Exercise 4?
- Does it use one of the introduction techniques suggested in Exercise 5?

5f Aquarium on Wheels

Video

The program really means a lot to me because I want to major in marine biology.

Before you watch

1 Work in groups. Look at the title of this video and the photo and discuss the questions.

1 Why do you think the video is called *Aquarium on Wheels*?
2 Do you think aquariums can teach children about more than just sea life?
3 What might the program teach young people?

2 Work in pairs. Mark what you think you will see.

a kid dressed as a monkey			a computer
a crocodile	a diver	a fish tank	a frog
a necklace	seashells	a tiger	a toy snake

While you watch

3 Watch the video and check your answers from Exercise 2.

4 Watch the first part of the video (to 02:17). Choose the correct option to complete the sentences.

1 The students in the video are:
a employees of the Aquarium on Wheels program.
b visitors to the National Aquarium.

2 The students want to teach about:
a recycling. b conservation.

3 The students perform a play about:
a snakes. b monkeys.

4 The children laugh because the actor says that:
a fighting is going to make his hair look messy.
b he doesn't have any leaves to eat.

5 Aquarium administrators want to give students:
a training in marine biology.
b lessons for life.

5 Watch the second part of the video (02:18 to the end). Answer the questions.

1 What kind of skills do the students need?

....

2 What haven't the people in their family done?

....

3 What does DejaNé Jones say is the most important thing the program has taught her?

....

4 What did performing the play teach them?

....

5 What does George Faulk want to be?

....

6 Why is the program personally important to Martha Schaum?

....

After you watch

6 Roleplay an interview with Martha Schaum

Work in pairs.

Student A: Imagine you work for a local newspaper. Use the information below to prepare questions to ask Martha Schaum about the Aquarium on Wheels program.

Student B: Imagine you are Martha Schaum. A reporter from a local newspaper is going to interview you. Look at the information below and think about what you are going to say.

- the overall objectives of the Aquarium on Wheels program
- who is involved with the program
- what the student employees have been doing
- what the program gives the student
- what Martha gets out of the program personally

Act out the interview, then change roles and act out the interview again.

7 At the end of the video, the narrator says: "The Aquarium on Wheels program is having a powerful impact on more than just the rain forests." What does that mean? Why do you think the program is so successful?

8 Work in groups and discuss these questions.

1 What kind of education about the environment do young children in your country receive? Is it effective?
2 The overall goal of the Aquarium on Wheels program is to entertain and educate. Do you think these two aims are compatible? Can you think of examples that meet both aims successfully?

advantageous (adj) /ˌædvən'teɪdʒəs/ having a good effect
camouflage (n) /'kæməˌflɑʒ/ something an animal uses to make it difficult to see
major (v) /'meɪdʒər/ get a college degree in
mess up (v) /'mes 'ʌp/ make something look disorganized
overall (adj) /'oʊvərˌɔl/ general
poison dart (n) /'pɔɪzən 'dɑrt/ a small arrow covered with poison at one end which is fired from a long tube by blowing

UNIT 5 REVIEW

Grammar

1 Work in pairs. What is the main industry in your town or city? How has this affected the character of the city?

2 Read the interview and answer the questions.

1 What is the new industry that has emerged?
2 How does this resident feel about it?

3 Complete the interview with the correct form of the verb: *-ing*, infinitive or base form.

I = Interviewer; R = Resident

I: So, are you enjoying [1] ________ (live) here again after a fifteen-year absence? Has Berlin changed a lot since you were last here?

R: Of course. There has been a huge amount of development. They have kept on [2] ________ (build) and [3] ________ (redevelop) since the early nineties. In many ways that is great for the city, but I regret [4] ________ (say) that its character has changed, and not for the better.

I: What do you mean by that?

R: Well, there are as many as 9 million tourists a year. It's as if the city government has decided [5] ________ (turn) Berlin into a vacation destination.

I: But surely tourists are a good thing? If they stopped [6] ________ (come), the city would lose a lot of jobs and income. I heard that tourism will help [7] ________ (create) 50,000 new jobs.

R: I'm not anti-tourist. I understand that tourism means [8] ________ (earn) good money, but a lot of this money goes straight to private companies. I think the city should ask tourists and tourism companies [9] ________ (pay) a tax for visiting Berlin. Then this money could be invested in real jobs for residents.

I CAN	
use verbs with *-ing* and infinitive	☐
use verbs with both *-ing* and infinitive but with different meanings	☐

Vocabulary

4 Match the words (1–6) with their meaning (a–f).

1 convert	a bring up to date
2 spoil	b change completely
3 modernize	c rebuild
4 demolish	d damage
5 transform	e turn into
6 redevelop	f destroy

5 Work in pairs. Use a different verb in each space.

1 Green spaces can really ________ a city.
2 In the 1970s and 1980s, there was a tendency to ________ older buildings downtown and replace them with high-rise buildings.
3 It's a good idea to ________ downtown areas into pedestrian zones.
4 People complain that the character of many famous cities has been ________ by ________ them with luxury apartments and expensive stores.

6 Discuss with your partner if any of the items in Exercise 5 are features of your city. Do you agree with the statements? Why?

I CAN	
talk about the different features of a city	☐
describe changes in a city	☐

Real life

7 Work in pairs. Complete each opinion with a verb.

1 What do you ________ of the idea to restore the downtown area to the way it was 200 years ago?
2 I ________ it amazing that no one has thought of doing it before.
3 If you ________ me, it's not a good idea.
4 No, that doesn't ________ right to me either.
5 The way I ________ it, if it's good for the local economy, then it's a good thing.
6 I think it ________ on what local people want.
7 Yes, I'd ________ along with that.

8 Work in small groups. Decide if it is better to restore old buildings or knock them down and start again.

I CAN	
reach a decision by expressing opinions and agreeing or disagreeing	☐

Speaking

9 Work in pairs. Tell each other about a large development project you know about (transportation, redevelopment, new town, sports or recreation complex). Cover these points:

- the project's benefits
- whether it is sustainable or not
- who supports the project; who opposes it
- your opinion

Unit 6 Alternative travel

The Hotel de Glace, Quebec, Canada; the only ice hotel in North America
Photograph by Ralph Lee Hopkins

FEATURES

1 Look at the photo. What do you think there is to do in this hotel? Would you like to stay here? Why?

2 Work in pairs. Choose the correct option(s). Then ask each other the questions.

1 How much *vacation / days off* do you get each year?
2 When you make a hotel reservation, do you usually ask for a room with a *sight / view*?
3 Do you generally take a lot of *suitcase / luggage* when you travel, or do you prefer to travel light?
4 What is your favorite kind of *scenery / countryside*: the ocean, forest, mountains, or desert?
5 Do you generally enjoy the *travel / trip* as much as actually getting there?
6 Which *airplane / airline* do you prefer to fly with?
7 On your last vacation, how long did it *take / last* to get to your destination?

6a Staycations

Speaking

1 Work in pairs. Ask each other these questions about your capital cities and their attractions.

1 Can you name five important tourist attractions?
2 How many have you visited?
3 Have you ever taken a bus tour or walking tour of the city?
4 Have you ever been to a famous market in the city?
5 How often do you visit the city's main museums or galleries?
6 Do you know the name of a good, reasonably-priced hotel in the city?

2 Are there parts of your local area that you haven't ever visited or feel that you don't know? Would you consider taking a vacation there? Why?

Reading

3 Read the blog. Are the sentences true (T) or false (F)?

1 Staycationers always sleep at home.
2 Staycationers go out and do different activities during their staycation.
3 Staycations have all the stresses of normal travel.
4 Staycations simulate traditional vacations.

4 Now use the information in the blog to complete these statements.

1 Staycations got started because...
2 They are good for the local economy because…
3 Some people think that visiting local attractions isn't as exciting as…
4 Without leaving New York, Karen Ash was able to have a…

STAYCATIONS

You probably don't like the term "staycation." Neither do I. But don't let that bother you. As a concept, staycations are a pretty good idea. Maybe you've already had one, but didn't know what it was called. Staycations don't just mean staying in and relaxing at home. They involve getting out more by taking day trips to see local sights. If you don't want to stay home, you can vacation locally—for example, at a local campsite.

Staycations first became popular after the financial crisis of 2008, when people were looking for ways to cut back on their spending. Apart from the savings, let's not ignore the other benefits: you don't have any of the problems associated with travel, such as packing, long drives, delays at airports, and so on; and you put money back into the local economy, by eating out, for example.

Some staycationers who base themselves at home like to follow a set of rules, such as setting a start and end date, planning their activities ahead of time and avoiding routine. You don't have to do these things, but it helps to create the feel of a traditional vacation. Others, aware that a visit to the local zoo may not match the thrill of foreign travel, take it a step further. Take, for example, Karen Ash, whose story appeared in the *Wall Street Journal*.

A resident of New York, Ash decided not to go to Japan, as she had originally planned, but instead took a weeklong Japanese vacation in her own city. This included buying postcards and souvenirs at a Japanese market, admiring bonsai plants, eating ramen (even speaking Japanese when ordering), all without leaving New York. Her itinerary also involved joining in at a traditional Japanese tea ceremony, attending a taiko drumming concert, and watching Japanese soap operas on DVD. I don't think many people would want to take this much trouble to create their staycation, but you get the idea!

Vocabulary phrasal verbs with *in* and *out*

5 Work in pairs. Find two phrasal verbs in the article with *in* and two with *out*. Discuss what they mean.

6 Complete the sentences using *in* and *out*.

1 I'd like to try ________ that new restaurant downtown. I've heard it's excellent.
2 Should we eat ________ tonight? We've got food.
3 I'm going to drop ________ on Uncle Joe and see how he is feeling. He's stuck at home with a broken leg and he is probably really bored.
4 All I seem to do is work and sleep these days. I need to get ________ more.
5 My daughter stayed ________ until 3 a.m. last night. I was really worried.
6 Please fill ________ this form with your name, address, and passport number.

> **WORDBUILDING phrasal verbs with *in* and *out***
>
> Some verbs can be used with both *in* and *out*. Sometimes they give opposite meanings and sometimes they give different meanings. Other verbs may only be used with either *in* or *out*.
>
> *eat in, eat out; drop in, drop out; join in, ~~join out~~*

7 Ask each other the following questions.

1 Do you feel you get out enough? If not, what would you like to do more of?
2 How often do you eat out?
3 What do you usually do in the evenings, if you are staying in?
4 If you saw some people in the park playing volleyball, would you watch or join in?
5 How late were you allowed to stay out when you were fifteen years old?
6 Do you like to try out new types of food?
7 Do you like it when people drop in on you, or do you think they should be invited to come to your house?
8 What is your ideal weekend night like? Do you go out or stay in?

Grammar *not*

8 Underline these examples in the article and comment on the position of *not* in each case:

1 a negative infinitive (para 4)
2 a negative sentence using *want* (para 1)
3 the opposite of *must* (para 3)
4 a negative sentence using *think* (para 4)
5 a negative sentence using *let* (para 2)

> **NOT**
>
> **Negative infinitive**
> *It's cheaper not to go abroad.*
>
> ***want***
> *I didn't want to stay in…* *~~I wanted not to~~ stay in…*
>
> ***must not* and *don't have to***
> *You must not book a vacation without comparing prices first.* (Note that in British English, the contracted form *mustn't* is commonly used in place of *must not*.)
> *You don't have to spend a lot of money to enjoy your vacation.*
>
> ***hope* and *think***
> *I hope it doesn't rain.* *~~I don't hope it rains.~~*
> *I don't think that's right.* *~~I think that's not right.~~*
>
> ***let's***
> *Let's stay home this year. Let's not go abroad.*
>
> For more information and practice, see page 163.

9 Look at the grammar box. Then make each sentence express the opposite idea using negatives.

1 Let's spend a lot of money on a foreign vacation.
2 I want to stay in a big modern hotel.
3 Staycations can replace foreign vacations.
4 I hope the hotel is near the river.
5 I told them to wait until the last minute.
6 We must go swimming—if you want to, that is.

10 Look at these tips from a travel magazine. Choose the correct option.

> Let's [1] *don't forget / not forget* that the main reason for choosing a staycation is to save money. For example, if you [2] *don't want to spend / want not to spend* a lot on eating out, just take a picnic with you when you go on a day trip. It [3] *must not / doesn't have to be* a cheap picnic; you can still treat yourself to a few luxuries.
>
> Try [4] *to not choose / not to choose* only activities that cost money. One idea is to plan a two- or three-day walk and take a tent with you. If you [5] *don't think you'll enjoy / think you don't have to enjoy* camping, then look up some motels you could stay in instead.
>
> The most important thing is to be adventurous. The fun of any vacation is discovering new places and there is no reason why a staycation should be any different. I [5] *hope it isn't / don't hope it's* a disappointment!

Speaking

11 Work in small groups. Plan a five-day staycation in your own area or the area you are studying in. Try to give the staycation a theme, like the foreign theme in the article. Make a short itinerary of at least five activities.

12 Work with another group. Compare your staycation ideas. Have a class vote on which staycation sounds the most fun and practical.

6b Voluntourism

Listening

1 Work in pairs. What do you think the saying below means? Do you have a similar saying in your language? Do you think it's true?

"A change is as good as a rest."

2 19 Voluntourism is when people travel to a foreign location to work for free. Look at the photo. What sort of volunteering do you think people do here? Listen and check.

3 Which of the statements best summarizes Katie Samuel's opinion of what a good volunteer vacation should be?

a a working vacation where you learn practical and useful skills
b a cultural experience where both the visitor and the host benefit
c an enjoyable way to help others less fortunate than yourself

4 19 Listen again and complete these sentences with one word per space. Then discuss what each expression means.

1 You probably thought that kind of vacation was for eighteen-year-olds in **their** ______ **year**.
2 Wouldn't people who only get **a few weeks** ______ **a year** prefer a more relaxing option?
3 This should be **a** ______ **travel experience**, not just **a work** ______.
4 In return, the locals take them for ______ **walks**, which are like mini-safaris.
5 They have to pay for their flight and **their** ______ **expenses**.
6 The CRTP helps to restore **cultural** ______ **sites** around the world.

5 Work in groups. Discuss the questions. Then tell the class.

1 What do you think of this type of vacation?
2 Should people have to pay to volunteer?
3 What other ways can you think of to get close to local people on a vacation?

Grammar negative and tag questions

6 There are various ways of phrasing a question. Look at these examples (1–4) and match each one to the answer the speaker wants (a–c).

1 Have you ever thought of doing a little building work during your vacation?
2 You probably thought that kind of vacation was for eighteen-year-olds, didn't you?
3 Wouldn't most people prefer a more relaxing option?
4 It's not really a vacation as we know it, is it?

a Doesn't expect a particular answer (*yes* or *no*)
b Expects the answer to be *yes*
c Expects the answer to be *no*

7 Work in pairs. Find more examples of questions that expect a particular answer in the audioscript on page 177.

Elephants are often the victims of poaching; a project in Kenya helps local people find other ways to make a living.

> **NEGATIVE and TAG QUESTIONS**
>
> **Open questions (no confirmation of opinion demanded)**
> *Do you like visiting new places?*
> *Yes, now and then.*
>
> **Negative questions**
> *Don't you like visiting new places?*
> *No, not at all.*
>
> **Tag questions**
> *You like visiting new places, don't you?*
> *Yes, I love it.*
> *You don't like visiting new places, do you?*
> *No, you're right. I don't.*
>
> For more information and practice, see page 164.

8 Look at the grammar box. Convert these open questions into negative or tag questions that fit the answers.

1 Do you like the idea of volunteer vacations? (tag question)
....?
Yes, I do, very much.

2 Do you think it's an interesting idea? (negative question)
....?
No, I don't.

3 Have you been on a volunteer vacation? (tag question)
....?
Yes, two years ago.

4 Did it seem strange to pay money in order to work? (negative question)
....?
No, not really.

5 Will you be going again this year? (tag question)
....?
No. We're taking a staycation this year.

9 Pronunciation intonation in questions

a 20 Look at the grammar box. Listen to the sentences and answer the questions.

1 Does the speaker's intonation rise or fall at the end of an open question?
2 Does the speaker's intonation rise or fall at the end of a negative question?
3 Does the speaker's intonation rise or fall at the end of each tag question?

b 21 Work in pairs. Practice saying the converted questions in Exercise 8 with the correct intonation. Then listen and check your pronunciation.

10 The Great Continental Divide is a biking and hiking trail that crosses North America from Mexico to Canada. Read this telephone conversation and convert the sentences in bold into negative or tag questions. Then check your answers with your teacher.

A: Hi, I'm interested in helping out on the Great Continental Divide this summer. My friend did four days last summer. [1] .... **(I / can / work / for / just a few days)**
B: Absolutely. Anything from two days to two months.
A: That's great. I have about a week in June. How much does it cost to take part?
B: It's free.
A: Sorry? [2] .... **(I / have to / pay / for / my accommodation)**
B: No, it's completely free. You just have to register.
A: [3] .... **(I / can / do / that / online)**
B: Sure, you can. It's on our website. [4] .... **(you / have / visited / our website)**
A: Yes, I took a quick look. And where on the trail can I work?
B: New Mexico, Montana, Wyoming...
A: [5] .... **(you / have / got / something / in Colorado)** That's where I live.
B: Yes, we do. We have opportunities in Winfield.
A: [6] .... **(and / you / provide / training / first)**
B: It's on-the-job training, unless it's very specific. We're looking for a chef at the moment. [7] .... **(you / want / to be / a chef)**
A: No. I just want to help build some trails.

Speaking

11 Ask negative or tag questions to try to persuade others of your opinions about these items.

- beach vacations
- experiencing local culture
- traveling alone
- trying out local food
- volunteer vacations
- working abroad

6c Unusual places to stay

Reading

1 Work in pairs. Make a list of what you look for in a vacation destination (comfort, a beautiful setting, modern facilities). Then compare your list with another pair.

2 Read part of a travel magazine's guide to unusual places. Answer the questions.

1 Which seem like comfortable places to stay?
2 Which seem to have the most disadvantages?

3 Read the article again. Choose the correct option to complete the sentences.

1 Karosta's own description of its hotel:
a is surprising. b is not truthful.
2 The writer thinks the cost of a night in prison:
a is too high. b is about right.
3 For a long time after the gold rush Virginia City:
a was uninhabited.
b was a rich town.
4 The cabins at the Nevada City Hotel are:
a all newly built.
b a mix of old and new.
5 The caves of Sassi di Matera have always been:
a lived in. b used to store things.
6 The new owners have tried to keep the original:
a furniture. b feel of the caves.
7 In a lot of art hotels the art is not:
a very good. b very prominent.
8 The different rooms at the Propeller Island City Lodge are decorated:
a in a dramatic way.
b in a similar way.

4 All these words describe parts of a building. Find them in the article and discuss their meaning with your partner. Use a dictionary if necessary.

balcony	balustrade	corridor
earth roofs	saloon	vaulted ceilings

5 Which of these places would you prefer to stay in? Why? Tell your partner.

Critical thinking claims and justifications

6 Each of these hotels claims to offer an authentic experience. For each hotel, say what the experience is, which facts support this claim, and which facts, if any, don't support it.

Hotel	Claims to be…	Supporting facts	Contradictory facts

7 Work in pairs. Discuss the questions.

1 Does it matter that some of the claims the hotels make are not always justified?
2 Does it make you less likely to trust them?
3 Does it make you less likely to stay there?

Word focus *mind*

8 Work in pairs. Find two expressions with the word *mind* in the text. Discuss whether they are nouns or verbs and what they mean. Then work out what these other expressions with *mind* mean.

1 I am **of two minds** about whether to stay at a hotel or drive home.
2 If you **change your mind** about coming with me, let me know before Friday.
3 I'm sure you can think of a solution if you **put your mind to it**.
4 Sorry I haven't got back to you about the weekend. I've had a lot **on my mind** lately.
5 Sorry, I know I've heard his name before but my **mind's gone blank**.

9 Write three sentences with different phrases with *mind*, but leave a blank where the phrase should be. Exchange sentences with another pair and fill in the blanks.

Speaking and writing

10 Work in small groups. Create your own idea for an unusual place to stay. Discuss:

- where the hotel is
- how your hotel is different
- whether it should be luxurious or basic
- what facilities you can offer that fit with the theme

11 Write a short description of it. Then present your idea to the class. Vote for which one sounds the most interesting.

Unusual places to stay

PRISON HOTELS Built in 1905, Karosta naval jail in Latvia was originally home to mutinous Russian sailors. In the 1970s, it housed political prisoners. In direct contrast to most hotel publicity, the website describes Karosta proudly as "unfriendly, unheated, and uncomfortable." They are not lying. This is more of a jail experience than a hotel stay. "Reception" is a dark corridor where a former prison guard explains the rules to you (no luggage except a toothbrush, no attempts to escape), and then fires his gun in the air to show you he is serious. After a meal of bread and sweet Russian tea, "guests" are given five minutes to bathe before making up their own beds from wooden benches and thin mattresses. Sound unpleasant? It is. But for $12 per night, what do you expect?

PERIOD HOTELS Would you like to experience life in America's Wild West 150 years ago? Virginia City, Montana, a former gold-rush town, was a ghost town until it was restored in the 1950s for tourism. Owned largely by the state government, the town now operates as a large open-air museum. Nearby is the Nevada City Hotel and cabins where you can hang up your Stetson hat and enjoy life as a cowboy. The rooms feature period Victorian furniture, and downstairs the saloon has a true Wild West feel. The cabins look extremely rustic from the outside—two even have their original earth roofs—but inside they have large double beds and private bathrooms. Bear in mind that if you book mid-week, you might be disappointed because the city only comes to life on weekends, when actors in period costumes play sheriffs, cowboys, and gold prospectors.

CAVE HOTELS If you had more primitive accommodation in mind, try the caves of Sassi di Matera on the toe of Italy, inhabited since the Bronze Age. During the Renaissance, they developed into more sophisticated rooms with stone walls, vaulted ceilings, and balustrades. But more recently they were the poor homes of peasants who lived there with their animals until as late as 1952. Now, however, they have been renovated to provide hospitality in a historical setting. Although visitors to Le Grotte Della Civita must do without television or fridges, the rooms are comfortably furnished with antique furniture and period terracotta tiles. The owners wanted the caves to feel as authentic as possible, so they built the furniture into the walls and left in place the iron rings where peasants tied up their animals. Prices start at $300 per night.

ART HOTELS A modern art gallery is a place where you can lose yourself in an artist's vision of the world. A hotel is essentially a place where you can spend the night, in either more or less comfort, according to your budget. As its advertising promises, Propeller Island City Lodge in Berlin manages to combine the two. Housed in a former apartment block, the hotel is a collection of individually designed rooms—the upside-down room, the all-orange room, the mirror room—which are often so extreme that you have no choice but to get into the spirit of it. In some art hotels, you can forget the art and simply enjoy the comfort of your surroundings. That's not the case with Propeller Island. The rooms can be small and claustrophobic (although some have balconies) and often you have to share a bathroom with other guests. But if you don't mind that, it may be the next best thing to spending the night in a gallery.

6d Couch surfing

Real life getting around

1 Work in pairs. Take one minute to read this description of couch surfing. Then discuss how couch surfing works. Is it something you would do? Why?

2 You are going to listen to a conversation between a couch surfer and a host. Look at the box. Who do you think says each expression?

3 **22** Listen to the conversation. Check your answers from Exercise 2.

4 **22** Listen again. Complete the expressions.

GETTING AROUND

I'm coming in by [1] ________________ .
I wanted to pick you up, but [2] ________________ .
That's [3] ________________ , but I can find my own way.
How do I get to [4] ________________ ?
You could just catch [5] ________________ .
Alternatively, you can hop on [6] ________________ .
Look out for the [7] ________________ on your right.
It's only a twenty-minute [8] ________________ .
The easiest thing is to [9] ________________ .
I'll come out and [10] ________________ .
If I get held up, I'll [11] ________________ . But otherwise, expect a call around six thirty.

5 **Pronunciation intonation in sentences with two clauses**

a **23** Listen for these two sentences with *but*. Notice how the speaker's intonation rises at the end of the first clause, indicating that they have not finished speaking.

I wanted to pick you up, but my car's in the garage that day.
You could just catch a taxi, but it's about eleven miles from downtown.

b Practice saying these sentences using the same intonation.

1 I'll try to be home by six, but I can't promise I will.
2 Normally it's a ten-minute drive, but the road work has made it longer.
3 I can't make it today, but I'll come tomorrow.
4 It's nice of you to offer, but we can find our own way.
5 The bus is cheap, but the train is much quicker.

6 Work in pairs. Take turns playing the roles of couch surfer and host. As the guest, call your host and ask about the best way to get to his/her home from another city.

Originally the idea of a New Hampshire student who emailed 1,500 students at the University of Iceland asking if he could spend the night on their couches, couch surfing is now an established worldwide practice. This is how it works. When you have made your travel plans, you contact people on the couch-surfing network by email to find out if they can offer you a bed for the night in the places you are going to visit. There's no fee. The only obligation on your part is to be able to offer a place to stay at your home when someone asks in the future. Aside from being free, the benefit is that you meet people with local knowledge. If you're lucky, some might even become long-term friends.

6e A disappointed customer

Writing a letter of complaint

1 Have you ever had a bad experience on vacation that caused you to complain? What happened and what was the outcome?

2 Read this complaint and answer the questions.

1 Why is the customer unhappy?
2 What does she want the hotel to do about it?
3 Does her complaint seem justified?

44 Ascot Street
New Haven, CT 06511

Sweet Hotel Group
Via Central 150
Miraflores
Lima, Peru 15001

Dear Sir or Madam:

I am writing to express my dissatisfaction with my stay at the Grau Hotel on April 12. I made a reservation through another website which was offering one night for two people with dinner for $110. However, when we arrived at 5:30 p.m., we were informed that there was no table available in the restaurant and that we could find another restaurant in town.

We got a strong impression that because we used a discounted offer, we did not receive the same level of hospitality as regular, full-paying guests. The situation was both embarrassing and inconvenient. After some discussion with the staff, we were able to have dinner at the hotel restaurant, but much later than we wanted to, at 9:30 pm. No one apologized for this.

Given the circumstances, compensation is not my principal concern. Rather, I would ask you to investigate the matter thoroughly to ensure this does not happen to other guests.

Sincerely

Ann Dunhill

3 Work in pairs. Formal letters follow certain conventions. Answer the questions.

1 What is the correct position for each address?
2 Where is the reason for writing mentioned?
3 Where is the request for action?

4 Writing skill formal language

a Find the formal words or phrases in the letter that say the following:

1 to say I was unhappy
2 we were told
3 a cheap deal
4 after we talked to
5 what worries me most
6 look into
7 make sure

b Convert the phrases in bold in these sentences into more formal language. Use the letter to help you.

1 We **want** to **tell you how unhappy we were** with the standard of the food on the cruise ship.
Example:
We wish to express our dissatisfaction with the standard of the food on the cruise ship.
2 I **told** the receptionist that I **had booked the room** for two nights, not one.
3 After **I'd talked to** the manager, she **said she was sorry** and promised to **look into** the problem. **But** no action was taken.
4 I expected the safety of the guests to be what the staff **were most worried about**.
5 Given the **trouble** this caused us, we expected to **get some money back**.
6 The manager said no other rooms were **free**, but if the opportunity **came up**, she'd move us.

5 Read the situation and then write a letter of complaint to the hotel.

You recently stayed at a small hotel in downtown Chicago. During the night, you were awakened by some noisy people in the room next door. You went down to the reception desk to tell a member of the hotel staff, but no one was there. You are angry and upset that no one was on duty during the night.

6 Exchange letters and read your partner's letter. Use these questions to check their letter.

- Does it begin with the reason for writing?
- Does it end with what action is expected?
- Does it use rhetorical or other types of questions to be persuasive?

6f East Timor

Video

East Timor: for the intrepid few, an emerging tourism destination with unspoiled natural beauty

Before you watch

1 Work in groups. Look at the photo of East Timor and discuss the questions.

1 What do you know about East Timor?
2 Why do you think the caption says that East Timor is "for the intrepid few"? What does this suggest about the country?

2 What do you think you will see in this video? Check the items below.

a a person sunbathing on a tropical beach
b builders renovating a damaged building
c a group of people pulling in fishing nets from the sea
d tourists having drinks in a hotel bar

While you watch

3 Watch the video and check your answers from Exercise 2.

4 Watch the first part of the video (to 00:45). Complete the conversation between a journalist (J) and Ann Turner (A).

J: Hi Ann, where do you work?
A: 1 ....
J: Why did you first come to East Timor?
A: 2 ....
J: When did you decide you wanted to stay?
A: 3 ....
J: What four things impressed you most?
A: 4 ....
J: How many fish species are there?
A: 5 ....
J: Why is there such a huge diversity of fish species here?
A: 6 ....

5 Watch the second part of the video (00:46 to the end). Answer the questions.

1 What is the main problem on East Timor?
....
2 How long has East Timor been independent?
....
3 What happened after people in East Timor voted for independence?
....
4 What is the government worried about?
....
5 What policies is the government working on?
....
6 What should people who want to start a tourism business in East Timor do?
....

6 Watch the whole video again. Number the quotes in the order you hear them.

a The subsequent recovery effort has been painfully slow.
b Welcome to East Timor, one of the world's newest countries.
c It faces an age-old predicament: how to make the most of its natural assets without destroying them.
d East Timor is a former war zone.
e We are still developing policies and regulations.

After you watch

7 **Roleplay talking about a new project**

Work in pairs.

Student A: Imagine you are a foreigner living in East Timor. You want to build a small beach hotel. Look at the ideas below. Think about what you are going to say to a government official.

- what you hope to do
- how you will protect the environment
- how your hotel will benefit the local economy

Student B: Imagine you are an East Timor government official. Look at the information below. Think about what you are going to tell a business person.

- You are interested in attracting tourism but you also want to protect the environment.
- Find out how the beach hotel will do both.

Act out the conversation. Then change roles and act out the conversation again with a new business. Decide whether the business is a good idea or not.

8 Work in groups and discuss these questions.

1 Which areas of your country attract tourists?
2 How does tourism contribute to the economy of your country?
3 What impact does it have on natural assets?
4 Do you think the government does enough to protect the natural assets of your country?

asset (n) /'æset/ a valuable possession
emerging (adj) /ɪ'mɜrʤɪŋ/ in the process of becoming
expatriate (n) /eks'peɪtriət/ someone who lives in a foreign country
infrastructure (n) /'ɪnfrəˌstrʌktʃər/ basic services that are necessary for a community to function
intrepid (adj) /ɪn'trepɪd/ brave, willing to take risks
meager (adj) /'migər/ small
militia (n) /mə'lɪʃə/ an armed group
rampage (v) /'ræmpeɪʤ/ behave in a wild and violent way
ruin (v) /'ruɪn/ destroy
unspoiled (adj) /ʌn'spɔɪld/ in a natural state

UNIT 6 REVIEW

Grammar

1 Work in pairs. Look at the photo. What kind of tourist attraction do you think this is?

2 Read the conversation and see if you were right. Then complete it using phrases with *not*.

M = Meka; P = Pauline

M: You're planning to go to Mexico for your vacation, [1] ________ ?

P: That was the plan, but I've [2] ________ (decide / go) now. I thought to myself, You're always traveling to exotic places. Why [3] ________ (you / explore) your own country?

M: That's interesting. That's called a staycation, [4] ________ ? You'll certainly save a lot of money.

P: Well, I hope so. But I [5] ________ (want / stay) at home. I'm going to travel around the north of France. Giverny, the garden where Monet painted his water lilies, is one place I'd really like to go. I [6] ________ (hope / rain) a lot.

M: Where are you going to stay? Or [7] ________ (decide) yet?

P: I'll take a tent with me, but I [8] ________ (think / I will use) it all the time. Let's [9] ________ (be) too ambitious! I'll stay in guest houses sometimes.

M: Well, I think it sounds like a great idea. It means you [10] ________ (must / worry) about visas and changing money and all.

3 What is Pauline's next vacation going to be? Why?

I CAN	
use *not* correctly with *hope*, *think*, *want*, *let*, *must*, and *have to* in the infinitive	☐
make negative questions and negative tag questions	☐

Vocabulary

4 Put the correct preposition in each space.

1 Do you prefer to cook for yourself or do you generally eat ________ when you're on vacation?
2 Do you like to try ________ new food?
3 Do you generally join ________ with group activities and organized excursions or do you prefer to do things alone?
4 If you had two weeks ________, how far would you travel?
5 Have you ever had to fill ________ an immigration form?
6 Do you stay ________ later than usual when you're on vacation?

5 In pairs, ask each other the questions above.

I CAN	
use phrasal verbs with *in* and *out*	☐
talk about vacations and travel	☐

Real life

6 Match each phrase in list A with its ending in list B.

A	B
I'm coming in	in traffic.
The easiest thing is to hop	my own way.
I'll pick you up	ride.
I'll call if I get held up	to your house?
Look out for the Hoover building	by train.
I can easily find	on a bus.
It's only a ten-minute	on your right.
How do I get	from the station.

7 Tell your partner how to get to a well-known meeting point in your town by public transportation.

I CAN	
describe the best way to get from one place to another	☐
ask for directions and travel advice	☐

Speaking

8 Work in pairs. What do you look for when choosing a vacation destination? Tell each other which of these matters more to you and why:

- the comfort OR the experience
- the journey OR the destination
- familiarity with the place OR not knowing anything about it
- relaxation OR being active

Unit 7 Natural resources

This photo taken half above, half under water shows fishermen on an Indonesian coral island. *Photograph by David Doubilet*

FEATURES

1 Work in pairs. Look at the photo. How many natural resources can you identify?

air	soil
animals	sunlight
fossil fuels (coal, oil, gas)	trees
minerals	water
plants and fruits	wind

2 Match the words (1–5) to their definitions (a–e). Then discuss which words apply to the natural resources in Exercise 1.

1 abundant	a nature can replace what is used
2 exhaustible	b in plentiful supply
3 inexhaustible	c can be used up
4 renewable	d difficult to find
5 scarce	e will never be used up

3 The three Rs of saving natural resources are: Reduce, Reuse, and Recycle. What examples can you give of each of them? Do you do any yourself?

7a Water conservation

Speaking

1 Work in pairs. Why do we need to save water when over 70 percent of the Earth's surface is covered by water? Read the article and see if your answer was similar.

So what if people waste a lot of water—we've got enough, don't we? Well, we may have a lot of ocean water, but we are using fresh water faster than nature can replace it. So instead we are forced to recycle waste water, cleaning it and then piping it into people's homes. That process requires a lot of energy—running a tap for five minutes uses the same energy as burning a 60-watt light bulb for fourteen hours—and a lot of money. Also, when underground natural water reservoirs (or aquifers) get low, they can become contaminated with high concentrations of natural minerals like arsenic, or man-made chemicals from the ground. To prevent this, we need to keep these reservoirs well-stocked. Here's where our water goes:

A six minute shower	15 gallons (55 liters)
A hamburger	660 gallons (2,500 l)*
A serving of goat meat	11 gallons (42 l)
A bar of chocolate	372 gallons (1410 l)
A serving of chicken	153 gallons (580 l)*
A cup of coffee	36 gallons (135 l)
Flushing the toilet	2 gallons (8 l)
500 sheets of paper	6,000 gallons (22,500 l)
A slice of bread	11 gallons (40 l)
1 lb (½ k) of clean wool	22,500 gallons (85,000 l)

* in the case of the farm animals, only a few gallons were drunk by the animals or used in processing; the majority of the water went into the grain they were fed during their lives.

2 Look at the facts and answer the questions.

1 Are you surprised by any of the facts? Why?
2 What are the best ways to save water?

Listening

3 24 Listen to speakers from the United Kingdom, the United Arab Emirates, the United States, and Mexico talking about water. What does each say about:

1 their own attitude toward water use?
2 what will happen if water is not conserved?

4 24 Listen again and answer the questions.

Speaker 1
1 How does Liam describe Manchester?
2 What does he do when he brushes his teeth?
Speaker 2
3 What is the problem with desalinating water?
4 What is Gemal researching?
Speaker 3
5 How has the Colorado Delta changed in the last 100 years?
6 What is the river water used for?
Speaker 4
7 What practical water saving measures does Carmen do at home?
8 What does she suggest about other people's attitudes toward water use?

5 Are there similar situations in your country?

Grammar mixed conditional sentences

6 Work in pairs. Look at the *if* sentences (1–6). Answer the questions (a–c).

a Which sentences describe present situations and present consequences?
b Which describe past situations and past consequences?
c Which are a mixture of the two?

1 If we had known the facts, we would not have wasted so much water in the past.
Example:
B. We didn't know the facts in the past, so we wasted a lot of water in the past.
2 If I had been brought up in Saharan Africa, I would be more aware of my water use.
3 If we used less water, we wouldn't have to use so much energy treating it.
4 If not for desalination, this country would not have been able to develop.
5 If you had visited the area around the old delta in Mexico 100 years ago, you would be shocked to see it now.
6 If more people thought and acted like me, things would not have come to this point.

MIXED CONDITIONAL SENTENCES

First conditional (for present or future situations)
If + simple present,... *will* + base form

Second conditional
If + simple past,... *would* + base form

Third conditional
If + past perfect,... *would have* + past participle

Mixed second and third conditional
If + simple past,... *would have* + past participle

Mixed third and second conditional
If + past perfect,... *would* + base form

For more information and practice, see page 165.

7 Look at the grammar box. Then make conditional sentences based on the information in these situations.

1 We bought a cheap dishwasher that wasn't very efficient so we ended up using a lot more water than we need to.
2 I don't use the dishwasher much, because no one told me that you use more water washing dishes by hand.
3 You wasted a lot of water in the past because you washed your car every week.
4 Automatic carwashes are really expensive. As a result, I haven't used them very often.
5 Our water use is way above the average because we built a big swimming pool.
6 We water the garden when the temperature is cool so that the water doesn't evaporate.
7 The United States has a water shortage because they tried to cultivate areas with a desert climate.
8 We changed our habits after we saw a TV show about how much water is wasted.

8 Finish these sentences with the correct tense.

1 If we hadn't used so much water,...
2 If you'd visited this area twenty years ago,...
3 If they don't act now,...
4 If people'd been more careful,...
5 If there's no rain,...

9 Use the conditional forms in the grammar box to make hypotheses based on these facts.

1 The Aral Sea in central Asia (a huge freshwater lake) is now one-tenth of the size it was in the 1960s because water has been used by farmers to irrigate their fields.
2 As a desert town, Las Vegas has to import a lot of water. But a lot of it goes to watering green spaces, particularly the 50 golf courses that have been built around the city.
3 Sixteen million tourists visit Greece each year, causing shortages of water on many of its islands.
4 In the 1970s, Britain found a lot of gas in the North Sea. But rather than use it carefully, they used it immediately. Now more than 50 percent of Britain's gas is imported.

The Aral Sea

Vocabulary and speaking

10 Work in pairs. Match each verb in A with as many nouns in B as you can. Then tell each other if you do any of these actions or support others who do.

A

conserve	consume	preserve	protect
run out of	save	spend	waste

B

animals	food	forests	land	money
energy	gas	time	water	

11 Think about how your country has saved or wasted resources and write conditional sentences about them. Then talk to the other students and tell each other your ideas. Choose the best idea and tell the class.

7b The minister for no oil

One thing you do not expect an oil minister to do is to block the development of his own country's oil fields. But that is exactly what Alberto Acosta did when he was appointed Ecuador's Oil Minister in 2007.

For a relatively poor country whose main income is from oil exports, this proposal seemed crazy. But if Ecuador is not rich by economic standards, in terms of biodiversity, it is one of the richest places on Earth. When scientists studied trees in the Yasuni National Park in Ecuador's unspoiled rain forest, they found over 650 different species of tree in just one hectare—more than the total number in all of the continental US and Canada combined.

Mr. Acosta said he would rather the oil companies did not destroy these natural riches. His innovative idea was to leave the oil reserves beneath Yasuni Park untouched, in return for compensation of half their value. The oil is worth more than $7 billion, so Ecuador asked the international community to pay $3.6 billion not to extract it.

But the plan has met with problems, both inside and outside of Ecuador. The state oil company, Petroecuador, opposes the plan and many suspect that President Correa now wishes he had never supported it. At the same time, only a few countries have shown interest, with only Germany promising $800 million over thirteen years.

Ecuador is not the only country trying to get richer nations to pay for not exploiting their forests. Both Nigeria and Guatemala are hoping they will be able to make similar deals. A spokesperson for local environmental groups explained, "If only people in developed countries appreciated that these forests absorb a lot of the CO_2 that their industries produce. I just wish they would take a longer-term view of this problem. If we don't do something to protect biodiversity and prevent climate change, we will all be losers—with consequences I'd rather not even think about."

Vocabulary oil

1 How many of these expressions do you know? Which is shown in the photo above?

oil field, oil refinery, oil reserves, oil rig, oil slick, oil tanker, oil well

WORDBUILDING collocations related to one word

There are some nouns that have many words that collocate with them: *oil well, oil tanker, oil field*

2 Work in pairs. Discuss the questions.

1 How much is a gallon or liter of gas in your country?
2 Are people more careful these days about how they conserve oil or gas?

Reading

3 Read the article and choose the phrase (a–c) that best summarizes Acosta's idea.

a for Ecuador to use money from oil exports to protect its forests
b for Ecuador to be paid not to extract its oil
c for Ecuador to keep the oil underground until it really needs the money

4 Answer the questions.

1 Why did Acosta's proposal seem crazy?
2 In what way was the price Acosta asked other countries to pay a fair one?
3 What has been the reaction of the international community to the plan?
4 What has been the reaction of local environmental groups?

5 Fill in each space with a word from the article.

1 Ecuador's riches are in its ________ .
2 In Yasuni park, Ecuador has oil ________ worth $7 billion.
3 The Ecuadoran ________ opposes the plan.
4 There are other countries who would like to be paid not to ________ their natural resources.
5 People in the developed world don't ________ the forests' role, in preventing climate change.
6 People need to think about what will happen in the ________-________ .

6 Work in pairs. What do you think of Acosta's idea? Is it helpful for Ecuador? Is it unrealistic?

Grammar *wish, would rather,* and *if only*

▶ *WISH, WOULD RATHER,* and *IF ONLY*

Wish about a present situation
wish + noun/pronoun + simple past

Wish about a past situation
wish + noun/pronoun + past perfect

Wish for someone to do something about a present situation
wish + noun/pronoun + *would*
(The subject of *wish* and noun/pronoun cannot be the same.)

Strong wishes about a present or past situation
Use *if only* in place of *I wish*

Stating what you would prefer to do
would rather + base form

Stating what you would prefer someone else to do
would rather + noun/pronoun + simple past

For more information and practice, see page 166.

7 Look at the grammar box. Look at these sentences. Then choose the option that describes the actual situation.

1 Mr. Acosta said he would rather the oil companies did not destroy these natural riches.
The oil companies *destroy / don't destroy* these natural riches.
2 President Correa now wishes he had never supported it.
President Correa *supported / didn't support* it.
3 If only people in developed countries appreciated that forests absorb a lot of CO_2.
People in developed countries *appreciate / don't appreciate* that forests absorb a lot of CO_2.
4 I just wish they would take a longer-term view of this problem.
They *will / won't* take a longer-term view of this problem.

8 Choose the correct form to complete the sentences below.

1 I wish people *stopped / would stop* complaining about the price of gas these days.
2 I wish they *didn't cut down / hadn't cut down* those trees in the park to make a playground.
3 Would you rather *walk / walked* or would you prefer we *go / went* by car?
4 Most oil companies wish they *had / would have* the freedom to extract oil from wherever they wanted.
5 If only we *didn't have / wouldn't have* to rely on our cars so much out here in the countryside.
6 If only I *could speak / would speak* another language, I could work abroad.
7 Suri wishes that she *had taken / would take* a job with Exxon when she had the chance. She'd much rather *work / worked* for them than Shell.
8 I wish people *woke up / would wake up* to the problems of climate change.

Speaking

9 Look at these situations and make two sentences for each one with *wish, if only,* or *would rather.* Then read your sentences to your partner.

1 Your car is old and uses a lot of gas. You don't have enough money to buy a new one.
2 You would like to travel more, but you only get three weeks' vacation.
3 Your trip to work takes you an hour a day, so you never get home in time to do any exercise, which you would love to do.

7c A world of its own

Reading

1 Work in pairs. Look at the facts on page 87 about the island of Madagascar for two minutes and then cover the page. Get your partner to ask you three questions about these facts. Then get them to cover their books and ask them three other questions.

2 Read the article. Answer the questions.

1 Which of Madagascar's natural resources is the author most worried about?
2 How is this resource collected and used?
3 What examples of sustainable ways of making money from Madagascar's natural resources are mentioned?

3 Choose the correct option (a–c) to complete the sentences.

1 Madagascar has unusual ....
a flora b fauna c both
2 The Madagascan people are ....
a poor
b anxious
c wealthy
3 Cultivating crops meant ....
a clearing the forest carefully
b setting fire to forests
c getting government permission
4 President Ravalomanana was ....
a ecologically-minded
b an inexperienced politician
c popular with the military
5 The new government passed a law allowing people to ....
a cut down hardwood trees
b import hardwood from China
c sell wood from fallen hardwood trees
6 For many Madagascans, cutting down hardwood trees is ....
a an easy way to make money
b necessary to make furniture
c against their beliefs
7 Other types of trees are cut down to ....
a protect the rivers
b make medicines
c transport the hardwoods
8 The forest offers locals other ways to make money, such as ....
a developing new medicines
b taking tourists on guided walks
c exporting flowers

Critical thinking emotive language

4 Often, when writers feel very strongly about an issue, they will use strong or emotive language to try to make the reader feel as they do. Find emotive words or phrases that convey:

1 how individual Madagascar is (para 1)
2 how hard the lives of the local people are (para 2 and 5)
3 how strongly ecologists feel about the situation (para 3)
4 how inconsiderate the loggers are (para 4)
5 how impressive and special these hardwood trees are (para 4)
6 how hopeless the situation is (para 7)

5 Do you think that by using such language, the writer helps his argument? Or would it be better to give a more balanced argument? What facts or information would you include to do this?

Vocabulary strong feelings

6 Replace the words in bold with a word from the article to make these sentences more emotive.

1 A lot of efforts are being made to preserve this **individual** place. (para 1)
2 She was **anxious** to get the job. (para 2)
3 Li **disapproves of** logging. (para 3)
4 A number of oil companies now want to **take** oil **from** the Arctic. (para 4)
5 It is a beautiful view, with the **tall and elegant** mountains in the background. (para 4)
6 Archaeology is much more **physical and tiring** than most people think. (para 5)
7 With no prospect of a job, many young people think the future looks **hopeless**. (para 7)
8 All environmentalists seem **very interested in** climate change. (para 7)

7 Work in pairs. Think of a place that is very special and should be protected (like a local green space, a traditional community). Write a short description of it (100–150 words) using emotive language. Then read your description to the class. Vote on which description is the most persuasive.

A world *of its* own

Madagascar, the world's fourth largest island, at over 225,000 square miles, is a unique place that has been blessed with exceptional riches. Roughly 90 percent of its flora and fauna is found nowhere else on the planet. The spectacle of its carrot-shaped baobab trees and ghostly lemurs makes even the most well-traveled visitors wide-eyed with amazement and delight.

But its rare beauty hides the desperate situation of its people. The typical Madagascan lives on about a dollar a day, even though you would not guess this from the cheerful and optimistic Malagasy, the island's main ethnic group. Since the first humans arrived in Madagascar some 2,300 years ago, loggers and developers have destroyed nearly 90 percent of the island's original forest habitat, harvesting it for timber or burning it down to create room for crops and, more recently, cattle.

Considering that Madagascar's population is growing by three percent a year, this tension between rich land and poor residents is increasing daily. Alarmed ecologists have named Madagascar a biodiversity hot spot, deploring the practice of slash-and-burn agriculture. In 2002, the global environmental community rejoiced when green-friendly Marc Ravalomanana was elected president. But only seven years later, in the spring of 2009, the military replaced Ravalomanana with a former radio disc jockey who seemed to have little interest in protecting the environment.

Needing money, the new government reversed a ban on the export of precious hardwoods, making it legal to sell wood from trees which had already been cut down or had fallen during the cyclones that regularly hit the island. Yet in reality they did little to control the loggers who continued to rob the forests of new wood. The main targets of this environmental crime are the rosewood and ebony trees. The wood from these majestic trees is in high demand: in China, it is used to make exotic imperial-style furniture for the new middle class; in Europe and America, it is a valued material in the manufacture of expensive musical instruments.

The locals are caught in a trap. Poverty and the high value of rosewood—at $3,000 per cubic meter it is ten times as valuable as oak—have driven them to cut down trees that are traditionally considered sacred. It is dangerous and back-breaking work. Using hand axes, in a few hours they bring down a tree that has stood tall for many centuries. Then they cut the trees into logs and drag them several miles to the nearest river.

The rare hardwood trees are not the only casualties. In order to transport the heavy rosewood logs downriver, rafts must be built from other wood. For each raft, the loggers cut down four or five lighter trees near the river, causing the earth to erode and silt up the rivers. Animals' habitats have also been disturbed, putting their survival at risk.

In this bleak landscape, one man's work offers hope. Olivier Behra, who first came to Madagascar from France in 1987, believes that the only solution is to give local people economic alternatives. Almost single-handedly, he has stopped deforestation in the Vohimana forest by encouraging the locals instead to collect medicinal plants, which they never imagined had any monetary value, and sell them overseas. The village lemur hunter has been retrained as a guide for tourists obsessed with lemurs. The same tourists also pay to visit the wild orchid conservatory that Behra has set up. Can small-scale and sensitive initiatives like this compete with the rosewood mafia of Madagascar? Only time will tell.

MADAGASCAR IN NUMBERS

FOURTH-LARGEST island in the world after Greenland, New Guinea, and Borneo

22 MILLION people from 18 different Asian and African ethnic groups living here

90 PERCENT of its flora and fauna is found nowhere else on Earth

70 different species of lemur found only on Madagascar

300 YEARS: the time it takes a rosewood tree to reach maturity

Number 1 producer of vanilla in the world

27,000 TONS of ebony and rosewood exported in 2009, much of it illegally

7d The climate change debate

Real life making your point

1 Work in pairs. What causes climate change? Is it man-made or a natural phenomenon? Use the expressions below to help you.

CO_2 emissions	natural weather cycle
fossil fuels	the greenhouse effect
global warming	

2 25 Listen to four people discussing climate change. Which two people would change their habits to help prevent climate change?

Speaker 1: Elena ☐ Speaker 3: Jim ☐
Speaker 2: Anne ☐ Speaker 4: Rick ☐

3 25 Listen again. Complete the expressions (1–6) that the speakers use to make their points.

▶ MAKING YOUR POINT

Giving examples
Take…, for example…
Let me give you an example…
Imagine [1] ______ hair…

Stressing a point
The point is that…
I, for one, [2] ______ in how I pollute…
Look, there's no doubt that [3] ______…
To be honest with you,…

Rejecting an argument
I don't accept that.
I used to believe [4] ______, but…
Yeah, but that's not the point.
I (don't) believe it simply because [5] ______.

Challenging the question itself
The whole starting point for this debate is wrong.
We're approaching this debate all wrong by saying [6] ______ problem.

4 25 Discuss which of the techniques (a–e) each speaker used to make a point. Listen again and check.

a humor
b challenging the question itself
c speaking clearly and slowly
d illustrating with examples/stories
e anticipating counter-arguments

5 Which technique did you find most effective? Which technique do you prefer yourself? Tell your partner.

6 Pronunciation sentence stress

a 26 When making their point, each speaker uses word stress to emphasize the important words. Listen to this example.

I don't know and I'm not sure **anyone** knows for sure. (2 words)

b 27 Underline the words which you think are most stressed. Then listen and check.

1 We don't know that we're causing it, but some people say we might be... (2 words)
2 …scraping ice off the inside of my windows rather than the outside. (2 words)
3 Regional temperatures may be lower, but average global temperatures keep on rising. (2 words)
4 Because it's not just an environmental problem. It's an economic problem, a social problem, even an ethical problem. (4 words)

7 Work in pairs. Choose one of the solutions to climate change given below. Work out arguments in favor of this solution. Think about the techniques you will use to make your point and the examples you could give. Then debate another pair who have a different solution.

The solution to climate change is:
- reducing energy use by inreasing fuel prices
- paying poor countries to protect their forests
- finding a technological solution to cool the Earth (like putting millions of tiny mirrors in space to reflect the sun's rays)
- getting all countries to sign an international agreement to limit CO_2 emissions

7e Waste of energy

Writing a letter to the editor

1 Do you ever read the letters section of newspapers, local or national? Have you ever written a letter to the editor yourself?

2 Read the letter. Answer the questions.

1 Who wrote the letter?
2 Why did they write it?
3 Do you find it persuasive? Why?

Financial News **Published: March 20**

To the Editor:

James Anderson (Travel section, March 15) writes about the waste of energy in hotels: overheated rooms, lights left on all night, towels used once and washed. He is right, but why stop with hotels? Wouldn't it be better to mention all the other mindless waste that characterizes modern life?

In the morning, I walk downtown past stores whose doors are wide open, blowing hot air into the street. At night, I walk home past fully-lit, empty office buildings, when the workers have already left; past enormous flashing screens where advertisers try to go one better than the competition. At the supermarket, I take my frozen vegetables from open freezer bins. My children leave their computers on when they go out, and their phone chargers plugged in with no phone on the other end (though they should know better).

All this waste illustrates two simple facts. First, that energy is too cheap and we had better increase its price substantially to make people more energy-conscious. Second, that no one really considers the public interest anymore.

Just as it is in the public interest that we have speed limits on our roads—though some of us may not like it—so would we be better off if we were forced by our government to conserve energy.

V. Dupeyrat
Head of Energy Services
DEF Energy, Seattle

3 Work in pairs. How is the letter organized? Match the functions (a–d) with each paragraph. Discuss whether they could be organized differently.

a Examples that illustrate the problem
b A recommendation or call to action
c The reason for writing
d A summary of the problem

4 Word focus *better*

Underline all the phrases using the word *better* and match them with the definitions (a–e) below. Compare answers with your partner.

a not be so stupid
b in an improved (often economic) situation
c more useful or desirable
d improve on the effort of another
e really ought to

5 Writing skills giving vivid examples

a What does the writer say about lights and towels to illustrate his argument?

b Find more examples of energy waste in the first two paragraphs.

6 Look at this list of things that annoy people about modern life. Expand three of them to explain what is annoying about it, as in the example. Then compare with your partner.

Example:
magazines that… *are full of news about celebrities*

airlines which…
cell phones that…
TV shows about…
supermarket food that…
computer programs which…

7 Write a short letter (150 words) to the editor, talking about one of the items in Exercise 6. Make sure you include the same elements as in the sample letter. Then exchange letters with your partner. Do they agree with the way you feel?

8 Read your partner's letter. Use these questions to check their letter. Is it correctly organized?

- Does it use enough examples?
- Does it end with a summary?
- Is it persuasive?

7f Galapagos energy

Video

Naturalist Charles Darwin once called the Galapagos "a little world within itself."

Before you watch

1 Work in groups. Look at the photo and discuss the questions.

1 What do you know about the Galapagos Islands? Make notes about:
   a their location.
   b the population.
   c what the islands are famous for.
2 What do you think Darwin meant when he called the Galapagos "a little world within itself"?

2 Complete the video summary with words from the glossary below.

The Galapagos Islands are home to many unique species of plants and animals. However, recently human beings have invaded this tropical [1] ________ . Tourism has [2] ________ and workers from the [3] ________ have followed. This has created pollution from vehicle [4] ________ , the energy people use, and the trash they produce, which harms the islands. Now, [5] ________ , corporations, and the government are working to minimize human impact.

While you watch

3 Watch the video and check your answers from Exercises 1 and 2.

4 Watch the first part of the video (to 02:41) and answer the questions.

1 Why did the animals on the Galapagos evolve into unique species?

   ____

2 What do people always say about the islands?

   ____

3 What do the volcanic eruptions tell scientists?

   ____

4 How long have humans been living on the islands?

   ____

5 What is one positive aspect of tourism?

   ____

6 What happened after the recent oil spill?

   ____

5 Watch the second part of the video (02:42 to the end). Mark the things you see.

a bird with a blue beak	a bicycle	boats
a bird with a red beak	black sandals	a bus
a recycling bin	a motorbike	a seal
a blue dress	a pink T-shirt	a turtle

6 Watch the second part again and answer the questions.

1 What is the goal of the program that international organizations and the Ecuadoran government are working on?

   ____

2 What four examples of conservation projects does the video show?
   a ________
   b ________
   c ________
   d ________

After you watch

7 **Roleplay an interview with Leopoldo Bocheri More**

Work in pairs.

Student A: Imagine you are going to interview Leopoldo Bocheri More. Read the information below and prepare a list of questions.

Student B: Imagine you are Leopoldo Bocheri More. A journalist is going to interview you. Look at the information below and think about what you are going to say the journalist.

- the problems the Galapagos have
- what the government is doing
- what other help is needed

Act out the interview. Then change roles.

8 Work in groups and discuss these questions.

1 What natural areas in your country have been adversely affected by human activity?
2 What can be done to protect such places?

conservationist (n) /ˌkɑnsərˈveɪʃənɪst/ a person who works to preserve nature
contaminant (n) /kən'tæmɪnənt/ something that pollutes
emissions (n) /ɪ'mɪʃənz/ smoke and gas from machines
haven (n) /'heɪvən/ a place people or animals can escape to
leak (n) /lik/ liquid or gas that escapes through a hole
mainland (n) /'meɪnˌlænd/ a large area of land that is not an island
oil spill (n) /'ɔɪl ˌspɪl/ when oil accidentally escapes from the place it is stored
old-timer (n) /'oʊld 'taɪmər/ a person or animal who has lived in a place for a long time
pristine (adj) /prɪs'tin/ in perfect condition
relic (n) /'relɪk/ something left over from the past
revenue (n) /'revəˌnu/ money earned
run aground (v) /'rʌn ə'graʊnd/ hit rocks or the bottom of the sea
skyrocket (v) /'skaɪˌrɑkɪt/ to go up very quickly
wake-up call (n) /'weɪk ʌp ˌkɔl/ a warning to pay attention

UNIT 7 REVIEW

Grammar

1 Work in pairs. Do you think that young people are more or less aware of the need to conserve resources than their parents' generation?

2 Read part of a blog discussing young people's attitude toward resources. What kind of things are they aware of? And not aware of?

3 Complete the text with the correct form of the verbs.

The younger generation seems very aware of global problems with natural resources. If you ask them about the rain forests, for example, they [1] *will say / would say*: "Oh, I wish people [2] *stopped / would stop* cutting them down. They're destroying the planet."
But on a personal level, they don't seem to be so aware. For example, it seems they would rather [3] *leave / left* the computer in sleep mode than [4] *turn / turned* it off. If the central heating was on too high, they [5] *would be / would have been* more likely to open a window than turn it down!
We parents are partly to blame for this. If we [6] *were / had been* stricter with our children when they were young, they [7] *would know / would have known* how to act now. I wish that they [8] *had / had had* more energy-saving education at school. As parents, we'd all rather schools [9] *teach / taught* these things because when we try, our children just think we are nagging!

I CAN	
hypothesize about present and past situations using mixed second and third conditionals	☐
express wishes and preferences about the past and future with *wish, if only, would rather*	☐

Vocabulary

4 Work in pairs. Find the odd one out in each group of words. Explain why it doesn't fit.

1 conserve, waste, save, preserve
2 natural, abundant, scarce, inexhaustible
3 oil refinery, oil slick, oil rig, oil tanker
4 sunlight, minerals, air, wind
5 majestic, tall, obsessed, desperate

5 Work in small groups. Think of two natural resources that are scarce. Discuss what we can do to protect them.

I CAN	
talk about natural resources	☐
use nouns, verbs, and adjectives about using and conserving natural resources	☐

Real life

6 Work in pairs. Which speakers (1–5) agree with this sentence and which disagree?

We should force developing countries to consume resources more carefully.

1 "Worry about developing countries? I have enough trouble remembering to turn off the lights!"
2 "The point is that the developed nations have used resources as they wished, so why shouldn't developing countries do the same?"
3 "If a rich person in India wants to own four cars and a mansion, who am I to say he can't?"
4 "I know you'll say that it's *everyone's* duty not to waste resources, but I don't accept that."
5 "It's not about what's fair; it's about what's necessary. We all need to conserve."

7 Which technique (a–e) does each speaker use to make their point?

a humor
b challenging the question itself
c using emphasis
d using examples/stories
e anticipating counter-arguments

8 Choose one of the techniques in Exercise 7 and make your own point about the need to conserve resources.

I CAN	
use different techniques to make my point in a debate	☐

Speaking

9 Work in small groups. Discuss the following issues.

- a regret you have about harming the environment
- a consequence of not protecting natural resources in your area
- an action to help conserve a natural resource

Unit 8 The news

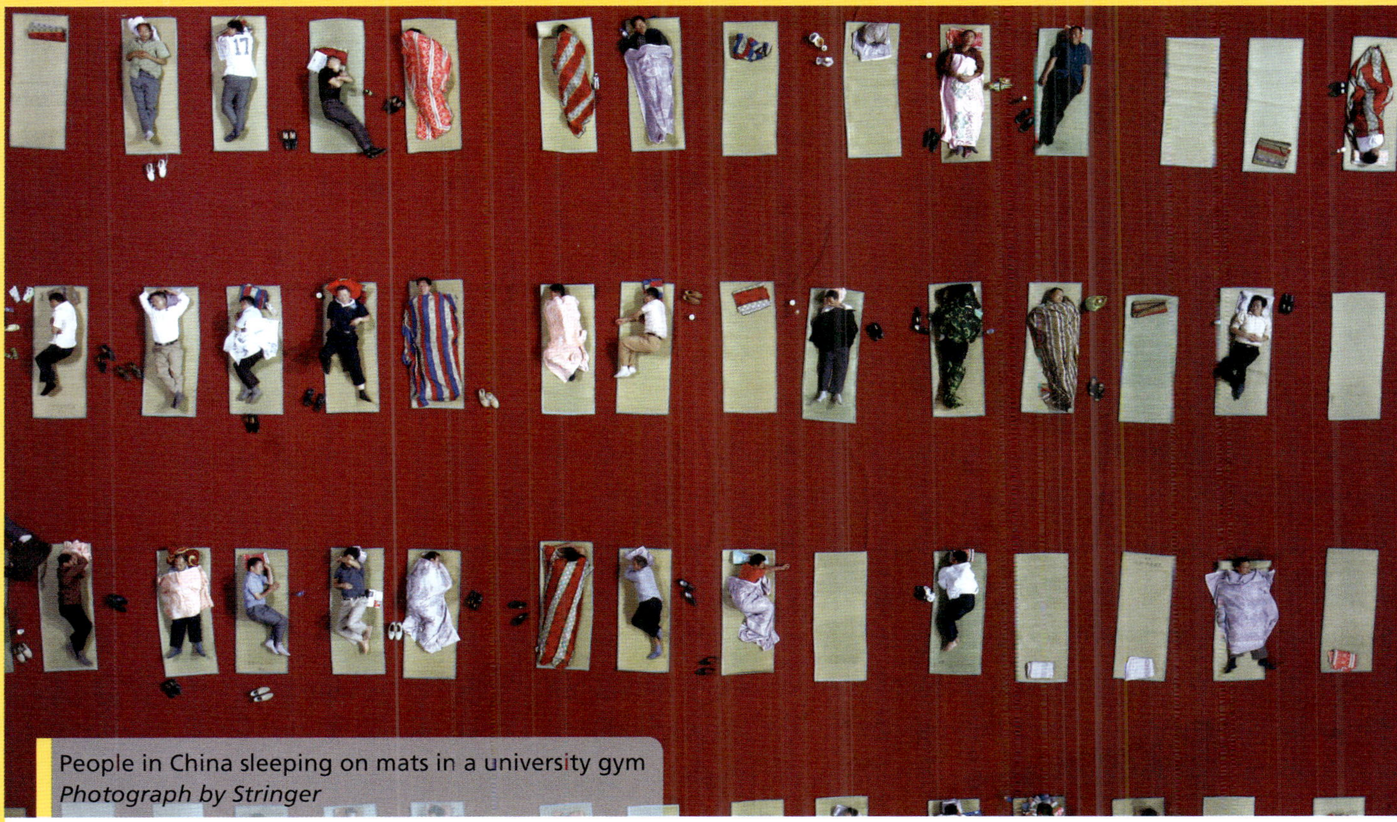

People in China sleeping on mats in a university gym
Photograph by Stringer

FEATURES

1 Match the phrases to complete these English sayings about the news. What sayings about news do you have in your language?

1 Good news… a is good news.
2 Bad news… b doesn't sell.
3 No news… c travels fast.

2 Work in pairs. Look at the photo and caption. Why do you think these people are sleeping in the gym? Think of a news story to explain the photo. Share your answers with the class.

3 Do the following fall into the category of hard news (serious, urgent) or soft news (less serious, not urgent)? Discuss.

- a column with celebrity gossip
- a local news story about a new housing development
- an editorial about a political scandal
- business news about interest rates
- a travel feature about Nicaragua
- a science news story about a cure for Alzheimer's disease

8a A life revealed

Vocabulary photography

1 Read the quotations. Find the following:

- 3 words that mean *a photograph*
- 2 words for parts of a camera
- 3 verbs that describe what a camera does with an image

2 Which is your favorite quotation? Why?

A picture is worth a thousand words. - *Fred R. Barnard*

What you have caught on film is captured forever… it remembers little things, long after you have forgotten everything. - *Aaron Siskind*

There is one thing the photograph must contain: the humanity of the moment. - *Robert Frank*

Look and think before opening the shutter. The heart and mind are the true lens of the camera. - *Yousuf Karsh*

I see no reason to record the obvious. - *Edward Weston*

A great photographer takes 100 shots and keeps just one. - *Anon*

Seeing and composing the beauty is what separates the snapshot from the photograph. - *Matt Hardy*

Reading

3 Work in pairs. Look at the two photos and discuss the questions. Then read the article and check your answers.

1 Have you seen either of these photos before?
2 Where are these people from?
3 How old are they?
4 What is the relationship between them?

4 Complete these sentences by finding the contrasting facts in the article.

1 Sharbat Gula let McCurry take her picture, even though…
2 The picture became world famous, even though…
3 McCurry recognized 29-year-old Gula immediately, even though…
4 Gula does not complain about her life, even though…

A LIFE REVEALED

She remembers the moment the photographer took her picture. The man was a stranger, but he asked if he could, and she agreed to let him take it. She had never been photographed before and, until they met a second time seventeen years later, she was not photographed again.

The photographer, Steve McCurry, remembers the moment too. It was 1984 and he was recording the lives of Afghan refugees in a camp in Pakistan. She was staring out of the school tent and he admits thinking at the time that the picture would be nothing special. Yet the "Afghan girl," as the portrait is now known, became one of the most iconic images of our time. McCurry used her intense expression, so untypical of an average, carefree twelve-year-old girl, to warn us not to ignore the victims of war, especially its young victims.

In 2002 National Geographic persuaded McCurry to return to Pakistan to look for the girl. After showing her photo around the refugee camp, he found a man who had known her as a child and knew where to find her. He offered to get her from her home in the Tora Bora mountains and after three days returned with Sharbat Gula, a woman perhaps 29 years old. McCurry knew at once that this was her.

Time and hardship had erased her youth. Her skin was weathered. Yet her eyes still burned with the same intensity. Her brother explained the story of their lives, blaming the war for forcing them and many other Afghans out of their homeland. When Sharbat was six years old, they fled to the mountains, hiding in caves and begging people to give them food and blankets. She married when she was sixteen and now her time is occupied with bringing up her three children, cooking, cleaning, and caring for them. Yet she does not complain about having a hard life. More amazingly, she is not aware of the impact that the photo of the young Sharbat with her sea-green eyes had on the world.

iconic (adj) /aɪˈkɒnɪk/ well-known and admired everywhere

Grammar reporting verbs

5 Look back at the article and complete these sentences using reporting verbs. Note the form that follows the reporting verb in each case.

1 She **agreed** ________ him take her picture.
2 He **admits** ________ at the time that the picture would be nothing special.
3 McCurry used her intense expression to **warn** us ________ the victims of war.
4 In 2002 National Geographic **persuaded** McCurry ________ to Pakistan.
5 He **offered** ________ her from her home in the Tora Bora mountains.
6 Her brother **blamed** the war ________ them out of their homeland.
7 They **begged** people ________ them food and blankets.
8 She does not **complain** ________ a hard life.

6 Work in pairs. What is being reported in Exercise 5? Discuss what the person actually said at the time. Then compare answers with another pair.

1 She agreed to let him take her picture.
Yes, you can take my picture.

REPORTING VERBS

Verb + infinitive
She agreed to let him take her picture.

Verb + someone + infinitive
National Geographic persuaded McCurry to return to Pakistan.

Verb + -ing
He admits thinking at the time that the picture would be nothing special.

Verb + preposition + -ing
She does not complain about having a hard life.

Verb + someone + preposition + -ing
Her brother blamed war for forcing them out of their homeland.

For more information and practice, see page 167.

7 Look at the grammar box. Use the verb given to report each of these statements.

1 You've taken some amazing photos!
She ________. (complimented)
2 You should think seriously about doing this professionally.
She ________. (encouraged)
3 You are far too modest about your own talents.
She ________. (accused)
4 Why don't you take a better photograph?
She ________. (suggested)
5 I'll also introduce you to my friend, who is a wildlife photographer.
She ________. (promised)
6 In fact, I'm sorry I haven't introduced you to him sooner.
She ________. (apologized)
7 You really should enter that photo competition in National Geographic.
She ________. (urged)
8 I can lend you my camera, if you don't think yours is good enough.
She ________. (offered)

8 Complete the article about the ethics of taking photos of other people. Put the verbs in the correct form. (You may need a preposition.)

Photographers who take pictures without their subject's knowledge are accused [1] ________ (be) sneaky or even unethical. A photographer who uses a telephoto lens to take a picture of someone at home cannot deny [2] ________ (do) wrong—they invaded someone's privacy. Newspaper reporters are often criticized [3] ________ (do) this kind of thing, not that it stops them.

But isn't this the same as taking pictures of strangers without permission? They haven't said it's OK for you [4] ________ (take) their picture. Maybe they would feel uncomfortable if you asked them [5] ________ (pose) for a shot; they might even refuse [6] ________ (let) you do it.

A lot of photographers insist [7] ________ (be) invisible so that their shots are more natural. They object [8] ________ (ask) their subject for permission first because this would spoil the moment. But I disagree. I always advise photographers [9] ________ (talk) to their subjects first. In fact, I strongly recommend [10] ________ (get) to know their subjects' story, because it gives the shots more meaning.

Speaking

9 Work in small groups and discuss the questions.

1 Do you like having your photo taken? Why?
2 What is the best way to get a good photo of someone?
3 Do you ever take photos of people you don't know? How do you approach this?
4 Have you ever felt uncomfortable about taking a photo of someone you didn't know?

8b And finally...

Vocabulary the feel-good factor

1 News programs often like to end with a good news story. Look at the adjectives that describe how this type of story can make people feel and match each one to a definition.

amusing	appealing	charming	encouraging
inspiring	odd	optimistic	quirky

1 ...., ...: hopeful
2 ....: makes one smile or laugh
3 ....: shows what people can achieve
4 ...., ...: unusual or strange
5 ...., ...: delightful

WORDBUILDING forming adjectives from verbs

We can add *-ing* to many verbs to form adjectives.
amuse → amusing, encourage → encouraging

2 Work in pairs. Think of an example of a good news story you have heard recently. Tell your partner. Use one of the adjectives in Exercise 1.

I saw a really inspiring local news story on TV about a five-year-old boy who raised money for his sick sister by...

Listening

3 **28** Listen to four feel-good news stories and complete the summaries.

1 People thought that the ...., but they were wrong because .... As a result in the future we will see ....
2 Researchers believe they have found .... When people took ...., the result was that ....
3 The world's largest .... says they have invented .... But doctors ....
4 Costa Rica is .... because it has .... Countries like .... on the other hand, ...

4 Work with a student from another group and retell the stories to each other. Which story did you find the most optimistic? Quirky? Inspiring?

Grammar passive reporting verbs

5 Look at these two examples of passive reporting verbs and answer the questions.

It *was thought* that the large blue butterfly was extinct.
It *is estimated* that 20,000 large blue butterflies will be seen this summer.

1 What do/did people actually say or think?
2 When do/did they say or think this?

PASSIVE REPORTING VERBS

Typical reporting verbs
say, think, believe, report, consider, know, estimate, expect, claim

It **+** ***is*** **+ passive reporting verb +** ***that*** **+ sentence...**
It is thought that people are more healthy these days. (present report of present event)
It is thought that people were less healthy in the past. (present report of past event)
It is thought that people will be healthier in the future. (present report of future event)

It **+** ***was*** **+ passive reporting verb +** ***that*** **+ sentence...**
It was thought that the butterfly was extinct. (report and event at same time in past)
It was thought that the butterfly had disappeared. (past event before past report)
It was thought that the butterfly would not return. (past report of a future event)

For more information and practice, see page 167.

6 Work in pairs. Look at the grammar box. Then look at the audioscript on page 179 and underline more sentences with passive reporting verbs. For each one decide:

- when the reporting happened
- when the reported event happened

1 ....

2 ....

3 ....

4 ....

5 ....

6 ....

7 ....

7 Transform these sentences into passive reporting sentences using *it*.

1 People report: "Large blue butterflies are everywhere now."

Example:

It is reported that large blue butterflies are everywhere now.

2 30 years ago people said: "The large blue butterfly is a common species."
3 People said: "Hunters caused the butterfly to die out."
4 The announcer said: "People thought the butterfly was extinct."
5 I said: "I take zinc and I haven't had a bad cold in a year."
6 In the past people thought: "Costa Rica is a poor country."
7 Scientists claim: "Taking zinc helps if you have a cold."
8 They said: "None of the previous experiments has been conclusive."
9 Experts claimed: "Eating the new chocolate will improve your health."
10 But people know: "Eating too much chocolate is actually bad for you."

8 Look at these other news items and facts and make sentences using the passive reporting verbs given. Tell your partner whether you think each one is true or not. Then check your answers on page 155.

1 It / believe / that chewing gum when you peel onions / prevent / you from crying.
2 It / say / Google's name / come / from "googol," a number with 100 zeros.
3 It / know / that laughing regularly / increase / life expectancy by up to ten years.
4 In 2008, it / report / that air pollution in the US / fall / by 40 percent since 1980.
5 It / claim / recently that scientists studying the zebrafish / discover / a way for the human heart to heal itself.
6 In 2011, it / report / that a man whose house had been crushed by a huge rock in the New Zealand earthquake /sell / the rock for $10,000.

Writing and speaking

9 Work in groups of three and prepare a feel-good news story. Choose a theme of your own or one from the list below. Then write the story together, using at least two passive reporting verbs. When you have finished, practice reading it aloud. Then each person should join a new group of three and read their stories to the other students.

- a person rescued by an animal
- the discovery of a valuable painting or antique
- a child's remarkable musical ability
- the invention of a new clothing fabric
- a couple who are celebrating their 90th wedding anniversary
- a dentist that people actually enjoy visiting

8c From hero to zero

Reading

1 Work in pairs. Look at the headlines below, as they appeared over several months. Discuss what you think happened.

HERO BA PILOT PETER BURKILL SPEAKS: I THOUGHT WE'D DIE IN HEATHROW CRASH

"I AM NOT A HERO"
SAYS BA CRASH PILOT CAPTAIN PETER BURKILL

REAL HERO OF BA FLIGHT 38
IS COPILOT JOHN COWARD

HERO PILOT "FORCED OUT OF BA"

FALLEN HERO: THAT DAY CHANGED MY LIFE FOREVER

OFFICIAL REPORT SAYS ICE FAULT CAUSED BA AIRPORT CRASH

2 Read the story quickly. Then check the sequence of key events with your partner. How did the story differ from your answer in Exercise 1?

3 Mark the statements true (T) or false (F).

1 Burkill's copilot was at the controls when the engines failed.
2 Some passengers were badly hurt.
3 At the time of the accident, Burkill was a single man who liked to enjoy himself.
4 Burkill's crew read BA's internal report.
5 Burkill was praised in the AAIB report.
6 He was too loyal to BA to work for another airline.

4 Complete the sentences with words from the article.

1 Burkill went from being a hero to being a (opposite of *hero*) *villain* . (para 1)
2 When the plane crash-landed, (incredibly) ________ it stayed upright. (para 2)
3 Perhaps his colleagues believed he was (no good at his job) ________ . (para 3)
4 The press portrayed Burkill as irresponsible: he (failed) ________ the people he was supposed to be responsible for. (para 4)
5 Burkill felt (completely unsupported) ________ by his colleagues. (para 5)
6 After the official report was published, Burkill was (given as a prize) ________ a medal for his actions. (para 7)

Critical thinking different perspectives

5 Each participant had a different perspective and a different motivation for acting as they did after the accident. Make notes to complete the table.

People involved	Their view of Burkill's role	Motivations for their actions
Peter Burkill	*he did what any pilot would have done*	*to clear his name and keep his job*
BA staff		
BA management		
AAIB*		
the newspapers		

*Air Accidents Investigation Branch

6 Who do you believe? Who do you think the newspapers' readers believed?

Word focus *word*

7 Find four expressions in the article with *word*. Match each one with the definitions below.

1 make the final point in an argument and win it
2 news or a rumor starts to circulate
3 no evidence other than what two sides claim to be true
4 no news about something

8 Work in pairs. What do these other expressions with *word* mean?

1 "The new gallery is amazing. But **don't take my word for it**: go see for yourself."
2 "When my husband handed me the keys to a new car for my birthday, I was at a loss **for words**."
3 "The hotel doesn't advertise at all. It just relies on **word of mouth** to get new customers."
4 "I can't believe they're closing the library. They **gave their word** that they wouldn't."

Speaking

9 Work in groups. Discuss the media in your country.
1 How respectful are reporters towards politicians?
2 How balanced is the reporting of public scandals?
3 Are people interested in reading about the private lives of famous people?

FROM HERO TO ZERO

In January 2008, hours after saving his plane from crashing at Heathrow Airport, Captain Peter Burkill was being praised as a hero. Only days later, when reports appeared in the press accusing him of freezing at the controls, he became a villain. How did this extraordinary transformation come about?

Peter Burkill was the pilot on flight 38 from Hong Kong and ultimately responsible for the lives of its 152 passengers. Seconds before landing, two of the plane's engines failed. With the plane losing height fast, Burkill let his copilot John Coward take the controls while he himself adjusted the wing flaps to help the plane reach the runway. His risky decision worked. The plane missed some houses and landed heavily on the grass just short of the runway. After skidding for a few hundred feet, it miraculously came to a stop without turning over. The passengers escaped without serious injury. As far as Burkill was concerned, he had done what any captain would have done. The rest was luck.

However, this was not the version of events that began to circulate among BA's staff in the following days, whether because they just liked to gossip or felt Burkill was incompetent. Word went around that rather than taking control of the plane, Burkill had frozen. Worse, it was reported that he had failed to issue a mayday call and had not evacuated the passengers correctly.

Some newspapers, sensing a chance to sell more copies, picked up the story, claiming that John Coward was the real hero. They published details of Burkill's colorful past, painting a picture of a well-paid pilot who had lived the life of a playboy, and—when it mattered—had let down his crew and passengers. Worse still for Burkill, it wasn't even his word against theirs. British Airways banned him from speaking about the events until the full investigation by the Air Accidents Investigations Branch (AAIB) was complete.

Overnight, Burkill's life changed. Before the accident, he had had everything: a great job, a beautiful home, a loving family, and the respect of his colleagues. Now he felt betrayed and desperate. The stress put enormous pressure on his family. In the weeks that followed, he spent more time at home helping his wife, Maria, to look after their young children. But he became depressed. He begged the company to issue a statement to clear his name, but they refused, clearly anxious to avoid bad publicity in case the official investigation found Burkill guilty. Even when they published their own internal report in May 2008, clearing him of any wrongdoing, it was only read by the senior management. No word of it reached his close colleagues, and rumors circulated that crew members were afraid to fly with him. He wrote to BA's chief executive asking for help, but got no reply.

The official AAIB report, the result of a completely independent inquiry, was finally published in February 2009. It concluded that ice had formed in the fuel system during the approach to Heathrow, cutting the fuel supply to the engines. The actions of the crew had saved the lives of all on board, it said, in particular Captain Burkill's split-second decision to reduce the flap setting.

The pilots and thirteen cabin crew were awarded the British Airways Safety Medal and the story of Peter Burkill the hero once again made the headlines. But the damage had been done. In August 2009, Peter Burkill took voluntary retirement from the company he had served for 25 years. He began applying for jobs with other airlines, but he was not invited to a single interview.

So did his critics win? No. Burkill himself had the last word. BA said that he was and always had been welcome in the company and in September 2010, BA invited him to come back and fly for them. Burkill accepted their invitation.

Captain Peter Burkill (right) and copilot John Coward

mayday call (n) /ˈmeɪdeɪ ˌkɔl/ a call for help in an emergency
runway (n) /ˈrʌnˌweɪ/ the part of an airport where planes land and take off
skid (v) /skɪd/ to slide without any control
voluntary retirement (n) /ˈvɑlənˌteri rɪˈtaɪərmənt/ to agree to leave your job in exchange for payment

8d Spreading the news

Real life reporting what you heard

1 29 Listen to two neighbors discussing an incident. Choose the picture that best illustrates what happened.

2 29 Work in pairs. Discuss the questions. Then listen again and check.

1 Why didn't Phil see the incident?
2 Who did Jess learn about the incident from?
3 How could the argument between the drivers have been avoided?
4 Who was one of the drivers identified as?
5 What happened in the end?

3 29 Look at the box. Complete the phrases Jess (J) uses to report what someone said and Phil (P) uses to say how reliable this source was. Then listen again and check.

1 J: ________ that it was an argument between two drivers and ________ it got pretty nasty.
2 J: ________ one of the drivers became really aggressive.
3 P: I'd take what Tara says with ________ . She tends to ________ things ________ .
4 J: She ________ that if the police hadn't arrived, there would have been a fight.
5 J: Someone ________ they had seen one of the drivers before. ________ , he is a local politician.
6 P: I think I'd take ________ ; he's not the type to ________ .
7 J: ________ Chris, they took them both away.

REPORTING WHAT YOU HEARD

I heard that…
Someone said that…
They figure that…
According to (somebody)…,
It seems that…
Apparently,…
Supposedly,…

Expressing belief and disbelief

I'd take his/her word for it.
He/She generally gets his/her facts right.
He's/She's not the type to spread gossip.
Don't pay attention to what he/she says.
It's been blown out of proportion.
I'd take that with a grain of salt.

A

B

C

4 Pronunciation the schwa

30 Unstressed syllables often produce the schwa sound /ə/. Listen for these examples and repeat. The stressed syllable is underlined.

/ə/ /ə/ apparently
/ə/ /ə/ generally
/ə/ /ɪ/ supposedly
/ə/ happened

5 You are going to spread news around the class. Follow these steps:

- Tell your partner two facts (one true, one false) about yourself or something you did.
- Talk to other students in the class and tell at least three people what you heard.
- Return to your partner and report the new information you heard.
- Discuss which ones you think are true or not. Use the expressions in the box.
- Tell the class what you thought and see if you were right.

8e A residents' meeting

Writing minutes from a meeting

1 Read this report of a residents' meeting on a street where a traffic incident occurred. Answer the questions.

1 What three ideas were suggested to avoid confrontations between drivers?
2 Which one was chosen as the best idea and why?

Flores Street residents' association

From: Antonia Perez

Re: Residents' meeting about road rage incident

Thanks to all of you who wrote and apologized for not being able to attend Tuesday's meeting. Here are the minutes.

We met to discuss what to do about traffic on our street following last week's incident. Various ideas were discussed about how we could prevent drivers from getting into these angry confrontations. One proposal was to make Flores a one-way street, but most people thought that this wouldn't be good for residents. Another suggestion was to reduce the number of parking spaces to allow more places for cars to pass each other. The objection to this was that it would force residents to park in neighboring streets and just move the problem to another street.

In the end, it was agreed that the best thing would be to put some signs at each end of the road asking drivers to drive with care and consideration. Terry Miles offered to write a letter to town hall asking if this would be possible. A draft copy will be posted next week for comment before it is sent.

2 Which of these elements are included in the report? In what order do they appear?

- the aim of the meeting
- what action was decided
- who said what
- who attended the meeting
- follow-up action

3 Writing skill impersonal language

a Underline the phrases that the writer uses to avoid naming people directly when reporting what was said. Why does she do this? Compare your answers with your partner and discuss.

b Rewrite the sentences using the words given to make them less personal.

1 Hannah suggested that we should put speed bumps on the street.
One ______ . (suggestion)
2 Everyone thought this was a terrible idea.
It ______ . (decided / good)
3 Dan thought the speed limit should be reduced to 15 mph.
Another ______ . (idea)
4 But several people said that probably no one would keep to this speed limit.
It ______ . (agreed)
5 Javi proposed having a sign with arrows giving priority to drivers from one direction.
Another ______ . (proposal)
6 Sofia argued that this would be impossible to enforce.
The ______ . (objection / difficult)

4 Read the description of a local problem. Discuss possible solutions with your partner. Look at the suggestions on page 153. Write a report of a meeting at which these solutions were discussed. Say which one was chosen and describe the follow-up action.

The city's university has recently bought four houses on your street to accommodate students, because they don't have enough rooms at their main dorm. The students are making a lot of noise at night, playing loud music and shouting in the street. This is a problem for local residents, many of whom have young children.

5 Exchange your reports with another pair. Answer these questions.

- Did they choose the same solution as you?
- Does their report seem too personal or direct?
- Does it follow the model in Exercise 1?
- Is it missing any important information?

8f Mount Fuji

Video

Climbing Mount Fuji is a mind exercise. It's mind over matter more than anything.

Before you watch

1 Work in groups. Look at the photo and discuss the questions.

1 Where are the people in the photo?
2 Why do you think they are there?
3 What do you think the caption tells us about the people in the photo?

2 Mark the things you think you are going to see in this video.

a bear	a rollercoaster
a bulldozer	snow
clouds	sunflowers
drums	a sunrise
food vendor	umbrellas

While you watch

3 Watch the video and check your answers from Exercise 2.

4 Watch the video again and describe these things.

1 Mount Fuji

....

....

2 the fire and water festivals

....

....

3 the weather when Karen Kasmauski climbs the mountain

....

....

5 Watch the first part of the video (to 02:07). Are these sentences true (T) or false (F)? Correct the false sentences.

1 Karen Kasmauski is enjoying perfect weather for her photo shoot.
2 Karen thinks Japanese people worship Mount Fuji because it is so beautiful.
3 Mount Fuji is worshipped with fire and water festivals.
4 Karen starts her photo shoot in the forest at the base of the mountain.
5 You can buy crackers and cakes at Mount Fuji.
6 Climbing Mount Fuji is seen mostly as something tourists have to do.

6 Watch the second part of the video (02:08 to the end). Make notes about these things. Then compare your notes with a partner.

1 How Karen feels when she gets to the top.

....

....

2 How Mount Fuji was different in the past.

....

....

3 Managing Mount Fuji.

....

....

4 What happens at the end of the climbing season.

....

....

After you watch

7 Roleplay interviewing a National Geographic photographer

Work in pairs.

Student A: Imagine you are a photographer for National Geographic. You are going to be interviewed by an amateur photographer. Make notes about the items below.

Student B: Imagine you are an amateur photographer. You are going to interview a photographer for National Geographic. Prepare questions based on these items.

- lifestyle of a photographer
- the advantages and disadvantages of the job

Act out the interview, then change roles.

8 Karen Kasmauski says that climbing Mount Fuji is "a national bonding experience." What do you think she means? Are there any symbols of national unity in your country?

9 Work in groups and discuss these questions.

1 Are there any special places in your country where people like to go and take photographs?
2 What makes an interesting photograph for you: the place, the people, or what is taking place?
3 Is there any famous place in the world you would like to photograph? Why?

appease (v) /ə'piz/ keep a person or a thing calm
bento box (n) /'bentoʊ ˌbɑks/ a wooden or metal box, divided into compartments, used in Japan for storing a meal
bonding (n) /'bɑndɪŋ/ the process of becoming emotionally close to other people
bulldozer (n) /'bʊlˌdoʊzər/ a large machine that moves earth
conical (adj) /'kɑnɪkəl/ shaped like a cone
pilgrimage (n) /'pɪlgrɪmɪʤ/ a journey to a holy place
purification (n) /pjʊərɪfɪ'keɪʃən/ the process of making something clean
typhoon (n) /taɪ'fun/ a very strong tropical storm
vending machine (n) /'vendɪŋ məˌʃin/ a machine that sells things, for example, drinks or food

UNIT 8 REVIEW

Grammar

1 Work in pairs. Look at the photo of a new development. What do you think the designers are trying to create?

2 Read the news article below and see if you were right.

3 Complete the article with the correct form of the verbs. Use prepositions where necessary. Then check your answer to Exercise 1.

Big cities are often criticized [1] ________ (be) big polluters. But it is generally considered that Singapore [2] ________ (be) an exception to this rule. For a long time the government has encouraged developers and conservationists [3] ________ (think) of ways to increase the island's green spaces. Recently green groups suggested [4] ________ (turn) the old KTM railway corridor into a nature trail. But perhaps the most striking project is Gardens by the Bay, a futuristic park which includes eighteen Supertrees. When it is complete, it is said that each of the eighteen trees [5] ________ (be covered) in more that 200 varieties of plants.

The government invited various companies [6] ________ (submit) ideas for the project and this was chosen as the most exciting. A spokesman for the government complimented the designers [7] ________ (come) up with a "truly innovative" design. The Supertrees are between 80 and 160 feet tall and mimic the function of real trees, absorbing sunlight through photovoltaic cells and collecting rainwater. The photographer who took this picture admitted [8] ________ (feel) skeptical about the project until he saw it for himself. "It looks like something from the movie *Avatar*: almost too good to be real!"

I CAN	
report speech with reporting verbs and the correct dependent verb form	☐
report what is generally said or thought with passive reporting verbs	☐

Vocabulary

4 Work in pairs. Find the odd word out in each group. Explain your choice.

1 movie, photo, snapshot, picture
2 column, feature, scandal, editorial
3 inspiring, amusing, optimistic, encouraging
4 lens, shutter, flash, camera
5 urge, promise, encourage, persuade
6 objection, suggestion, proposal, recommendation

5 Work in pairs. Describe a news photo that had a big impact on you. What was the story behind the picture?

I CAN	
talk about photography	☐
relate feel-good news stories	☐

Real life

6 Put each phrase into the right category: reporting what someone said (R), expressing belief (B), or expressing disbelief (D).

1 They figure that half a million people came to the free festival.
2 I'd take that with a grain of salt.
3 Apparently, a lot more people came than expected.
4 I think the number has been blown out of proportion.
5 According to official reports, around 250,000 attended.
6 It seems that the organizers were only expecting 150,000.
7 You can take the organizer's word for it.
8 Don't pay attention to what the promoters say. They just want publicity.

7 Work in small groups. Discuss an event, local or national, people have been talking about recently. Tell each other what you believe to be the real facts.

I CAN	
report what I heard	☐

Speaking

8 Work in pairs. Create a short news item about an event in your class or institution. Include at least two verbs reporting what people said.

Unit 9 Talented people

A mahout (elephant driver) bathes his elephant.
Photograph by Robert Harding

FEATURES

1 Work in pairs. Match the words in the box to the definitions (a–g).

background	experience	knowledge	degrees
qualities	skills	talents	

a strong natural abilities
b abilities developed by practice
c (generally positive) characteristics
d certificates which show you have learned something
e what you've done in your life
f what you know
g your past in general (birthplace, education, places lived)

2 Look at the photo and the caption. What qualities, skills, knowledge, and experience do you think a mahout needs to do their job well? Discuss.

3 Make short notes on your own background, experience, knowledge, and talents. Then ask each other questions.

9a An ordinary man

Reading

1 Work in pairs. Look at the photo and read the title of the article. Do you know who Neil Armstrong is? Tell your partner what you know.

2 Read the article and say in what ways Armstrong was an ordinary man and in what ways he was extraordinary.

3 Read the article again. Answer the questions.

1 Why is Armstrong called "the ultimate professional"?
2 Who paid for his college and what did they get in return?
3 What motivated Armstrong?
4 What does "the rest is history" mean?
5 What did Armstrong do to avoid publicity after the Apollo 11 mission? Why?
6 According to Armstrong, who was responsible for the success of the Apollo 11 mission?

An ORDINARY man

Neil Armstrong, the most famous of the astronauts on Apollo 11, has been called the ultimate professional. He was hired to do a job. He did the job and then he went home and kept quiet about it. In 40 years, he gave two interviews. He died in August 2012. But how could the man who first set foot on the Moon, a hero to millions of people, have remained such a mystery?

People like Armstrong often develop their interests at a young age. He pursued a career built on a passion for flying that he developed during his childhood in the 1930s. He learned to fly before he had graduated from high school in Wapakoneta, Ohio. He then took courses in aerospace engineering at Purdue University in Indiana, sponsored by the United States Navy. In return, Armstrong served as a naval pilot for three years. He saw action almost immediately, flying 78 missions in the war in Korea.

He left the Navy in 1952, and two years later got a job with the Lewis Flight Propulsion Laboratory, where he flew experimental aircraft. He reached speeds of 4,000 MPH and altitudes of over 200,000 feet. When he decided to become an astronaut is not clear. Certainly, it was not his ambition to be famous. An extremely talented pilot, he wanted simply to push the boundaries of flight.

He was selected for a space training program in 1960, and shortly after, news began to circulate that NASA was looking for astronauts for their Apollo program. Incredibly excited, he applied for the job and was accepted in 1962. The rest, as they say, is history.

When the astronauts returned from the Apollo 11 Moon landing of July 1969, Armstrong was a worldwide celebrity and could have done anything he wanted: TV shows, public speaking, etc. Instead, he became a professor at the University of Cincinnati. On weekends, he went flying to get away from all the attention. He subsequently worked for two private avionics companies until he retired in 2002. In 40 years he only gave two interviews. Why did Armstrong avoid publicity? Certainly he felt fortunate to have had the chance to fulfill his dream, but he did not feel any more special than the thousands of people who worked on the Apollo space program. He was just the pilot.

Astronaut Buzz Aldrin photographed on the Moon by Neil Armstrong (visible in Aldrin's visor)

Vocabulary careers

4 Work in pairs. Find verbs in the article that collocate with each of these nouns. Then identify the different steps in Armstrong's career.

1 to .... a career
2 to .... a school or college
3 to .... a course
4 to .... in the Navy
5 to .... an astronaut
6 to .... a company
7 to ...., ..., ... a job

WORDBUILDING verb (+ preposition) + noun collocations

pursue a career
graduate from a school/college

Grammar articles: *the* or no article?

5 Look at how *the* or no article are used in the paragraph. Match the words in bold (1–7) with the uses of *the* and no article (a–g).

Neil Armstrong, (1) **the most famous** of (2) **the astronauts** on Apollo 11, has been called the ultimate professional. He was hired to do a job. He did (3) **the job** and then he went (4) **home** and kept quiet about it. In 40 years, he gave two interviews. But how could (5) **the man** who first set foot on (6) **the Moon**, a hero to (7) **millions** of people, have remained such a mystery?

a to talk about an already mentioned thing
b to talk about something unique
c before a superlative adjective
d to talk about a specific thing or person
e to talk about specific things or people
f to talk about things or people in general
g before certain familiar places (like work)

6 Work in pairs. Find one more example of each use in the rest of the article.

ARTICLES: *THE* or NO ARTICLE?

definite article
the + singular/plural count nouns, noncount nouns = specific things

no article
– + plural count nouns, noncount nouns = things in general
Note: We don't use *the* with most time expressions or place names. However, there are some exceptions.

For more information and practice, see page 158.

7 Find an example in the article of the following:

1 no article with:
a) a country
b) a subject of study
c) a month
2 *the* with:
a) a country
b) a professional group
c) a period of time

8 Complete these sentences by inserting *the* where necessary.

1 While flying for .... Navy in .... Korea, Armstrong had to eject into .... sea when one of .... wings on his plane was damaged.
2 Armstrong and Aldrin only spent one day on .... surface of .... Moon.
3 Armstrong retired from .... NASA in .... 1972, but he helped with .... crash investigations in .... later years.
4 .... first investigation was in .... May 1970 following an explosion on .... Apollo 13.
5 .... other investigation involved .... space shuttle Challenger, which broke into .... pieces over .... Atlantic Ocean near .... Florida.
6 In .... nineties, Armstrong stopped signing .... autographs, because .... dealers were selling each for $1,000.

Speaking

9 Draw a path of your own (or a parent's) career. Begin with your interests as a child. Finish with future ambitions. If it is not an obvious linear progression, show how the direction changed. Then explain the path to your partner.

When I was a kid, I really liked to draw. But my parents wanted me to be a lawyer, so I started college for law in 2013.

But now you're in art school!

Yes… I hated it, so I took a year off and then dropped out!

9b Pushing the boundaries

Listening

1 31 Listen to an interview about the National Geographic Emerging Explorers program and answer the questions.

1 What is the aim of the program?
2 How does National Geographic help those selected?
3 What kind of fields do Emerging Explorers work in?

2 31 Are the sentences true (T) or false (F)? Listen again and check.

1 Emerging Explorers are people who are not yet fully established in their careers.
2 Emerging Explorers get money and publicity for their work in the magazine.
3 They generally have a scientific background.
4 Storytellers are explorers who record traditional stories from different cultures.
5 Alexandra Cousteau's father filmed other Emerging Explorers.
6 Alexandra is interested in how new technology can help to spread the environmental message.

Grammar relative clauses

3 Work in pairs. Look at the relative clauses in bold from the interview (a–e). Then discuss the questions (1–4).

a Each year, between eight and fifteen explorers, **whose work is really outstanding**, are selected.
b Emerging Explorers are generally people **who are at an early stage of their careers**.
c National Geographic awards each one of them $10,000, **which is intended to go towards further research**.
d The magazine is a place **where other interested people can read about their work**.
e There are all these people doing important work out there in the various fields **that I have described**.

1 In which sentence is the relative pronoun the subject of the relative clause?
2 In which sentences does the relative clause explain who or what is being talked about?
3 In which sentences does the relative clause give extra information and how does the punctuation help you know this?
4 In which sentence could the relative pronoun be omitted?

RELATIVE CLAUSES

Relative pronouns: *who* (*that*), *which* (*that*), *where*, *whose*
Subject: *She's the woman who won the award.*
Object: *That's the award which/that the woman won.*
OR *That's the award the woman won.*

Defining relative clause
This clause contains essential information for identification.
She's the woman who won an award for her photography.

Non-defining relative clause
This clause contains extra information, separated by one or two commas.
Her husband, who is also a photographer, accompanied her on the trip.

***that* or no pronoun**
The article (that) I read about her was good.

For more information and practice, see page 169.

4 Look at the grammar box. Then complete these sentences about Emerging Explorer Alexandra Cousteau by inserting the correct relative pronoun and any commas that are missing.

1 Alexandra Cousteau ________ is a conservationist believes water will be the most important issue of the 21st century.
2 Alexandra Cousteau ________ father was an oceanographer is a great advocate for environmental protection.
3 Cousteau says that the environmental movement uses communication tools ________ are old-fashioned.
4 She is currently planning an expedition ________ aim is to research different water ecosystems around the world.
5 She is currently working on a book ________ she hopes will teach people how to live on a "Water Planet."
6 The problem ________ she says was created by people is a problem ________ people can only solve by working together.

Grammar reduced relative clauses

5 An alternative to a relative clause is a reduced relative clause. Look at the participles in bold in these sentences. Which are active and which are passive?

1 We have so many different types of explorers, **chosen** from diverse fields.
2 There are all these people **doing** important work out there in the various fields.
3 That's the skill of the storytellers, **communicating** important facts about the planet.
4 She works as a conservationist, **trying** to persuade people to protect resources like water.
5 Alexandra Cousteau, **inspired** by her father's success as a storyteller, is researching ways in which the environmental community can use new media.

REDUCED RELATIVE CLAUSES

Present participle
researching
She works at Harvard, ~~where she is~~ researching sharks. (active)
Past participle
researched
It's a subject ~~which is~~ researched by only a few people.
(passive)

For more information and practice, see page 169.

6 Look at the grammar box. Then rewrite the reduced relative clauses in Exercise 5 as relative clauses.

7 Complete the profiles of other Emerging Explorers below by inserting the missing information as a reduced relative clause where possible and if not, as a relative clause.

1 She has been called the real-life Lara Croft by the *New York Times*.
2 She cycled a distance of 700 miles.
3 They threatened to harm her.
4 He is fascinated by the truly big questions.
5 He plays music to take his mind off problems.
6 He spends his time diving into water caves deep under the ground.
7 The caves have been undisturbed for 3.5 million years.
8 Knowledge is provided by these dark and wonderful places.

8 Work in pairs. Circle the eight adjectives in the profiles that describe people's strengths and qualities.

9 Which of these people would you most like to meet? Tell your partner.

Speaking and writing

10 Think of someone you admire for the work they do. Write a short description of their achievements and qualities. In groups, read your descriptions and ask questions.

Kira Salak, [1] ...., doesn't want to tell travel stories you have already heard. Independent and adaptable, she has traveled across Papua New Guinea on foot, and Alaska on a bicycle, [2] .... It is not easy traveling alone as a single woman in remote and dangerous regions. In Mozambique, she escaped soldiers [3] .... But she does not regret such experiences because she says they have helped her discover her strengths.

Stephon Alexander is a theoretical physicist [4] .... like "how did space and time begin?" It's an unusual job because you need to be not only analytical and patient, but also daring and a risk taker, because to answer such questions you have to make guesses. Often you can be completely wrong. But when you are right, he says, the feeling is amazing. The work can be mentally tiring, but Alexander is quite an easy-going type. He is also a jazz musician, [5] ....

Kenny Broad is an extreme explorer [6] .... These "blue holes," [7] ...., are like time capsules, full of interesting scientific evidence about the way life on our planet has evolved. The caves are also important reservoirs of fresh water. An articulate and passionate speaker, Broad promotes the idea that by working together, scientists from different backgrounds can benefit from the knowledge [8] ....

9c The king herself

Reading

1 Work in pairs. Look at the title of the article. What is strange about the words *king* and *herself* together?

2 Read the article and put these events about Hatshepsut's life in the correct chronological order.

a Her mummy was discovered in a minor tomb.
b The monuments she built were destroyed.
c Thutmose III became pharaoh.
d She ruled Egypt as king for 21 years.
e Her mummy was identified and put in the Royal Mummy Rooms.
f She married Thutmose II.
g She was born, the eldest daughter of Thutmose I and Queen Ahmose.

3 What were the different roles that Hatshepsut fulfilled (like pharaoh)?

4 Choose the correct option (a–c) to complete the sentences.

1 Hatshepsut's mummy was not identified at first because it:
  a was badly damaged.
  b was not in a royal tomb.
  c had another name with it.
2 Hatshepsut was very worried that people would:
  a realize she was a woman.
  b not think she was royalty.
  c not remember her.
3 Thutmose III did not want people to know that Hatshepsut had been:
  a king.
  b queen.
  c related to him.
4 Thutmose II's children consisted of:
  a one son and one daughter.
  b one son.
  c one daughter.
5 According to tradition, the queen regent was supposed to:
  a make offerings to the gods.
  b help until the king was ready.
  c be a politician.
6 In later statues and images, Hatshepsut appears male from:
  a her body shape.
  b the way she stands.
  c the dress she wears.

Critical thinking weighing the evidence

5 Find evidence that supports each sentence (1–6). If the sentence is definitely true, write 100%. If there is no evidence, write 0%. Put percentages in between if it is not clear.

1 When Hatshepsut's sarcophagus was first found in 1903, it was empty.
2 The mummy called KV60a was Hatshepsut's body.
3 Hatshepsut wanted to produce a male heir, but failed.
4 Hatshepsut had a greater claim to become pharaoh than Thutmose III.
5 Hatshepsut wanted her subjects' approval.
6 The king in waiting, Thutmose III, was angry that Hatshepsut had assumed the role of king.

6 Work in pairs. Compare your scores and your evidence.

Word focus *long*

7 In the article, find these six phrases (1–6) with the word *long* and match each one to its definition (a–f).

1 at long last	a soon
2 as long as	b over a long period of time
3 long for	c after much waiting
4 long after	d provided that
5 before long	e much, much later
6 in the long term	f desire very much

8 Complete the sentences using phrases with *long*.

1 Hatshepsut clearly ………… people to remember her.
2 The grand monuments she built ensured she would be remembered ………….
3 ………… people believed she had a divine right to be pharaoh, Hatshepsut felt safe.
4 Hatshepsut died in 1458 BC and …………, Thutmose III had destroyed most references to her as king.
5 Experts in hieroglyphs ………… uncovered the truth.
6 Thutmose III ruled for another 34 years, ………… Hatshepsut had died.

Speaking

9 Work in small groups. Say who you would expect to find doing these jobs: mostly men, mostly women, or an equal number of men and women. Give reasons.

company director	cleaner	nurse	teacher
IT technician	doctor	plumber	
machine operator	florist	secretary	
prime minister	lawyer	senior civil servant	

10 Look at the statistics on page 154. Which job in Exercise 9 fits in which category? Compare and discuss your answers.

THE KING *Herself*

Today she is in the Royal Mummy Rooms at the Egyptian Museum in Cairo, reunited at long last with her family of fellow pharaohs, with a sign saying she is Hatshepsut, the king herself (1473–1458 BC).

But in 1903, when the archaeologist Howard Carter found Hatshepsut's sarcophagus in the Valley of the Kings, it was empty. Had her mummy been stolen or destroyed? The truth only came out a century later when Egyptian scientists positively identified a mummy called KV60a, discovered more than a century earlier in a minor tomb, as that of Hatshepsut. None of the treasures normally found with pharaohs' mummies were with it. It was not even in a coffin.

For Hatshepsut, a pharaoh who did not fear death as long as she was remembered, the irony is great. As one of the greatest builders in one of the greatest Egyptian dynasties, she raised numerous temples and shrines. She commissioned hundreds of statues of herself and left accounts in stone of her titles, her history, even her hopes and fears. Inscribed on an obelisk at Karnak are the words: "Now my heart turns this way and that, as I think what the people will say. Those who see my monuments in years to come, and who shall speak of what I have done."

But following her death, her successor and stepson Thutmose III set about erasing her memory. At Deir el Bahri, at the temple designed to be the center of Hatshepsut's cult, her statues were smashed and thrown into a pit. Images of her as queen were left undisturbed, but wherever she proclaimed herself king, the destruction was careful and precise. Why?

Hatshepsut was the eldest daughter of Thutmose I and Queen Ahmose. But Thutmose also had a son by another queen, and this son, Thutmose II, became pharaoh when his father died. As was common among Egyptian royalty, Thutmose II married his sister, Hatshepsut. They produced one daughter; another, less important wife, Isis, gave Thutmose II the male heir that he longed for, but Hatshepsut was unable to provide.

When Thutmose II died not long after from heart disease, his heir, Thutmose III, was still a young boy. As was the custom, Hatshepsut assumed control as the young pharaoh's queen regent. And so began one of the most intriguing periods of ancient Egyptian history.

At first, Hatshepsut acted on her stepson's behalf, respecting the convention that the queen should handle political affairs while the young king learned the ropes. But before long, she began performing kingly functions, like making offerings to the gods. After a few years, she assumed the role of king of Egypt, supreme power in the land. Her stepson was relegated to second-in-command and "the king herself" proceeded to rule for an amazing 21 years.

What caused Hatshepsut to break so radically with the traditional role of queen regent? A social or military crisis? A desire for power? A belief that she had the same right to rule as a man? No one really knows. Maybe she felt, as a direct descendant of the pharoah Thutmose I, she had a greater claim to the divine line of pharaohs than Thutmose III. At first she made no secret of her sex—in images her body is unmistakably a woman's—but later she is depicted as a male king, with headdress and beard, standing imposingly with legs apart.

Her hieroglyph inscriptions have frequent references to "my people" which suggest that she knew she had broken with tradition and wanted her subjects' approval. Whatever their opinion was, there is no doubting the frustration of Thutmose III. After Hapshepsut's death, he took his revenge, wiping his stepmother's reign as pharaoh out of history. But in the long term it is she, the king herself, who achieved the greater fame.

coffin (n) /ˈkɒfɪn/ a box in which a dead body is put to be buried
commission (v) /kəˈmɪʃən/ to order and pay for something to be made
divine (adj) /dɪˈvaɪn/ related to God
heir (n) /eər/ a successor

9d Right for the job

Real life describing skills, talents, and experience

Shelterbox is a charity which sends boxes of essential items needed in an emergency—a tent, tools, cooking utensils, a water purification kit—to places where disasters, such as earthquakes and floods, have struck. Boxes are prepared in the US and delivered immediately by Shelterbox employees to anywhere in the world where they will help save lives.

1 Read the description of Shelterbox. What kind of organization is it and what service does it offer?

2 **32** Listen to someone being interviewed for a job at Shelterbox. Answer the questions.

1 What aspect of Shelterbox's work is the candidate interested in?
2 What is the interviewer concerned about?

3 **32** Look at these phrases from the interview describing the candidate's suitability for a job. Note the prepositions used in each case. Then listen to the interview again and complete each one.

DESCRIBING SKILLS, TALENTS, AND EXPERIENCE

I'm familiar with your work because I have a friend who [1] ....
I'm really interested in [2] ....
I specialized in [3] ....
I think I would be well-suited for [4] ....
I'm good at coping with [5] ....
I have quite a lot of experience [6] ....
I'm pretty good with [7] ....
I'm comfortable with all [8] ....
I'm serious about wanting to [9] ....
I need to become more knowledgeable about [10] ....

4 Work in pairs. Discuss: did the candidate do a good job of selling himself to the interviewer?

5 **Pronunciation difficult words**

a **33** The spelling of a word in English is not always a clear indication of its pronunciation. How confident are you that you can pronounce these words from the interview? Mark each word confident (✓), somewhat confident (?), and not confident (×). Then listen and check.

although	comfortable	environments
foreign	knowledgeable	months
specialized	suited	world

b **34** Listen to and spell eight more words.

6 Work in pairs.

Student A: Choose one of the jobs below that interests you and think about the skills, talents, and experience you have that would help you do it. Try to convince Student B why this would be a good job for you.

Student B: Interview Student A for the job. Then swap roles.

- a travel guide for walking tours
- a sales assistant in a children's bookstore
- an outreach director for a charity that helps the homeless
- an assistant to a cameraman who makes films about plants and wildlife

9e Professional networking

Writing an online profile

1 Do you use any professional networking sites? Why?

2 Read the profile and summarize in no more than nine words what this person's main skills and qualities are. How effective was his profile in putting across the key points?

3 Read the tips on how to write a profile on a professional networking site. Put a check mark (✓) next to each tip that has been followed, a cross (✗) next to those which have not, and a question mark (?) if the tip has only been partly followed.

Tips:

1 Include a personal photo and recommendations from others.

2 Give a heading and summary so that readers can get the main idea quickly.

3 Say what you're doing now.

4 List all the places where you have worked or studied; someone from there may be looking at your profile!

5 Job titles may mean nothing to others, so always describe what you did in each job.

4 Writing skill writing in note form

a Look at these four phrases from the profile. Which are proper sentences? Which are written in note or shortened form? Why is this?

1 responsible for new products

2 Learning is my passion.

3 published *Learning in the 21st Century*

4 Developing innovative e-learning program for the car industry

b Insert the necessary words (pronouns, articles, auxiliary verbs) to show what the phrases in note form would look like as full sentences.

Profile

Tom Vasquez
Managing Director of EverReady Learning

Location: Chicago, IL
Industry: Online learning
Current: Developing innovative e-learning program for the car industry

Past

- Head of development, Faheys Educational: responsible for new products
- Editorial Director, York Books; published *Learning in the 21st Century*
- Director of Business Studies, Carston University

Education: Stanford University

Summary
Learning is my passion. I specialize in the design and management of online learning programs for industry, but I am also a writer, editor, blogger, educator, and business consultant. My work has brought me into contact with many companies and I am now skilled at identifying and responding to the learning needs of any business sector, from cosmetics to car-making. If my experience has taught me one thing, it's that learning is the key to improvement for all of us.

c Convert these statements from other profiles into a shorter, more concise form by deleting the unnecessary words.

1 I worked as a personal assistant to the Marketing Director.

2 I am currently writing an article for *National Geographic* magazine.

3 I was in charge of organizing corporate social events.

4 I took the official photos for the Boston Ballet.

5 I am working for various charities.

6 I was hired to raise money for a local college.

5 Write your own short professional profile, similar to the one above. Think about the message you would most like the reader to be left with. When you have finished, exchange profiles with another member of the class. Read them once quickly and tell each other your main impression.

6 Read your partner's profile again. Check the following points:

- Has the profile been laid out correctly?
- Have the tips in Exercise 3 been followed?
- Has note form been used in places to make the profile more concise?

9f Queen of Egypt

Video

She has a reputation for beauty, power, controversy, and ultimately, tragedy.

Before you watch

1 Work in pairs. Make notes about what you know of Cleopatra.

- who she was
- when and where she ruled
- important events in her life

2 You are going to watch a video about the story of Cleopatra. Write down three kinds of images you think you might see which help to tell this story.

While you watch

3 Watch the video and check your ideas from Exercises 1 and 2.

4 Watch the video again and answer the questions.

1 Why was Cleopatra forced from power?

....

2 How did she first meet Julius Caesar?

....

3 How did Cleopatra's relationship with Caesar help her?

....

4 Why did Octavian go to war with Mark Antony and Cleopatra?

....

5 In what year and what battle was Mark Antony beaten?

....

6 How did Mark Antony die?

....

7 How did Cleopatra die?

....

5 Match the sentence beginnings (1–7) with the endings (a–g). Then watch the video again to check.

1 Julius Caesar arrived in Alexandria
2 Cleopatra's relationship with Caesar kept Rome
3 After Caesar's murder
4 Cleopatra and Antony shared
5 Mark Antony's Roman rival, Octavian
6 Cleopatra spread numerous
7 Antony's followers carried him to Cleopatra

a from taking direct control of Egypt.
b false rumors of her death.
c where he died in her arms.
d in pursuit of a rival Roman general.
e her position became uncertain.
f went to war against them.
g a hunger for power.

After you watch

6 Roleplay **first meeting with Caesar**

Work in pairs.

Student A: Imagine you are Cleopatra. You arrive in Caesar's court hidden in a rug. You need to charm Caesar so that he will help you become queen again. Read the information below and make notes.

Student B: Imagine you are Caesar. Cleopatra arrives in your court hidden in a rug. Read the information below and make notes.

- how you feel (surprised, excited, curious)
- what you want from the other person
- how you can help the other person
- what you decide to do

Act out your meeting, then change roles and act out the meeting again.

7 At the end of the video, the narrator says: "Cleopatra lives on in history through her personal story of love and tragedy." Why do you think her story has lasted for so long? Do you think her story teaches us anything about love and power today?

8 Work in groups and discuss these questions.

1 Do you think Cleopatra was an admirable woman? Why?
2 Are there any similar characters in the history of your country?
3 Would you like to have lived in Cleopatra's time? Why?

charmed (adj) /ʧɑrmd/ fascinated by
controversy (n) /'kɑntrəˌvɜrsi/ disagreement about something
court (n) /kɔrt/ the place where a ruler lives and works
distort (v) /dɪs'tɔrt/ change something from its normal shape
dynasty (n) /'daɪnəsti/ a family that rules a country for several generations
grief (n) /grif/ great sadness
infuriate (v) /ɪn'fjʊriˌeɪt/ make very angry
overjoyed (adj) /ˌoʊvər'ʤɔɪd/ extremely happy
pursuit (n) /pər'sut/ the act of chasing someone or something
rival (n) /'raɪvəl/ a person or group that competes with another
rug (n) /rʌg/ a small carpet
seize (v) /siz/ take by force

UNIT 9 REVIEW

Grammar

1 Complete this text with *the* where necessary.

Constance Adams has had an unusual career path. She studied [1] ________ architecture at [2] ________ Yale University before working as an architect in [3] ________ Berlin and [4] ________ Japan. She then joined [5] ________ Johnson Space Center in [6] ________ US, where she helped design TransHab, a module for [7] ________ International Space Station. The idea of [8] ________ module was to provide [9] ________ living quarters for [10] ________ astronauts during their stay in [11] ________ space. In [12] ________ 2005 she became a National Geographic Emerging Explorer.

2 Complete the text with relative pronouns in 1–5 and present and past participles in 6–10.

Adams explains that the TransHab module was intended to be a habitat for a crew of six astronauts, [1] ________ mission was to reach Mars. The team had to design a module [2] ________ would be only 14 feet in diameter when it was launched. But once in space it needed to be three times that size to house the six astronauts [3] ________ lived there. So they made a structure [4] ________ could inflate and unfold in space to become a three-level "house" [5] ________ astronauts could eat, sleep, and work.

The outer shell of the module, [6] ________ (compose) of over twenty layers of different materials, had to resist the space debris [7] ________ (hit) the spaceship all the time. This debris can hit the spaceship seven times faster than a bullet, [8] ________ (cause) great damage. The outer layers were made of a kind of foam [9] ________ (use) in chairs and cushions. The inner shell was made of Kevlar, a material [10] ________ (wear) by soldiers and police for body protection.

3 Work in pairs. Discuss what was special about the module's size, shape, and materials.

I CAN	
use *the* and no article	☐
use relative clauses and reduced relative clauses	☐

Vocabulary

4 Complete the sentences with these nouns and the correct form of the verbs.

background	become	do	experience
pursue	graduate	knowledge	degree
quality	serve	skills	take

1 My main academic ________ is in physics and I got it when I ________ from Duke University.
2 I have a lot of ________ organizing things. I ________ in the army for four years.
3 I think my main ________ is that I'm adaptable. I can ________ many different jobs.
4 I have good computer ________ . I ________ a course in advanced computing last year.
5 My ________—both my parents are scientists—meant scientific research was a natural career for me to ________ .
6 My ________ of astrophysics helped me to ________ a space scientist.

5 Work in pairs. Use the nouns and verbs to describe your own skills and experience.

I CAN	
talk about my experience and skills	☐
describe my career path	☐

Real life

6 Put the correct preposition into each space.

1 I'm familiar ________ most design software.
2 I specialized ________ mechanical engineering.
3 I think I am well-suited ________ working abroad.
4 I'm good ________ people.
5 I'm good ________ persuading people.
6 I'm serious ________ pursuing a career in art.
7 I'm not very interested ________ sitting all day.
8 I am pretty knowledgeable ________ mechanics.

7 Work in pairs. Tell each other about a job that would be right for you and one that wouldn't.

I CAN	
describe what kind of work I am suited for	☐

Speaking

8 Work in small groups. Describe the work of someone you admire. Include these points:

- a description of their qualities and talents
- what they have achieved

Unit 10 Customs and behavior

Two generations of Chinese visitors visit Beijing's Forbidden City.
Photograph by Nigel Swinn

FEATURES

1 Work in pairs. Look at the photo. What is it about the behavior of the younger tourists that surprises the older pair?

2 Look at the quotation below. Discuss what you think it means. Do manners make you a better person, or more socially acceptable—or both?

"Manners maketh man." *William of Wykeham (1324–1404)*

3 Complete these phrases about manners with words from the box. Check your answers with your teacher. Then discuss whether you think these things are important to teach children. What would you add?

chew	courtesy	inappropriate	interrupt
offensive	point	well-behaved	stare
talk	slouch		

1 Don't ________ with your mouth full.
2 Don't ________ when grown-ups are speaking.
3 Don't ________ or ________ at people.
4 Don't ________ gum.
5 Don't wear clothes that are ________ or ________.
6 Be polite, ________-________, and show ________ to others.

10a Cruel to be kind

Reading

1 Work in pairs. Answer the questions.

1 What is happening in the photo?
2 How would you describe the mother's attitude: strict, intense, something else?
3 How strict were your parents? Are you happy that they were this way or not?

2 Work in small groups. Which of these things should parents control strongly? A little? Which should the child decide?

- watching TV
- playing computer games
- practicing a musical instrument
- going out to play with friends
- doing homework
- choosing what subjects to study at high school
- choosing extracurricular activities

3 Read the article and find out who "tiger mothers" are. How do their attitudes to the first five items in Exercise 2 compare to Western attitudes?

4 Does the writer approve of the "tiger mother" approach to child-rearing? Do you?

Vocabulary raising children: verbs

5 Work in pairs. Look at the pairs of verbs below and discuss the difference between them. You will find the first verb in each pair in the article.

1 *bring up* and *educate* children
2 *praise* and *reward* good behavior
3 *rebel against* and *disobey* your parents
4 *push* and *discipline* yourself
5 *give in to* and *spoil* your children
6 *nag* and *pester* someone
7 *shame* and *punish* someone

CRUEL TO BE KIND

Is there a right way to bring up children? Some parents read guides to find an answer, many just follow their instinct. Whatever they do, a doubt always remains: could I have done a better job?

A recent contribution to the subject is Amy Chua's controversial book *Battle Hymn of the Tiger Mother*, which describes the approach to child-rearing of an ambitious Chinese parent living in the West. According to Chua, Western mothers are far too soft on their children. She says they are always praising their children for every effort they make, even if the result is coming last in a race or playing a piano piece badly. These are the kind of parents who will give in to their children's demands to go out and play rather than do their homework, if they protest loudly enough.

The "tiger mother" method is very different and the key is total control. Tiger mothers will accept nothing less than perfect grades in every subject—failure to achieve these is just proof that children have not worked hard enough. They will encourage not with praise and reward, but by punishing and shaming. Chua told her daughter that she would give her doll's house to charity if she failed to master a difficult piano piece. She even rejected a homemade birthday card because her daughter had drawn it in a hurry.

But that highlights another difference, says Chua, which is directness and honesty. A tiger mother will not hesitate to tell her children that they are lazy, whereas Western parents are always telling their children not to worry, that they will do better next time, even if they think they have been lazy.

The constant nagging of the tiger mother, the banning of TV and computer games, seems harsh, but perhaps it works. Chua's children have not rebelled, and they don't resent their strict upbringing. They regularly get the top grades at school and are proficient at violin and piano—stereotypical symbols of success, critics would say. By contrast, children with more freedom and more laid-back parents will often lack self-discipline and will fail to push themselves to achieve more.

Grammar habitual actions: present tenses, *will*

> **SIMPLE PRESENT, PRESENT CONTINUOUS, and *WILL* FOR REPEATED ACTIONS**
>
> **Simple present**
> *Some parents read guides to find an answer.*
>
> **Present continuous with *always***
> *She says they are always praising their children for every effort they make.*
>
> ***will***
> *These are the kind of parents who will give in to their children's demands.*
>
> For more information and practice, see page 169.

6 Work in pairs. Look at the sentences in the grammar box. Which tense is used to describe:

1 typical behavior?
2 a habit which the speaker finds annoying?
3 a simple fact or general truth?

7 Find and underline:

1 an example of tiger mothers' typical behavior; an example of typical behavior of Western mothers' children.
2 a simple fact about Chua's children.
3 something Chua finds annoying about Western mothers.

8 Complete these comments by underlining the correct verb forms. Sometimes there is more than one possibility. Then discuss which ones you sympathize with and which you don't.

1 My parents *will always tell / are always telling* me to practice the piano and it just makes it a chore.
2 In my experience, children *will do / do* as little work as they can. So you have to make them do it.
3 Children *will want / want* to be loved. It's also true that they *will perform / perform* much better in a loving and secure environment.
4 All parents *will hope / hope* that their children will be successful, but they *won't always admit / aren't always admitting* it to their children or even themselves.
5 You have to have a different approach with different children. Some *will respond / respond* better to gentle encouragement; others *will need / need* to be pushed and challenged.
6 I don't like parents who *will always try / are always trying* to be friends with their children. There are too many parents who *will buy / buy* their children presents and let them do what they want just to get on their good side.

9 Read the anecdotes below and put the verb in the right form. Then check your answers with your teacher.

I've seen this kind of situation so many times in Mexico when children [1] ______ (beg) their parents for some candy. At first the parent [2] ______ (say) no. So then the child [3] ______ (pester) and pester until the parent finally gives in—which they always do. It's against all the rules of parenting.

I teach in a school in San Francisco where we have quite a lot of ethnic Chinese and Japanese kids. By and large, they [4] ______ (do) what you tell them. But the other kids [5] ______ (always / misbehave). You have to tell them ten times to sit down.

Where I live in India, it is common for young children to work. Kids still [6] ______ (depend) on their parents, but they have a different attitude toward responsibility. Just as children in every culture [7] ______ (play) naturally, so children in India naturally [8] ______ (assume) responsibility for working and earning money.

Speaking

10 Work in pairs. Discuss the situations in Exercise 9. How familiar is each one to you? Does the behavior seem right or wrong?

11 Think of three more examples of children's and parents' behavior in your country: a simple fact about the way children or parents behave; an example of typical behavior; an example of behavior that annoys you or seems wrong.

12 Describe your examples to another pair. Are they similar to theirs?

10b A matter of taste

Listening

1 What is the strangest thing you have ever eaten? Why did you eat it? What did it taste like?

2 **35** Listen and answer the questions.

1 Where is the Nochmani tribe from?
2 What do they eat mostly?
3 How do they make sure there is enough of this food?

3 **35** Listen again and choose the correct word or phrase to complete the statements.

1 We live in an age when people are very ________ what they eat.
 a nervous about b conscious of
 c careless about
2 In the past it was thought that the Nicobar Islands contained ________ .
 a no inhabitants b no fresh water
 c no fish
3 The Nochmani didn't want to eat ________ .
 a sweets and cakes b meat
 c any of the food they were offered
4 Insects have a lot of ________ in them.
 a carbohydrates b vitamins
 c protein
5 The speaker thinks we could all benefit from eating ________ .
 a less meat b more insects
 c alternative types of food

4 What do you think of the diet of the Nochmani? Do you think what we eat is just a matter of habit? Why? Can we learn to eat anything if we have to, or are there some things we can never eat?

Grammar *used to, usually, be used to,* and *get used to*

5 Match each verb form in bold (1–5) to the meaning (a–e).

1 We **didn't use to worry** so much about food.
2 People **usually need** mammals in order to live.
3 The Nochmani **were not used to eating** meat.
4 If you **are used to** something, you prefer it.
5 We should **get used to eating** insects.

a refers to something that was strange or abnormal for someone
b refers to something that happens regularly or is generally the case
c refers to learning to cope with something difficult or unfamiliar
d refers to what someone did regularly in the past, but doesn't do anymore
e refers to something that is normal and not strange

USED TO, USUALLY, BE USED TO, and *GET USED TO*

Past habits	**Present habits**
used to + infinitive	*(not) usually* + simple present
I used to eat…	*I usually eat…*
I didn't use to eat…	*I don't usually eat…*
Did you use to eat?	*Do you usually eat?*
Familiar (and unfamiliar) habits	**Habits that are becoming familiar**
be used to + noun or *-ing* form	*get used to* + noun or *–ing* form
I am used to (eating) Italian food.	*I am getting used to (eating) American food.*
I am not used to…	*I am not getting used to…*
Are you used to… ?	*Are you getting used to… ?*

For more information and practice, see page 170.

6 Look at the grammar box and then choose the right form to complete sentences 1–9 in A, B, and C. Note that we use *be used to* and *get used to* for things that are not strange or difficult to do.

A In China, people [1] *do not usually finish / didn't use to finish* everything on their plate, because it is a sign that they have not had enough to eat. Visitors from the West find it difficult to [2] *be used to / get used to* this, because they [3] *usually eat / are used to eating* everything to show that they like it. When a Chinese host sees their empty plates, he [4] *usually assumes / is used to assuming* that they want more.

B Fifty years ago, people in the US [5] *used to sitting / used to sit* down for meals with their families each evening. Families nowadays [6] *usually eat / used to eat* together only three times a week, because busy lives and TV get in the way. But it is believed that if more families could [7] *be used to dining / get used to dining* together, it would strengthen family relationships.

C Eating a traditional English breakfast of eggs, bacon, and sausages [8] *used to be / was used to being* a common thing in the UK. A big breakfast was important because people [9] *didn't use to eat / weren't used to eating* so many snacks during the day.

7 Put the verb in the most appropriate form to complete these sentences.

1 We ________ (eat) out a lot, but restaurants are so expensive that we don't anymore.
2 I ________ (have) a tuna salad sandwich for my lunch.
3 I ________ (take) sugar in my coffee, but now I have a sweetener. It took a little while to ________ (get used to) the taste, but now I can't tell the difference.
4 When I was staying with my friends in Iowa, we ate at six o'clock in the evening. It was strange, because I ________ (eat) much later.

8 Are any of the sentences in Exercise 7 true for you? Have you had similar experiences? Discuss with a partner.

I also used to eat out a lot, but now I try to get home for lunch.

Not me, I usually buy a sandwich… not tuna, though!

9 In pairs, ask each other these questions.

1 What is something you have gotten used to doing recently?
2 Do you usually do your homework in the mornings or the evenings?
3 Are you used to eating dinner with your family or do you usually eat on the go?
4 What is the best way to get used to a new place?
5 What is something that you used to do that you don't do anymore? Why did you stop?
6 What is something that you are used to doing that you wish you could change? Why?

Vocabulary and speaking

10 Work in pairs. Place these four items of food into the correct category. Think of two more items for each category. Then compare your list with another pair.

breakfast cereal	chocolate bars
rice	yogurt

dairy products (like milk)	processed food (like frozen peas)	staple foods (like potatoes)	snacks (like potato chips)

11 Complete these sentences with information about eating habits in your country. Go around the class and exchange your information with at least three other people. Then work with your partner. Tell each other the two most memorable statements you heard.

1 When I was growing up, a lot of families used to…
2 The main staple food is… People aren't used to eating…
3 For breakfast, people usually…
4 I think visitors find some of our eating customs strange, because they are not used to…
5 People in my country don't usually eat…
6 Young people find it difficult to get used to…

10c A universal language

Reading

1 Work in pairs. Put the actions in the box into the correct category of body language. Then demonstrate the actions to each other. What is the meaning of each?

a handshake	standing with arms crossed
biting your bottom lip	waving
sitting back in your chair	
smiling	

posture: ....

gesture: ....

facial expression: ....

2 Read the article. Which sentence best summarizes the author's view?

a We need to learn how people from different cultures use body language.
b The differences in body language between cultures are small but important.
c There are more similarities than differences in body language between cultures.

3 According to the writer…

1 Making comparisons between cultures can be:
a fun. b useful. c dangerous.
2 Standing too close to someone of another culture can:
a cause arguments. b cause discomfort. c be a serious insult.
3 A lot of the facts given in travel guides are:
a very important. b wrong. c not of much practical help.
4 Looking away from the speaker is a sign of:
a sadness. b boredom. c both.
5 To avoid making mistakes in body language with other cultures, people need to be:
a sensible. b sensitive. c both.
6 Differences in body language between people start at:
a an individual level. b a cultural level. c an emotional level.

4 With your partner, demonstrate to each other:

- the two gestures described in paragraph 3
- the two greetings mentioned in paragraph 4
- the body language associated with boredom and anger described in paragraph 6

5 Do you agree with the writer's view about cross-cultural communication? Is your culture one that generally shows its emotions or not?

Critical thinking sources

6 The article gives a lot of information about body language and customs. But how do you know how reliable this information is? Underline the examples of different cultures' body language and customs in the article.

7 Work in pairs. Find the author's source for each example. Mark the source according to this scale: 3 = very credible; 2 = quite credible; 1 = incredible; and 0 = no source.

Word focus *common*

8 Match the meanings of the word *common* (1–2) with the sentences (a–d).

common (adj)
1 something usual or normal
2 something that is shared by two or more people

a It is quite common in European countries to sit with your legs crossed.
b The things that we all have in common…
c There are also common factors when people are bored.
d If we all just apply a little sensitivity and common sense,…

9 Now do the same for these expressions.

e In a negotiation, always try to find common ground between you and the other party.
f It is a common misconception that English people drink only tea, not coffee.
g Don't worry about mispronouncing my name; it's a common mistake that everyone makes.
h It's common knowledge that many Asian cultures use chopsticks, not knives and forks.

Speaking

10 Work in pairs. Describe the following customs in your country. Then compare your answers with another pair. How similar were they?

- The most common form of greeting
- Common gestures that visitors are not used to
- Common eating customs
- Common misconceptions foreigners have about your country

A *universal* language

People love to compare and contrast. In most parts of England, you buy your bus ticket on the bus. In France, you buy it at a metro station. In Australia, you can buy it at a newsstand. We all find this kind of comparison entertaining. Books on cross-cultural communication exploit our curiosity by focusing on differences between people around the world, including the significance of their body language.

Proxemics, the study of different standards of personal space, is one example. How close I stand when speaking to people depends not only on my relationship to them, but also on my culture. This is important because if people are not used to standing as close as I do when we are talking, they might feel uncomfortable. Statistics tell us that the average distance at which two people stand in a social context—neighbors chatting, for example—is somewhere between 4 and 11 feet. In Latin cultures (like South America and Italy), and also in China, this distance tends to be smaller, while in Nordic cultures (like Sweden and Denmark), people usually stand farther apart.

The messages sent by your posture and gestures is another case in point. For example, it is quite common in European countries to sit with your legs crossed and the top foot outstretched. But, as I know from personal experience, people in Arab countries hardly ever sit this way because they might show you the bottom of their shoe, which is a serious insult. It is said that in the Philippines, people often greet each other by raising their eyebrows quickly. In the US, this is a sign of surprise.

Such information fills the pages of guide books, but I would really question the usefulness of what are presented as must-know facts. Clearly it is important to know a little about eating customs, tipping, and the rules concerning basic greetings—whether you should bow or shake someone's hand. But beneath the surface, we are not so different. Many signs are universal in the emotions that they communicate. Focusing on them is a much more profitable route than focusing on our differences.

Smiling is the best known sign, but not the only one. Behaviorists have proven that all over the world, people show sadness in a similar way. The face falls, the mouth becomes downturned and the eyes begin to look glassy. The person will probably look down or away and seem distracted.

There are also common factors when people are bored. They will look at other things, their feet will begin to move restlessly indicating that they want to escape, and they will tap their fingers or scratch their heads. Anger can also be read quite easily: the facial muscles tense up, often causing people to frown; the eyes stare, fixing themselves on the target of their anger; blood rushes to the face, turning it red. If the anger is great, the body will also tense up as if preparing itself for a physical fight.

Understanding these universal signals and reacting appropriately is the real key to cross-cultural communication. If we all apply just a little sensitivity and common sense, we are unlikely to cause lasting offense by making the wrong gesture or invading a stranger's personal space. Of course, some cultures show their emotions more openly and others prefer to keep them more hidden. But isn't that also the case within cultures, from one individual to another?

frown (v) /fraʊn/ to lower your eyebrows, causing lines to appear on your forehead
scratch (v) /skrætʃ/ to move your fingernails backwards and forwards across your skin
stare (v) /steər/ to look intensely and for a long time at something
tap (v) /tæp/ to hit something lightly with a finger or hand

10d A pre-wedding ritual

Vocabulary weddings

1 What pre-wedding customs or events are traditional for the bride-to-be in your country?

2 Work in pairs. Look at the words related to weddings and answer the questions.

bride	groom	bachelorette party
bachelor party	veil	

1 Which word means a pre-wedding party for the man? And for the woman?
2 Which word means the woman on her wedding day? And the man on his?
3 Which word means a piece of fine cloth that covers the woman's face?

WORDBUILDING word pairs

Some words have a natural partner or make a matching pair. *bride* and *groom*, *host* and *guest*

Real life describing traditions

3 36 Listen to the description of a traditional pre-wedding henna night in eastern Turkey. Then complete the first four phrases in the box below.

DESCRIBING TRADITIONS

1 It takes place ________ .
2 It marks the ________ .
3 It is an occasion for ________ .
4 It symbolizes the ________ .

It's traditional / customary for this to be done by...
Typically / As a rule / Usually the women from...

Describing the sequence of events
The ceremony begins with the...
Then,... / After that,... / Next,... / Finally,...

While this is happening / During this part, the guests...
After / Once the bride's head has been...
On the morning of the wedding, a...

4 37 Listen to the rest of the description. Number the items in the order they occur.

a A child presents the hennaed coin to the groom.
b The bride's head is covered with a red veil.
c The guests sing separation songs.
d The bride's hands and feet are hennaed.
e A gold coin is put into the remaining henna.
f The henna is prepared by the daughter of another couple.

5 38 Retell the events to each other using the linking words in the box to help you. Then listen and compare.

6 **Pronunciation the letter *s***

a 39 Listen to these words and for each one say if the letter *s* is pronounced /s/ or /z/. Note the spellings that produce each sound.

custom	dress	friends
music	suppose	weddings

b 40 Work in pairs. Practice saying the words, then listen and check. Think of three more words for each sound. Then compare words with another pair.

across	eastern	lose	place
rings	single	spends	surprise

Speaking

7 What special events take place before or after a wedding in your country? Describe one using the box to help you. Think about:

- when it takes place
- the sequence of the events
- its significance
- any special symbols used

8 Working in small groups, describe these customs to each other. When each person has finished their description, ask them questions.

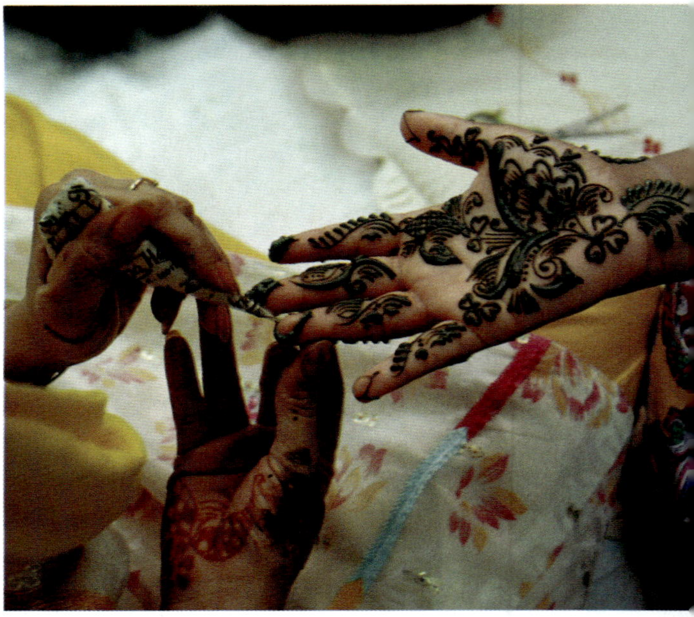

10e Business customs

Writing an informal email (2)

1 Imagine you are about to go on a business trip to a country you haven't visited before. What would you want to know about the customs there?

2 Read the first email. What is Paul asking for? What is he worried about?

3 Read Dominic's reply. Which pieces of advice should calm Paul's worries?

> Hi Dominic
>
> Good to see you briefly the other day. Forgot to tell you I'm going to China next week. Not sure what to expect. I know you have experience doing business there. Don't want to make any mistakes with any potential business partners. Could you let me know what I should be particularly aware of?
>
> Thanks,
> Paul

> Hi Paul,
>
> Glad to hear you're going to China. Think you'll enjoy it. Is it Shanghai? Let me know. Maybe I can fix you up with a couple of contacts. Anyway, my advice:
>
> - Take plenty of business cards; Chinese people will always give you theirs (make sure you read them carefully). It's embarrassing not to give one in return.
> - Keep the name and address of your hotel on you at all times. Visitors are always getting into trouble because they can't remember where they're staying.
> - The Chinese love their food and are very proud of it. They'll offer you some unusual dishes. Be adventurous and be grateful!
>
> Good luck and talk to you soon,
> Dominic

4 Writing skill elision in informal writing

a Look at the two emails again. Underline four phrases in the first email and four in the second email where words have been omitted to save time.

b Rewrite the sentences and phrases by inserting the missing words to make them more formal.

Example:

It was good to see you the other day.

c Convert these sentences into a more economical style by removing unnecessary pronouns, auxiliary verbs, or the verb *be*.

1 I hope we can meet up soon.
2 It was too bad that you didn't get the job.
3 I'll be back next Tuesday night.
4 This is my address in New York…
5 I will look forward to hearing all about it.
6 It went pretty well, didn't it?

5 Write a response to this email.

> Hi there,
>
> Wondered if you could help. I'm flying over next week to meet some clients. Will have to take them out to dinner and talk to them a little socially. Can you give me some advice about how things are done over there? Eating customs, what to talk about, etc. Sorry to ask, but very grateful for any information you can provide.
>
> Thanks!
> Sara

6 Work in pairs. Exchange emails. Read your partner's reply and answer the questions.

- Is it written in an informal style?
- Has the writer given some useful tips?
- Is the content short and to the point?
- Has the writer used some elision?

10f Eating insects

Video

Larry Peterman is a candy man on a mission.

Before you watch

1 Work in groups. Look at the photo and discuss the questions.

1 What do you think a candy man is?
2 How does the photo make you feel? Do you think most people would feel the same as you?
3 What do you think Larry Peterman's mission is?

2 Work in pairs. Think about the candy you used to eat when you were a child. Describe them to your partner.

3 You are going to watch a video about eating insects. Answer these questions.

1 Which countries include insects in their diets?
2 Do you think eating insects is a new habit?
3 Are insects good for you?
4 Is producing insects better for the environment than producing meat?

While you watch

4 Watch the video and check your answers from Exercise 3.

5 Watch the video again. Number the foods in the order you see them.

a banana, cream, and cockroach dessert
b salt-water taffy
c lollipop with cricket
d cricket cocktail
e mealworm-covered apples
f stir-fry
g caramels
h caterpillars

6 Answer the questions.

1 Where is Hotlix?

....

2 How long has Larry been trying to get Americans to eat insects?

....

3 According to Larry, why do most Americans not like eating insects?

....

4 How many species of insects are eaten around the world?

....

5 How does Larry compare insects to wine?

....

After you watch

7 **Roleplay a meal at Larry's restaurant**

Work in groups of three.

Student A: Imagine you are Larry. Prepare an interesting insect menu. Then give the menu to your customers. Explain what each dish is and answer their questions.

Student B: You don't like the idea of eating insects but are prepared to try. Ask Larry about the menu and order your meal. Also ask Larry why he is so interested in promoting insect foods.

Student C: You love the idea of eating insects. Order a meal.

Act out the conversation, then change roles. Prepare a different menu.

8 At the end of the video, Larry predicts that gourmet insects will have "snob appeal." What do you think that means?

9 Do you think Larry will eventually win people over to eating insects? Why?

10 Work in groups and discuss these questions.

1 Are there any unusual dishes or foods in your country?
2 What types of foods do people in your country avoid eating generally? Why?
3 Are there any foods you don't like? Why?

advocate (n) /ˈædvəkɪt/ a person who supports something
brim (v) /brɪm/ be full of
bug (n) /bʌg/ insect
munch (v) /mʌntʃ/ eat
niche (n) /niʃ/ a specialized business opportunity
revolting (adj) /rɪˈvoultɪŋ/ disgusting
snob (n) /snɑb/ a person who thinks he or she is better than other people
swat (v) /swɑt/ hit

UNIT 10 REVIEW

Grammar

1 Work in pairs. Look at the photo. What do you know about the eating habits of the Spanish: when they eat, what they eat?

2 Read the paragraph from a travel guide. What times are Spanish meals?

3 Underline the correct forms.

People visiting Spain for the first time can find it difficult to [1] *be used to / get used to* the eating customs of the Spanish. It's not so much the food itself, but the timing of the meals that visitors [2] *aren't used to / don't get used to*. I [3] *was used to living / used to live* in Cadiz, and I actually liked the way they did things. Breakfast is a light continental affair—just a roll and some coffee usually—eaten between 8 and 9:30 a.m. The main meal of the day is lunch, which people [4] *are used to eating / usually eat* sometime between 1 and 3:30 p.m. Quite a few of the shops, museums, and galleries [5] *close / are closing* around this time, because the locals like to take time over lunch. They [6] *are always resting / will rest* for a short time afterwards, although the traditional afternoon siesta is not as common as it [7] *was used to being / used to be*. People eat late in the evening—rarely before 9 p.m.—and on the weekend, the locals often [8] *aren't eating / won't eat* before 11 p.m. or even midnight.

I CAN
- use *used to, be used to,* and *get used to* correctly ☐
- talk about habits and typical behavior with simple present, present continuous, and *will* ☐

Vocabulary

4 Work in pairs. Which word doesn't belong in each group? Explain your choices.

1 punish, discipline, nag, spoil
2 educate, bring up, look after, raise
3 encourage, shame, praise, reward
4 bread, cheese, rice, pasta
5 sit back, shake hands, wave, point
6 interrupt, stare, smile, chew gum
7 well-behaved, offensive, polite, courteous

5 Tell each other what postures, gestures, or facial expressions you often use and in what situations.

I CAN
- talk about bringing up children ☐
- talk about eating habits ☐
- talk about body language ☐

Real life

6 Work in pairs. Find the correct ending from list B for each phrase in list A.

A	B
It marks	people give adult presents to the child.
It takes place	the moment when a child becomes an adult.
It is an occasion	the child to stand up and give a short speech.
It symbolizes	the parent walking into the hall with the child.
It's customary for	people in the audience can also say some words.
Typically the ceremony begins with	on the child's 16th birthday. for celebration.
After the child's speech	leaving childish things behind.

7 Tell your partner about a special celebration in your country and the traditions that surround it.

I CAN
- describe traditions and customs at special events ☐

Speaking

8 Work in small groups. How is children's upbringing these days different from when you were a child? Look at the quote. Do you agree with this speaker?

My parents were quite strict. They used to expect us to do jobs around the house. I think children these days have it much easier, although they are always complaining that their parents expect a lot from them.

Unit 11 Knowledge and learning

Students processing their DNA at a museum learning lab
Photograph by Rajat Bansal

1 Work in pairs. Match each technique of acquiring knowledge or learning (1–4) to a definition (a–d). Which technique are the students using in the photo?

1 by authority
2 by observation
3 by reasoning
4 by trial and error

a experimenting
b using logic
c judging from what you see or hear
d reading or listening to an expert

2 Match these phrases with their definitions.

1 You have **a basic grasp** of chemistry.
2 You need **to find out** when the paper is due.
3 You're working with a tutor **to pick up** some test-taking tips.
4 You need to read through your notes and **process** them before writing your paper.
5 You're not sure what the right answer is, but you chose A because of a **gut feeling**.

a You are going to learn some strategies from an expert.
b You need to learn the date.
c You understand the fundamental principles.
d You need to internalize and reflect on the information.
e You picked an answer based on instinct.

3 Intuition is something we know without having to learn it. Tell a partner about a time when you used your intuition to make a decision.

11a Knowledge conservation

Reading

1 Work in pairs. Look at the photo in the article below of a botanist in the field. What does a botanist do?

2 List the plants or plant products you use on a daily basis. Then compare your list with another pair. Which uses did your lists have in common?

Example: *cotton in my clothes*

3 Read the article and answer the questions.

1 How is Maria Fadiman's interest in plants different from that of a traditional botanist?
2 Where does she work?
3 What two uses of plants are mentioned in the article?

4 What does the article say about:

1 the way Fadiman collects knowledge from local people?
2 the way that local people often pass their knowledge on?
3 the way Fadiman passes her knowledge on to her students?

5 Do you think that Fadiman's idea of recording traditional plant knowledge is useful? Why? What knowledge has been passed down to you by your parents or grandparents? Tell your partner.

▶ WORDBUILDING IDIOMATIC EXPRESSIONS

Often there are idiomatic expressions that can replace basic verbs like *think, realize*
It struck me that... = I realized that...

KNOWLEDGE CONSERVATION

Dr. Maria Fadiman is an ethnobotanist: she studies how people use plants. "Looking at plant conservation without including people is a fantasy," she says. "The focus of my work is finding a balance where people use resources in a sustainable way."

It struck Fadiman early on that this was what she wanted to do. "I was born with a passion for conservation and a fascination with indigenous cultures," she explains. "Ethnobotany lets me bring it all together. On my first trip to the rain forest, I met a woman who was in terrible pain because the people in her village weren't able to remember which plant would cure her. I saw that traditional plant knowledge was being lost, and at that moment I knew conserving this kind of knowledge was what I wanted to do with my life."

Visiting the Ecuadoran rain forest, Dr. Fadiman was amazed at the variety of plants. "It looked like one big, green mish-mash," she says. "But the people who lived there were able to pick out the right plants for medicine and could distinguish not only the plants that were safe to eat, but also the right part of each plant."

The problem often is that such knowledge is stored only in local people's minds and it is passed down from generation to generation. Fadiman managed to persuade inhabitants of the Ecuadoran rain forest to let her record the information in written form. "They are excited by this idea because suddenly their knowledge is valued."

But conservation doesn't just mean protecting indigenous plants. If bringing in non-native plants, including cash crops like coffee, is beneficial to people and the environment, then that's fine too. In the Galapagos Islands, where overfishing was a real problem, environmentalists like Fadiman succeeded in getting local people to think about alternatives, like growing coffee.

By forming close relationships with local people and joining in with their way of life, Fadiman has inspired her own students at Florida Atlantic University. Students who couldn't easily absorb facts and statistics said they were able to engage much more easily with the subject when they heard her stories of going to the river to brush her teeth or sitting around a cooking fire.

indigenous (adj) /ɪnˈdɪdʒənəs/ native to a particular country or area
mish-mash (n) /ˈmɪʃˌmæʃ/ a confusing mixture or collection of things

Grammar *could, was able to, manage to,* and *succeed in*

6 Work in pairs. Underline the sentences in the article where the following forms (1–6) are used. Then match each form to the uses (a–c). Note that some forms can have more than one use.

1 *could*
2 *was / were able to (do)*
3 *couldn't*
4 *wasn't / weren't able to*
5 *managed to (do)*
6 *succeeded in (doing)*

a to describe success in a task on a particular occasion in the past
b to describe a general ability in the past
c to describe an inability to do something in the past

> **COULD, WAS ABLE TO, MANAGE TO, AND SUCCEED IN**
>
> ***could*** **+ base form**
> *He could tell which plants were safe.*
>
> ***couldn't*** **+ base form**
> *I couldn't remember the name of the plant.*
>
> ***was / were able*** **+ infinitive**
> *We were able to learn a lot from the local people.*
> *He wasn't able to explain how he knew it was right.*
>
> ***manage*** **+ infinitive**
> *After two hours climbing, we managed to reach the top.*
>
> ***succeed in*** **+ *-ing***
> *We succeeded in finding a guide to take us.*
>
> For more information and practice, see page 171.

7 Look at the grammar box. Then complete the sentences.

1 In the past, people could ______ (distinguish) plants more than they can now.
2 Recently, a group of children who were asked where cotton came from weren't able ______ (say) whether it was from an animal or a plant.
3 People were able ______ (use) this knowledge to find food and medicines.
4 They also managed ______ (work) out which plants were good for certain purposes.
5 But they didn't always succeed ______ (pass) this knowledge on to the next generation.
6 So people couldn't ______ (keep) some of this knowledge from being lost.

8 Underline the correct form in each of these sentences. Sometimes both forms are possible.

1 By specializing in ethnobotany, Fadiman *was able to combine / succeeded in combining* an interest in plants with her interest in people.
2 She also studied geography, which meant she *could look at / managed to look at* people and the land.
3 In Ecuador, Fadiman *could record / managed to record* plant data that hadn't been written down before.
4 In Yucatan, Mexico, local women taught Fadiman how to weave, something that she *wasn't able to do / didn't manage to do* before.
5 On a recent trip to Ecuador, she *could visit / was able to visit* a lot of places in a short time by using a helicopter rather than buses and canoes.
6 Fadiman was impressed by how indigenous people *were able to make / succeeded in making* use of the plants around them.

Vocabulary learning

9 Work in pairs. Find pairs of words in this group with the same meaning.

absorb	acquire	be ignorant of
connect with	engage with	grasp
inspire	motivate	not know
pick up	take in	understand

10 Complete these sentences about your own learning at school using one of the forms in the grammar box. Ask and answer these questions.

1 Which teachers ______ (inspire) you at school?
2 What kind of facts ______ (absorb) most easily?
3 Which subjects ______ (engage with)?
4 ______ (pass) all your exams?
5 What knowledge ______ (acquire) that has been useful in later life?
6 Was there anything that ______ (not / grasp) that you wished you did now?

Speaking

11 Work in pairs. Think of a subject you know a lot about. How did you acquire that knowledge? Have you managed to record or pass it on in any way?

11b Memory

Speaking

1 Work in pairs. Look at the picture below for ten seconds. Then turn your book over and list the objects you can remember.

2 Compare your results with another pair. What techniques did you use to remember the items?

Items left at the Vietnam Memorial, Landover, Maryland

Listening

3 What things do you commonly forget? Which failures of memory annoy you the most?

4 **41** Listen to the first part of a talk on memory by a psychologist and note the common failures of memory that he mentions. Were any of them the same as yours?

5 **42** Listen to the rest of the talk and answer the questions.

1 What is AJ good at remembering?
2 How does she feel about her good memory?
3 Why are people's memories not as good as they used to be?

6 **43** Complete each statement with the missing word. Then listen and check.

1 AJ's memory is stimulated by .... in the same way that our memories can be stimulated by certain ....
2 Having a good memory should make people feel more ....
3 Our memories are selective: they remember mostly .... things and .... things.
4 We should be .... for all the things that our memories hide.
5 Technology has become "our .... memory."
6 Now medical science is trying to address the problem of .... memory.

7 Work in pairs. Discuss how much you rely on your internal memory to remember things as compared to aids such as Post-it notes, your computer, or diaries. Do you agree with the speaker that our memories are getting worse?

Grammar future in the past

8 44 Listen to the first part of the talk again and complete the first half of these sentences with the correct verb forms.

1 You ________ to make a comment at a meeting and then...
2 You ________ to send a friend a card for his birthday, but then...
3 You recognized someone in the street and ________ spoken to her, but...
4 You promised you ________ mail a letter for someone and two days later...
5 You ________ to write down a great idea you had, but when you found a pen and paper,...

9 Work in pairs. What happened next in each case? Were any of these actions completed? Why?

10 Choose the right verb form to complete this description of another memory patient.

One interesting patient couldn't form new memories. He could only remember events before 1960. I [1] *was going to interview / would interview* his doctor about how someone with no memory managed to cope with daily life, but she suggested I interview him instead.
Our appointment [2] *was supposed to be / would be* at 2 p.m., but it made no difference since he lived only in the present. I [3] *would tell / would have told* him my name and why I was there, but I realized there was no point: [4] *it was going to mean / it would have meant* nothing to him. So I began by asking him about his past and he talked about his time as a child during the Second World War. Then the telephone rang. When he came back, I [5] *was about to ask / would ask* him to continue, but I realized he had completely forgotten our earlier conversation. I thought he [6] *was about to be / would be* frustrated by this but not at all. He seemed happy for not being burdened by memory.

▶ FUTURE IN THE PAST

going to* and *about to
I was going to call you, but I forgot.
I was about to call you, but I was interrupted.

would* and *would have
He said he would call me.
I would have called you, but I didn't have your number.

supposed to
He was supposed to call you. Did he forget?

For more information and practice, see page 172.

11 45 Look at the grammar box. Transform these original plans into future in-the-past forms. Then listen and check your answers.

1 "I'm going to ask Sanjip to come."
I ________, but I asked Kumar instead.
2 "She's supposed to be in Cairo this week."
She ________ in Cairo this week, but she's sick.
3 "I'll definitely send you the original."
He promised he ________ me the original, but he sent me a copy.
4 "We will be there by ten o'clock."
We ________ there by ten o'clock, but the train didn't get in until eleven fifteen.
5 He's about to announce that he will retire.
He ________, but now he thinks he'll stay another year.
6 "The city planners will build a new shopping mall downtown."
The city planners ________ a new shopping mall downtown, but residents opposed it.

12 Pronunciation contrastive sentence stress

a 45 Work in pairs. Underline the words in each sentence in Exercise 11 that highlight the contrasting facts. Listen again and check. Then practice saying each sentence.

b Complete each of these sentences with a contrasting idea. Underline the words in the sentence that highlight the contrast. Then say your sentences to your partner. Ask them which words they thought were stressed.

1 I was going to order a steak, but...
2 They were supposed to be going on vacation, but...
3 I would have driven, but...
4 He said he would wait for me, but...
5 We were about to buy a new TV, but...

Speaking

13 Work in pairs. Choose a situation below. Think of a good excuse to explain why it happened. Then change pairs and explain your excuse again.

- You were 30 minutes late for an important business meeting and didn't call to say so.
- You borrowed someone's car and were supposed to return it the following day, but they had to call you to find out where you were.
- It was a close friend's birthday two days ago. You didn't send a card or get them a present.

11c A clever bird

Reading

1 Work in pairs. Do you know a domestic animal which is particularly intelligent? How does this intelligence show itself?

2 Read the article and say how Alex the parrot's intelligence showed itself.

3 Mark the sentences true (T), false (F), or not answered (NA).

1 People are right to believe that animals have thoughts and emotions.
2 Pepperberg's idea was to let Alex communicate to her how he saw the world.
3 Pepperberg didn't want people to think she had chosen Alex for his intelligence.
4 Alex showed that he could distinguish between colors and shapes but not numbers.
5 Pepperberg concluded that cognitive skills were necessary for survival in the wild.
6 Alex felt very proud of his ability to communicate in English.

4 In pairs, discuss if you were surprised by Pepperberg's results, and why.

Critical thinking reinforcing ideas

5 Often when writers express an idea, they reinforce it, to make sure the reader understands, by:

- saying the same thing in other words
- giving examples
- quoting someone who also made this point

Find and underline the ideas expressed below by the author. Note how each one is reinforced.

1 How can we find out if animals can think?
2 Pepperberg's idea was to ask the parrot for his thoughts.
3 Researchers had no confidence in her idea.
4 She wanted to get inside the parrot's head.
5 Alex's cognitive abilities are not typical of all animals.
6 Alex's cognitive abilities are necessary to cope with his environment.
7 Alex worked through various mental tests.
8 Alex behaved like a bored teenager.

6 Which method of reinforcing an idea did you find the most effective?

Word focus *learn*

7 Work in pairs. Find these three expressions in the article with the word *learn*. Discuss what each one means.

1 learn as you go along
2 learn by heart
3 learn the hard way

8 Look at the expressions in bold with *learn* in the sentences below and figure out what each one means from its context. Which one means the same as "learn the hard way"?

1 If you work with an experienced chef, you can **learn some tricks of the trade**.
2 You're not ready to design the new brochure. You have to **learn to walk before you can run**.
3 It's **never too late to learn**. My grandfather took up the piano when he was 73.
4 I've **learned my lesson**. I'm never going to try to build a piece of furniture again without reading the instructions first.
5 I hate it too, but we're going to have to **learn to live with it**.
6 You'd think that the government would **learn from its mistakes**, but it never does.

9 Choose two of the expressions from Exercise 8 and use them in sentences about your own learning experiences. Read your sentences to your partner, omitting the expressions with *learn*. Can your partner figure out the missing expressions?

Speaking

10 Work in pairs. Take the quiz on page 154 to find out what type of learner you are. The answers are on page 155.

11 Work in small groups. Discuss how your learning style affects your language learning. What things can you do to learn more effectively? Look at the ideas below and add any others you can think of:

- watching English-language movies with subtitles
- reading stories (in English newspapers, books, magazines) and retelling them
- keeping a vocabulary book and drawing illustrations of each new word

A clever bird

How does a scientist find out to what extent an animal is capable of thinking? What evidence is there that it is able to acquire information about the world and act on it, learning as it goes along?

In 1977, Irene Pepperberg, a recent graduate of Harvard University, decided to investigate the thought processes of another creature by talking to it. In order to do this, she would teach a one-year-old African gray parrot named Alex to reproduce the sounds of the English language. "I thought if he learned to communicate, I could ask him questions about how he sees the world."

Pepperberg bought Alex in a Chicago pet store. She let the store's assistant choose him because she didn't want other scientists to say that she had deliberately chosen an especially smart bird. Given that Alex's brain was the size of a walnut, most researchers thought Pepperberg's communication study would be futile. "Some people actually called me crazy for trying this," she said.

But with Pepperberg's patient teaching, Alex learned how to imitate almost 100 English words, including the names of food. He could count to six and had learned the sounds for seven and eight. But the point was not to see if Alex could learn words by heart. Pepperberg wanted to get inside his mind and learn more about a bird's understanding of the world. She couldn't ask him what he was thinking about, but she could ask him about his knowledge of numbers, shapes, and colors.

In one demonstration, Pepperberg placed Alex on a wooden perch in the middle of the room. She then held up a green key and a small green cup for him to look at.

"What's the same?" she asked.

Without hesitation, Alex's beak opened: "Co-lor."

"What's different?" Pepperberg asked.

"Shape," Alex said. His voice had the sound of a cartoon character. But the words—and what can only be called the thoughts—were entirely his. Many of Alex's cognitive skills, such as his ability to understand the concepts of "same" and "different," are rare in the animal world. Very few animals share these skills. But parrots, like humans, live a long time in complex societies. And like humans, these birds must keep track of the dynamics of changing relationships and environments.

"They need to be able to distinguish colors to know when a fruit is ripe or unripe," Pepperberg explained. "They need to categorize things—what's edible, what isn't—and to know the shapes of predators. And it helps to have a concept of numbers if you need to keep track of your flock. For a long-lived bird, you can't do all of this with instinct; cognition must be involved."

In the demonstration, Alex then ran through various tests, distinguishing colors, shapes, sizes, and materials (wool versus wood versus metal). He did some simple arithmetic, such as counting the yellow toy blocks among a pile of mixed colored blocks. And then, as if to offer final proof of the mind inside his bird's brain, Alex spoke up. "Talk clearly!" he commanded, when one of the younger birds Pepperberg was also teaching mispronounced the word "green." "Talk clearly!"

Alex knew all the answers himself and was getting bored. "He's moody," said Pepperberg, "so he interrupts the others, or he gives the wrong answer just to be difficult." Pepperberg was certainly learning more about the mind of a parrot, but like the parent of a troublesome teenager, she was learning the hard way.

11d Keep learning

Real life getting clarification

1 Look at the list of short courses offered by an adult education college. Use a dictionary if you need to. Which of the courses interest you and why?

2 46 Listen and answer the questions.

1 What kind of course is Ahmad interested in taking?
2 What course does Liz suggest for him instead? Why?
3 What does Ahmad decide to do?

3 Look at the expressions used by Ahmad. Which are used for repetition (R) and which are used for explanation (E)?

GETTING CLARIFICATION

What do you mean by… ?
Can you speak up a little?
Can you explain what…?
I'm not really with you.
Are you saying that… ?
Could you give me an example of… ?
What was… again?
Hang on a second. That's too much to take in all at once.
I didn't catch…
Did you say… ?

4 46 Listen again. Complete the unfinished sentences in the box.

5 **Pronunciation linking in question forms**

a 47 In certain commonly used combinations (*did you, could you, what do you*) the words are strongly linked together. Listen to these examples.

Are you saying the course is full?
Can you speak up a little?
Could you give me an example?
Did you say Tuesday?
What do you mean?

b Work in pairs. Practice saying these sentences.

Can you explain what you mean?
Could you repeat that?
Did you mean September?
What are you trying to say?
What do you think?

6 Work in pairs. Act out a conversation, inquiring about the course. Then change roles.

Student A: You are a prospective student. Choose one of the courses in Exercise 1 or another course you would like to take. Ask Student B about your choice.

Student B: You are a college administrator. Prepare what you are going to say about Student A's chosen course.

ROUSHAM
ADULT EDUCATION CENTER

COURSE TITLE	FREQUENCY	EXAM COURSE
Basic car mechanics *Apr 5, 10 wks*	1 x 2hrs	✗
Psychology of human behavior *Jan 22, 18 wks*	1 x 2hrs	✓
Public speaking *Apr 11, 8 wks*	1 x 1.5hrs	✗
First aid *Apr 12, 4 wks*	2 x 1.5hrs	✓
Desert and jungle survival *Mar 1, 12 wks*	1 x 1.5hrs	✓
Ikebana: Japanese flower arranging *Jan 22, 18 wks*	1 x 2hrs	✗
Art appreciation *Apr 5, 10 wks*	1 x 2hrs	✗
Screenwriting *Jan 21, 18 wks*	1 x 2hrs	✗
Surfing *Apr 12, 6 wks*	1 x 3hrs	✓
Investing in stocks and buying shares *Apr 11, 8 wks*	1 x 1.5hrs	✗

11e The wrong course

Writing an email about a misunderstanding

1 Work in pairs. Read the email from a student to an adult education college. Answer the questions.

1 What is the misunderstanding about the course?
a the timing b the level c the subject
2 How would you describe the student's feelings?
a angry b offended c frustrated
3 How would you describe the tone of the email?
a complaining b reasonable c apologetic

Dear Sir or Madam:

I enrolled in your course "car mechanics 1" in August and have attended three sessions. When I originally inquired about the course, I was told that it was suitable for people with no previous knowledge of car mechanics. But in fact, everyone else in the course seems to know a lot already. So despite the fact that the lessons generally start with a basic concept, they move very quickly onto more complicated ideas.

I don't blame the teacher. On the contrary, he does his best to explain concepts to me. But I feel that I am just holding everyone else back. They know how an engine works already, whereas I have no background at all in mechanics.

I was going to wait a couple of weeks more before saying anything, but in the last session I felt so out of my depth that I have decided to write now and ask for a refund. While I understand this isn't really anyone's fault, I hope you will appreciate how frustrating the situation is for me.

I look forward to hearing from you.
Karen Redman

2 If you were an administrator at the college, how would you react to this email?

3 Writing skill linking contrasting ideas

a Find the words or phrases in the email that link these contrasting ideas.

1 The course should be for beginners. No one else is a beginner.
2 Each lesson starts with a simple idea. It progresses quickly to difficult ideas.
3 The teacher is not at fault. He helps me as much as he can.
4 The other students know a lot. I know nothing.
5 No one is to blame for this. I still feel it is unfair.

b Match these words and phrases to the ones in the email that they could replace.

1 although
2 in actual fact
3 but on the other hand
4 but in reality

c Complete these sentences with appropriate linking phrases.

1 .... the brochure says the start date is September 12, the first real class is a week later, on the 19th.
2 The course is advertised as "practical," .... you learn a lot of theory as well.
3 .... the course fee is quite high, it's a great investment in your future.
4 The course isn't much fun, ... , you would expect a course in lifesaving to be serious.
5 The French conversation class focuses on everyday French. .... in the advanced French class you cover literature.
6 Surfing is not an easy skill to learn. .... , you need to have a lot of perseverance.

4 Imagine you enrolled in one of the other courses on page 136. Think of a misunderstanding that occurred with the course. Write an email to the college explaining the misunderstanding and asking for a refund.

5 Exchange letters with your partner and check the following items:

- Does the email make clear what the misunderstanding was?
- Is the tone reasonable?
- Has the writer used linking words and phrases correctly?
- Do you think the email will get the desired response?

11f Paraguay shaman

Video

Paraguay's renowned healers, called "shamans," have a deep knowledge of local medicinal plants.

Before you watch

1 Work in groups. Look at the photo and discuss the questions.

1 What do you know about shamans?
2 What techniques do you think they use?

2 You are going to watch a video about medicinal plants. Answer these questions.

1 What problem do you think faces these plants?
2 What solution to the problem might the video suggest?
3 Write down three kinds of people you're going to see in the video.

While you watch

3 Watch the video and check your answers from Exercise 2.

4 Cross out the wrong information in these sentences. Then rewrite the sentences correctly.

1 When the scientists arrive, Gervasio, the local shaman, is collecting plants in the forest.

....

2 Gervasio and the team set off to look for an insect the scientists are interested in.

....

3 The local people eat the root raw.

....

4 Later, back in the village, Gervasio shows the team a book he has written.

....

5 Watch the video again and answer the questions.

1 What illnesses are mentioned in the video?

....

2 How do traditional folk healers in Paraguay help scientists?

....

3 Why is it important to record shamans' knowledge urgently?

....

4 Why does Gervasio use chants and prayers before going into the forest?

....

5 Why are the scientists interested in the suruvi root?

....

6 What does the scientists' book set out to do?

....

6 Number these in the order you hear them.

a Recording and analyzing Paraguayan plants for possible medical cures is urgent business.
b To reach Gervasio, a group of researchers set out on a long journey through the reserve.
c Somewhere in this forest, maybe in this plant or that herb, there might be a cure for an illness.
d When he feels ready, Gervasio and his wife lead the group on the search.
e The rain forests of Paraguay have long been a source of medicinal cures.

After you watch

7 Roleplay interviewing a scientist

Work in pairs.

Student A: Imagine you are a National Geographic reporter. You are going to interview the scientist who made the documentary about Gervasio. Use the information below to prepare questions.

Student B: Imagine you are the scientist who made the documentary about Gervasio. Look at the information below and think about what you are going to say to the reporter.

- the journey to the reserve
- the journey to Tekoha Ryapu
- what it feels like to work with Gervasio
- the importance of Gervasio's knowledge
- what they were able to achieve on this trip
- how the book might help

Act out the interview, then change roles.

8 Work in groups and discuss these questions.

1 Do you know of any modern medicines that originated from rain forest plants?
2 Do you think traditional medicines from plants are effective?
3 What do you think about other forms of traditional medicine, for example acupuncture, massage therapy, and homeopathy?

chant (n) /tʃænt/ a kind of rhythmic song that uses only one or two notes
deforestation (n) /dɪˌfɔrɪˈsteɪʃən/ cutting down trees
folk healer (n) /ˈfoʊk ˌhilər/ a person who uses traditional methods to cure illnesses
multiply (v) /ˈmʌltɪˌplaɪ/ reproduce quickly
renowned (adj) /rɪˈnaʊnd/ famous
reserve (n) /rɪˈzɜrv/ an area of land where plants or animals are officially protected

UNIT 11 REVIEW

Grammar

1 Work in pairs. What is the maximum number of languages someone can speak fluently? Does speaking one language help you to learn another?

2 Underline the correct option below.

When police in Brazil arrested an illegal immigrant speaking an unrecognizable language, they immediately called Ziad Fazah, the world's greatest linguist. Fazah realized quickly that the man was speaking a dialect used in Afghanistan. With Fazah's help, the man [1] *explain / was able to explain* that he had escaped Afghanistan and was seeking asylum in Brazil. At that time, Fazah, originally from the Lebanon, [2] *could speak / managed to speak* 54 languages. He also [3] *could get / succeeded in getting* his name into the Brazilian *Guinness World Book of Records* as the world's greatest living polyglot. Fazah had done a lot of interpreting for the police, but unfortunately they [4] *couldn't pay / didn't manage to pay* him.
When Fazah was 17, his talents were recognized by the Lebanese government, who [5] *were going to use / would use* him as an interpreter, but soon after, he moved to Brazil. Eventually he began giving private language lessons. Fazah [6] *would remain / would have remained* unknown, but in 2006 his language abilities were tested on a Spanish television show and he got international attention. Then people began to question his abilities. [7] *Was he really able / Did he really manage* to speak over 50 languages? The show [8] *was supposed to show / would have shown* that he could, but the evidence was not convincing.

3 Answer the questions.

1 What is a polyglot?
2 What is Fazah's regular job?
3 How many languages is he really fluent in?

I CAN

describe past abilities with *could, was able to, managed to,* and *succeeded in* ☐

talk about past intentions and predictions with the future in the past ☐

Vocabulary

4 Work in pairs. Complete the paragraph. The first letter of each missing word is given.

There are many ways to [1] a________ knowledge: by [2] t________ and error, from an authority, by reasoning, and by [3] o________ (in other words, just by watching). Some things, like bringing up children, are more instinctive; you have a gut [4] f________ about the right way to do things. Some things, like playing a musical instrument, you can [5] p________ up as you go along. But other things need to be taught. For example, you might have a basic [6] g________ of mathematics, but still be completely [7] i________ of how calculus works. For this type of learning, you need an authority like a book or a teacher that can help you to [8] e________ with the subject and understand it.

5 Tell each other how you learned to do two things (like cook or play an instrument).

I CAN

talk about learning and knowledge ☐

Real life

6 Work in pairs. Match 1–5 to a–e.

1 What do you mean by that?
2 Could you give me an example?
3 Can you speak up a little?
4 What was that again?
5 I'm not really with you.

a I didn't catch that.
b I don't really understand.
c For instance?
d Can you explain that?
e I can't hear you very clearly.

7 Think of something you can do, but your partner probably can't. Give your partner some instructions. As you receive the instructions ask for clarification and repetition.

I CAN

get clarification by asking someone to repeat or explain ☐

Speaking

8 Work in small groups. Tell each other about a good or bad learning experience.

At school we had a great art teacher who could inspire anyone. He had really good ideas, such as…

Unit 12 The economy

A woman in a pink mink coat next to her pink Rolls Royce, Hong Kong
Photo by Jodi Cobb

FEATURES

1 Work in pairs. Look at the photo. What does a matching luxury car and fur coat say about a person? Do rich people in your country like to show off their wealth?

2 Match the word (1–7) with its synonym (a–g).

1 afford	a poor
2 hard up	b have enough money
3 income	c expensive
4 loaded	d a good price
5 pricey	e very rich
6 reasonable	f comfortable
7 well-off	g earnings

3 Work in small groups. What is the definition of "poor" in your country? How would you define *rich* and *poor*? Can you be rich without having a lot of money?

12a Saving for a rainy day

Reading

1 Work in pairs. What do you know about Norway: its landscape, its people, its industry? Look at the photo for ideas.

2 Read the article. In what ways is Norway a "rich" country?

3 Complete these summaries of each paragraph. Then compare answers with another pair.

1. For a long time, Norway has had a better .... than other countries.
2. The three reasons for Norway's success are: big oil reserves, ..., and ....
3. For Norwegians, being rich means ....
4. Norway is saving money for ....

4 Do you think that the Norwegians are right to save their money? Why?

Grammar focusing adverbs *only, just, even*

> **FOCUSING ADVERBS *ONLY, JUST, EVEN***
>
> ***only***
> *Only Luxembourg and a couple of other countries are richer.*
>
> ***just***
> *Just 80 years ago, Norwegians were emigrating to the US.*
>
> ***even***
> *This isn't even a competition anymore.*
>
> For more information and practice, see page 172.

5 Work in pairs. Look at the grammar box. Which of these statements (a–c) is true of *only, just,* and *even*?

a they always come directly after the word they are emphasizing.
b they always come directly after the main verb.
c they always come directly before the word they are emphasizing.

6 Find other examples of these words in the article. Do they follow the same rule?

SAVING FOR A RAINY DAY

Come on, Norway; this isn't even a competition anymore! For the last eight years, Norway has registered the highest quality of life among the world's nations. It is one of the wealthiest countries in the world; only Luxembourg and a couple of others are richer. Norwegians can also expect to get a good education, find the job they want (unemployment is only 2.5 percent), enjoy good health, and live a long life. People say the prisons are quite comfortable too!

Norway has not always been a rich country. Just 80 years ago, Norwegians were emigrating to the US by the thousands, in search of a better life. The rise in oil prices in the 1970s changed all that. But Norway's success is not only the result of its huge reserves of oil. Other countries have had such riches and squandered them. It is also due to the Norwegians' thrift and their strong work ethic.

When you arrive in Oslo for the first time, don't expect to be met with Dubai-style skyscrapers, entrepreneurs in designer suits, and rows of Ferraris and Porsches. Norway may be rich, but it is modest in its wealth. Norwegians also work hard and are always near the top in surveys of global worker productivity rates. But in today's high-tech world, where work seems to follow us wherever we go, the people of Norway are redefining what wealth means. Laws just recently passed by the government emphasize the importance of family and time off, offering generous maternity and paternity leave, subsidized childcare, and long vacations as well.

Also, the country is saving for the future. Every dollar earned from oil is put straight into what is now the world's biggest pension fund, worth over $200 billion. Extraordinarily, none of this money is allowed to be spent on state infrastructure projects. It is not even invested in new schools and hospitals. But at a time when most other countries are wondering how they will finance the pensions of a growing retired population, Norway is sitting pretty.

leave (n) /liv/ time off from work
sitting pretty (v) /ˈsɪtɪŋ ˈprɪti/ in a good or comfortable situation
squander (v) /ˈskwɑndər/ waste
thrift (n) /θrɪft/ carefulness when spending money

7 Discuss the meaning of each sentence (1–8), then match it to what follows logically (a–h).

1 Only visitors think Norway is expensive.
2 Visitors only think Norway is expensive.
3 Visitors think only Norway is expensive.
4 Among the Scandinavian countries, I have visited Norway just once.
5 Among the Scandinavian countries, I have visited just Norway.
6 Even fathers are given time off to be with their new babies.
7 Fathers are even given time off to be with their new babies.
8 Fathers are given time off even to be with their new babies.

a Of course mothers are given a lot of time off too.
b I have visited the others several times.
c They are also given time off to move and to look after elderly parents.
d …but all the Scandinavian countries are.
e …but actually it's quite reasonable.
f I haven't visited the others at all.
g The residents themselves find it reasonable.
h ...in addition to extra money.

8 Complete these sentences by putting a focusing adverb in the right place. Then compare answers with your partner. Tell them whether these facts are true of your country.

1 Many people work long hours during the week, so they see their children on weekends.
2 People with college degrees are finding it difficult to get jobs these days.
3 For most people, a job is a way to make money, not something they particularly enjoy.
4 The rich represent about five percent of the population.
5 You don't see extreme poverty. Poor people usually have food and somewhere to live.
6 The state pension gives you enough to live on, but not to live very comfortably.

Grammar focusing adverbs *too, as well, also*

9 Work in pairs. Look at the position of *too* and *as well* in these sentences. Find the same sentences in the article, but with the word *also*. What do you notice about the position of *also*?

1 Norwegians can expect to get a good education too.
2 It is due to the Norwegians' thrift as well.
3 Norwegians work hard too.
4 The country is saving for the future too.

FOCUSING ADVERBS *TOO, AS WELL, ALSO*

sentence + *too*	*also* + main verb
sentence + *as well*	*be* + *also*
Also, + sentence	auxiliary verb + *also* + main verb

For more information and practice, see page 172.

10 Look at the grammar box. Which patterns from the box can you find in the article? Underline them. Then compare your answers with your partner.

11 Rewrite the sentences using the focusing adverbs given. Compare your answers with another pair.

1 Norwegians like their secure pensions, but they would like to see the government increase spending on healthcare. (*as well* / *also*)
2 Most countries have high public borrowing and a lot of debt. Norway has neither. (*too* / *also*)
3 Teachers in Norway receive a good salary and if they teach "heavy" subjects, they get extra payments. (*also* / *too*)
4 Artists can get a grant—not a loan—from the government of around $20,000 a year and support with childcare. (*also* / *as well*)
5 Food prices seem very high to outsiders and fuel is expensive. However, house prices are relatively low and so property is a good investment. (*too* / *also*)
6 Nurses in Norway get 42 weeks' maternity leave at full pay. They can use the hospital's day care when they return to work (*as well* / *also*)

Vocabulary money

12 Look at the verbs below and find the right noun in Exercise 11 to make phrases with the same meaning.

1 pay money = make a ________
2 invest money = make an ________
3 borrow more money = increase your ________
4 spend less money = reduce your ________
5 be lent money = take out a ________
6 owe money = have a ________
7 earn money = receive a ________
8 be given money (by the government) = receive a ________

Speaking

13 Work in pairs. Prepare questions to ask each other about the economy in your country or countries (the cost of living, work-life balance, government spending, government grants for certain professions). Use the items in Exercise 11 to help you get ideas.

14 Now change partners with another pair and ask and answer your questions.

12b Don't do it yourself

Vocabulary domestic help

1 Work in pairs. Which of the domestic workers listed below is the person in the photo? What do the other jobs involve?

au pair	babysitter
cleaner	cook
dog walker	gardener
handyman	maid
nanny	personal shopper

2 Discuss these questions about the jobs in Exercise 1.

1. Have you done any yourself?
2. Have you (or your family) employed anyone in these roles?
3. Which jobs involve the greatest skill?
4. Would you like to do any of them? Why?

Listening

3 48 Listen to the interview with the author of a book called *The Servant Economy*. Answer the questions.

1. How many domestic workers are there in the US today? Who are they?
2. Does the author think the growth of the servant economy is good or bad?

4 48 Listen again and identify:

1. which jobs from Exercise 1 the speakers mention.
2. what other jobs are mentioned.
3. whether many people or only the rich employ such workers.

> **WORDBUILDING *the* + adjective**
>
> We can refer to a group of people using *the* + adjective.
> *the rich, the poor*

5 Work in pairs. What did the interviewer find strange about hiring someone to install a Christmas tree? Do you agree?

6 Complete Hilaire Belloc's quotation. Do you agree with it? Why?

"It is the duty of the .... man to give .... to the artisan." *Hilaire Belloc*

Grammar causative *have* and *get*

7 Look at the forms in bold (a–d). Answer the questions (1 and 2). Then look at the transcript on page 181 and find one more example of each type of phrase.

a Thirty years ago, the idea of **getting a worker to hand wash** your car was unthinkable.
b Nowadays, you can **have it washed** for $6.
c You don't have to be rich **to have a cleaner come** once a week.
d Another example would be **getting your windows cleaned** every few months.

1. Which phrases mean someone does a job for you?
2. Which phrases tell you who actually does the job?

▶ CAUSATIVE *HAVE* and *GET*

have/get **+ something + past participle**
I had/got the fence fixed yesterday.

have **+ someone + base form**
I had the gardener fix the fence.

get **+ someone + infinitive**
I got the gardener to fix the fence.

For more information and practice, see page 173.

8 Look at the grammar box. Then complete the paragraph.

Nearly half of all homes in Britain get outside staff [1] .... (do) their domestic chores for an average of six hours per week. The most common reasons that people gave for having someone [2] .... (help) around the house were their own long working hours and to avoid arguments with their partner. A third of people said if they didn't have help, nothing would get [3] .... (do). The most popular domestic jobs are having the house [4] .... (clean) regularly, getting someone [5] .... (do) the gardening and having a handyman [6] .... (fix) things when they are broken. Some of these services do not come cheap either. People pay up to $800 per week to have a personal assistant [7] .... (organize) their appointments or have their young baby [8] .... (care) for.

9 Look at these things that a rich couple gets other people to do for them. Complete the sentences with causative forms. Note that you can complete the sentences in two different ways.

1 When they had a party last month, someone organized everything for them.
They .... everything for them. (get)
2 A personal trainer takes their children to the park to play.
They .... to the park to play (have)
3 A driver picks their children up from school.
They .... from school. (have)
4 A travel agent plans their vacations for them.
They .... for them. (have)
5 A nanny looks after their children.
They .... (get)
6 Someone even packs their bags for them.
They even .... for them. (get)

10 Write down one thing that you would never consider getting someone else to do and one thing you would always get someone else to do. Compare lists with your partner.

11 Pronunciation the sounds /ʃ/, /tʃ/, /ʒ/, and /dʒ/

a 49 Listen carefully to how the underlined letters are pronounced in the following words. Then practice saying them with your partner.

/ʃ/	/tʃ/	/ʒ/	/dʒ/
carwa<u>sh</u>	<u>ch</u>ores	deci<u>s</u>ion	chan<u>ge</u>
<u>sh</u>elves	ri<u>ch</u>er	gara<u>ge</u>	colle<u>ge</u>
<u>sh</u>opper	wat<u>ch</u>	plea<u>s</u>ure	fri<u>dge</u>

b 50 Listen to these words. Discuss which of the four sounds above each one contains. Then practice saying them.

agent	arrange	champagne	cheese
choice	fashion	general	January
sugar	television	usual	

Vocabulary and speaking

12 Work in pairs. How many DIY (do-it-yourself) jobs can you make by matching verbs in A with nouns in B?

A

assemble	clean
decorate	fix
hang	plaster
put up	tile

B

a bed	the bathroom
a carpet	some curtains
a picture	the roof
a tap	some shelves
a wall	

13 Look at the room in the photo. First make a list of all the things that need to be done before you can live in it. Then decide what you will do yourself and what you will get professional help to do. Explain your plans to another pair.

12c The gift economy

Reading

1 How do you think a gift economy works?

2 Read the article and see if you were right. Then find three examples of the gift economy.

3 Choose the correct option (a–c).

1 The false understanding of human nature mentioned is that we are all trying to:
  a compete to get as much as we can.
  b be individuals.
  c keep from being hungry.
2 Hunter-gatherers:
  a had plenty and needed plenty.
  b had little and needed little.
  c had plenty and needed little.
3 American companies found it difficult to recruit Japanese employees because they:
  a couldn't offer good conditions.
  b couldn't offer job security.
  c didn't understand Japanese culture.
4 The message of the 4th paragraph is that Japanese employers are involved in:
  a organizing employees' vacations.
  b their employees' lives.
  c the quality of employees' work.
5 According to the author, the Internet has made it easier for people to:
  a get to know each other.
  b discuss problems.
  c give and receive help.
6 The message of the last paragraph is that big organizations need to:
  a be made smaller.
  b think about the common good.
  c give more of their profits back.

4 Look at these pairs of words from the article. Which definition (a or b) matches each word?

1 gain / reward
  a profit b compensation
2 strive / thrive
  a do well b do your best
3 common / mutual
  a shared by two b shared by many
4 abundance / excess
  a too much b plenty
5 prospects / aspects
  a future possibilities b characteristics
6 accuracy / promptness
  a being precise b being on time

5 Work in small groups. Tell each other what kind of relationship exists between employer and employees in your country. Is it more like the American system or the Japanese relationship?

Critical thinking signposts to key information

6 There are certain phrases that act as signposts to key information (just given or about to follow). Find the following phrases in the article and then draw out the key information they refer to.

at the heart of... not only... rather...
the main... the real...

7 Work in pairs. Compare your answers. Did you agree on what the key information was?

Word focus *hard*

8 Work in pairs. Find three expressions in the article containing the word *hard*. Discuss their meaning.

9 With a partner, try to guess the meaning of each expression with *hard* from its context. Then compare your answers with another pair.

1 I'm sorry the boss didn't like your idea and preferred mine. **No hard feelings**, I hope.
2 Fran and Chris are pretty **hard up** these days. They've been unemployed for a year.
3 Did you hear that **hard-luck** story about the people who lost all their savings?
4 Don't **be hard on** Jake. It's not his fault he was late. His car broke down.
5 I tried to get him to sympathize with our situation because we're newly established, but he's a pretty **hard-headed** businessman.

Speaking

10 Work in groups of three. Discuss the customs of gift giving and exchange that you are familiar with. Think about:

- specific occasions (like weddings, dinner parties)
- visiting people
- help and favors
- business gifts
- returning home after a trip abroad

The banking crisis of 2008 again raised concerns that our economy is based too much on individual greed. Such an economic model, critics say, comes from a false understanding of human nature. Human society is not made up of individuals pursuing private gain through competition with each other. The real essence of human nature lies in the social bonds that we make through family, friendships, professional associations, and local communities. These bonds produce a sense of common purpose and shared values, in which groups of people strive for the common good: a sound education, a pleasant environment to live in, a healthy population. It is this idea of shared social interests that is at the heart of the gift economy.

Gift economies thrived in earlier times when people lived in a world of greater abundance and when their wants were fewer. Stone Age hunter-gatherers had shelter and enough food, and did not need many possessions, just a few weapons for hunting and clothing for warmth. They shared food and tools without any expectation of payment or immediate reward. But this is not only an idea that applies to a more primitive way of life. There are also many recent examples of the gift economy at work.

In the past, American companies operating in Japan found it difficult to attract Japanese recruits, even though, compared with Japanese employers, they offered more generous wages, shorter work hours, and better promotion prospects. But these factors were traditionally not so important to Japanese employees, who did not think of their services as being "bought." Rather, they felt they were entering into a long-term "gift exchange" relationship with their employer, which was of mutual benefit.

This relationship had many aspects. At its most basic it involves the simple exchange of physical gifts. For example, if an employee gets married, the company sends a gift and even a departmental manager to represent it at the wedding. Or the company gives its employees a yearly company vacation. On these organized weekends, coworkers share dormitories, eat together, and visit the same attractions, largely at the company's expense. For their part, the main gift employees give their company is their hard work, and this is why each Japanese employee pays such great attention to accuracy, quality in their work, and promptness in its delivery. Even the simplest tasks are carried out with extraordinary care.

Elsewhere, the Internet is facilitating the re-emergence of the gift economy. Neighborhood groups use online networks to share tools and skills. If you need a long ladder to repair your roof, you don't have to go out and buy one; simply put a message on the neighborhood discussion board and soon a neighbor will offer one. You probably will even get help with the repair, because helping and giving is part of human nature. On the Internet, knowledge and advice about almost everything are shared, from how a nuclear reactor works to building your own canoe.

"Fine," I hear you say, "but these are hard times. Helping our neighbor with his roof isn't going to pay the bills." But in an indirect way it is. The point is that by stressing the cooperative side of human nature, the gift economy helps us all. It keeps in check the excesses of big commercial organizations that seek to exploit situations for their own gain. So the big supermarket chains must understand that it is in the common interest not to force small shopkeepers out of business. Big industrial farms must realize that they cannot go on intensively farming the land until there is nothing left in it. Large companies should not always seek to drive the hardest bargain possible with their suppliers, but just pay them fairly. That is the real lesson of the gift economy.

The Gift Economy

12d The bottom line

Real life negotiating

1 Read this advice about negotiating. Do you agree with it? How does it relate to your own experience?

"A famous negotiator's advice was to "Care, really care... but not that much." In other words, don't let the other person see how much you want the thing or you will be at a disadvantage."

2 51 Listen, and answer the questions.

1 How much does each person seem to care about agreeing on the lease?
2 On what point do they have trouble agreeing?
3 What does the woman suggest to get around this problem?
4 How does the negotiation end?

3 51 Work in pairs. Listen again and complete the expressions in the box.

NEGOTIATING

To be honest, it's absolutely [1] ________ .
A key thing for us is how long we'd be [2] ________ the lease.
I was hoping we could [3] ________ .
If you look at it from our point of view, we're a [4] ________ .
Let's face it, fifteen years is [5] ________ .

If your client could [6] ________ on that...
I think what you have to appreciate is that our client's main concern is...
At the end of the day, it gives them some security.
To tell you the truth, that's why the rent [7] ________ .
That's somewhat of a sticking point.
Is there no way around that?
Maybe if we signed... , then we could pay...
If I were in your shoes, I think I'd just [8] ________ .
When all's said and done, it has to [9] ________ .

4 Work in pairs. Look at the expressions in the box and discuss which are used to:

- say what the important thing is
- be direct
- talk about an obstacle to the agreement
- ask the other person to see your side

5 How do you think each person could have done better in the negotiation? Tell your partner.

6 **Pronunciation sentence stress in idiomatic phrases**

a 52 Listen to these phrases and underline the one or two words that are most stressed in each phrase.

1 To be honest...
2 A key thing for us is...
3 Let's face it...
4 At the end of the day,...
5 To tell you the truth...

b 53 Work in pairs. Look at these other phrases. Mark the words where you think the stress falls. Then listen and check.

1 The bottom line for us is...
2 The long and the short of it is...
3 The fact of the matter is...
4 One thing that's bothering me is...
5 To be frank,...
6 Am I right in thinking that... ?

7 You are spending eight months in a foreign country and want to get a car to use while you are there. You see a second-hand one advertised in the newspaper. It seems to be exactly what you are looking for. Work in pairs and negotiate the sale of the car. Student A look at page 153; Student B look at page 155.

12e This is what I propose

Writing a report

1 Work in pairs. Look at this quotation by the French mathematician Blaise Pascal. Discuss what he was saying about the art of writing.

> I'm sorry I wrote you such a long letter; I didn't have time to write a short one.

2 Look at these elements of a good report. Which is the one referred to by Blaise Pascal?

clear aims | clear recommendation | conciseness | good organization

3 Read the report below. What is the aim of the report? What is the recommendation? Tell your partner.

Summary

I visited our potential new offices at 1 Paradise Square yesterday, May 4, and was very impressed. They seem ideal for our needs, but the lease is for fifteen years, much longer than the six or seven we agreed on at our last meeting. These are the details:

Advantages

- Space — 2,000 ft^2 of flexible office space
- Low rent: only $67,000 per year
- Central location: close to stores and train station
- Maintained: cleaning, repairs are included

Disadvantages

- Long lease: fifteen years
- Maintenance fee is high: $17,000 annually

Recommendation

I propose taking these offices. We have been looking for five months and these are the best offices I have seen at a reasonable rent. If we have to leave before the end of the lease, I am confident that the remaining part of the lease can be sold to a new tenant.

4 Writing skill subheadings and bullet points

a The writer of the report has organized it into sections using subheadings and bullet points. What do you notice about the language after each bullet point?

b Read this first paragraph of a report on a language training course. Rewrite the report, dividing it into two sections with subheadings. Then break the points in the second section into bullet points.

> Last month the company sent me to a two-week "professional English" course at Falcon Business Language Training in Chicago. I stayed with a host family. Although the course did not focus on my particular job as an engineer very much, it was well organized. On the positive side, I was made to speak English all the time, both in the school and with my host family. The teachers were very professional and had a good knowledge of the business world. We were put in small groups of three to four students, which meant that we got a lot of individual attention.

c Work in pairs. Compare your answers. Did you organize your reports in the same way?

5 Now write the second half of the report including any negative comments and a recommendation. When you have finished, exchange your report with your partner.

6 Read your partner's report. Check the following:

- Is the report concise and clear?
- Has it been broken down into clear sections using subheadings and bullet points?
- Does it end with a clear recommendation?

12f Japan
Video

It is a land of dual identities.

Before you watch

1 Work in groups. Discuss the questions.

1 What do the photos show? Describe each one.
2 What two identities do you think the caption refers to?

2 Work in pairs. Write down things you associate with Japan.

While you watch

3 Watch the video and check your ideas from Exercise 2. Which of the things that you wrote down appeared in the video?

4 Watch the first part of the video (to 02:04). What do these numbers and dates refer to?

1 127 million ....
2 4 ....
3 35 million ....
4 1868 ....
5 1941 ....
6 1945 ....

5 Watch the second part of the video (02:05 to the end). Answer the questions.

1 What gave Japan political stability after the war?
....
2 What has helped it become a world leader in technology, manufacturing, and finance?
....
3 What does the tea ceremony emphasize?
a ....
b ....
c ....
4 Who did painters like Hiroshige influence?
....

6 Match the sentence beginnings (1–5) with the endings (a–e).

1 Japan is a country that harmonizes the forces of what is Western and modern
2 The bustling urban area of greater Tokyo is
3 It looked to the West for a new, more modern
4 Although it is a land of few natural resources, Japan has become
5 Beyond the bullet trains and neon of Tokyo,

a with those that are traditional Japanese.
b political and industrial model.
c there lies a rich cultural tradition.
d the largest metropolitan area on Earth.
e one of the most industrialized countries in the world.

7 Work in pairs. Describe the snow scene painting by Hiroshige.

....
....

After you watch

8 **Roleplay a conversation between two different generations**

Work in pairs.

Student A: Imagine you grew up in a small village in pre-war Japan. Look at the information below and think about what you are going to say to your grandchild.

- what life was like (the work you did, how you got around, the food you ate)
- the differences between life then and now
- the war years

Student B: Imagine you are a young Japanese business person talking to one of your grandparents. Look at the information below and think about what you are going to say to him/her.

- what life is like in the city (the work you do, how you travel to work, the food you eat)
- how you combine modern and traditional life in the city

Act out the conversation. Compare life in Japan pre- and post-war. Then change roles.

9 Work in groups and discuss the questions.

1 How has your country changed culturally and economically in the last 100 years?
2 Do cultural traditions always support economic innovation?
3 Are economic advances always beneficial? Why?

bustling (adj) /'bʌslɪŋ/ busy
feudal (adj) /'fjud(ə)l/ relating to a social system where most people work and fight for more powerful people who own the land
forge (v) /fɔrdʒ/ make something under difficult conditions
glitz (n) /glɪts/ the quality of being shiny and superficially attractive
neon (n) /'niɑn/ a kind of brightly colored artificial light
raid (n) /reɪd/ an unexpected attack
shrine (n) /ʃraɪn/ a place where people go to meditate or pray
ubiquitous (adj) /ju'bɪkwɪtəs/ present everywhere
wrestling (n) /'reslɪŋ/ a sport where the contestants try to throw each other on the ground

UNIT 12 REVIEW

Grammar

1 Read the article and say why Japan has had a problem of relative poverty in recent years.

2 Insert the focus adverb into the right place in each sentence.

When we picture poverty we often think of people in under-developed countries without food or shelter. [1] But the so-called advanced economies of the world have their share of poverty (even). [2] Japan, for example, a few decades ago was enjoying an economic boom (just). [3] Yet by 2000, it had one of the highest rates of relative poverty among developed countries, with the US having a higher rate (only). [4] One reason was that Japan had one of the highest rates of non-regular workers (also). This means people who are working without proper social protection. [5] An increasingly elderly population—people who were not actively working—contributed to the problem (as well). [6] Making savings last when you live to be over 90 is a problem that people in developed countries will face in the coming years (even).

3 Put the verbs in the right form to complete this advice to people who are long-term unemployed.

1. The first thing to do is rewrite your resume and then get it ________ (check) by an expert.
2. Practice your interview technique. Have a friend ________ (play) the part of the interviewer and get them ________ (ask) you tricky questions.
3. Try to look professional when you go for an interview. Get your hair ________ (cut) and make sure your clothes are suitable. Again, get a friend ________ (help) you with this.
4. Call employers and go to see them in person. Show enthusiasm and get them ________ (see) that you are eager to work.

I CAN
- use focus adverbs to add emphasis ☐
- talk about things that others do for me with *have* and *get* ☐

Vocabulary

4 Find a synonym or close synonym in B for each word/expression in A.

A	B
hard up	paint
hang	au pair
decorate	earnings
borrow from the bank	reasonable
cheap	take out a loan
income	put up
nanny	poor
owe money	be in debt

5 Work in pairs. Make a list of domestic help that you think most people can afford now and again.

I CAN
- talk about money and the economy ☐
- talk about getting domestic jobs done ☐

Real life

6 Work in pairs. Put this conversation between a travel agent (TA) and customer (C) in order.

TA: To tell you the truth, they're not the kind of hotels you can negotiate with.
TA: So we're suggesting one week in the north of the island and one week in the south. Is this the kind of vacation you were looking for?
TA: OK, I'll give them a call and see what I can do.
TA: I understand that, and if I were in your shoes, I think I'd just go for it. At the end of the day, you only get one honeymoon.
TA: What you have to appreciate is that you've chosen two top hotels which aren't cheap.
C: I was hoping we could negotiate the price.
C: I know they aren't, but the key thing for us is to have nice accommodations.
C: Perhaps if we stayed at just one of them for the full two weeks we could get a better deal.
C: Yes it is, but to be honest, it's much more expensive than we expected.

7 Take the roles of travel agent and customer and finish the negotiation.

I CAN
- state my position and negotiate from it ☐

Speaking

8 Work in small groups. Do you think the idea below for a domestic service would work? Think of another idea. Then tell it to others in the class.

What about offering a cooking service where busy couples can have a meal prepared for them at home rather than eating out or getting takeout?

UNIT 3c, Exercise 11, page 38

Instructions

- Form a group of three or four people and ask the teacher which product you are going to present.
- Read the product description on page 154 or 155.
- Together prepare a brief presentation of the product: what it is, how it works, what it is appropriate for, and why it is special.
- Choose one person to give the presentation (the others will have to answer questions). Think about the questions you may be asked.
- Give and listen to the presentations, asking and answering questions as you go.
- Have a class vote for best product.

UNIT 4a, Exercise 10, page 47

Participation by art form

Art form	Creative participation %	Receptive participation %	Total participation %
Visual Arts & Crafts	22	38	49
Theater & Dance	7	40	42
Reading/ Creative Writing	16	84	84
Music	15	57	62

Participation in music

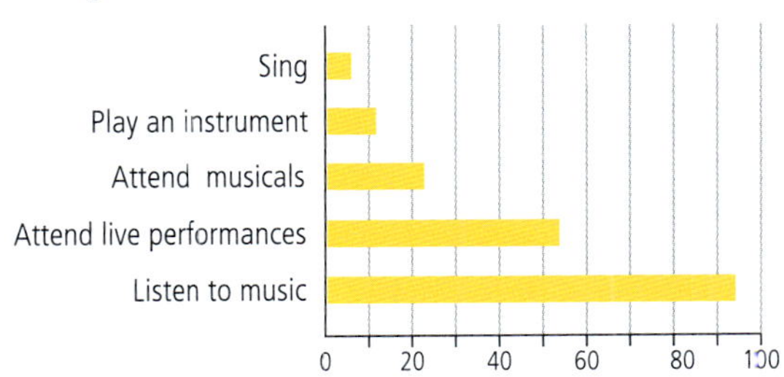

Reasons for non-participation

Reason	Non-participants %
difficult to find the time	54
not really interested	43
costs too much	41
not enough opportunities nearby	28

UNIT 8e, Exercise 4, page 101

- write to the university and ask them to speak to students about being considerate neighbors
- threaten to call the police if the students make noise after midnight
- have a friendly meeting with the students
- complain to town hall and ask them to put pressure on the university to find another solution

UNIT 5d, Exercise 5, page 64

Aston Homes for the Elderly

The bank gave the Aston Housing Association (AHA) a loan of $9 million in September 2009 to convert eight residential houses into groups of self-contained apartments for elderly people in the community who did not want to go into nursing homes.

Work started in December 2009, and so far five of the houses have already been converted, creating 40 self-contained apartments. The AHA has sold 30 of these, raising $4.5 million. It has also made repayments to the bank correctly and on time.

However, there have been complaints from local residents that AHA has sold some of the apartments to people who are not so elderly (one lady was in her late fifties), and that they have allowed people from outside the area to buy them. It seems that the price of the apartments is too high for many local people.

The AHA now intends to convert two more houses in the same area and is asking for an additional loan of $2.2 million.

UNIT 12d, Exercise 7, page 148

Student A

You want to buy this car. It is a seven-year-old VW Golf and the advertised price is $8,000. It is in good condition but has a lot of miles on it (100 000). Obviously you would like to get it for less, if you can. The problem is you have been looking for a long time and want to get a car quickly so that you can drive to work each day.

UNIT 3c, Exercise 11, page 38

Description 1

Portable Clay Cooler
Building on an ancient food-storage technique, the pot-in-pot system uses evaporation from a layer of wet sand between two pots to help keep produce fresh. Tomatoes can last weeks instead of days, meaning more income for farmers.

Developed by: Mohammed Bah Abba
Website: none available
Launch country: Nigeria

UNIT 9c, Exercise 10, page 110

* numbers in tens of thousands

UNIT 11c, Exercise 10, page 134

Quiz

Answer the questions then look at page 155 to see what type of learner you are. Do you agree?

1 WHEN I STUDY GRAMMAR, I LEARN BEST BY:
A reading clear rules. B writing down examples.
C putting it into practice in conversation.

2 IN CLASS, I PREFER:
A discussing. B looking at pictures, maps, diagrams, or videos.
C doing something practical.

3 I REMEMBER NEW VOCABULARY BEST WHEN IT IS ACCOMPANIED BY:
A a clear definition. B an image. C a demonstration.

4 IF I AM DISTRACTED IN CLASS, I USUALLY:
A hum or sing to myself. B doodle (draw) in my notebook.
C play with a pen or pencil.

5 WHEN LEARNING A NEW SKILL, I PREFER THAT:
A someone explain it to me. B someone demonstrate it.
C I just be allowed to get on with it myself.

6 WHEN I'M NOT SURE HOW TO SPELL A WORD, I:
A say the word aloud to myself. B try to visualize it in my mind.
C write down different versions.

7 I PREFER TO READ STORIES WITH LOTS OF:
A dialogue and conversation. B descriptive passages.
C action or adventure.

8 I PROBABLY LEARN THE MOST ENGLISH BY:
A listening to others. B watching movies.
C trying to use it.

UNIT 3c, Exercise 11, page 38

Description 2

Sugarcane Charcoal

Burning wood and dung, the main fuel sources for many in the developing world, has contributed to deforestation and breathing problems among inhabitants. These briquettes made from crushed sugarcane stalks not only make use of a local resource, they also burn more cleanly and allow residents to start a charcoal business for less than $50.

Developed by: MIT D-Lab
Website: http://d-lab.mit.edu/resources
Launch country: Haiti

UNIT 3c, Exercise 11, page 38

Description 3

Water Container

In poor rural areas, clean water is often miles away, leaving people vulnerable to diseases in unclean water. The strong Q Drum holds thirteen gallons in a rolling container that makes it easy to transport safe drinking water, a task that is usually done by women and children.

Developed by: P. J. and J. P. S. Hendrikse
Website: http://www.qdrum.co.za
Launch country: South Africa

UNIT 12d, Exercise 7, page 148

Student B

You want to sell this car. It is a seven-year-old VW Golf and the advertised price is $8,000. It is in good condition but has a lot of miles on it (100,000). You would like to get as close to the asking price as you can. However, it has been advertised for two months and you would like to sell it soon.

UNIT 11c, Exercise 10, page 134

Answers to quiz

Mostly As: you have an auditory learning style; you remember best when you hear things.

Mostly Bs: you have a visual learning style; you remember best when you see things.

Mostly Cs: you have a kinesthetic learning style; you remember best when you do things or when things are acted out.

UNIT 3c, Exercise 11, page 38

Description 4

Solar Wi-Fi Streetlight

The StarSight system consists of a series of pylons that use solar panels to power streetlamps, a Wi-Fi box for wireless Internet access, and if needed, closed-circuit TVs for security surveillance. The result is an integrated system of electricity and communication, plus better street lighting, which has been shown to help reduce crime.

Developed by: Kolam Partnership Ltd.
Website: http://www.starsightproject.com
Launch countries: Nigeria, South Africa, Turkey

UNIT 5b, Exercise 10, page 61

Questionnaire

1 HOW SATISFIED DO PEOPLE SEEM WITH THE AMOUNT OF MONEY THEY HAVE?

2 DO PEOPLE HAVE A GOOD BALANCE BETWEEN WORK AND FREE TIME?

3 HOW HAPPY ARE PEOPLE WITH THE EDUCATION THEY RECEIVE?

4 HOW CONFIDENT ARE PEOPLE IN YOUR COUNTRY'S HEALTH SYSTEM?

5 DO PEOPLE EAT HEALTHY FOOD?

6 HOW ENGAGED ARE PEOPLE POLITICALLY?

7 HOW OFTEN DO PEOPLE PARTICIPATE IN CULTURAL ACTIVITIES?

8 ARE PEOPLE TOLERANT OF OTHERS?

UNIT 8b, Exercise 8, page 97

1 false
2 true
3 half-true; it does increase life expectancy but no one can say how much
4 true
5 false; the zebrafish can heal its own heart, but not humans—yet!
6 true

UNIT 1

Present tenses review

Form

Simple present

Affirmative	Negative
I/you/we/they **live**	I/you/we/they **don't live** (don't = do not)
he/she/it **lives**	he/she/it **doesn't live** (doesn't = does not)

Interrogative	Short answer
do I/you/we/they **live**?	Yes, I/you/we/they **do**. No, I/you/we/they **don't**.
does he/she/it **live**?	Yes, he/she/it **does**. No, he/she/it **doesn't**.

Present continuous

Affirmative	Negative
I'm living ('m = am)	**I'm not** living ('m not = am not)
you**'re**/we**'re**/they**'re** **living** ('re = are)	you/we/they **aren't living** (aren't = are not)
he**'s**/she**'s**/it**'s** **living** ('s = is)	he/she/it **isn't living** (isn't = is not)

Interrogative	Short answer
am I **living**?	Yes, I **am**. No, **I'm not**.
are you/we/they **living**?	Yes, you/we/they **are**. No, you/we/they **aren't**.
is he/she/it **living**?	Yes, he/she/it **is**. No, he/she/it **isn't**.

Present perfect

Affirmative	Negative
I**'ve**/you**'ve**/we**'ve**/ they**'ve lived** ('ve = have)	I/you/we/they **haven't lived** (haven't = have not)
he**'s**/she**'s**/it**'s lived** ('s = has)	he/she/it **hasn't lived** (hasn't = has not)

Interrogative	Short answer
have I/you/we/they **lived**?	Yes, I/you/we/they **have**. No, I/you/we/they **haven't**.
has he/she/it **lived**?	Yes, he/she/it **has**. No, he/she/it **hasn't**.

Note the spelling rules for *-ed* endings:
*work → work**ed**; play → play**ed**; die → di**ed**; lie → li**ed**; try → tri**ed**; study → studi**ed**; stop → sto**pped***
Some verbs have irregular past participles, for example:
do → done; find → found; have → had; make → made

Present perfect continuous

Affirmative	Negative
I**'ve**/you**'ve**/we**'ve**/ they**'ve been living** ('ve = have)	I/you/we/they **haven't been living** (haven't = have not)
he**'s**/she**'s**/it**'s been living** ('s = has)	he/she/it **hasn't been living** (hasn't = has not)

Interrogative	Short answer
have I/you/we/they **been living**?	Yes, I/you/we/they **have**. No, I/you/we/they **haven't**.
has he/she/it **been living**?	Yes, he/she/it **has**. No, he/she/it **hasn't**.

Note the spelling rules for *-ing* endings:
work → working; play → playing; live → living; have → having; stop → stopping; run → running; die → dying; lie → lying

Use

Simple present

We use the simple present to talk about:

- facts or things which are generally true. *Orangutans **eat** fruit and leaves. The Earth **doesn't move** around the Moon. Where **do** polar bears **live**?*
- daily routines and habits. *I **work** in that factory every day. I always **take** a shower in the morning.*
- a permanent state or situation. *She **doesn't play** the piano. **Do** you **live** in Bahia?*

We often use adverbs of frequency (*always, usually, often, sometimes, rarely, never*) and expressions of frequency (*once a week, on Fridays, on the weekend, in the summer, every Saturday*) with the simple present to talk about how often we do something.
*We **always** play football on Saturday morning.*
*She **never** talks to strangers.*

Present continuous

We use the present continuous to talk about a situation in progress or things which are happening now or around now. With the present continuous, we often use these time expressions: *at the moment, (right) now, this week, this summer.*
*The boys **are playing** tennis in the park.*
*Paul **isn't living** in San Miguel this summer.*
***Are** you **doing** your report, Vikram?*

Present perfect

We use the present perfect to talk about a recent action or situation which started in the past. The situation may also continue into the present or have a result in the present.
*Michael can't come with us because he **hasn't renewed** his passport.*
***Have** you **visited** your grandparents lately?*

Present perfect continuous

We use the present perfect continuous to talk about an action or situation that was in progress in the recent past. The situation may also continue into the present or have a result in the present. We use the present perfect continuous, not the present perfect, to emphasize the duration of an action.

*I've **been working** here for months.* (And I still am.)
*They've **been behaving** like this since they arrived.*
*What **have you been doing** since I last saw you?*
*She **hasn't been working** hard enough lately!*

We often use the present perfect and present perfect continuous with *since* and *for* to talk about how long a situation has continued. We use *since* with the point of time when the activity started, for example *since Monday, since I was a boy*. We use *for* to talk about a period of time up to now, for example *for an hour, for a long time*.

*We've been friends **since** we were twelve years old.*
*We've been playing at the club **since** 2010.*
*I've lived in this house **for** six months.*

Practice

1 Choose the correct option.

Can you believe these other amazing and unlikely friendships between animals?

- A baby hippo [1] *has been living* with a giant tortoise since a devastating tsunami in 2004. They [2] .... and [3] .... together.
- One intrepid explorer says that his Eskimo dogs [4] .... an extraordinary relationship with some polar bears. They [5] .... together each year since 2008, when the dogs first traveled through the Arctic lands of Canada.
- Ellie, a dog, and Hattie, an elephant, [6] .... the best of friends since they met in 2009.
- At a reserve in South Africa, a leopard cub and a dog often [7] .... together, and at the moment, they [8] .... in the same kennel.

People are amazed by these friendships. "It's true to say that there has been an evolution in the animal kingdom recently," says one animal expert.

1 a has been living b has lived c is living
2 a are eating b have eaten c eat
3 a are sleeping b have slept c sleep
4 a have been b have been getting c have got
5 a are playing b have played c have been playing
6 a become b are becoming c have become
7 a play b are playing c have played
8 a sleep b are sleeping c have slept

The passive voice

Form

We form the passive voice with the correct tense? of the verb *to be* + past participle.

Tense	Active	Passive
Simple present	makes/make	is/are made
Present continuous	is/are making	is/are being made
Present perfect	has/have made	has/have been made

Use

We use the passive voice when we want to focus on an action or the object of the action, rather than the person doing the action. The object of the active sentence becomes the subject of the passive one.

Active: Parents (subject) are questioning the new values (object).
Passive: The new values (subject) are being questioned by parents (object).

In a passive sentence, we can say who did the action (the agent) using *by*. We use *by* + agent when it is important to know who did the action. It isn't always necessary to use *by* + agent. We don't usually use the agent when it is obvious who has done the action, when we don't know, or when it isn't important.

*The best products are selected **by the product manager**.*
Guests are asked ~~by the hotel~~ to sign the visitors' book.

We also use the passive when we don't want to identify the agent.

I'm sorry, but the window has been broken ~~by my son~~.

Practice

2 Rewrite the sentences in the passive voice. Use *by* + agent where appropriate.

1 They are changing people's lives every day.
People's lives are being changed every day.
2 We make new plans all the time.
....
3 The government is making some new laws.
....
4 They have changed the whole system since I was a student.
....
5 Young people are forgetting the old way of life.
....
6 We haven't seen good manners for a long time.
....
7 We are still respecting a lot of the old customs.
....
8 Are they respecting the way that people used to live?
....

UNIT 2

Simple past and present perfect

Form

Simple past

We add *-ed* to regular verbs to form the simple past.

Affirmative	Negative
I/you/he/she/it/we/they **worked**	I/you/he/she/it/we/they **didn't work** (didn't = did not)

Interrogative	Short answer
did I/you/he/she/it/we/they **work**?	Yes, I/you/he/she/it/we/they **did**. No, I/you/he/she/it/we/they **didn't**.

Note the spelling rules for other regular verbs:

- for verbs ending in *-e*, we add *-d*: *realize* → ***realized***
- for verbs ending in *-y*, we change the *-y* to *i* and add *-ed*: *carry* → *carr**ied***
- for verbs ending in vowel + consonant (not *-w*, *-x*, or *-y*), we double the consonant: *plan* → *pla**nned***

Some verbs have an irregular affirmative form in the simple past:
be → *was/were; do* → *did; go* → *went; see* → *saw; write* → *wrote*

Present perfect

We form the present perfect with the simple present of the verb *to have* + past participle.

See page 156: Present perfect

Use

Simple past

We use the simple past to talk about finished actions in the past when there is a clear link to a specific time in the past. We often use a time phrase (*yesterday, last week, five years ago*) with the simple past.
*He **finished** the movie script two hours ago.*
*They **didn't go** to the movies last night.*
***Did** you **meet** Alex earlier?*

We use the simple past to talk about someone's life when they are dead.
*He **fought** as a soldier in the Civil War.*

Present perfect

We use the present perfect to talk about a recent action or situation which started at some time in the past. The situation may also continue into the present or have a result in the present. We use the present perfect when the experience is more important than the time, and the time is not stated.
I've seen a lot of different movies in the last five years.
He hasn't seen the new Lord of the Rings *movie yet.*

We also use the present perfect to talk about life experiences (when the people are still living).
I've never been to Peru. Have you ever gone?

When we talk about a period of time that is not finished, we use the present perfect, even if the action itself is finished.
Have you talked to him today? (It is still today.)

When the period of time is finished, we use the simple past.
Did you talk to him earlier? (It is now later.)

Practice

1 Choose the correct option.

1 I *saw* / *have seen* a very interesting movie yesterday.
2 *Did you ever read* / *Have you ever read* poetry?
3 I *didn't like* / *haven't liked* the end of the movie.
4 They *enjoyed* / *have enjoyed* watching the play last night.
5 Elena *didn't study* / *hasn't studied* literature for a long time.
6 The students *wrote* / *have written* some very original short stories in last year's class.
7 Lately his parents *told* / *have told* him a lot of funny anecdotes from when he was a child.
8 When *did you find out* / *have you found out* about the stories of Borges?

Past tenses review

Form

See page 158: Simple past

Past continuous

Interrogative	Short answer
was I/he/she/it **working** there?	Yes, I/he/she/it **was**. No, I/he/she/it **wasn't**.
were you/we/they **working** there?	Yes, you/we/they **were**. No, you/we/they **weren't**.

Past perfect

Affirmative	Negative
I**'d**/you**'d**/he**'d**/she**'d**/it**'d**/we**'d**/they**'d worked** ('d = had)	I/you/he/she/it/we/they **hadn't worked** (hadn't = had not)

Interrogative	Short answer
had I/you/he/she/it/we/they **worked**?	Yes, I/you/he/she/it/we/they **had**. No, I/you/he/she/it/we/they **hadn't**.

Past perfect continuous

Affirmative	Negative
I**'d**/you**'d**/he**'d**/she**'d**/it**'d**/we**'d**/they**'d been working** ('d = had)	I/you/he/she/it/we/they **hadn't been working** (hadn't = had not)

Interrogative	Short answer
had I/you/he/she/it/we/ they **been working**?	Yes, I/you/he/she/it/they **had been working.** No, I/you/he/she/it/they **hadn't been working.** (hadn't = had not)

Use

Simple past

We use the simple past to talk about the sequence of the main events of a story.
*Giles **got up** at six o'clock and **left** the location early.*

Past continuous

We use the past continuous to describe a background event which was in progress around the time of the main event. We often use the past continuous with the simple past.
*The sun **was coming up** as Paul arrived at the park.*

Past perfect

We use the past perfect to talk about what happened earlier, before the main event.
*When Julieta saw the animals, she remembered what the trainer **had said** the day before.*

Past perfect continuous

We use the past perfect continuous to describe an action that was in progress before or up to the main event in the past.
*When Salma arrived, the other actors **had** already **been rehearsing** for two hours.*

We don't usually use stative verbs in either the past continuous or the past perfect continuous.
*I **knew** the route well.* (Not *I ~~was knowing~~ the route well.*)
*I **had known** him for ten years.* (Not *I ~~had been knowing~~ him for ten years.*)

Practice

2 Complete the text with the correct past tense form of the verbs.

Elena [1] .... (walk) in the park near her home. It [2] .... (be) a beautiful evening. The sun [3] .... (shine) all day and now it [4] .... (set) behind some tall trees by the river. Suddenly she [5] .... (hear) a scream. She thought that it [6] .... (come) from the direction of the river so she [7] .... (run) there as fast as she could. When she [8] .... (reach) the river, she [9] .... (see) a young boy in the water. He [10] .... (slip) on the muddy bank and [11] .... (fall) head first into the water. Now he [12] .... (struggle) and unable to swim. Elena quickly [13] .... (take) off her shoes and [14] .... (jump) in. She [15] .... (catch) the boy by the arm and [16] .... (drag) him out.

UNIT 3

Future forms review

Form

will

Affirmative	Negative
I/you/he/she/it/we/they**'ll** go ('ll = will)	I/you/he/she/it/we/they **won't** go (won't = will not)

Interrogative	Short answer
will I/you/he/she/it/we/ they go?	Yes, I/you/he/she/it/we/they **will**. No, I/you/he/she/it/we/they **won't**.

going to

Affirmative	Negative
I**'m going to** visit	I**'m not going to** visit
you**'re**/we**'re**/they**'re going to** visit	you/we/they **aren't going to** visit
he**'s**/she**'s** /it**'s going to** visit	he/she/it **isn't going to** visit

Interrogative	Short answer
am I **going to** visit?	Yes, I **am**./No, I**'m not**.
are you/we/they **going to** visit?	Yes, you/we/they **are**. No, you/we/they **aren't**.
is he/she/it **going to** visit?	Yes, he/she/it **is**. No, he/she/it **isn't**.

about to

Affirmative	Negative
I**'m about to** start	I**'m not about to** start
you**'re**/we**'re**/they**'re about to** start	you/we/they **aren't about to** start
he**'s**/she**'s**/it**'s about to** start	he/she/it **isn't about to** start

Interrogative	Short answer
am I **about to** start?	Yes, I **am**./No, I**'m not**.
are you/we/they **about to** start?	Yes, you/we/they **are**. No, you/we/they **aren't**.
is he/she/it **about to** start?	Yes, he/she/it **is**. No, he/she/it **isn't**.

See page 156: Simple present, Present continuous

Use

will

We use *will* to talk about:

- a prediction. *I expect he'**ll** be here in a minute.*
- a decision we have made at the time of speaking. *"I can't start my car." "Don't worry. I'**ll give** you a ride."*
- a future event in an *if* or *when* clause. *If the population increases, there **won't be** enough food.*

going to

We use *be* + *going to* + base form

- to talk about a plan or intention for the future. This has been decided before the moment of speaking. *When I'm in Chile, **I'm going to travel** to Arica.*
- to make a prediction about the future based on present information. *My team is playing very badly. They**'re going to lose** this game.*

about to

We use *be* + *about to* to talk about an event in the immediate future.
*I can't talk to you now—**I'm about to go** into a meeting.*

We often use *just* in front of *about to*.
*Tell me the details later—**I'm just about to go** into town.*

Present continuous

We use the present continuous to talk about:

- an intention or previously made decision or arrangement. *They **aren't coming** to the theater.*
- a formal arrangement. *They**'re coming** at noon.*

We often use the present continuous with a specific (or understood) time in the future.
*I'm traveling to New York **on Thursday evening**.*

Simple present

We use the simple present to talk about:

- a scheduled event. *The concert **starts** at eight o'clock. What time **does** the train **leave**?*
- a simple statement of fact. *Water **boils** at 212°F.*

Practice

1 Complete the conversation with the correct future tense of the verbs.

A: The first talk [1] ________ (start) at five.
B: [2] ________ you ________ (go) to it?
A: No, I think I [3] ________ (pass). It's not really a subject that interests me.
B: Really? I think it [4] ________ (be) really interesting.
A: Well, I [5] ________ (meet) a colleague in half an hour anyway to discuss the presentation we [6] ________ (give) later.
B: Oh. When does that [7] ________ (start)?
A: It [8] ________ (be) at 2:00 p.m.
B: Oh good. I [9] ________ (try) to come to that.
A: Great! Anyway, you'd better go. Your talk [10] ________ (be) to start.

Future continuous and future perfect

Form

Future continuous

We form the future continuous with *will be* + *-ing*.

Affirmative	Negative
I/you/he/she/it/we/they **will be doing**	I/you/he/she/it/we/they **won't be doing**

Interrogative	Short answer
will I/you/he/she/it/we/they **be doing**?	Yes, I/you/he/she/it/we/they **will**. No, I/you/he/she/it/we/they **won't**.

Future perfect

We form the future perfect with *will have* + past participle.

Affirmative	Negative
I/you/he/she/it/we/they **will have done**	I/you/he/she/it/we/they **won't have done**

Interrogative	Short answer
will I/you/he/she/it/we/they **have done**?	Yes, I/you/he/she/it/we/they **will**. No, I/you/he/she/it/we/they **won't**.

Use

Future continuous

We use the future continuous to talk about an action which you know or think will be in progress at or during a certain period of time in the future.
*In five years' time, everyone **will be using** HD phones.*
*This time tomorrow I **won't be sitting** in this office.*
*What **will** scientists **be researching** ten years from now?*

Future perfect

We use the future perfect to talk about an action which is going to be completed at or before a certain point of time in the future.
*In 50 years' time, people **will have stopped** using cash.*
*He **won't have finished** the work by the weekend.*
***Will** you **have sent** that email by five o'clock?*

Practice

2 Choose the correct option.

1 Next year people *will be using* / *will have used* wind power for their electricity.
2 By next January the company *will be designing* / *will have designed* a smaller computer chip.
3 Scientists *will be making* / *will have made* some important breakthroughs by 2020.
4 It is predicted that *we will be living* / *will have lived* on Mars in the next 50 years.
5 I expect that I *will be working* / *will have worked* in a laboratory next month.
6 I'm sure he *will be studying* / *will have studied* biology all his life.

UNIT 4

Expressions of quantity

Form

***(not) many, (a) few, a (small/large) number of, several* + plural count noun**

There were ***not many people*** *at the concert.*
Eda has only been to ***a few*** *classical* ***concerts****.*

***(not) much, (a) little (of) a (large/small) amount of* + noncount noun**

There isn't ***much live music*** *at the festival.*

***a lot of, lots of, plenty of, loads of, (a) lack of, (almost) no, (not/hardly) any, some, enough* + plural count or noncount noun**

You can buy ***plenty of food and drink*** *at the show.*
There were ***hardly any cars*** *in town today.*

Use

We use quantifiers with count or noncount nouns to talk about quantity (how much or how many of something).

Large quantities

To express large quantities, we use:

- *a large number of, a huge number of* with plural count nouns
- *a large amount of, a huge amount of* with noncount nouns
- *some, a lot of, lots of, loads of, plenty of* with plural count or noncount nouns

An enormous number of *people are involved.*
Some *visitors return three or four times a year.*
There were ***a lot of/loads of*** *great bands at the festival.*
Note that *loads of* is less formal than *a lot of/lots of.*

Small quantities

To express small quantities, we use:

- *(not) many, (a) few, a (small) number of, several* with plural count nouns.
- *(not) much, (a) little (of), a small amount of* with noncount nouns.
- *some, a lack of, (almost) no, (not/hardly) any* with plural count or noncount nouns.

In most towns, there are ***a few*** *interesting places to visit.*
Hardly any *artists become rich in their lifetime.*

We use *little/a little* and *few/a few* to talk about small quantities in affirmative statements. *A little* and *a few* have a positive meaning (= some, but not many). *Little* and *few* have a negative meaning (= only a small number of).
A few *people watched his latest play.* (= at least some, if not many)
Few *people watched his latest play.* (= almost none)
They arrived very late so they only saw ***a little*** *of the show.* (= some, but not much)
He ate ***little*** *of his dinner in the restaurant because he didn't like seafood.* (= almost none)

We don't usually use *much* in affirmative statements. We normally use *a lot of/lots of.*
They don't have much knowledge of the local area.
We have a lot of brochures about the area.

Several usually means three or more things or people.
There were ***several*** *people in the audience.*

enough

We use *enough* to say we have the correct or sufficient quantity. We use *not enough* to say we have less than we want or need.
There are ***enough*** *members of the orchestra now.*
There ***aren't enough*** *artists signed up for the festival yet.*

We can use *a large amount, enough, plenty, several, not much, not many* without nouns when the meaning is clear.
Do you have many theaters in your town? Yes, we have ***several****. / No, there* ***aren't many****.*

Practice

1 Choose the correct option.

1 There aren't *much / many / a little* movies playing this week.
2 There is *a few / several / lots of* gas in the car.
3 Is there *many / much / a few* interest in art?
4 *Few / Not much / A little* people were there.
5 *Much / Many / Some* art books are on the shelf.
6 There is only *a little / lots of / plenty of* talent among these new actors.
7 The exhibition had *a little / not much / almost no* good paintings.
8 Are there *a bit of / enough / not much* bands playing at the festival?

Determiners

Form

***each, every, either, the whole* + singular noun**

Each visitor *to the gallery receives a plan of the exhibition.*
Every exhibit *in the museum is catalogued.*
People can buy ***either*** *a one-day or a season ticket.*

***all, both* + plural noun**

All *the shortlisted artists gained a lot of publicity.*
Both *artists exhibited three pictures.*

***any, no* + singular or plural noun**

Have you seen ***any*** *good movies this month?*
They received ***no*** *complaints.*

all, any, no + noncount noun

All *literature has value.*
Can we use ***any*** *material we like?*
No *culture is superior to another.*

Use

every, each, all

We use *every, each,* and *all* to talk generally about people or things.
Every *musician played well.*
Each *artist had some interesting work on display.*
All *the paintings were very good.*
We use *each* and *every* to refer to the individuals or individual parts of a group. We use *all* to refer to the whole group.

We use *every* (+ singular noun) and *all, all the, all of the* (+ plural noun/noncount noun) when the plural noun refers to **three** or more people or things.
Every *person had the opportunity to be an artist for a day.* (There were three or more people.)
All of the *participants wrote a poem about nature.* (There were three or more participants.)
We use *each* (+ singular noun) to talk about **two** or more people or things.
Each *member of the group made some form of contribution.* (There were two or more people.)

both, either

We use *both* and *either* to talk about **two** things or people. We use *both/both of the* (+ plural noun) to say the same thing about two people or things. We use *either* (+ singular noun) to say there are two possible options.
Both (of the) *sculptors made three works of art.*
They could choose to use ***either*** *stone or clay.*

We use *neither* to express the opposite of *both.*
Neither *contestant made it to the final.*

(not) any, no

We use *(not) any* or *no* to talk about a negative idea.
They ***didn't*** *allow* ***any*** *graffiti on the walls at all.*
There are ***no*** *original ideas left in art.*

We can use *(not) any* without a noun when the meaning is clear.
Did you get the tickets? No, there ***aren't any left.***

Practice

2 Complete the sentences with a suitable determiner. More than one answer is possible.

1 There were ten pianists in the competition, and they were <u>*all*</u> very good.
2 .... member of the band is talented.
3 Gilberto and Jorge work as a pair, but .... men are artists in their own right.
4 They were both good players, so .... of them could have won.
5 .... performer was better than the others.
6 .... student was asked to bring a sketch.

UNIT 5

Verb + infinitive or *-ing*

Form

Verb + infinitive	
verb + infinitive	*They **wanted to create** a luxury resort.*
verb + *someone* + infinitive	*He **asked his father to lend** him the money for the deposit.*
verb + *someone* + base form	*She **helped her friend establish** a new theme park.*

Verb + *-ing*	
verb + *-ing*	*I **enjoy going** to shopping malls.*

Use

verb + infinitive

After certain verbs we use infinitive. This is often to talk about hopes, intentions and decisions.
He offered ***to draw*** *the plans for the redevelopment.*
They didn't want ***to work*** *on the project any more.*
Common verbs which are followed by infinitive include: *agree, appear, arrange, choose, decide, expect, hope, intend, manage, need, offer, plan, prepare, pretend, promise, refuse, seem, want, wish, would like.*

verb + *someone* + infinitive

Some verbs are followed by an object and infinitive.
He reminded ***his employees to arrive*** *early.*
They'd like ***the contractors to submit*** *their proposal.*
Common verbs which are followed by *someone* + infinitive include: *allow, ask, expect, force, help, invite, like, need, remind, teach, tell, want, would like.*

verb + *someone* + base form

Some verbs are followed by an object and the base form.
She ***helped her daughter expand*** *her business.*
Common verbs which use this form are: *feel, hear, help, notice, see, watch.*

verb + *-ing*

We use verb + *-ing* after certain verbs.
The architect ***suggested adding*** *some green space.*
Common verbs which are followed by *-ing* are: *avoid, can't help, like, love, enjoy, prefer don't like, hate, can't stand, (not) mind, keep, miss, practice, risk, suggest.*

Practice

1 Choose the correct option.

1 I always enjoy *going* / *to go* to work.
2 Dubai *growing* / *grows* richer every day.
3 Ana asked them *sending* / *to send* help.
4 We decided *to invest* / *investing* in property.
5 The ministers suggested *to start* / *starting* an investment bank.
6 The government refused *giving* / *to give* them planning permission.

Verb + *-ing* or infinitive

Form

verb + *-ing* and verb + infinitive (two different meanings)

*He **remembered listening** to the program.*
*They **remembered to record** the program.*

verb + *-ing* and verb + infinitive (no change in meaning)

*He **continued traveling** around Asia.*
*He **continued to travel** around Asia.*

Use

Some verbs can be followed by either *-ing* or infinitive but the meaning changes.
*Jan **stopped talking** to journalists.* = action has ended (Jan used to talk to journalists but then he stopped.)
*Jan **stopped to talk** to a local resident.* = the reason for stopping (Jan stopped so that he could talk to a local resident.)
Common verbs which can be followed by *-ing* or infinitive with a change in meaning are: *forget, go on, mean, regret, remember, stop, try*.

Some verbs can be followed by either *-ing* or infinitive with very little or no change in meaning.
*Lizze **likes reading** business economics books.*
*Lizzie **likes to read** business economics books.*
Common verbs which can be followed by *-ing* or infinitive with little or no change in meaning are: *begin, continue, hate, love, prefer, start*.

Practice

2 Complete the sentences with the correct form of these verbs.

ask bring borrow ~~buy~~ change inform

1 I forgot *to buy* some milk.
2 I don't remember .... any money from Mike but he says I did.
3 We regret .... you that your bank account has been closed.
4 I meant .... them if the water was safe to drink or not.
5 Did you remember .... the plans with you?
6 If we want the company to be profitable, it means .... our prices.

UNIT 6

not

Form

Negative infinitive

We form the negative infinitive by putting *not* in front of the infinitive. Note that *not* goes before *to*.
*We decided **not to go** abroad on vacation this year.*

want, would like

To make a sentence negative with *want* or *would like*, we make the main verb negative.
*She **didn't want** to visit India.*
*They **wouldn't like** to work there.*

must not* and *don't have to

The negative form of *must* is *must not* and the negative form of *have* to is *don't/doesn't have to*. (Note that in British English, the contracted form *mustn't* is commonly used in place of *must not*.)
*You **must not** travel without your passport.*
*You **don't have to** go.*

hope* and *think

The negative forms of *hope* and *think* are different. When we form a negative sentence with *hope*, we make the verb that follows negative. When we form a negative sentence with *think*, we use *don't/doesn't think*.
*I **hope he isn't** late.*
*He **doesn't think** she should travel alone.*

let's

To form the negative of *let's*, we use *let's not*.
***Let's not** go on vacation this year.*

Use

Negative infinitive

We often use the negative infinitive to give advice or orders about what **not** to do.
*It would be better for you **not to meet** him tomorrow.*

want, would like

We use *don't/doesn't want* and *wouldn't like* to talk about a wish not to do something in the future.
*I **don't want** to go.* (Not *I ~~want not~~ to go.*)
*I **wouldn't like** to read that book again.*

must not and *don't have to*

We use ***must not*** to say that it is important not to do something.
*You **must not** forget to apply for your visa.* (= It's important that you not forget.)

We use *don't/doesn't have to* to show that something is not important or essential.
*He **doesn't have to** get a new passport before he goes.*

hope and *think*

*I **hope** my vacation **won't be** a disappointment.* (not *I ~~don't hope~~…*)
*I **don't think** her hotel **will be** cheap.* (not *I think her hotel ~~won't be~~ cheap.*)

let's

We use *let's not* + base form when we want to make a negative suggestion: ***Let's not** go out.*

Practice

1 Complete the sentences using *not* and the correct form of the verb. Use contractions where possible.

1 He told me *not to spend* (spend) too much.
2 Bo ________ (want) to go to the museum.
3 Let's ________ (tell) Ping about it—it will upset him.
4 Orel asked me ________ (book) the flights.
5 We ________ (think) the airplane will take off on time.
6 We decided ________ (stop) off in Managua on the way.

Negative and tag questions

Form

Open questions (no confirmation of opinion demanded)

We form open questions using an auxiliary verb (like *do, have*) and inverting the subject and verb.
***Do you enjoy** traveling by train?*
***Has he played** tennis before?*

Negative questions

We form negative questions using the negative form of the verb. We usually use the contracted form.
***Don't you enjoy** traveling by train?*
***Hasn't he played** tennis before?*

Tag questions

To form tag questions, we use the auxiliary of the verb in the main sentence. When the main verb in the sentence is affirmative, the tag question is negative:
*They were at the party, **weren't they**?*
When the main verb in the sentence is negative, the tag question is affirmative:
***He didn't** stay late, **did he**?*

When you write tag questions, put a comma between the main sentence and the tag.

Note that when the subject is a pronoun, we repeat it in the tag question. When the subject is a noun, we use an appropriate pronoun in the tag question.
***It**'s very interesting, isn't **it**?*
***Mike** travels to South Africa every year, doesn't **he**?*

Tense	Positive-negative	Negative-positive
to be (am, is, are, was, were)	***It's** a long way, **isn't it**?* ***I was** bad, **wasn't I**?*	***It isn't** a long way, **is it**?* ***I wasn't** bad, **was I**?*
Simple present (*do*/*does*)	***She works** there, **doesn't she**?*	***She doesn't work** there, **does she**?*
Present continuous (*am, is, are*)	***They're arriving** soon, **aren't they**?*	***They aren't arriving** soon, **are they**?*
Simple past (*did*)	***She went** there, **didn't she**?*	***She didn't go** there, **did she**?*
Past continuous (*was, were*)	***They were eating, weren't they**?*	***They weren't eating, were they**?*
Present perfect and present perfect continuous (*has, have*)	***You've been** here before, **haven't you**?* ***They've been studying** late, **haven't they**?*	***You haven't been** here before, **have you**?* ***They haven't been studying** late, **have they**?*
Past perfect (*had*)	***They'd gone, hadn't they**?*	***They hadn't gone, had they**?*
will	***You'll do** it, **won't you**?*	***You won't do** it, **will you**?*
Modals (*must, should, can, would*)	***I can go, can't I**?* ***He should** know, **shouldn't he**?*	***I can't** go, **can I**?* ***He shouldn't** know, **should he**?*

Use

Open questions

We use open questions when we don't know what the answer will be or when we don't expect a particular answer.
Are you going on vacation this year? (Possible answers: *Yes, I am. No, I'm not. Well, maybe. I don't think so.*)
Did he tell you where he was going? (Possible answers: *Yes, he did. No, he didn't. I can't remember.*)

Negative questions

We use negative questions to check information that is probably true. We answer with *yes* or *no*.
***Don't** you always visit your parents on Sunday? Yes, I do.*
***Wouldn't** you prefer to stay in a hotel? No, I wouldn't.*

We also use negative questions.

- to show surprise. *Don't you enjoy eating out?*
- to make a suggestion. *Don't you need to go now?*
- to request something, especially when we expect a negative answer. *Can't I have a different room?*

Tag questions

We use tag questions to ask for information, or to check and confirm information.
*We're meeting at two o'clock, **aren't we**?*

Practice

2 Complete the negative and tag questions.

1 *Don't* you want to stay here? It's nice.
2 India is a very diverse country, *isn't it* ?
3 Ana didn't go out, ________ ?
4 ________ you booked the flights yet? I thought I asked you to last week.
5 The group won't be taking a train to Cuzco, ________ ?
6 They wouldn't be much use, ________ ?
7 ________ he pay for his hotel before he arrived?
8 ________ she like to go somewhere else for a change?

UNIT 7

Mixed conditional sentences

Form

	If-clause	Main clause
First conditional	*If* + simple present	*will* + base form
	***If** it **rains**, the drought **will end**.*	
Second conditional	*If* + simple past	*would/could/might* + base form
	***If** we **recycled**, we **could reduce** our trash.*	
Third conditional	*If* + past perfect	*would/could/might have* + past participle
	***If** they **had saved** more water, there **wouldn't have been** a drought.*	
Mixed second and third conditional	*If* + simple past	*would have* + past participle
	***If** the policy **worked**, the government **wouldn't have needed** extra food.*	
Mixed third and second conditionals	*If* + past perfect	*would/could/might* + base form
	***If** the water **hadn't been stored**, there **wouldn't be** a harvest this year.*	

Remember, we can use *if* in two positions:

- *If*-clause first: *If we use less water, we should be able to provide enough for the whole population.*
- Main clause first: *We should be able to provide enough water for the whole population if we use less water.*

When the *if*-clause is at the beginning of the sentence, we use a comma to separate it from the main clause.

Use

First conditional

We use the first conditional to talk about a possible future action or situation. We can also use it to talk about things that are generally true.
*If they **pollute** the water, we **won't be able** to drink it.* (It's possible that they will pollute the water in the future. Then we won't be able to drink the water.)

Second conditional

We use the second conditional to talk about hypothetical situations in the present or future.
*If they **changed** their environmental views, perhaps they **would get** the contract.* (This is a possible situation in the future.)
Note that when we use the simple past with *if*, it refers to the present or future. It does not refer to the past.
We can also use *could* and *might* instead of *would* in the main clause.
*If they **changed** their environmental views, they **might/could get** the contract.*
*Fossil fuels **might not** run out if people conserved more.*

Third conditional

We use the third conditional to talk about imagined past situations or events that did not happen and their hypothetical consequences.
*If they **had built** the dam, those villages **wouldn't have flooded**.* (But they didn't build the dam and the villages were flooded.)

We can use *could/might (not) have* to speculate on a possible consequence of the imagined past situation.
*If they had built the dam, those villages **might not** have flooded.* (They did not build the dam; it's possible that the villages wouldn't have been flooded but we are not certain.)

Mixed conditionals

We use mixed conditionals to talk about unreal situations when the *if* clause and the main clause don't refer to the same time.

We use mixed second and third conditionals to talk about an imagined situation in the present or future with the hypothetical past result or consequence.
*If the pro-forest organization **didn't exist**, more of the Amazon forests **would have disappeared**.* (But the organization does exist, and so more of the Amazon forests didn't disappear.)

We use mixed third and second conditionals to talk about an imagined situation or action in the past, with the imagined consequence in the present or future.
*If the activists **hadn't intervened**, the Amazon **would be** much smaller now.* (But the activists did intervene, so the Amazon is bigger than it would have been without their help.)

Practice

1 Complete the sentences. Use mixed conditionals.

1 Rafa didn't say anything at the summit meeting because he didn't know anything.
If Rafa *had known* (know) anything, he *would have said* (say) something.
2 They didn't dam the river because people protested about it.
If people ________ (not protest) about it, the river ________ (be) dammed today.
3 The job required environmental knowledge. Katrin doesn't know about the environment, so she didn't apply.
Katrin ________ (apply) for the job if she ________ (know) about the environment.
4 They need people with experience in conservation, but I don't have any.
If I ________ (have), I ________ (join).
5 I worked hard on the mining project, so I felt I needed a rest that weekend.
If I ________ (not work) so hard on the project, I ________ (be) tired that weekend.
6 You were writing reports last week. You're feeling very tired today.
If you ________ (not write) so many reports, you ________ (not feel) so tired today.

wish, would rather, and *if only*

Form

***wish / if only* + noun/pronoun + simple past**
*I wish / If only I **knew** more about the plan.*

***wish / if only* + noun/pronoun + past perfect**
*I wish / If only he **hadn't signed** the contract.*

***wish / if only* + noun/pronoun + *would* + base form**
*I wish / If only they **would approve** the plan.*

***would rather* + base form**
*They **would rather save** the rain forest than mine for oil.*

***would rather* + object + simple past**
*The company **would rather you proposed** a more energy efficient solution.*

Note that when we use the verb *to be*, we use *was* in everyday speech; we use *were* in formal speech and writing, for example:

- Informal spoken: *I wish I was on vacation.*
- Formal spoken/written: *I wish I were on vacation.*

Use

We use *wish* and *if only* to talk about regrets and to describe an imaginary situation which is the opposite of the real situation.

- To express a wish about a present situation, we use *wish / if only* + simple past.
I wish I knew the answer. (But I don't.)
- To express a wish about a past situation, we use *wish / if only* + past perfect.
I wish I'd bought a smaller car. (But I didn't.)
- To express a wish for someone to do something differently in the present or future, we use *wish / if only* + noun/pronoun + *would* + base form.
I wish you would be more environmentally friendly. (You won't be more environmentally friendly, but I want you to be.)
Notice that you can't use the same subject in both clauses with *would*. You can't say: *I wish I would be more environmentally friendly.*

We use *would rather* + base form to talk about preferences.
*I **would rather use** my car less.*

When we use *would rather*, we can also include *than* + an alternative.
*I'd rather use my car less **than** spend more on gas.*

We use *would rather* + object + simple past to state what we would prefer someone else to do.
***I'd rather you used** energy-saving lightbulbs.*

Practice

2 Complete the sentence using the correct conditional form of the verbs.

1 If only there *were* (be) a way to stop people from using fossil fuels, but there isn't.
2 I wish they ________ (stop) using pesticides on crops, but they won't.
3 If only the river ________ (not flood) their village, things would be OK now.
4 I wish they ________ (understand) how to protect their environment, but they don't.
5 If only people ________ (consider) the consequences before cutting down the forest, but they didn't.
6 I wish there ________ (not be) a nuclear power station here, but there is.
7 I wish they ________ (leave) the downtown area alone, but they didn't.

UNIT 8

Reporting verbs

Form

Reporting verbs use different patterns.

verb + base form
She ***promised to investigate*** *the story.*
Reporting verbs with this pattern include: *agree, offer, promise, refuse, threaten.*

verb + someone + base form
He ***asked the photographer to send*** *the files.*
Reporting verbs with this pattern include: *advise, ask, convince, encourage, invite, persuade, remind, tell, urge, warn.*

verb + *-ing*
He ***admitted faking*** *the document.*
Reporting verbs with this pattern include: *advise, admit, deny, mention, propose, recommend, suggest.*

verb + preposition + *-ing*
He ***complained about working*** *long hours.*
Reporting verbs with this pattern include: *apologize (for), complain (about), insist (on), object (to).*

verb + someone + preposition + *-ing*
The editor ***blamed him for not checking*** *his facts.*
Reporting verbs with this pattern include: *accuse (+ of), blame (+ for), compliment (+ on), congratulate (+ on), criticize (+ for), forgive (+ for), thank (+ for), warn (+ about).*

Other common verb patterns are:
verb + someone + *that*
He ***warned us that*** *the journey would be difficult.*
Reporting verbs with this pattern include: *advise, persuade, tell, warn.*

verb + *that*
We ***agreed that*** *she was the best candidate.*
Reporting verbs with this pattern include: *admit, agree, explain, deny, know, realize, say, think, warn.*

Use

Say, tell, think, and *ask* are the most common reporting verbs, but we often use others to report what people said. When we decide what reporting verb to use, we think about the function or the purpose of the speaker's words.
"Remember to download your photos." = **remind** *(He reminded me to download my photos.)*
"I'll sign up later." = **promise** *(She promised to sign up later.)*

Practice

1 Report the statements using these verbs. You may need to use a preposition after the verb.

admit apologize complain invite offer tell thank urge

1 I really think you should go to the meeting.
Ki *urged me to go to the meeting.*
2 It was me that informed the press.
Rebecca ....
3 I'm really grateful that you read my article.
Fatima ....
4 I really dislike having to write business reports.
Leo ....
5 I'm sorry, but I made a mistake.
Clara ....
6 Please come to my house tomorrow.
Ji-hu ....
7 I'll give you a ride to the press conference.
Jaime ....
8 Don't send that email.
Aisha ....

Passive reporting verbs

Form

Passive reporting verbs are formed with *It* + *be* + past participle of reporting verb + *that* + clause.

When we report ideas in the present, we use the verb *be* in the simple present.
It ***is*** *believed that…*

For a present report of a present event, we use the simple present in the *that*-clause.
It is said that people ***are*** *less happy nowadays.*

For a present report of a past event, we use the simple past in the *that*-clause.
It is believed that they ***lived*** *unknown to the outside world for over 200 years.*

For a present report of a future event, we use *will* + base form in the *that*-clause.
It is understood that reporters ***will leave*** *them alone.*

When we report ideas in the past, we use the verb *be* in the simple past.
It ***was*** *believed that…*
It ***was*** *reported that…*

For a report and event at the same time in the past, we use the simple past in the *that*-clause.
It was claimed that the break-in ***happened*** *that morning.*

For a report in the past of an event that happened before the report, we use the past perfect in the *that*-clause.
It was believed that the break-in ***had happened*** *earlier.*

For a past report of a future event, we use *would* + base form in the *that*-clause.
It was understood that the survivors ***would go*** *straight to the hospital when they returned.*

Use

We use passive reporting structures to talk about events when the speaker is unknown or unimportant, or when someone wishes to remain anonymous. We can report ideas in the present or in the past.
It ***is*** *said that people consume on average 50 times more sugar than they did ten years ago.*
It ***is*** *believed that tickets will be available soon.*
It ***was*** *reported that there had been violence.*
It ***was*** *thought that there wouldn't be enough money.*

For passive reporting, we use verbs such as *believed, claimed, considered, estimated, expected, known, reported, said, suggested* , *thought*, and *understood*.

Practice

2 Write sentences using the prompts.

1 Present report about a present event: report / story / not be / true
It is reported that the story is not true.

2 Present report about a past event: understand / those people / live / there / for twenty years
....

3 Present report about a future event: suggest / people / travel / to Mars / next year
....

4 Past report about a past event: think / women / be / less intelligent
....

5 Past report about a distant past event: said / men / not see / the Arctic ice / then
....

6 Past report of a future event: not believe / newspapers / become / so powerful
....

UNIT 9

Articles: *the* or no article?

Form

Definite article *the*:
Armstrong walked on ***the*** *Moon.*

No article:
He was a hero to ***millions****.*

Use

We use *the* + singular count noun, plural count noun or noncount noun:

- to refer back to the same thing or person. *I applied for a job. It was* ***the*** *perfect job for me.*
- when there is only one. *He was the youngest person to cross* ***the*** *Atlantic Ocean by boat.*
- before a superlative adjective: *That was* ***the*** *most terrifying experience I've ever had!*
- to talk about a specific thing or things, person or people.
Did you see ***the*** *space shuttle landing earlier?*
I have a lot of admiration for ***the*** *relief workers there.*
- to talk about professional groups. *He worked in* ***the*** *navy for many years.*
- with certain countries, place names, geographical regions, oceans and seas, deserts, mountain ranges and rivers, for example: *the USA, the UK, the Republic of China, the Philippines, the United Arab Emirates, the Great Wall, the White House, the Middle East, the Antarctic, the Pacific, the Indian Ocean, the Atacama Desert, the Andes, the Himalayas, the Amazon.*

We use no article + plural count and noncount nouns:

- to talk in general about things or people. *Do you use computers in your job? I don't like potatoes.*
- before certain familiar places (*work, home, college, school*). *What time do you go to work?*
- before most cities, countries, continents, lakes, mountains, languages, and names of people. *Have you ever been to* ***Beijing****? She lives in* ***Bolivia****. He worked in* ***India*** *for many years.* Other examples are: *New York, Lima, Argentina, China, Asia, South America, Lake Titicaca, Mount Everest, Mandarin, Spanish, Japanese, Christopher Columbus.*
- before certain time expressions. *I'll meet you* ***next week****. He was born in* ***1953****.*

Notice that there are exceptions, for example:
time expressions: *in* ***the*** *sixties, on* ***the*** *weekend, in* ***the*** *summer, in* ***the*** *18th century*

Practice

1 Complete the text with *the* or no article (–).

I was listening to [1] *the* news at ten o'clock [2] .... last night, when it was reported that [3] .... President of [4] .... United States was on [5] .... vacation for [6] .... two weeks. They said that he was visiting [7] .... town where he was born. Apparently he doesn't like going to [8] .... places where there are lots of people, preferring [9] .... peace and quiet. [10] .... reasons why someone in his position does this are obvious!

Relative clauses

Form

Relative pronouns introduce defining relative clauses. To give information about:

- people, we use *who* or *that*. *He's the man **who** got the job.*
- things, we use *which* or *that*. *That's the network **which** is used for public access.*
- places or times, we use *where or when*. *This is the place **where** the information is stored. It was a time **when** space was unknown.*
- possession, we use *whose*. *She's the person **whose** job was advertised.*

Reduced relative clauses

We can sometimes shorten relative clauses by omitting the relative pronoun and using a present or past participle.
If the verb in the relative clause is in the active, we use the present participle.
*People **who visit** the area have admired its lakes.*
*People **visiting** the area have admired its lakes.*

If the verb in the relative clause is in the passive, we use the past participle:
*It is a subject **which is studied** by many people.*
*It is a subject **studied** by many people.*

We can't use a reduced relative clause when the relative pronoun is the object of the relative clause.
The expedition, which I am leading, is in June.
Not: ~~The expedition leading is in June.~~

Use

We use a relative clause to give more information about a noun in the main clause of the sentence.
We use a **defining** relative clause when the extra information in the relative clause is essential for identification. The meaning in the main clause is unclear without it.
*This is the forest **where the new species was discovered**.*

We use a **non-defining** relative clause when the extra information is not essential. The meaning of the main clause is still clear. The non-defining relative clause is separated from the main clause by commas.
*Stefano Calabrio, **who is eighty-five,** still works as a mountain guide.*
The ship Arctic Krestrel*, **which was built in Glasgow,** is registered in Russia.*

The relative pronoun in a relative clause can be:

- the subject of the clause. *Explorers are people who make discoveries.*
- the object of the clause (with a noun or pronoun following it). *He's the explorer who I met in Laos.*

We can omit the relative pronoun when it is the **object** of a **defining** relative clause.
That's the explorer (who) I met in Laos.
We cannot omit the relative pronoun when it is the subject of a defining relative clause or in a non-defining relative clause.

We often use reduced relative clauses in announcements and reports.
Passengers ~~who are~~ traveling to Mumbai, please proceed to gate 25.
Due to the bomb scare, all bags ~~which were~~ left unattended were removed and destroyed.

Practice

2 Write sentences using relative clauses. Use reduced relative clauses where possible.

1 He is an explorer. He likes traveling to remote places.
He's an explorer who likes traveling to remote places.

2 This is the lake. The fish was discovered here.

....

3 Equipment is often left on Mount Everest. It is regularly removed.

....

4 That is the biologist. Her papers were lost in the storm.

....

5 Lake Titicaca is very large. It is on the border of Bolivia and Peru.

....

6 GreenSpace created the prototype. The prototype was copied by a rival company.

....

UNIT 10

Simple present, present continuous, and *will* for repeated actions

Form

Simple present

Adverbs of frequency come before the main verb with the simple present, but after the verb *be*.
*We **always have** a family celebration at Thanksgiving.*
*He's **usually** on time for his extra class.*

Present continuous with *always*

Always comes between the verb *be* and the *-ing* form of the verb.
*They're **always** criticizing their children.*

will

*Children **will** naturally choose to play rather than study.*

Use

We use the simple present for repeated actions (often with adverbs of frequency) or to talk about a simple fact or general truth.

*He **listens** to the radio news every morning.*
*Water **freezes** at 32° Fahrenheit.*

We use the present continuous with *always* to talk about a habit which we find annoying or which we wish to criticize.

*I try to avoid Zhang at work. He **is always talking** about his children's achievements.*
*She**'s always complaining** about work.*

We use *will* to talk about typical behavior.

*Westerners **will** often avoid unfamiliar food.*

Practice

1 Write sentences using the prompts. Use the simple present (SP), present continuous (PC) with *always*, and *will* (W).

1 (SP) Mary / read / detective novels
Mary always reads detective novels.
2 (W) Cats don't like swimming. They / do / anything to avoid getting wet
....
3 (SP) James / ride/ his bike everywhere
....
4 (PC) Ria / talk / with / her mouth full
....
5 (SP) Kumar / stay / at work until 7:00 or 8:00 at night
....
6 (W) Cats / sleep / all day / rather than go out
....
7 (PC) My mom / complain / about my messes
....
8 (SP) Li Wei / get / to work early most days
....

used to, usually, be used to, and *get used to*

Form

Affirmative	Negative	Interrogative
used to + base form I/you/he/she/it/we/they **used to** live	I/you/he/she/it/we/they **didn't use to** live	**did** I/you/he/she/it/we/they **use to** live?
usually + simple present I/you/we/they **usually play**	I/you/we/they **don't usually play**	***do*** I/you/we/they ***usually*** play?
he/she/it **usually plays**	he/she/it **doesn't usually play**	**does** he/she/it ***usually*** play?

be used to + noun or *-ing* **I'm used to** playing	**I'm not used to** playing	**am I used to** playing?
you're/we're/they're used to playing	you/we/they **aren't used to** playing	**are** you/we/they **used to** playing?
he's/she's/it's used to playing	he/she/it **isn't used to** playing	**is** he/she/it **used to** playing?

be getting used to + noun or *-ing* **I'm getting used to** playing	**I'*m not getting used to*** playing	**am I getting used to** playing?
you**'re**/we**'re**/they**'re getting used to** playing	you/we/they **aren't getting used to** playing	**are** you/we/they **getting used to** playing?
he**'s**/she**'s**/it**'s getting used to** playing	he/she/it **isn't getting used to** playing	**is** he/she/it **getting used to** playing?

Use

We use *used to* (+ base form) to talk about past habits, situations, and states.

*I **used to go** out to eat a lot when I lived in Paris.*
*She **didn't use to enjoy** opera when she was younger.*

We use *usually* + simple present to talk about present habits.

*We **usually have** dinner with my parents on Sundays.*
***Do** you **usually go** shopping on Friday nights?*

We use *be used to* to talk about familiar (and unfamiliar) habits and situations.

***Is** he **used to using** his new laptop yet?*
*He **isn't used to** his new laptop yet.*

We use *get used to* to talk about habits that are becoming familiar.

*Sara **is getting used to working** in the store now.*
*Sara **is getting used to** the store now.*

Practice

2 Choose the correct option.

1 Since his illness, he .... very healthy food.
a usually eats
b used to eat
c is getting used to eat
2 Paul has worked for a multinational company for years, so he .... now.
a usually travels
b used to travel
c is used to traveling
3 They both .... golf when they were boys.
a usually play
b used to play
c are used to playing

4 Li .... at her new college.
a usually studies
b used to study
c is getting used to studying

5 Didn't Jana .... to her co-director every day?
a usually speaks
b usually speak
c is getting used to speaking

6 Jorge .... different food since he went to Thailand last week.
a used to
b is used to trying
c didn't use to try

7 Petra's worked here for years, so she ....
a used to get up early
b is used to getting up early
c is getting used to getting up early

8 My brother .... very late on Saturday nights.
a usually stays out
b is used to staying out
c is getting used to staying out

UNIT 11

could, was able to, manage to, and *succeed in*

Form

Affirmative	Negative	Interrogative
could + infinitive base form I/you/he/she/it/we/they **could do**	I/you/he/she/it/we/they **couldn't do**	**could** I/you/he/she/it/we/they **do**?
was/were able + infinitive I/he/she/it **was able to do** you/we/they **were able to do**	I/he/she/it **wasn't able to do** you/we/they **weren't able to do**	**was** I/he/she/it **able to do**? **were** you/we/they **able to do**?
manage + infinitive I/you/he/she/it/we/they **managed to finish**	I/you/he/she/it/we/they **didn't manage to finish**	**did** I/you/he/she/it/we/they **manage to finish**?
succeed in + *-ing* I/you/he/she/it/we/they **succeeded in making**	I/you/he/she/it/we/they **didn't succeed in making**	**did** I/you/he/she/it/we/they **succeed in making**?

Use

To talk about a general ability in the past, use *could*.
*He **could swim** when he was three years old.*
*He **couldn't find** the herbal medicine he was looking for.*

We use *was / were able to, manage to* + base form and *succeed in* + *-ing* to talk about the ability (or lack of ability) to successfully complete a particular task or activity, but not to talk about general ability.
*She **was able to find** the quickest route immediately.*
*They **weren't able to finish** the journey.*
*He finally **managed to publish** his book.*
*Did she **manage to get** that scholarship in the end?*
*We **succeeded in raising** enough money for our trip.*
*Unfortunately, she **didn't succeed in getting** the job.*
We use *manage to* + base form only with people or living things.
The plant managed to grow without light.
Not: ~~The car didn't manage to accelerate.~~
We often use expressions such as *finally* and *in the end* with *manage to* and *succeed in* to emphasize that the activity was an effort.
*I **finally** managed to pass my exams.*
***In the end**, I succeeded in becoming a doctor.*

Practice

1 Look at the sentences (a and b) and choose the best option.

1a Did you manage to find out about the Mexican cure for blisters?
1b Could you find out about the Mexican cure for blisters?
2a In the past, people didn't succeed in accessing as much information about plants as they can today.
2b In the past, people weren't able to access as much information about plants as they can today.
3a A recent survey found that most people in the US weren't able to identify common plants.
3b A recent survey found that most people in the US didn't manage to identify common plants.
4a The medicine didn't always succeed in treating the illness.
4b The medicine didn't manage to treat the illness.
5a Sally didn't manage to publish her latest article. She submitted it too late.
5b Sally couldn't publish her latest article. She submitted it too late.

Future in the past

Form

***going to*: See page 159**

***about to* + base form: See page 159**

Affirmative	Negative	Interrogative
would + base form I said (that) I/you/he/she/it/we/they **would do**	I said (that) I/you/he/she/it/we/they **wouldn't do**	they asked if I/you/he/she/it/we/they **would do**
would have + past participle I/you/he/she/it/we/they **would have made**	I/you/he/she/it/we/they **wouldn't have made**	**would** I/you/he/she/it/we/they **have made?**
be supposed to + base form I/he/she/it **was supposed to finish** you/we/they **were supposed to finish**	I/he/she/it **wasn't supposed to finish** you/we/they **weren't supposed to finish**	**was** I/he/she/it **supposed to finish?** **were** you/we/they **supposed to finish?**

Use

We use *was / were going to* to talk about:

- an intention which may or may not have been fulfilled. *I **was going to call** you, but I got too busy.*
- a plan or arrangement which changed. *We **were going to meet** at 2:00 but came late.*

We use *be about to* to say that we were very close to doing something, but were prevented at the last moment.
*I **was about to leave** the house when the telephone rang.*

We use *would* to report what somebody said they would do.
*Jane said that she **would work** that evening.*
*He promised he **would send** me the report.*

We use *would have* to refer to a future action in the past which didn't happen.
*I **would have bought** it, but I didn't have enough money.*

We use *supposed to* to talk about actions which people should have done, but didn't.
*They **were supposed to get** here at eight o'clock! Where are they?*

Practice

2 Complete the second sentence so it has the same meaning as the first. Use the words in bold.

1 He planned to tell you, but he didn't see you.
going He *was going to tell* you, but he didn't see you.

2 "I'll work harder next week."
would John said that he ________ harder next week.

3 She intended to tell you, but she forgot.
would She ________ you, but she forgot.

4 Maria was going to bring enough food for everyone! Where is it?
supposed Maria ________ enough food for everyone! Where is it?

5 They intended to start studying tomorrow, but they went out instead.
going They ________ studying tomorrow, but they went out instead.

6 He wanted to say something, but decided not to.
about He ________ something, but decided not to.

7 Why didn't you ask? She wanted to tell you.
would She ________ you if you had asked.

8 "I'll remember."
would Lin said that she ________.

UNIT 12

Focusing adverbs: *only, just, even, too, also, as well*

Form

only, just, even

Only, just, and *even* always come directly before the word they are emphasizing.
***Only/Just** Dave knows how hard they worked.*
*It is **only/just** two days since I saw him.*
*A lot of people don't **even** have any savings.*

too, also, as well

- sentence + *too*:
  We *can invest in that company* ***too**.*
- sentence + *as well*:
  *We bought a new iPad **as well**.*
- *Also* + sentence:
  ***Also**, she runs a successful accounting business.*
- *also* + main verb:
  *Most people **also** want to plan for their future.*
- be + *also*:
  *He's good at tennis. He's **also** a good badminton player.*
- auxiliary verb + *also* + main verb:
  *They are **also** going to the game.*

Use

We use focusing adverbs to emphasize a particular piece of information. Sentences which include focusing adverbs can exist without them.

Only and *just* focus on one particular thing to the exclusion of all others.

***Only/Just** she and I know her secret.*

*It's **only/just** banks that accept travelers checks.*

We use *even* to show that we think something is unusual or surprising.

*The question was so easy that **even** Bill knew the answer.*

***Even** football doesn't interest him any more.*

We use *also, as well,* and *too* to emphasize an additional piece of information in a sentence. *Also* comes before most verbs, but after the verb *to be*, or at the beginning of a sentence. *As well* and *too* come after the verb (and the object if there is one).

*He likes sports, but **also** enjoys playing chess.*

*He likes sports, but enjoys playing chess, **as well/too**.*

Practice

1 Choose the correct option.

1 I *only* / *too* heard about his financial situation yesterday.
2 Did you want to go to the bank *even* / *too*?
3 He *even* / *too* asked the accountant about it!
4 He usually works late on Thursdays *even* / *as well*.
5 They *only* / *as well* have a few thousand dollars left.
6 The money has *just* / *as well* been deposited in your account.
7 The boys *also* / *too* wanted some of the money.
8 The recession is a big problem for us *too* / *only*.

Causative *have* and *get*

Form

have/get + something + past participle

*I **had/got my car repaired** last week.*

have + someone + base form

*I **had a gardener help** me with the garden.*

get + someone + infinitive

*I **got a gardener to help** me with the garden.*

Use

We use *have/get something done* to explain that we asked someone to do something for us but we don't say who. We often pay for the work.

*She **has her house cleaned** by a cleaning company.*

*We **get our car serviced** every six months at the local auto shop.*

We use *have someone do / get someone to do* to explain that you have asked someone to do something for you. With these expressions, we say who does the job. Notice that with *get* we use infinitive. With *have* we use the base form.

*I **have a gardener mow** the lawn.*

*I **get a window cleaner to clean** the windows.*

Practice

2 Write sentences using the prompts. Use causative forms.

1 I / get / hair cut / yesterday
I got my hair cut yesterday.

2 I / have / accountant / go over / my accounts / on Saturday
....

3 We / get / mortgage rate / fix / last week
....

4 She / get / neighbor / pay for / new fence / this afternoon
....

5 He / get / friend / open / an account / last summer
....

6 She / have / new credit card / send out / this morning
....

Unit 1

1

It's known that animals often cooperate in their own social groups, helping each other to hunt or raise their young. Some highly intelligent animals, like elephants, go even further than this, and help other animals who are not in their own family group. But cooperation between animals of different species is unusual, so that's why the story of Suriya, the orangutan, has attracted a lot of interest.

Suriya lives with his keepers at the Institute of Greatly Endangered and Rare Species in Myrtle Beach, South Carolina, which is a kind of sanctuary for rare animals. Recently this orangutan has made an unlikely friend in a local hound dog. Now most dogs avoid apes because they are scared of them basically, but these two have formed a strong bond.

Each day the dog comes into the compound and searches out Suriya. When he finds him, they carry on like long-lost friends, wrestling and hugging and playing together. They've been doing this every day since they first met, and their friendship has attracted the curiosity of millions of viewers on the National Geographic Channel. The founder of the institute, Dr. Antle explains: "It's clear they are having the time of their life. What is more striking is that Suriya has also understood that the hound dog is very hungry, so he regularly shares his monkey biscuits with him. Orangutans are very generous creatures. If you give one a piece of candy, often they will break it in half and hand one piece back to you."

So how does he explain the fact that their relationship has a lot of the characteristics of what we call friendship? Antle says that the two animals are fulfilling a basic social need in each other that perhaps we don't normally associate with animals. "It's a relationship with attributes of fun and interaction that they are not getting from anyone else."

2

G = Greta; T = Tan

G: Tan, hello! Imagine bumping into you here! How are you?
T: Greta! Wow, what a surprise! Hi!
G: It's been a long time. What have you been up to?
T: I know. It's been way too long. Umm, I've been working abroad for the last eighteen months.
G: Anywhere exciting?
T: Yes, in India, actually. I had a contract with the consulate to do teacher training.
G: Well, it obviously suits you: you're looking very tanned and relaxed.
T: Oh, thanks, it's been a lot of fun. And you? You're looking well too. How are things?
G: Oh, you know, busy as ever. I've been completely swamped with work the last few months, trying to get my online shoe store off the ground.
T: Is it going OK?
G: Well, you know. It has its ups and downs. But we're getting there.
T: And what about Amanda? Do you see much of her?
G: Yeah, we still get together now and then. She was asking about you the other day, actually.
T: Oh. Well, I probably won't have time to look her up this time. I'm only back for a week. But do tell her I said hi.
G: I will.
T: And the next time I'm back, maybe we can all meet and catch up.
G: Yeah, that'd be great. How long will you be gone for?
T: I've just got to do another two months over there. Then I'll be back in the US for a while, I hope.
G: OK. Well, give me a call when you're back. You've got my number, don't you?
T: Yes, if it's still the same one.
G: Yeah, it is. I'll look forward to that. Is Shan going out there with you?
T: She has been with me, but uh, she's not coming this time.
G: Oh. Well, say hello to her from me. Look, I don't mean to be rude, but I need to get back to work—but it was really nice seeing you. Hope the trip goes well.
T: Thanks. Yeah, I've got to run too. Anyway, great to see you too, Greta. Take care… and see you soon. Good luck with the business.

3

1 Imagine bumping into you here.
2 I had a contract with the consulate.
3 Is it going OK?
4 Do you see much of her?
5 We still get together now and then.
6 I'm only back for a week.

Unit 2

4

P = Presenter; M = Mark Mowlam

P: Take a best-selling book, a great storyline and a great cast, add an experienced director and a large budget and what do you get? A box office success, you would think. Think again. There's no guarantee that a book that has enjoyed great success will make a good movie. Some movie adaptations have worked, others have flopped. So what's the secret? That was the question I put earlier to film critic Mark Mowlam, who's followed the progress of many book-to-film adaptations in his time and has recently reported on the making of Tolkien's *The Hobbit*.

M: Well, the goal is really to make a good movie that remains true to the spirit of the book. There are many examples of adaptations which have failed because they tried to remain too faithful to the plot and the characters of the book. Probably because at the time, the producers worried that they'd alienate loyal readers if they departed too much from the original text. But in fact, that's a mistake: what works well on the page doesn't necessarily work well on the screen; you have to give the screenwriter freedom to create a script that flows, even if that means changing the original. So what we find is a lot of good films—*Sense and Sensibility*, *The Shining*, for example—that are completely unlike the original book. And readers are generally OK about this because they think of books and movies as two separate works of art. But there are movies that have managed to stay true to the book and still be good. What they've done—a little like in cooking, I suppose—is to put in all the book's good ingredients and then boil them down to a concentrated mixture that's packed with the flavor of the original work. Probably the best example of this is *The Lord of the Rings* trilogy by Peter Jackson. The central theme of the book—which is a struggle between the forces of good and evil—perhaps wasn't so difficult to portray, but J.R.R. Tolkien created a very original other world and reproducing that was a much more difficult task, because each reader has his or her own very distinct idea of what this world was like. I think Jackson did a fantastic job, using the spectacular scenery of New Zealand for the film's location. The other thing about the *The Lord of the Rings* is that it's a very substantial work—three books, each containing over twenty long chapters—so Jackson had to leave some elements of the story out. To compensate for this, he took the most important scenes and then put all the emotional force behind them. The result is that it has become one of the most successful movies of all time, a blockbuster that has grossed almost $3 billion.

5

1 I haven't been to India.
2 It isn't far.
3 You aren't allowed.
4 It doesn't matter.
5 I hadn't noticed.
6 They weren't late.
7 She hasn't called.
8 We didn't care.

6

Conversation 1

A: The bus broke down on the highway, so we were all left stranded until help could arrive.
B: What did you do?
A: Luckily another bus came within about 15 minutes and we all transferred to that one.
B: That must have been a relief.

Conversation 2

A: My pants got caught on the door handle and as I walked away, they tore.
B: Oh, that's awful.
A: Yes, I had to walk right across the restaurant back to our table with my hands over the hole.
B: How embarrassing!

Conversation 3

A: I bent the key trying to force it into the lock and when I tried to straighten it, it snapped.
B: How did you get in?
A: I went to the neighbors', but they weren't at home, so I just had to wait 'til someone came home.
B: Yeah, something like that happened to me once.

Conversation 4

A: The elevator got stuck between floors twenty-five stories up, and two of the occupants were completely panic-stricken.
B: What a nightmare!
A: It was. Then the lights went off and one of them started screaming.
B: Yeah, I think I would have done the same thing.

Conversation 5

A: The tires on my bicycle were badly worn and when I hit a bump in the road, one of them burst.
B: Poor you!
A: Well, I fell off and cut my hand. Thank goodness there were no cars behind me.
B: That was lucky.

Conversation 6

A: My computer froze while I was working.
B: Really? How strange!
A: Yeah, I thought I'd lost about four hours' work, but I when I rebooted the computer, I searched for some of the key words in my document and found a temporary file which had most of the document in it.
B: That was good thinking.

7

That must have been a relief.

So what did you do?

8

1 What a nightmare!
2 Oh, that's awful.
3 How embarrassing!
4 Really? That's odd.
5 That was good thinking.
6 Something like that happened to me.

Unit 3

9

Hello everyone… one moment, I'll just adjust my microphone… OK, that's better. I can see a lot of hopeful-looking faces out there. I'm speaking to a government committee tomorrow and I hope they look as bright-eyed as you do… Let me just say that I'm afraid that those of you who have come looking for immediate answers to overpopulation are going to be disappointed, but I hope I can at least give you some cause for optimism. I'm not going to speak for too long because I'd like to hear what you have to say too, but let me tell you first how I see the situation…

In 1798, an English economist, Thomas Malthus, claimed that the population always grows faster than the food supply until war, disease, or famine arrive to reduce the number of people. A century and a half later in 1968, Paul Ehrlich wrote in his book *The Population Bomb* that medical science was keeping too many people alive and that we had failed to control the birth rate. He predicted that as a result hundreds of millions of people would soon starve to death.

But his bomb was a dud. Yes, medical science has extended life expectancy and the population carries on growing: around 7 billion today and it will probably peak at around 9 billion by 2050. But mass starvation? It hasn't happened. Why? Because science stepped in with better seeds and better pesticides to boost food production, and it's about to step in again with nanotechnology, which will help us to engineer safer and cheaper foods.

So what about overpopulation? Let me give you a fact: if in 2045 there are 9 billion people in the world, the population density will still be only half that of France today. And no one complains about overcrowding there: France is the world's favorite vacation destination! Some of the new megacities of Asia might not be such pleasant places to live… But the problem is not just the number of people. The problem is how people consume resources.

By 2030, more than a billion people in the developing world will belong to the "global middle class." That's a good thing, but it will be a bad thing for the planet if those people start eating meat and driving big cars every day. Some ultracautious people say we should bring in wartime emergency measures to conserve resources. I don't think that's the answer, but then I'm a scientist at heart even if I'm semi-retired now. For me the answer lies in innovations like biofuels and other alternative energy sources.

I'll talk about these specific solutions in the second part of my talk, but let's just go back to Malthus for a moment. People, he argued, are basically lazy. They won't do anything unless they are forced to by necessity. But what he didn't take into account is that faced with disaster, people are not lazy. Mankind and science will rise to the challenge—that is my sincere belief.

10

B = Ben; S = Sophie

B: Can you give me a hand? I'm having trouble printing this map.
S: Hang on, I'm just finishing a letter. I'll be with you in a second… OK. What do you want to do exactly?
B: I'm just giving directions to some friends who are staying in our house next week. I'm trying to paste this map into a Word document.
S: Are you going to email it to them? Because if so, you could just email them the link to the map.
B: No, I'm going to print it out and give it to them when they get here, because we're going away… The trouble is, it won't allow me to copy it.
S: Let me take a look. Oh, I see.. It's a Google map; you can't select and copy them, I'm afraid.
B: Oh… what should I do then?
S: Well, there are two possibilities. You can either take a screen shot or…
B: What does that involve?
S: Here I'll show you. Just press alt print screen like this, then open a new Word document and paste it in. That should do the trick.
B: Oh, I see, but it came out very small. That's going to be too hard for them to read. What else do you suggest?
S: Have you tried looking for a different map? If you do a search, you might find one that you can copy.
B: OK. I'll give that a try. Thanks.
S: Feel free to ask me again if that doesn't work.

11

What do you suggest?

What does that involve?

It won't allow me to copy it.

First select the picture,…

What are you trying to achieve?

What solution do you propose?

Did you attach the document?

Unit 4

12

"Nature has done everything for Sydney, man nothing; man has done everything for Melbourne, nature nothing," a visitor to Australia once noted. Herein lies the essential difference between Australia's two largest cities. Melbourne is Australia's second city, but it has plenty of first-class qualities, from a buzzing art scene to an enormous range of restaurants. It may have a few gray days, and a muddy river instead of a beautiful harbor, but don't let that worry you. The lack of natural attractions has meant that Melbourne has had to create its own man-made pleasures, and in doing so it has become Australia's cultural capital. Theater, music, street sculpture, fashion—in fact, there are hardly any forms of artistic expression which you can't find here. All thrive, alongside a cosmopolitan mix of cafés, restaurants, and bars.

What's great about Melbourne for the visitor is how accessible all these arts are. In addition to traditional museums and galleries like the National Gallery of Victoria and concert halls like Hamer Hall, there is an enormous number of smaller art spaces and venues which cater to every kind of taste. Art is not something for a small minority. In fact, for most inhabitants of Melbourne a weekly visit to the movie theater or an art exhibition is a routine event. Several festivals take place during the winter months, including the International Film Festival in July and the Fringe Festival in September, which has loads of interesting (even if not always good!) comedy, dance, and theater acts.

If the locals appreciate their art, they absolutely love their sport. Lots of people around the world will know the Australian Formula One Grand Prix and the Australian Open Tennis, which attracts over half a million spectators to Melbourne in a carnival atmosphere, but few people will be familiar with the sports Melburnians themselves follow. Australian Rules football and cricket enjoy a huge amount of support and, if you have enough time, a visit to see either is well worth it just for the atmosphere. If you're looking to participate rather than just watch, why not try some surfing or swimming? Biking, jogging, or a visit to one of Melbourne's many gyms are other possibilities. All this information is on our website…

13

a huge amount of support

a huge number of galleries

a lack of natural attractions

a lot of information

lots of people

14

I = Interviewer; W = Walid

I: OK, Walid, I'm going to fire some statements at you about what various people say art should be, and I want to know which of these you agree with. OK?

W: Uh, OK, but I'm already a little suspicious, because I don't really think that "should" has a lot to do with it. People have a very fixed idea about what art "should" be—a certain kind of portrait or landscape, very often—but, anyway, anyway, I'll play the game, so… let's hear what they say…

I: Good, here's the first one then: *Art should be pleasing for the viewer.*

W: Mmm, no, not necessarily—the artist's intention might be to make you feel uncomfortable, not to give you a warm feeling.

I: OK. What about this, then? *Art should involve effort on the part of the artist.*

W: Well, that's more interesting, but still the answer is "not necessarily." Monet did some of his paintings in five minutes.

I: Did he? I didn't know that. That's amazing! Well, that ties in with the next one, perhaps. *Art should involve technical skill.*

W: Um, I can think of quite a lot of examples of successful art that wasn't technically difficult, but was just based on a clever idea.

I: OK, *Art should have a social message or make a political point*.

W: No, certainly not. Is the Mona Lisa political? I don't think so. Look, an artist's role is simply to present an idea in a visual form. The viewer's role is to give that effort their time and attention and then say either "Yes, I really like that," or "That moves me," or "No, I'm afraid that doesn't do anything for me."

15

J = Jae; T = Tomas

J: Hey, Tomas, how was *The Lion King*?

T: I loved it, even though I'm not generally a fan of musicals.

J: No, me neither. I never feel particularly inspired by the music in them, which should really be the whole point of them, with a few exceptions maybe—like *West Side Story* or *Grease*, which have terrific music. So what was so good about it?

T: Well, visually it's absolutely stunning, the opening scene in particular. All the animals—giraffes, wildebeest, zebra, antelope—congregate on the stage to set the scene, which is the plains of the Serengeti where the story takes place. And they're in these fabulous costumes. They're difficult to describe, but the effect is that they actually seem to move like real animals. Everyone in the audience was spellbound.

J: But is the story the same as in the Disney movie? I remember there were a couple of pretty annoying characters in the movie, like that bird who's supposed to be there for comic effect—well at least I think it is—but after a while, really begins to annoy you.

T: You mean Zazu. Yeah, I know what you mean about that kind of Disney character. They can get on your nerves, but this production's different. It actually seems much more adult than the movie. It's very well done. I found the story really moving.

J: What about the music?

T: It's essentially the same score as the film—I think Elton John wrote most of it, but it's all based on African rhythms and vocals.

J: Doesn't really sound like my kind of thing.

T: Oh, well, I'm really into Elton John. I think he catches the mood of this really well. Have you heard *Circle of Life*?

J: Uh, no, I don't think so.

T: Well, I'm not going to sing it. Anyway, I really recommend it. It's not cheap to go, but if you get a chance you should. I can't stand the high prices they charge for musicals these days, but actually I didn't mind for this one. It was worth it.

Unit 5

16

I = Interviewer; J = Journalist

I: I know you like exotic places. Have you tried visiting India?

J: I was just there actually, in Kerala, in the southwest. I was meaning to go on to tour other parts of India, but Kerala was so fascinating I stayed longer.

I: Were you on vacation?

J: No. Well, it was meant to be a vacation, but it actually turned into more than that.

I: Oh dear…

J: Oh, no! I don't regret changing my plans! I became so interested in the place that I started to write an article about it for the newspaper I work for.

I: Really? Is it a travel article?

J: Not really. It's more sociological, I guess. I'm trying to show what a remarkable place Kerala is in the developing world. You see, it's a small state with a big population, and the average income is only about $300 a year. Usually that would mean people having a fairly poor quality of life, but that's not the case. In fact, Kerala stands out as a kind of model of social development. The population is highly literate and well-educated and they seem very well-off, compared to other parts of India. They're healthy and live almost as long as Americans or Europeans. It seems that infant mortality is also very low. Also, women, who've, uh, traditionally been the head of the household, continue to be very active (and equal) participants in society.

I: Huh, that's really interesting. I remember going there with my wife in the 1990s. But we were just tourists and my memories of it are as a very tranquil and beautiful place, with gorgeous beaches and lagoons.

J: Well, of course that's the part of it that tourists like to spend time visiting. But tranquil is not necessarily the adjective I would use. Trivandrum, the main city where we stopped to visit an Indian journalist I know—a highly cultured man, by the way—is absolutely hectic. The people there are very politically engaged: they never stop debating. There are often strikes on the buses or parades of demonstrators. Some medical students started protesting when we were there and went on protesting for four days.

I: So why do you think it's such a successful society?

J: Well, there are essentially two reasons, I think. The first is that the Keralites are naturally tolerant people: you find Hindus, Muslims, and Christians all living peacefully beside each other, and foreigners are treated no differently than anyone else. And second, the government has invested a lot in health and education and goes on investing a lot. The land is incredibly fertile and well managed. Small farmers cultivate every inch of it so none is wasted, which I regret to say is not always the case in some developing countries.

I: Sounds fascinating. Please remember to send me a copy of the article when it's published.

J: Of course I will.

17

1 state weight
2 low though
3 head said
4 course force
5 main plane
6 stopped opt
7 none fun
8 waste faced

18

P = Patricio; A = Ana; I = Isabel

P: OK, Ana, I believe you've prepared a brief summary of the Howard Park project. [**Ana:** Yup]. Could you just take us through the main points?

A: Yes, sure. Well, the Howard Park project began two years ago. We agreed to lend the local government $750,000 to redevelop a green space in the Howard's Hill area of the city. The aim was to give the local residents a nicer park, first of all, but also some new recreation facilities: a mini-golf course, two tennis courts, a small café, and a new children's play area. The play area was in terrible condition—full of trash—so it was actually pretty dangerous. So here we are two years later, and what progress have they made? Well, they've done a good job of cleaning the area up: they've planted trees and laid new grass, so it looks much, much better. They've also built the café and the children's play area. However, they've also done some things that weren't part of the original plan. For example, they've built a fountain near the café, and six months ago they also bought a sculpture, at a cost of $80,000, to place near the fountain. Now they've run out of money and are asking for a new loan of $250,000 to complete the tennis courts and mini-golf course. What do you think?

I: If you ask me, that's completely wrong. They've been spending money on things they had no right to. I don't think we should give them another cent.

P: Well, hang on a minute. Let's not be too hasty. I agree that they should have told us about these other changes, but we need to consider whether they are in the spirit of the original aims of the project.

A: That really depends on the opinion of the local residents. The way I see it, it's probably a good thing if residents like it and it means they'll use the park more.

I: Well, I just find it arrogant of them.

P: OK, so what should we do? Personally, I don't think we should lend them any more until we know what local people think of the work they've already done.

A: Yes, I'd go along with that. We need to ask them to conduct a survey of local opinion and then show us the results.

P: Exactly. Are we all in agreement, then?

I: Yes, I guess so. Yes, that seems fair to me.

Unit 6

19

P = Presenter; K = Katie Samuel

P: Now, have you ever thought of doing a little building work during your vacation? Or helping to look after animals on a wildlife preserve? You probably thought that kind of vacation was for eighteen-year-olds in their gap year, didn't you? But it seems more and more working adults are opting for volunteer vacations With us today is Katie Samuel, author of *Good Travel*, a guide to alternative vacations. Katie, I can see that this might attract a few people, but wouldn't most people who only get a few weeks off a year prefer a more relaxing option?

K: Well, that depends very much on how your volunteer vacation is organized. The good companies in this field are certainly conscious of the fact that this should be a rewarding travel experience, not just a work trip.

P: But isn't the whole point to go and lend a hand to people in need of help? It's not really a vacation as we know it, is it?

K: Well, no, perhaps it isn't, but it is more like what real travel should be about: a cultural experience where each side gives something and takes something. A good example is a program next to Kenya's Tsavo National Park, where volunteers help local people to find ways of making a living that don't involve poaching or killing local wildlife. So they help them to plant crops, build fences, develop ideas for tourist businesses, and so on. In return, the locals take them for bush walks, which are like mini-safaris, teach them about local wildlife, talk about the history of their community.

P: But the volunteers pay for the trip, don't they?

K: Yes, of course, they have to pay for their flight, their living expenses, and something to cover the organization's costs.

P: And do you need to be qualified to volunteer? I imagine organizations don't want people turning up to teach or build or whatever who have no idea of what they're doing, do they?

K: Again, it depends. There are a few projects which are only open to people with professional experience, uh, like people with a medical background, but for the most part, volunteers can be trained to do the work. The Cultural Restoration Tourism Project (CRTP), which helps to restore cultural heritage sites around the world, gives volunteers the chance to work with local architects and artists. They have a project restoring a 300-year-old monastery in Nepal where you can get training in doing wall paintings from a world-famous painter.

P: So, you could actually come back with a skill you didn't have when you left?

K: Absolutely. It might not be a skill you'll ever use again: helping to bottle-feed milk to orphaned lion cubs—that's a project in Zambia—is unlikely to be of direct use to you back at the office, but we all benefit from new and different experiences, wouldn't you agree?

P: Yeah, I'm sure that's true. So could you tell us a bit more about…

20

Do you like visiting new places? Yes, now and then.

Don't you like visiting new places? No, not at all.

You like visiting new places, don't you? Yes, I love it.

You don't like visiting new places, do you? No, you're right. I don't.

21

1 You like the idea of volunteer vacations, don't you?
2 Don't you think it's an interesting idea?
3 You've been on a volunteer vacation, haven't you?
4 Didn't it seem strange to pay money in order to work?
5 You won't be going again this year, will you?

22

M = Manuel; P = Paul

M: Hi Paul, this is Manuel, your host. You emailed me about staying next Thursday for a couple of nights.

P: Oh hi, hi Manuel. Thanks for getting back to me. Is that still OK?

M: No, that's all fine. I just thought I'd give you a call to explain how to get here, because it's a little complicated. How are you getting to Hamilton, first of all?

P: I'm coming in by train sometime in the afternoon.

M: OK. I wanted to pick you up, but my car's in the garage that day.

P: Hey, that's nice of you, but I can find my own way.

M: OK. Well, I'm at work 'til about five thirty, so feel free to come over any time after six.

P: That sounds perfect. And how do I get to you from downtown?

M: Well, you could just catch a taxi, but it's about eleven miles from downtown, so it won't be cheap. Alternatively, you can hop on a bus to Stoney Creek. Look out for the Stoney Creek Arena on your right and get off there. It's only a twenty-minute ride. From there, Cherry Heights is another fifteen minutes on foot, straight up King St. Once you reach the crossroads at Gray Road, the easiest thing is to give me a call and I'll come out and meet you.

P: So: bus to Stoney Creek, walk up King St. to Cherry Heights and call from there?

M: Yup. Call when you get to the crossroads at Gray Road.

P: OK, got it. That sounds great. If I get held up in any way I'll let you know, but otherwise expect a call around six thirty.

M: Great. See you next Thursday then. Bye.

P: Bye.

23

I wanted to pick you up, but my car's in the garage that day.

You could just catch a taxi, but it's about eleven miles from downtown.

Unit 7

24

Speaker 1: Liam from the United Kingdom

I live in Manchester, which is probably one of the wettest places in the UK. If I had been brought up somewhere like Saharan Africa, where I had to walk miles each day just to fetch water, I'd obviously be a lot more conscious of water conservation. But I'm afraid I don't set a very good example. I probably waste a lot—leaving the tap running when I brush my teeth and so on. Clearly we're not going to run out of water in the UK, but I know water conservation is important. If we all used less water, the water companies wouldn't have to use so much energy treating water to make it clean. And of course that would be more environmentally-friendly.

Speaker 2: Gemal from the United Arab Emirates

I'm not saying the idea of desalination plants is wrong. If desalination methods didn't exist, this country would not have been able to develop in the way it has. Nowadays we use water in our homes more or less as we want to. But I don't think we can continue like this. You see, the waste from the desalination process is a kind of brine with a dangerously high salt content which will eventually destroy life in the sea. I am interested in discovering farming techniques that use salt water. There are grasses and other types of plant that can grow with sea water. If we were to use more of these, it would give our natural fresh water springs a chance to recharge.

Speaker 3: Daniel from the United States

Americans (and I'm as guilty as the rest) use water like there is no tomorrow. I think it's well-known that the Colorado River doesn't reach the sea anymore. If you had visited the area around the old delta in Mexico 100 years ago—rich wetlands, full of wildlife—you'd be shocked to see it now. It's all dried up, a kind of salt flat. The reason is agriculture. The river has been dammed and diverted in various places along its route to irrigate fields and provide enough water for people living in the desert areas of Nevada and California. Unless we change the way we think about water and stop wasting so much, the river will keep on getting smaller.

Speaker 4: Carmen from Mexico

My water needs are the same as most people's, I think: I have a small vegetable garden; I have to wash myself and my clothes. I don't have to save water, but I want to, you know. I collect rainwater for the garden, I fill a basin to wash in rather than running the tap, I wash my dishes every other day. But now governments are discussing big projects for transporting water from one part of the world to another using huge pipes and tankers. I think if more people thought and acted like me, things would not have come to this point, you know.

25

E = Elena; A = Anne; J = Jim; R = Rick

A: Elena, what do you think about all these people who say that there's no proof that climate change is man-made?

E: My position is that I don't know if climate change is man-made and I'm not sure anyone can say for sure. Let me give you an example, an analogy. Imagine you were losing your hair and I told you that some people had found that if they ate a banana every day it prevented hair loss. Even though you had no proof it worked, you would probably try eating a banana every day, wouldn't you? Well, it's the same with global warming. We don't know that we're causing it, but some people say we might be, with all the fossil fuels we burn. And I, for one, am happy to be a little more careful in how I pollute in case they're right.

A: Mmm, well, I don't accept that. I used to believe in climate change, but the last few winters here in the US have been much colder than normal. To be honest with you, I'd believe it more if I wasn't getting up in the morning and scraping ice off the inside of my windows rather than the outside.

E: Yeah, but that's not the point, Anne, is it? You know, regional temperatures may be lower, but average global temperatures keep on rising.

J: Well, look, there's no doubt that the weather's changing, but I don't believe it's a man-made problem. It's just part of a natural weather cycle. Yeah, I know you'll say "Oh, that's just your excuse to drive a big car and fly to exotic places for your vacations," but actually that's not the reason. I don't believe it simply because no scientist has successfully proved it yet.

R: We're approaching this debate all wrong by saying "it's a big environmental problem that we need to address." Because it's not just an environmental problem. It's an economic problem, a social problem, even an ethical problem. We all need to do what we can to prevent climate change.

26

I don't know and I'm not sure anyone knows for sure.

27

1 We don't know that we're causing it, but some people say we might be.
2 …scraping ice off the inside of my windows rather than the outside.
3 Regional temperatures may be lower, but average global temperatures keep on rising.
4 Because it's not just an environmental problem. It's an economic problem, a social problem, even an ethical problem.

Unit 8

28

And finally… it was thought that the Large Blue butterfly was extinct in Britain, but it seems to have made a remarkable comeback. The Large Blue, which disappeared 30 years ago, is only found in certain fields. What these fields have in common is that their grass is very short because rabbits, sheep and cows graze there. Originally it was believed that greedy butterfly hunters had killed off the Large Blue, but it is now agreed that changes in farming techniques were responsible for its decline. As a result of recent efforts to protect its natural habitat, it is estimated that around 20,000 of these beautiful creatures will be seen in the British countryside this summer.

And finally, researchers believe they may have found a cure—or at least some relief—for the common cold. In tests, it was reported that people who started taking zinc at the first signs of a common cold got well sooner. There have been many previous studies into the effectiveness of zinc but they were inconclusive. The new study, involving over 1,000 people of various ages, found that, on average, people who took zinc supplements recovered from their colds one day earlier than those who took nothing. The effectiveness of zinc in preventing a cold in the first place was less certain, although it was said that those who took it regularly suffered less serious symptoms than those who didn't.

And finally, believe it or not, eating chocolate might be good for you after all. In the past it was thought that eating candy would result in tooth decay and weight gain. But now it is claimed that a new chocolate bar, invented by the world's largest chocolate maker, can actually slow the aging process of your skin. The special chocolate contains antioxidants, which help hydrate the skin and fight wrinkles. The market for healthy foods has grown by over five percent a year in recent years and it seems now that even the sellers of traditionally unhealthy snacks are trying to get in on the act. However, doctors have warned against rushing out to buy extra chocolate—good skin and chocolate are not generally natural partners, they say.

And finally, Costa Rica today has the honor of being named the world's happiest nation. According to the latest Happy Planet Index, it is said that Costa Rica has the best balance of human well-being—that is to say, good health, a long life, low levels of poverty—and a low ecological footprint, in other words the amount of natural resources it uses. In fact, Latin American countries took nine of the top ten places, while richer, so-called developed countries, like the US at number 74, were much further down in the list.

29

J = Jess (female); P = Phil

J: Hey, Phil. Did all that noise in the street wake you up last night?
P: No, it didn't, but then I'm a deep sleeper. What happened?
J: Well, I didn't see it myself but I heard that it was an argument between two drivers and supposedly it got pretty nasty.
P: Really? Who told you about it?
J: Tara at number 42. It seems that both drivers got out of their cars and started shouting at each other. She says they almost started fighting.
P: Well, I'd take what Tara says with a grain of salt, if I were you. She tends to blow things out of proportion.
J: No, I believe her actually—people do get very frustrated not being able to pass each other in this street. Anyway, the police were called…
P: The police? It wasn't that serious, was it?
J: Well, no. The cars didn't crash or anything. But Tara says that they got out of their cars and started arguing. She figures that if the police hadn't arrived, there would have been a fight.
P: Did the cars make contact?
J: No, they were just coming in opposite directions and they met where the street gets narrow and neither one would back up to let the other pass. So they just stayed there, in the middle of the road, with neither one giving way.
P: How childish.
J: Yeah, right? Someone said they'd seen one of the drivers before. Apparently he's a local politician.
P: It wasn't Tara getting her facts mixed up again, was it?
J: No, it was Chris. I think I'd take his word for it; he's not the type to spread gossip.
P: So what did the police do about it?
J: Well, according to Chris, they took them both away for questioning.

30

apparently	generally
supposedly	happened

Unit 9

31

Q: Can you tell us something about the Emerging Explorers program?
A: It's an awards program set up by the National Geographic Society to encourage young adventurers, scientists, photographers, and storytellers to continue their work and to realize their potential. Each year, between eight and fifteen explorers whose work is really outstanding are selected and given money to help them continue their research and exploration.
Q: So Emerging Explorers are generally young people?
A: Not necessarily. Emerging Explorers are generally people who are at an early stage of their careers. What they have in common is that they are all people who are pushing the boundaries of their field, whether that's exploring undiscovered deep-water caves or watching the stars through a telescope.
Q: And how does National Geographic encourage them?
A: Well, first of all National Geographic awards each one of them $10,000, which is intended to go towards further research and exploration. Of course their profiles are also raised by the articles and news that appear in *National Geographic*. In other words, the magazine is a place where other interested people can read about their work.
Q: And what kind of fields do the winners come from?
A: We have so many different types of explorer, chosen from fields as diverse as anthropology, space exploration, mountaineering, and music.
Q: You mentioned storytellers earlier. What did you mean by that, exactly?
A: Well, there are all these people doing important work out there in the various fields that I've described. And that's great, but it's also very important that everyone hears about this work. That's the skill of the storytellers: communicating with pictures and words important facts about the planet and life on the planet in a way that grabs everyone's attention. A really good example is Alexandra Cousteau, whose father Philippe Cousteau was well-known for his documentaries about marine life. She works as a conservationist, trying to persuade people to protect scarce resources like water. Alexandra, inspired by her father's success as a storyteller, is researching ways in which the environmental community can use new media—social networks, video games—to communicate its message.

32

S = Sarah; P = Panit

S: So, you're 24 years old, you graduated a year ago, and you're looking for work with a charity. What attracted you to Shelterbox?
P: Well, I'm familiar with your work because I have a friend who volunteered for you last year packing boxes, and I think it's a fantastic concept. But, umm, mainly I'm really interested in working abroad in foreign countries.
S: Mm, I see. And what makes you think you'd be suited for that? I see you studied economics at Stanford. Don't you think that's a pretty different world?
P: Yes, it's true that I specialized in economics but, actually, I'm good at coping with difficult environments. I spent three months helping to build a school in Chennai in India last

summer. And the year before that, I trekked across the Mojave Desert. So I think I'd be well-suited for the work.

S: OK, well, they're certainly not easy places to adapt to, although in fact you'd also be spending a good part of the time here in the office doing paperwork.

P: Yeah, that's also fine. I was expecting that. I have quite a lot of experience sitting at a desk for my studies. What sort of paperwork is it?

S: Well, each trip involves a lot of preparation and a certain amount of follow-up, too. Keeping spreadsheets, writing reports. Are you OK doing that sort of thing?

P: Yeah, I'm pretty good with computers. I'm comfortable with all the usual programs—Excel, Word, some financial software…

S: OK. There's just one thing that's worrying me though. You're clearly a bright person and you have a good degree. How do I know that you won't just do this job for a few months and then go and get a better-paid job with a bank or a consulting company?

P: That's a good question. It's actually what a lot of my friends from college have done, but I'll tell you why that's not for me. First, I'm really serious about wanting to help people in need. Second, I think I need to become more knowledgeable about the world, before I use my economics degree to do something else. If you put your faith in me, I will be absolutely committed to doing the best job that I can for two or three years at least.

33

although	comfortable
environments	foreign
knowledgeable	months
specialized	suited
world	

34

clothes	February	folk	island
lengths	receipt	surface	thorough

Unit 10

35

Different people's diets rarely surprise me these days. We didn't use to think so much about what we ate. But today, well, we live in an age when people are just very conscious of their diets. A day hardly ever passes without a story in the news about a particular food that's good for your health or bad for you if you eat too much of it.

So I was very interested to read a story the other day about the diet of the Nochmani tribe of the Nicobar Islands in the Indian Ocean. People used to think that these tiny islands—which are about 600 miles from the coast of India—that they were uninhabited by humans. But in 2004, aid workers in helicopters spotted some tribespeople on a mountainside. Scientists were particularly surprised that there were inhabitants there, because people usually need mammals—you know, cows, goats and so on—and their produce—meat, milk, et cetera—in order to live. But the Nicobar Islands have almost no mammals. So what were the Nochmani surviving on? Fish, perhaps? No. Amazingly, their diet consisted largely of insects, in particular beetles, of which there were over 1,700 varieties on the islands, but also other insects including spiders.

This presented a problem for the aid workers, who'd brought with them standard survival meals, including chicken, beef, and pork. The Nochmani, who weren't used to eating meat at all, were disgusted by these offerings. All they'd take from the aid workers were sweets and cakes. It wasn't just a matter of taste, either. If you're used to a certain type of food—even insects—other types may be completely indigestible.

Insects are, in fact, very nutritious: high in protein and fat and low in carbohydrates, making them an ideal food source for humans. But what was even more amazing was that just as we usually help our animals to live by providing food for them, so the Nochmani cultivate certain fungi and mosses to attract and feed the insects they eat. Perhaps we can learn from this tribe. If more of us could get used to eating unconventional foods such as insects, it might help the world's food problems.

36

M = Marie; E = Esther

M: I know of henna painting as a custom from Indian weddings, but you came across it in Turkey, didn't you?

E: Yes, in eastern Turkey when I was traveling there. It takes place a few nights before the wedding.

M: Was it a little like a bachelorette party?

E: Well, in the sense that it marks the last evening that a bride spends with female family and friends, I suppose it is a little like that. What happens, typically, is that women from both families get together with the bride, to celebrate with music, song, and dance. But it's not just a party. It's an occasion for sadness too, because it symbolizes the end of life as a single person and the start of another stage.

37

M = Marie; E = Esther

M: So what happens exactly?

E: Well, the ceremony begins with preparation of the henna. It's traditional for this to be done by the daughter of a couple who have had a successful marriage themselves. Then, after the bride's head has been covered in a red veil, her hands and feet are decorated with henna. After that, a gold coin is put into the remaining henna. While this is happening, the guests sing, umm, separation songs—these are rather sad, as you can imagine. The party continues well into the night. Then, on the morning of the wedding, a child presents the hennaed coin to the groom as a symbol of future prosperity and good fortune.

38

M: I know of henna painting as a custom from Indian weddings, but you came across it in Turkey, didn't you?

E: Yes, in eastern Turkey when I was traveling there. It takes place a few nights before the wedding.

M: Was it a little like a bachelorette party?

E: Well, in the sense that it marks the last evening that a bride spends with female family and friends, I suppose it is a little like that. What happens, typically, is that women from both families get together with the bride, to celebrate with music, song and dance. But it's not just a party. It's an occasion for sadness too, because it symbolizes the end of life as a single person and the start of another stage.

M: So what happens exactly?

E: Well, the ceremony begins with preparation of the henna. It's traditional for this to be done by the daughter of a couple who've had a successful marriage themselves. Then, after the bride's head has been covered in a red veil, her hands and feet are decorated with henna. After that, a gold coin is put into the remaining henna. While this is happening, the guests sing, umm, separation songs—these are rather sad, as you can imagine. The party continues well into the night. Then, on the morning of the wedding, a child presents the hennaed coin to the groom as a symbol of future prosperity and good fortune.

39

custom	dress	friends
music	suppose	weddings

40

across	eastern	lose	place
rings	single	spends	surprise

Unit 11

41

Have any of these things happened to you? You were about to give a speech or make a comment at a meeting, and then your mind went blank. You were supposed to send a friend a card for his birthday, but then you forgot. You recognized someone in the street and would have spoken to her, but you didn't because you couldn't remember her name. You promised you would mail a letter for someone and two days later you found it still in your pocket. You were going to write down a great idea you had, but when you found a pen and paper, the idea had gone. I could go on, but I won't because I'm sure everyone recognizes these common failures of memory.

42

We all would like to remember more but would it actually make us any happier?

I want to tell you the story of a 41-year-old woman from California known in medical literature as AJ, who remembers almost every day of her life since the age of 11. She remembers that at 12:34 p.m. on Sunday, August 3, 1986, a young man she was attracted to called her on the telephone. She remembers that on March 28, 1992, she had lunch with her father at the Beverly Hills Hotel. It's a bit like certain smells that evoke strong memories: AJ's memory is stimulated in the most intense way by dates.

You'd think that being able to retrieve facts and knowledge in this way would make us more confident and wiser. But in fact for AJ, an incredible memory is as much a burden as it is a benefit. That's because most memories are selective: they provide us mostly important things, and mostly good things too. AJ remembers every detail, good or bad, important or not.

So when we curse our poor memories for forgetting to send a birthday card, actually we should be grateful also for all the things that our memories hide away because they don't need to be remembered or thought about. Umm, technology, of course helps us with this. We don't need to remember the precise content of a report or the exact time of a meeting, because it's stored on our computer or in our smart phone.

But interestingly, the growth of this technology—what psychologists call our external memory—is having an effect on what and how much we remember. Even our memories of happy events—like parties or vacations—get stored in photograph albums on our computers. So our internal memories are probably worse than those of people 100 years ago. Medical science is trying to address the problem of poor memory and this is what I want to talk about next.

43

Have any of these things happened to you? You were about to give a speech or make a comment at a meeting, and then your mind went blank. You were supposed to send a friend a card for his birthday, but then you forgot. You recognized someone in the street and would have spoken to her, but you didn't because you couldn't remember her name. You promised you would mail a letter for someone and two days later you found it still in your pocket. You were going to write down a great idea you had, but when you found a pen and paper, the idea had gone.

I could go on, but I won't because I'm sure everyone recognizes these common failures of memory.

We all would like to remember more but would it actually make us any happier?

I want to tell you the story of a 41-year-old woman from California known in medical literature as AJ, who remembers almost every day of her life since the age of 11. She remembers that at 12:34 p.m. on Sunday, August 3, 1986, a young man she was attracted to called her on the telephone. She remembers that on March 28, 1992, she had lunch with her father at the Beverly Hills Hotel. It's a bit like certain smells that evoke strong memories: AJ's memory is stimulated in the most intense way by dates.

You'd think that being able to retrieve facts and knowledge in this way would make us more confident and wiser. But in fact for AJ, an incredible memory is as much a burden as it is a benefit. That's because most memories are selective: they provide us mostly important things, and mostly good things too. AJ remembers every detail, good or bad, important or not.

So when we curse our poor memories for forgetting to send a birthday card, actually we should be grateful also for all the things that our memories hide away because they don't need to be remembered or thought about. Umm, technology, of course, helps us with this. We don't need to remember the precise content of a report or the exact time of a meeting, because it's stored on our computer or in our smart phone.

But interestingly, the growth of this technology—what psychologists call our external memory—is having an effect on what and how much we remember. Even our memories of happy events—like parties or vacations—get stored in photograph albums on our computers. So our internal memories are probably worse than those of people 100 years ago. Medical science is trying to address the problem of poor memory and this is what I want to talk about next.

44

Have any of these things happened to you? You were about to give a speech or make a comment at a meeting, and then your mind went blank. You were supposed to send a friend a card for his birthday, but then you forgot. You recognized someone in the street and would have spoken to her, but you didn't because you couldn't remember her name. You promised you would mail a letter for someone and two days later you found it still in your pocket. You were going to write down a great idea you had, but when you found a pen and paper, the idea had gone. I could go on, but I won't because I'm sure everyone recognizes these common failures of memory.

45

1 I was going to ask Sanjip to come, but I asked Kumar instead.
2 She was supposed to be in Cairo this week, but she's sick.
3 He promised he would send me the original, but he sent me a copy.
4 We would have been there by ten o'clock, but the train didn't get in until eleven fifteen.
5 He was about to announce that he would retire, but now he thinks he'll stay another year.
6 The city planners were going to build a new shopping mall downtown, but residents opposed it.

46

A = Ahmad; L = Liz

A: Hi there, I'm interested in taking a class at your college—umm, the history of art course.
L: Is that the two-year advanced course?
A: Excuse me, what do you mean by advanced?
L: The advanced art history course is a two-year college-level course with exams at the end of each year.
A: Oh no, no, no! I don't want to take any exams. It's just for interest.
L: OK. In that case, we have a one-year art appreciation course.
A: Sorry. Can you speak up a little? I can't hear you very well.
L: Yes, we have a one-year art appreciation course.
A: Umm, can you explain what the course involves?
L: Yeah, it's a two-hour class once a week and, basically, it teaches you how to look at art so that you get the most from the experience.
A: No, sorry, I'm not really with you. Are you saying that it doesn't really deal with the history of art?
L: No, there's some history of art in it, of course, but it's mainly learning about composition, techniques, references and so on.
A: Hmm… Could you give me an example of the kind of thing students do in the class?
L: Sure. Typically, students look at works of art and then comment on them. Then they're told more about the artist, what he or she was trying to achieve, and then they look at their work again, with fresh eyes, so to speak.
A: Mmm, OK. It sounds pretty interesting. What was the course called again?
L: Art appreciation.
A: And when is it?
L: Every Tuesday from 7 p.m. til 9 p.m., starting on… one minute… yeah, starting on September 29th. The cost is $298 for the year, unless you're a registered student.
A: Hang on a second. That's too much to take in all at once. I'm trying to write

it down. I didn't catch the start date. Did you say November 29th?

L: No, September 29th.

A: OK. Well, thanks. I'll think about it, but it sounds good.

L: OK, bye.

47

Are you saying the course is full?

Can you speak up a little?

Could you give me an example?

Did you say Tuesday?

What do you mean?

Unit 12

48

I = Interviewer; D = David Stiles

I: Thirty years ago, the idea of getting a worker to hand-wash your car would have been unthinkable—except to the very rich. Either you washed it yourself at home on a Sunday morning, or you took it the carwash. Nowadays, you can have it washed inside and out by a team of willing and capable workers for as little as $6. So, what's changed? I have here with me David Stiles, author of *The Servant Economy*. David, are we just getting too lazy to do our own domestic chores. or is this part of some new economic phenomenon?

D: Well, first of all hi and thanks for having me on your show. In answer to your question, yes, it's said that in the US today there are more workers doing domestic jobs than there were in the 19th century—perhaps as many as two million: gardeners, nannies, maids. And this is a direct consequence of globalization and the freeing up of the labor market. You see, many of these workers are migrants—in the case of the US, mostly Latin Americans. Umm, and I think that in capitalist economies, anyway, the richer classes will always provide employment for the poorer classes. As the Victorian satirist Hilaire Belloc famously said, "It is the duty of the wealthy man to give employment to the artisan."

I: Yes, but that's the point, isn't it? A 19th-century-style servant economy actually emphasizes the inequalities between rich and poor in a society.

D: Well, yes, it can, but it also creates employment. You don't have to be especially rich to have a house cleaner come once a week. Quite a lot of working people do that. A lot of so-called ordinary people get their windows cleaned every few months. But there are some—uh, rich—people who get it into their heads that they're too busy or important to do any domestic chores. So they'll hire a personal shopper, and have someone walk their dog every day. If they're having a party at home, they'll get an outside catering company to prepare the food. I know some people who even have their Christmas tree installed in their living room and then decorated for them. That really *is* a statement of wealth.

I: Hmm… It seems more a statement of confused priorities to me. Walking the dog and decorating the Christmas tree are supposed to be a pleasure, aren't they?

D: Well, of course they are. But look at it another way: these are all things that create employment. As long as the staff are treated well—you know, as employees, not as servants—and are fairly paid and their skills are valued, just as you would show respect to your hairdresser when you get your hair cut, then I don't see a problem.

49

carwash	shelves
shopper	chores
richer	watch
decision	garage
pleasure	change
college	fridge

50

agent	arrange
champagne	cheese
choice	fashion
general	January
sugar	television
usual	

51

LA = Leasing agent; W = Woman

LA: So, you've had a look at the offices. What do you think?

W: Well, yeah, I really like the building. To be honest, it's absolutely perfect for our needs.

LA: That's wonderful! So you'd like to take it?

W: Well, yes, ideally I would but, umm, a key thing for us is how long we'd be tied into the lease.

LA: Well, it's a fifteen-year lease. I think that was in the details I sent you.

W: Yes, it was, but I was hoping we could negotiate that down. Because if you look at it from our point of view, we're a young business and we don't really know how things are going to go for the next few years. Who does? And let's face it, fifteen years is a big commitment. So if your client could give a little on that…

LA: Hmm… I think what you have to appreciate is that our client's main concern is securing a rental for a reasonable length of time. You know, at the end of the day, it gives them some security. To tell you the truth, that's why the rent is so low. The fifteen-year period is a kind of compensation for that. So I'm not at all sure we're going to get anywhere there.

W: Oh, that's somewhat of a sticking point then, isn't it? Is there no way around that?

LA: Uh, not that I can think of offhand. What did you have in mind?

W: Well, maybe if we signed a fifteen-year lease but with an exit clause after, say, six years, then we could pay some kind of penalty to get out of the contract.

LA: Umm, well, the normal penalty would be that you paid the remaining nine years' rent, so I don't really think that would work.

W: Oh, I see. Well, that's a shame because I really like it and we need a place pretty urgently.

LA: Look, we have other people interested in the premises, so someone will take it. If I were in your shoes, and found the terms of the lease difficult, I think I'd just leave it. When all's said and done, it has to feel right to you.

W: But that's just the problem, it does feel right to us. Give me a moment. I'm just going to call my business partner and see what he thinks.

LA: OK, no problem.

52

1 To be honest…
2 A key thing for us is…
3 Let's face it…
4 At the end of the day,…
5 To tell you the truth…

Inside Photo: 3 tl (Shivji Joshi), 3 tc (Dario Mitidieri/Hulton Archive/Getty Images), 3 tr (sellingpix/Shutterstock.com), 3 tl (EMANUELE PICCHIRALLO/National Geographic Creative), 3 tc (GEORGE STEINMETZ/National Geographic Creative), 3 tr (SUDRES Jean-Daniel / hemis.fr/Alamy), 3 cl (DAVID DOUBILET/National Geographic Creative), 3 c (CHINA OUT Reuters/Stringer/Reuters), 3 cr (Robert Harding Travel/Photolibrary Group/Getty Images), 3 bl (NIGEL SWINN/National Geographic Creative), 3 bc (GEORGE STEINMETZ/National Geographic Creative), 3 br (JODI COBB/National Geographic Creative), 8 tr (IS09908XU/Image Source / Alamy), 8 tc (Patrick Aventurier/Getty Images/News/Getty Images), 8 tl (Barry Bland/Barcroft Media/Getty Images), 8 bl (TIM LAMAN/National Geographic Creative), 8 bc (MICHAEL NICHOLS/National Geographic Creative), 8 br (David Ewing/INSADCO Photography/Alamy), 8 cr (Andrew Peacock/Aurora Open/Aurora Photos / Alamy), 9 t (© Regien Paassen/Shutterstock.com), 10 t (Stevi Calandra/National Geographic Channel/National Geographic Creative), 12-13 (RANDY OLSON/National Geographic Creative), 15 t (PAUL THOMPSON/National Geographic Creative), 16 br (Corbis), RF/Alamy), 17 b (© iStockphoto.com/hadynyah), 18 (Edwin Levick/ Hulton Archive/Getty Images), 20 cl (JOEL SARTORE/National Geographic Creative), 21 t (Dario Mitidieri/Hulton Archive/Getty Images), 22 b (Adam Woolfitt/Corbis), 24 b (STEVE WINTER/National Geographic Creative), 27 br (JOEL SARTORE/National Geographic Creative), 28 br (Oote Boe 2 / Alamy), 29 b (© Ralph Loesche/Shutterstock.com), 30 (John Springer Collection/Corbis), 32 tl (BEVERLY JOUBERT/National Geographic Creative), 33 t (© sellingpix/Shutterstock.com), 34 t (RANDY OLSON National Geographic Creative), 35 br (© Michael Rosskothen/Shutterstock.com), 36 b (OLIVER UBERTI /National Geographic Creative), 38 bl (RENEE COMET/National Geographic Creative), 38 bc (RENEE COMET/National Geographic Creative), 38 bc (Renee Comet/National Geographic Creative), 38 br (RENEE COMET/National Geographic Creative), 39 b (KENNETH GARRETT/National Geographic Creative), 44 bl (AMY WHITE & AL PETTEWAY/National Geographic Creative), 45 t (EMANUELE PICCHIRALLO/National Geographic Creative), 46 t (ANNIE GRIFFITHS/National Geographic Creative), 48 b (Alexandre Orion), 51 b (DAVID ALAN HARVEY/National Geographic Creative), 52 t (STEPHEN MORRISON/epa/Corbis), 53 tr (Justin Kase zfivez / Alamy), 54 (Patrick Aventurier/Getty Images), News/Getty Images), 56 cl (STEPHEN SHARNOFF/National Geographic Creative), 57 t (GEORGE STEINMETZ/National Geographic Creative), 58 b (Smar Jodha/National Geographic Creative), 60 tl (Frans Lanting/Frans Lanting Studio / Alamy), 60 tr (MICHAEL MELFORD/National Geographic Creative), 63 b (CHIEN-CHI CHANG/MAGNUM PHOTOS/National Geographic Creative), 64 b (© thebezz/Shutterstock.com), 66 (IS09908XL/Image Source / Alamy), 69 t (SUDRES Jean-Daniel / hemis.fr/Alamy), 70 br (CHRIS JOHNS/National Geographic Creative), 72 bkgd (©Fichugin Dmitry/Shutterstock.com), 73 tr (Ivo Roospold/Alamy), 75 tr (Ian Trower/Age Fotostock/Photolibrary Group/Getty Images), 75 tr (RICHARD NOWITZ/National Geographic Creative), 75 cr (Sextantio Press), 75 br (Juergen Henkelmann Photography / Alamy), 76 b (KEENFRESS/National Geographic Creative), 78 (David Ewing/INSADCO Photography/Alamy), 80 c (FARRELL GREHAN/National Geographic Creative), 81 t (DAVID DOUBILET/National Geographic Creative), 82 b (Liysa/Perspectives/Getty Images), 83 cr (GERD LUDWIG/National Geographic Creative), 84 t (PANORAMIC IMAGES/National Geographic Creative), 87 bkgd (©Nazzu/Shutterstock.com), 88 b (©Tinna/Shutterstock.com), 90 (TIM LAMAN/National Geographic Creative), 92 cl (XPACIFICA/National Geographic Creative), 93 t (CHINA OUT Reuters),/Stringer/Reuters), 94 cl (STEVE MCCURRY/National Geographic Creative), 94 bl (Steve McCurry/National Geographic Creative), 96 bl (IS098Q1KE/Image Source / Alamy), 96 inset (©Holger Wulschlaeger/Shutterstock.com), 96 bl (©withGod/Shutterstock.com), 96 bl (©Cheryl E. Davis/Shutterstock.com), 97 br (Corbis), Cusp/Alamy), 99 br (Cate Gillon/Getty Images News/Getty Images), 102 (Andrew Peacock/Aurora Open/Aurora Photos / Alamy), 104 tl (Wong Maye-E/Associated Press/Press Association Images), 106 b (courtesy of nasaimages.org/NASA), 109 t (Robert Harding Travel/Photolibrary Group/Getty Images), 109 t (Wes C. Skiles/National Geographic Creative), 109 bl (Kira Salak), 109 bc (Stephon Alexander/Diana Rogers), 109 br (Wes C. Skiles/National Geographic Creative),111 t (KENNETH GARRETT/National Geographic Creative), 111 b (Kenneth Garrett/National Geographic Creative), 112 tl (Shelterbox), 112 tl (Bjoern Bertheau/Synthesis International),113 tr (©wavebreakmedia/Shutterstock.com), 114 (Ben Ramos / Alamy), 117 t (NIGEL SWINN/National Geographic Creative), 118 br (Asiaselects/Alamy), 120 t (©jeep2499/Shutterstock.com), 123 t (STEFANO MASSAI/National Geographic Creative), 124 br (JAMES L. STANFIELD/National Geographic Creative), 125 (©zhu difeng/Shutterstock.com), 126 (Barry Bland/Barcroft Media/Getty Images), 128 cl (KRISTA ROSSOW/National Geographic Creative), 129 t (GEORGE STEINMETZ/National Geographic Creative), 130 cr (Renee Fadiman), 132 l (Maggie Steber/National Geographic Creative), 135 b (Vincent J. Musi/National Geographic Creative), 136 br (©Lisa F. Young/Shutterstock.com), 138 (MICHAEL NICHOLS/National Geographic Creative), 140 cl (©Michael Klenetsky/Shutterstock.com), 141 t (JODI COBB/National Geographic Creative), 142 br (LUKA TAMBACA/National Geographic Creative), 144 t (MARIA STENZEL/National Geographic Creative), 145 br (JOEL SARTORE/National Geographic Creative), 147 b (XPACIFICA/National Geographic Creative), 148 br (Sterba Martin/CTK / Alamy), 150 t (MATTIAS KLUM/National Geographic Creative), 150 bkgd (Sam Abell/National Geographic Creative), 152 t (Justin Guariglia/National Geographic Creative), 153 c (Motoring Picture Library / Alamy), 154 tl (RENEE COMET/National Geographic Creative), 154 cr (RENEE COMET/National Geographic Creative), 155 tl (Renee Comet/National Geographic Creative), 155 tr (Renee Comet/National Geographic Creative), 155 c (Motoring Picture Library / Alamy).

Illustration: Bob Lea P 42, Celia Hart P 100, David Russell P 40, National Geographic Maps/National Geographic Creative P 8.